OXFORD MEDICAL PUBLICATIONS

Refugee community health care

Photo of a wall hanging by an unknown Pakistani artist depicting Afghans crossing the border from Afghanistan into the safety of Pakistan.

Refugee community health care

Edited by

STEPHANIE SIMMONDS and PATRICK VAUGHAN
Ross Institute of Tropical Hygiene, London School of
Hygiene and Tropical Medicine

and

S. WILLIAM GUNN
Emergency Relief Operations,
World Health Organization,
Geneva

OXFORD   NEW YORK   TORONTO
OXFORD UNIVERSITY PRESS

Oxford University Press, Walton Street, Oxford OX2 6DP

Oxford New York Toronto
Delhi Bombay Calcutta Madras Karachi
Kuala Lumpur Singapore Hong Kong Tokyo
Nairobi Dar es Salaam Cape Town
Melbourne Auckland

and associated companies in
Beirut Berlin Ibadan Nicosia

Oxford is a trademark of Oxford University Press

Published in the United States
by Oxford University Press, New York

British Library Cataloguing in Publication Data
Refugee health care. − (Oxford medical publications)
1. Refugees − Medical care
I. Simmonds, Stephanie   II. Vaughan, Patrick
III. Gunn, S. William
362.1   HV640
ISBN 0-19-261407-X

Library of Congress Cataloging in Publication Data
Main entry under title:
Refugee health care.
(Oxford medical publications)
Bibliography: p.
Includes index.
1. Refugees − Medical care.   I. Simmonds, Stephanie.   II. Vaughan, Patrick.
III.   Gunn, Sisvan William Aram, 1926−   .   IV. Series.
[DNLM: 1. Refugees.   2. Community health services. W A 300 R332]
RA564.9.R43R43   1983   362.1'0880694   83-2198
ISBN 0-19-261407-X (pbk.)

Printed in Great Britain by
Thomson Litho Ltd., East Kilbride, Scotland

Foreword

DAVID BRADLEY

Professor of Tropical Hygiene and Director of The Ross Institute, London School of Hygiene and Tropical Medicine

The problems faced by and posed by refugees are great, and are increasing both in numbers and in complexity. The world's refugees, somewhere between 10 and 18 million of them, are enough to populate a sizeable country. Many people and organizations are involved in helping refugee populations to solve their health problems and this book attempts to facilitate the task.

Relief in times of disaster has often involved charitable organizations from outside the countries directly involved, but the short-term health staff recruited from among the nurses and doctors of developed countries have experience mainly of curative work. In the wake of an acute catastrophe that has created a refugee problem, surgical and traditional nursing skills are needed, but the problems of refugees are longer term and more complex. The need is to create a health care system which chiefly involves the refugee community itself and which will be viable without heavy external inputs of staff. To meet this need for training health workers in these extra community health skills, Stephanie Simmonds, who had widespread refugee experience and is a Ross Insititute staff, began a short annual course. This so clearly filled a need that it led on to this book and to the development of a refugee health group supported by the Edna McConnell Clark Foundation. Refugee health needs, in fact, resemble those of other communities with limited resources and a closely defined habitat, such as tea plantation communities with which the Institute had much experience. The outcome has been this manual which relates the area of disaster medicine to that of community health for the particular problems of refugees. It fills a need and will help to provide both practical help and a coherent philosophy of health among refugees as well as being of interest to all who work in public health in developing countries.

Preface

This book is intended for health workers who may become involved in the planning, implementation, and evaluation of health programmes in refugee populations. Whatever the size of the community, this presents an enormous challenge. We have suggested one possible approach to the problem based on community health care—which can have a positive impact both in the short- and the long-term. This approach is based on the combined wealth of experience of the contributors and has been implemented in countries such as Angola, Ethiopia, Somalia, and Thailand.

It would be very difficult, and it has not been our intention, to cover all aspects of health care in one book. Two areas not covered in depth are broader community development and political issues and secondly, more specific technical details. The bibliography in Appendix 1 gives references on these subjects.

Although we use a variety of terms to describe situations where refugees are grouped together, we emphasize that these are all populations which resemble the villages and towns that were left behind.

This book focuses particularly on aspects of health care specific to refugee communities that have been set up as a result of such disasters as famine, drought, or war. Refugees or displaced persons enter the camps during an initial emergency phase but, increasingly, remain there for years. Established communities such as these are best viewed from the overall perspective of Third World development.

We hope that this book will also be useful for teaching and reference. Each community will have its own particular problems and a great deal of flexibility will be necessary in order to adapt our suggestions to individual situations. We also hope that the contents will be of value to administrators, teachers, engineers, and others working in refugee communities.

Comments and criticisms would be appreciated as valuable contributions towards further revised editions of this publication.

London and Geneva   S.S.
March 1983   P.V.
                                                                         S.W.G.

Acknowledgements

Our colleagues in the Ross Institute, especially those in the Evaluation and Planning Centre and Refugee Health Group, spent a lot of time at workshops and seminars helping to develop this book. In this respect it is very much a team effort and the book has greatly benefited. Participants in the 1981 Ross Institute/World Health Organization/United Nations High Commissioner for Refugees course 'Health Care in Refugee Camps' also provided valuable comments, as have many refugees and national and international health workers in several different countries. We are extremely grateful for all these efforts.

It would have been extremely difficult to produce this book without the generous financial support of the Edna McConnell Clark Foundation of New York, USA, the Overseas Development Administration of the United Kingdom Government, the United Nations High Commissioner for Refugees, Geneva, Switzerland, and the Swedish International Development Agency.

Another colleague, Denise Ayres, used her great editorial skills and transformed a large and disjointed document into a recognizable book. Her expertise has proved invaluable.

We recognize a huge debt and give many thanks to Linda Bruhlmeier, Kathy Bird, and Pat Rumis, all of whom provided excellent secretarial support. Without complaining they revised chapter after chapter on the Word Processor.

All the photographs in the book were taken by Stephanie Simmonds, except those on pp. 20 and 126 which are reproduced by kind permission of the United Nations High Commissioner for Refugees.

Our warm thanks also to the many refugees whose wisdom, knowledge, and experience have influenced our work.

Contents

Contributors

David Bradley
Professor of Tropical Hygiene and Director of the Ross Institute, London School of Hygiene and Tropical Medicine (LSHTM), University of London.

Mapping and control of communicable diseases.

George Cumper
Senior Lecturer in Health Economics, Ross Institute, LSHTM.

Economic considerations.

William Cutting
Senior Lecturer in Tropical Child Health, Department of Child Life and Health, Edinburgh University.

Diarrhoea and the community.

William Gunn
Responsible Officer, Emergency Relief Operations, World Health Organization, Geneva.

Role of international agencies.

Malcolm Guy
Chief Medical Laboratory Scientific Officer, Ross Institute, LSHTM.

Laboratory service.

Pat Harman
Community Health Nurse, Tropical Child Health Unit, Institute of Child Health, University of London.

Family health care.

Peter Hawkins
Environmental Health Engineer, Ross Institute, LSHTM.

Environmental health.

Tim Lusty
Lecturer in Disaster Management, Ross Institute/Department of Human Nutrition, LSHTM.

Immunization and health management.

Carol MacCormack
Senior Lecturer in Social Sciences, Ross Institute, LSHTM.

Political, social, and cultural factors.

Donald Mackay*
Senior Lecturer and Deputy Director, Ross Institute, LSHTM.
Personal health care.

Anne Mills
Lecturer in Health Economics, Ross Institute, LSHTM.
Economic considerations.

David Nabarro
Lecturer in Nutrition in Developing Countries, Department of Human Nutrition, LSHTM.
Nutrition surveys and surveillance.

Stephanie Simmonds
Research Fellow and Honorary Lecturer in Community Health and Co-ordinator of the Refugee Health Group, Ross Institute, LSHTM.
Physical environment, planning process, assessment of needs, training refugee health workers, health education, practical considerations, and bibliography.

Peter Smith
Senior Lecturer in Tropical Epidemiology and Head, Tropical Epidemiology Unit, LSHTM.
Estimating refugee populations.

Claire Tafts
Lately, Health Visitor, Ubon Refugee Camp, Thailand.
Family health care.

Patrick Vaughan
Senior Lecturer in Health Care Epidemiology and Co-ordinator of the Evaluation and Planning Centre for Health Care, Ross Institute, LSHTM.
Physical environment, mapping, community health care, epidemiology and surveys, and control of communicable diseases.

Godfrey Walker
Senior Lecturer in Health Care Epidemiology, Ross Institute, LSHTM.
Clinical care.

Gill Walt
Research Fellow in Social Policy, Ross Institute, LSHTM.
Overview.

---

* As his many friends know Donald Mackay died suddenly. His contribution to this book reflects his support and interest in our work on refugee health care.

Tables

Figures

1 Refugees: a global perspective

Overview

In most situations there are few difficulties in identifying refugees. They are nearly always fleeing from areas torn by strife or from repressive regimes. Equally, drought, famine, or civil war may cause large communities to be displaced by having to move to different parts of their country.

REFUGEE STATUS

Most refugees take into exile only what they wear and carry, and are often totally dependent on others for survival. They may have no means of identification or proof of what they can do. They may be met with suspicion, hostility, pity, or embarrassment. There are different types of refugee, some of whom are recognized officially, while others are not. This book is largely

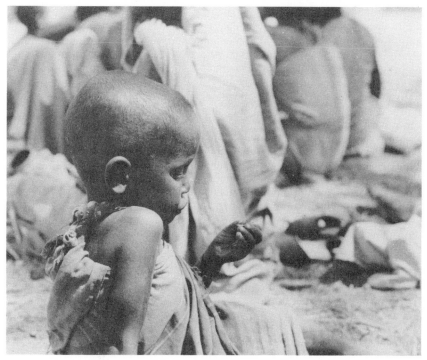

Fig. 1.1 Anyone can be a refugee.

concerned with refugees and displaced persons who are assisted in camps, at least initially, by the host country and by international organizations.

The official 1951 United Nations Convention, which was extended by the 1967 Protocol, defines a refugee as:

Any person who owing to a well-founded fear of persecution for reasons of race, religion, nationality, membership of a particular social group or political opinion is outside the country of his nationality and is unable or owing to such fear, is unwilling to avail himself of the protection of that country; or who, not having a nationality and being outside the country of his former habitual residence as a result of such events, is unable or, owing to such fear, is unwilling to return to it (UNHCR 1979).

In subsequent General Assembly resolutions, the mandate of the United Nations High Commissioner for Refugees (UNHCR) has been extended to include:

● Displaced persons who are outside their country of former habitual residence. They may not necessarily qualify as refugees within the terms of the Statute but are, nevertheless, in refugee-like situations.
● Former refugees and displaced persons repatriated to their country of origin.
● In specific cases persons displaced as a result of man-made disasters within their own country.

These definitions are still too narrow and many cases fall outside the legal responsibility of the United Nations. Non-governmental agencies can often meet the needs of these people.

Under the terms of its statute UNHCR must seek durable solutions for refugees. In order of preference these solutions are:

● Voluntary repatriation.
● Local integration in a neighbouring country of asylum.
● Resettlement in a third country of asylum.

Official requests for assistance by the receiving or host country are vital, because they entitle refugees access to aid. Many poor countries which are hosts—willingly or unwillingly—may be unable to help unless international aid is provided. Assessing a refugee situation may take a long time, especially if a country is inaccessible or closed to the outside world.

By 1982, 92 countries had become parties to the United Nations 1951 Convention and/or the 1967 Protocol. Even in those countries that have not yet become parties to either the Convention or the Protocol, the UNHCR Statute and generally recognized principles for the treatment of refugees are the basis for ensuring the refugees' basic human rights. The most important of the recognized principles is that of non-refoulement. According to this principle, no one may be forcibly returned to a country where he or she has

Fig. 1.2. A Cabindan refugee in Zaire with her document determining refugee status.

reason to fear persecution on the grounds of race, religion, nationality, or membership of a particular social or political group.

The determination or recognition of refugee status can be a complex issue. Many have argued that some of the Vietnamese 'boat people' of 1978 left more from fear of economic loss than 'fear of persecution'. A receiving country may be politically embarrassed to admit the existence of refugees from its more powerful neighbour. People fleeing their own country may settle over the border without seeking recognition. Indeed, they may avoid official assistance if it implies having to move into camps, although this will depend on what other help is available.

However, in most situations there are few difficulties in identifying refugees. They are nearly always fleeing from areas torn by strife or from repressive regimes. Equally, drought, famine, or civil war may drive large communities to be displaced by having to move to a different part of their country. In 1980–81 Ethiopia had to cope not only with displaced Ethiopians fleeing civil war and drought, but also with refugees and returnees.

NUMBERS OF REFUGEES

In 1951 there were about one and a quarter million officially recognized refugees in the world. In 1982, in Africa alone, at least five million people needed refugee assistance. In the same year there were about 10 million recognized refugees in the world, over half of whom were children. An

Fig. 1.3. Ethiopia 1980. The increased number of dead livestock was a good indicator of the severity of the drought that caused thousands of people to be displaced in the Ogaden desert.

unofficial estimate in 1982 was 18 million. In some countries, refugees may represent an overly high proportion of the total population, putting an enormous strain on the host country's resources. For example, in 1981, Somalia, with a population of about four million, had to cope with an estimated 600 000 refugees and displaced persons.

The last decade has seen an unprecedented rise in the number of refugee situations needing international aid. In 1971 over nine million inhabitants of East Pakistan, now Bangladesh, fled into India. During 1973, 1974, and again in 1975 famine displaced thousands of people in Ethiopia. In Angola, in 1978, not only was there civil war but about 100 000 refugees suddenly arrived in the north-east area, fleeing from the first of two wars within two years in the Shaba province of Zaire. That same year some 200 000 refugees from Burma streamed into Bangladesh. Then early in 1979 large numbers of refugees and displaced persons in Somalia gave cause for concern, as did the Indochinese 'boat people' stranded in camps and small islands stretching from Thailand to the Philippines. In 1980 some 300 000 starving, exhausted Khmer people fled Kampuchea into Thailand and severe drought again threatened hundreds of thousands of lives in East and the Horn of Africa. By mid 1982 there were an estimated 2.5 million Afghan refugees in Pakistan, of whom at least 1.7 million were receiving national and international assistance. More recently the political situation in Central America and in Southern Africa and the Middle East continues to generate yet more refugees and displaced persons.

The problem would appear to be growing, but as the scope of international aid has changed more people are included in official figures. Those refugees who cannot be voluntarily repatriated have to be resettled, either in the host country or elsewhere. For material or political reasons some receiving countries are reluctant to allow refugees to settle and offer only temporary asylum. Refugees may thus be in temporary camps before going to other countries to settle. A refugee's position is always tenuous because of the lack of international agreement over the granting of asylum. The needs of individual refugees are seldom considered above their perceived effect on the host country.

REFUGEE CAMPS

Refugees may find shelter with friends or relatives in urban squatter areas, government hostels, boarding houses, or in villages. When there are large numbers, they may be organized into a community which may be called a camp, village, shelter, or settlement. The difference between settlements and camps depends on the politics of the host country, its land resources, and the extent to which the problem is perceived as temporary or long-term. Thus a temporary camp may become a permanent settlement with its own land and assistance given for the development of farming and small scale industries, such as happened in Tanzania for refugees from Burundi.

Some communities may be enormous—60 000 people and more—others quite small. Some are well planned but others grow rapidly with little organization. There may be a constant movement as people are resettled and new refugees arrive. Their very existence may create a demand for places. It appears that this may have happened in Thailand near the Laotian border, where camps are being used by people who, it is alleged, are not really refugees but want assisted migration to the West. Other camps may arise because of an emergency and are then closed once the problem has been solved. The flight of the East Bengalis into India in 1971 ended in repatriation to their newly independent homeland, Bangladesh, and the closure of the camps within a year. Palestinian refugee communities illustrate how camps can become permanent settlements.

There may be great diversity among the refugees. Even among relatively homogeneous groups there will be some who are richer or have more skills than others. Refugee camps often mirror the social stratification of home villages or towns, but this may not be immediately obvious to outsiders.

Basic needs within these communities will always be the same: water, food, health care, shelter, and protection from being sent back to the country of origin. Some urgent medical services may also be necessary. One of the major problems confronting refugees is the lack of work; the apathy and hopelessness that this can cause can be debilitating. Aid organizations which do everything for refugees rather than with them unwittingly exacerbate the situation. The following chapters aim to make some positive suggestions for the health field that will enable refugees to be less dependent on outside help.

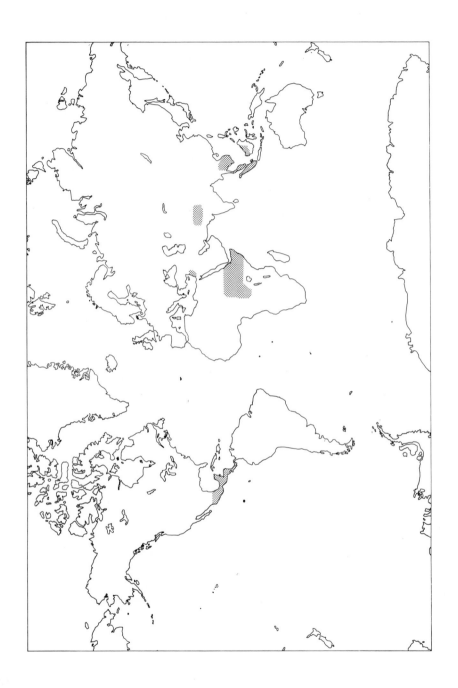

Fig. 1.5. Somalia. Refugees arriving at a camp.

◀ **Fig. 1.4.** January 1983. The five main refugee problem areas in the world.
Central America = 300 000 refugees
Horn of Africa and Sudan = 1 340 000 refugees
Pakistan = 2.5 million refugees
S.E. Asia = 320 000 refugees
Near East, numbers difficult to determine during the present problems
Total number of refugees by continent:

Africa = 5 million
Near East and Asia = 4 million
America and Europe = 1 million

Role of the United Nations and international agencies

Whatever the nature of the disaster that causes people to become refugees, the primary responsibility for caring for its victims rests with the government of the country where these victims are, whether or not they are nationals of that country.

Invariably, assistance will be required from outside the host country. This can be provided by one or more international agencies. These organizations fall roughly into the following groups:

● United Nations—including United Nations High Commissioner for Refugees (UNHCR), United Nations Relief and Works Agency for Palestinian Refugees in the Near East (UNRWA), World Health Organization (WHO), Food and Agriculture Organization (FAO), United Nations Children's Funds (UNICEF), United Nations Development Programme (UNDP), and United Nations Disaster Relief Organization (UNDRO).

● Bilateral Government agencies—such as the Overseas Development Administration of the United Kingdom Government (ODA), the European Economic Community (EEC), United States Agency for International Development (USAID), and the Swedish International Development Agency (SIDA).

● Non-governmental organizations—for example the Red Cross, OXFAM, CARITAS, and the World Council of Churches.

OVERALL RESPONSIBILITIES

United Nations (UN)

UNHCR has overall responsibility for the legal protection of refugees, a term which can now be extended to persons outside their country of origin in refugee-like situations, and for seeking a permanent solution to their problems. At the request of the General Assembly or the Secretary-General of the United Nations UNHCR's, responsibility may also be extended to cover persons who are still within their own country. Assistance to Palestinian refugees is provided by UNRWA.

Responsibility for mobilizing and co-ordinating the relief activities of the UN in natural and other disasters lies with UNDRO. This office also promotes the study, prevention, control, and prediction of natural disasters. UNDRO is represented in the field by the Resident Representative of UNDP and deploys staff as necessary to meet the needs of specific disasters.

There are certain types of disasters for which *ad hoc* arrangements are necessary to ensure an effective response from the UN system. Such situations include:

• Assistance to internally-displaced victims of man-made disasters who have been displaced within their own country, e.g. Uganda in 1980/81.

• Large and complex emergencies caused by a combination of man-made, economic, and natural disasters, sometimes affecting nationals of more than one country, e.g. Kampuchea in 1980.

Decisions on the allocation of UN co-ordinating responsibility for such disasters are made by the Secretary-General of the United Nations in consultation with the Executive heads of the other UN organizations concerned.

Bilateral agencies

Governments may prefer to extend assistance to a country directly on a bilateral basis. Some countries have agencies specifically for this purpose. Two of the largest of these that operate in refugee-like situations are USAID and SIDA. They may work through the UN or bilaterally with the host government. Food is one of the most common contributions, though other items such as drugs have also been supplied in the past. The EEC has a special Disaster Fund. In the UK, the Disaster Unit of the ODA is responsible for co-ordinating relief supplies and money. Certain governments also have special disaster units which can be deployed for a limited time at the request of the affected country.

The Red Cross

An important role in assisting refugees is played by the International Red Cross, that is, the International Committee of the Red Cross (ICRC), the national Red Cross and Red Crescent Societies, and the League of Red Cross Societies (LRCS) (the co-ordinating body of the national societies). The ICRC has particular responsibility for refugees in times of armed conflict. It provides a wide range of assistance, from relief to the reunion of dispersed families. The national Red Cross or Red Crescent Societies often play a central part in humanitarian and health assistance to refugees, as they are particularly well placed to give immediate help. In cases where the resources of the national society are insufficient, the LRCS organizes additional relief at international level. This may include the mobilization of extra personnel, so that LRCS delegates and teams may be working with the national society.

Non-governmental organizations (NGOs)

There are many NGOs which, although often fairly small, when combined together can make significant contributions. In particular, NGOs tend to provide health workers to work in refugee communities when the host governments do not have sufficient resources. Thus in Thailand and Somalia over 30 NGOs were involved, and were almost totally responsible for the implementation of health care at the camp level.

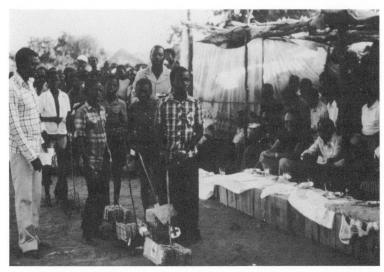

Fig. 1.6. Zairean children in a refugee village in Angola with hand-made toys, imitating the logistics work of the Red Cross.

RESPONSIBILITIES FOR SPECIFIC AREAS

While UNHCR and UNDRO are primarily concerned with emergencies, the majority of UN organizations work principally for development, and emergency response forms only a part of their responsibilities. Areas covered by other agencies include the following.

Health: WHO has Programme Co-ordinators in almost every developing country, working directly in or with the national Ministry of Health. In major refugee emergencies a UNHCR/WHO field health co-ordinator will generally be appointed to be responsible for:

- Developing appropriate health care.
- Monitoring the quality of the health services.
- Liaison and co-ordination of the activities of the UNHCR, Ministry of Health and participating organizations.

The WHO Emergency Relief Operations office in Geneva ensures co-ordination and broader action at headquarters level. In some countries there may be special WHO control programmes, for example, for malaria, tuberculosis, or diarrhoeal diseases, which may be of particular relevance to the health of the refugees. WHO also promotes prevention and preparedness for emergencies and refugee situations through epidemiological and field studies carried out in conjunction with its scientific Collaborating Centres.

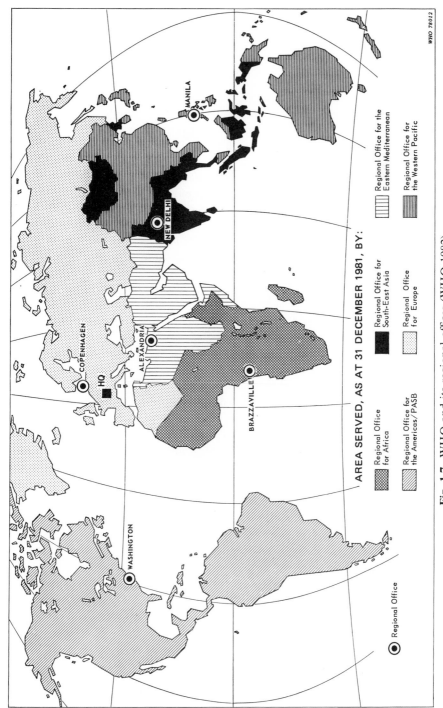

Fig. 1.7. WHO and its regional offices (WHO 1982).

In collaboration with UNHCR, WHO will provide readily packed emergency kits of drugs and clinic equipment sufficient for 10 000 refugees for three months (see Appendix 2).

Maternal and child needs: UNICEF promotes the welfare of mothers and children in conjunction with WHO, including the provision of drug supplies and development of drinking water programmes.

Vocational training: The International Labour Organization (ILO) may provide vocational training and re-training facilities.

Food supplies: WFP devotes a substantial part of its food aid to refugee emergencies. It co-ordinates all practical arrangements for food supply. Where there are particular nutritional problems, a feeding programme co-ordinator may be appointed, responsible for co-ordinating feeding programmes that provide adequate nutrition and evaluating their effectiveness.

Diseases of a nutritional nature, e.g. vitamin A deficiency, fall within WHO activities. FAO provides seeds and tools and advises on agricultural activities and land use in refugee communities. Animal health and husbandry, which can be crucial problems in displaced communities, also fall within the work of FAO.

Fig. 1.8. Zaire. An Angolan refugee enjoying the results of a nutrition demonstration on the best use of relief foods.

Education: The United Nations Educational, Scientific, and Cultural Organization (UNESCO) may be called upon to provide educational facilities, such as books, in long-standing refugee settlements. UNICEF is very active in the education of children, and will provide textbooks and visual aids for use in schools in refugee communities.

Logistics: To ensure that supplies from various sources arrive at the right place at the right time, UNHCR often assumes responsibility for a centrally co-ordinated operation. Organizations such as the ILO, Red Cross, and Crown Agents Emergency and Disaster Service (UK) also have particular expertise in this field.

General equipment, including medical supplies, can be obtained through the UNICEF Packing and Assembly Centre in Copenhagen (UNIPAC); most UNICEF and UNDP offices have the UNIPAC catalogue. WHO has emergency stockpiles of drugs, vaccines, and dressings in strategic areas of the world.

CO-ORDINATION

Whatever the circumstances that determine co-ordinating responsibility (for example, UNHCR for refugees, WHO for epidemics), all the organizations described above assist within their sphere of competence. How the various components of international response fit together will depend on the implementing arrangements desired by the host government for the actual delivery of assistance to the refugees. The following outline assumes a refugee

Fig. 1.9. Lessons for children in a refugee community in Somalia.

Fig. 1.10. Road conditions often make the distribution of supplies extremely difficult.

emergency for which UNHCR has overall responsibility. Many of the considerations would be valid whichever was the UN co-ordinating body, though there are obvious differences between arrangements for assistance to nationals, such as, flood victims, to those for refugees or displaced persons who are outside their country of origin.

Developing a relief programme

Where a government decides that the programme will be implemented through its own administration, UNHCR will concentrate on the co-ordination of UN assistance and the monitoring of its effectiveness. When a government does not wish to implement the programme, special arrangements have to be made. These may involve national or external non-governmental organizations, voluntary agencies, specialized units from other governments, and the Red Cross. These might have overall responsibility for refugees in a particular place, or a sectorial responsibility, for example, for health care. In certain circumstances, UNHCR itself may have to assume a high degree of direct operational involvement, at least initially. In the majority of refugee emergencies UNHCR relies considerably on non-governmental organizations for the implementation of the programme. Usually implementing responsibility is shared between government, national and international organizations, with, for example, local authorites administering the programme and NGOs responsible for health care.

Fig. 1.11. Co-ordination ensures that most refugees should remain healthy most of the time.

UNHCR will set up suitable overall co-ordination arrangements with the host government and the other UN organizations involved, while at the same time ensuring that the diplomatic representatives of interested governments, and particularly the donors, are kept informed. In some instances the non-governmental organizations may themselves form a co-ordinating committee, on which the government and UNHCR are represented. Working groups may be established for specific sectors, such as health care or water supply. Co-ordination at all levels with the appropriate government ministry or department is particularly important in the health sector in order to ensure that the type and level of care is appropriate, and integrated into existing national programmes, such as those for immunization, malaria, and tuberculosis control.

Financing the operation

The co-ordinating agency will seek contributions from national governments and international agencies. Certain UN organizations have emergency funds which can be used immediately. For example:

- UNHCR can make up to US$ 4 million available for any one emergency.
- WFP may be able to give substantial quantities of food.
- UNDP, UNDRO, and UNICEF can make more limited immediate cash contributions.

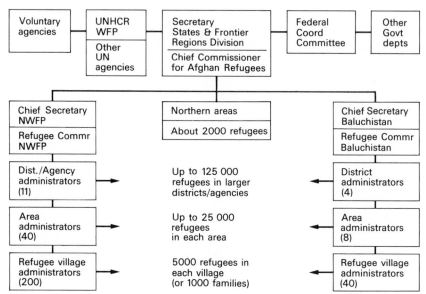

Note: Provincial Coord Committees and Regional Sub Offices of UNHCR, WFP and other UN/ Voluntary Agencies also function at Provincial Headquarters

Fig. 1.12. An example of governmental and international relationships in a refugee situation (Afghan refugees in Pakistan) (Government of Pakistan 1981).

● WHO can immediately release medicines and vaccines from stockpiles or mobilize funds for urgent medical supplies and health services.

Once the basic situation has been assessed, the co-ordinating agency will generally appeal to potential donors, setting out the requirements in cash or kind under such headings as:

● Shelter
● Health care
● Food
● Water
● Sanitation
● Social services
● Education
● Logistics and programme support

Close co-ordination with other fund-raising appeals, for example by the Red Cross, must be maintained in order to avoid duplication or gaps and to ensure that respective responsibilities are clear to potential donors. Non-governmental organizations may either contribute to the overall target or provide funding or supplies for the implementation of a part of the programme.

2 Refugee communities

Physical environment

The wet season is the worst time of the year. Food shortages are common, local food prices rise, and there is a high incidence of infections, like malaria and diarrhoea.

Refugees can rarely choose the environment where they have to live. They may find themselves in mountainous land, on an island, or in a semi-arid desert, all of which may be very different from their home surroundings. More often than not refugee communities are sited on land which is unwanted for normal agricultural or residential use, on frontiers or in no-man's land, in peri-urban areas, or possibly a 'green field' site selected by local political forces. Whatever the reasons for the chosen location, the immediate physical environment will have a pronounced effect on the health and welfare of the refugees.

LOCAL CLIMATE

Temperature, rainfall, humidity, and winds will obviously affect the choice of site. Officially-quoted climatic statistics are often daily or monthly averages

Fig. 2.1. Dancing is one way of relieving the stress of life in a camp.

and locally the ranges may be much wider. For people sleeping on the ground, temperatures can be 5–10 °C below those measured in weather stations. Even in the tropics, ground frosts are possible in sheltered hollows when night skies are clear. One severe tropical storm can cause more damage, disruption of services, and misery than a whole season of 'average' rainy weather.

Seasonal changes affect disease patterns, nutrition, insect vectors, the health of women and children, agriculture, irrigation, and social, economic, and political processes. The wet season is often the worst time of the year. Food shortages are common, local food prices rise, and there is a high incidence of infections, like malaria and diarrhoea. There is often a loss in body weight due to poor diet and an increase in neonatal and infant mortality. Illnesses increase throughout the whole community. These effects tend to be more obvious in refugee communities than amongst the local population. The practical implications include:

- Taking seasonal changes into account when planning,
- Ensuring an adequate quantity of water at the end of the dry season,
- Ensuring that each community has two or three weeks of food in store towards the end of the dry season and during the wet season, in case supplies fail because of poor roads or tracks,
- Giving attention to environmental health aspects of diseases such as diarrhoea and malaria, especially during and just after the rains,
- Making regular community assessments of the most prevalent symptoms and diseases which are dependent on seasonal changes, such as malnutrition and malaria.

SITUATION

Temporary camps often become permanent locations as time goes on and the refugees' investments in their shelters and surroundings assume substantial proportions. Therefore, when siting a temporary camp it is worth considering whether it may develop into a permanent settlement in future.

Intensely farmed agricultural areas will have the highest demand for rural labour, whereas access to a sizeable town or city will provide the best prospect for urban employment. Inevitably, some refugees will need to migrate to obtain work and access to transport routes is important in keeping costs to a minimum. Pastoralists need, however, access to pasture and local grazing. Some of the well-established camps for Palestinian refugees in the Middle East are a good example. Those near cities such as Damascus, and Amman, and Beirut before the armed conflict in 1982, have become fully integrated and prosperous urban or peri-urban communities, whereas the smaller, more remote rural camps are much poorer.

Apart from economic and administrative considerations, the site must be selected after careful analysis of environmental conditions:

• Water (particularly ground water) availability must be established. Special attention must be paid to climatic extremes between the wet and dry seasons. The risk of flooding may be great. The size of the community will be limited by the amount of water that can be supplied during the driest season.

• The slope of the site is important as it can provide natural drainage for rain water and waste, particularly on impervious ground. Drainage channels are needed in very flat sites. A high point where water can be stored is useful, as water can then be piped by gravity feed.

• The proximity of vector breeding sites, such as ponds, small streams, or swamps. Places harbouring rats and other rodents should be identified and either cleared or poison applied.

• Consideration must be given equally to the needs of the local inhabitants. The refugee community may produce a lot of refuse, waste water, and excreta, and impose an increased demand on sometimes scarce facilities, such as water or fuel.

• The type of local vegetation is important in providing shade and keeping down dust. It hardly ever lasts, however, unless precautions are taken to guarantee an adequate and continuous supply of fuel.

COMMUNITY LAYOUT

The way the community is planned should make it possible for refugees to lead a life similar to that to which they were accustomed. The layout will also be important in determining how to distribute water-points and latrines.

Whatever the layout, a camp is often divided into sections and sub-sections or community units for ease of administration. For example, a camp of 10 000 might be divided into four sections of 2500 each and each section divided into community units of 500 persons. Within these community units there might be groups of 50–100 families. At each stage there is usually an appointed chief or leader.

• A grid layout is often preferred when a sudden and massive migration occurs. However, it may destroy the refugees' incentive for participation and unless solid structures have been provided it does not last very long, because people soon re-organize themselves and chaos can follow.

• On the other hand, communities may attempt to reproduce the setting that people were used to. The refugees can then regroup according to their traditional customs. This will boost interest in participating in setting up facilities and in maintaining them. Figures 2.3 and 2.4 show such alternative layouts. The main health centre would be part of the centralized services with sub-clinics as part of the decentralized community services.

Fig. 2.2. A grid layout in a camp of Salvadorean refugees in Honduras (UNHCR, Cedan).

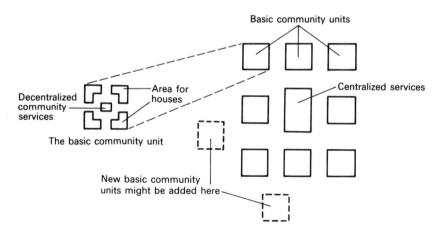

Fig. 2.3. Example of a cluster or cross-axis layout (UNHCR Handbook 1982).

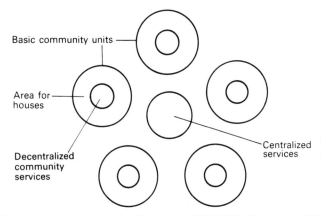

Fig. 2.4. Example of a circular layout (UNHCR Handbook 1982).

The provision of shelter

Whenever possible, housing should reproduce the traditional homes of the refugees. This can lead, however, to massive degradation of the nearby environment. When to allow permanent housing rather than temporary shelter is often a highly political issue.

Communal buildings as living quarters are often seen as an efficient way to occupy scarce space and can be set up quickly along the grid layout system. But they offer little privacy and may contribute to the spread of air-borne diseases such as whooping cough, measles, meningitis, pneumonia, and tuberculosis. International agencies often provide housing that is ill-suited to tropical environments.

The provision of blankets, mats, or groundsheets if culturally acceptable, in sufficient numbers is an essential part of shelter planning. In most circumstances the refugees will have to sleep on the ground, which can cool considerably at night, thus drawing heavily on energy requirements of individuals.

Communications

What may seem a perfectly adequate road, track, bridge, or river crossing point during the dry season may become totally impassable as soon as the rains start. This will obviously affect the supply of food and other commodities. Air transport has been used successfully in some relief operations—during drought conditions in Ethiopia, for example—but it is very expensive.

Two-way radios can be extremely useful when camps are miles from either regional or central headquarters. For security reasons permission should always be sought from the government before installing such a system.

Fig. 2.5. Traditional housing destroyed in Lebanon 1982 during the war, caused many thousands of Palestinians and Lebanese to be displaced.

Vegetation

There may be no suitable vegetation available for livestock and the different seasonal patterns disrupt attempts to grow food. Traditional doctors and midwives may not have access to the plants and herbs they normally use. Refugees can rapidly deplete the supply of local building materials and firewood for cooking. In some areas this can lead to serious soil erosion and rapid deforestation. Other forms of fuel, e.g. kerosene may need to be supplied for domestic use.

SUMMARY

The following points are most important when health workers are asked to help select a new site or to design the extension of an existing one:

- The main consideration must be the layout that the refugees prefer.
- To prevent overcrowding WHO recommends 30 m^2 per person, plus land for agriculture and livestock.
- All-weather roads must be nearby for the transfer of patients, food supplies, and goods.
- Hospital services capable of handling referred sick patients should be within a reasonable distance.
- The area should be free from major environmental hazards, such as malaria, schistosomiasis, or tsetse fly.

Fig. 2.6. Kerosene for the Afghan refugees in Pakistan is stored in tanks such as this.

• An adequate amount of suitable water, ideally 20–30 l per person per day, must be available at all times of the year. The maximum distance between houses and water distributing points should not be more than 100 m if possible.

• Protection against the cold must be ensured by providing adequate shelter and possibly groundsheets and blankets.

• The site must be above flood level and have suitable surface water drainage.

• Buildings and equipment should be protected from wind and rain damage.

• Suitable sites and soil should be available for the construction of latrines and sewage disposal. Allowance should be made for one latrine per 20 people and a latrine should not be more than 50 m away from the household.

• To prevent the spread of fires a 50-m wide break in buildings is recommended for every 300 m of built-up area.

• Consideration must be given to protecting the interests of the local population.

Political, social, and cultural factors

Indigenous ideas about the cause of illness and traditional treatments may bring positive benefits to the sufferer by allocating extra fluids, food, and efficacious local medicines.

THE REFUGEE COMMUNITY

Four groups interact in a refugee camp:

- the refugees
- the local population
- the administrators in the host country and
- the representatives of aid agencies

The refugee's home community is often internally structured by kinship, but family, clan, or neighbourhood groups may have been broken up in migration. Social structures may, therefore, need to be recreated or new ones promoted. There may be a low proportion of male refugees with a high percentage of children and elderly people. If there has been a traditional division of labour based upon sex, there may be further impediments to initiating and carrying out economic tasks. For example, in settled agricultural communities, men usually prepare the soil and women weed the crop. With men absent it is difficult, if not 'unnatural', for women to begin an agricultural cycle. Nomadic women, on the other hand, are more accustomed to being without their men for part of the year. People may grieve for the loss of their livestock and possessions.

Refugee communities are internally divided by such factors as ethnicity, caste, class, skills, and rural–urban background. The earlier groups to arrive in the host country may resent the later arrivals who compete with them for scarce resources. Political parties that existed at home may be reorganized and form the basis of different power groupings. Refugees may compensate for a sense of defeat by displays of sullenness or even clandestine guerrilla activity.

A refugee camp may not, therefore, especially early in its existence, be a 'community' in the traditional sense. Rather a collection of people under great emotional and physical stress, in adverse socio-economic and environmental conditions, whose patterns of society have been severely disrupted. This has important implications for community involvement in the development of the health services. For example, who will emerge as leaders among the refugees? How valid is their interpretation of the health needs and problems? How difficult will it be for the refugees to come to a community decision about who should sit on the health committee or who to train as a community health worker?

Refugees are looking for help and their despair may deepen when foreign donors give them inappropriate food and supplies. Aid of this kind often ends up in local markets because refugees have traded it for more familiar goods, and may eventually find its way to markets in major cities. Whenever possible, familiar foods and building materials should be obtained locally. The refugees may play off the donors against the local administrators by making complaints which may be well-founded or simply designed to further their own goals.

Male chiefs and elders often have positions of great power and influence in camps. Shamans and spirit mediums are of great value; they are the intellectuals in their own society experienced in treating 'sick souls', and will help people come to grips with their grief and depression. Some societies also have specialists in bone-setting, herbal remedies, and other aspects of health care. Indigenous ideas about the cause of illness and traditional treatments may bring positive benefits to the sufferer by allocating extra fluids, food, and efficacious local medicines. To understand the functional logic behind local ideas and build up further self-help education from this cultural base is very important. Peoples' beliefs and practices should never be rejected unless there is very good evidence that they do more harm than good.

Since there are often more women and children in the camps, health services and education should be largely for their benefit. If women come from a puritanical religious background, a high proportion of women health workers may be essential. Childbirth is usually within the domain of women's knowledge and competence.

Even in rather patriarchal societies many aspects of health may be largely the women's responsibility. Traditional midwives may have a recognized social role and offer their help in distributing iron tablets and other materials to pregnant women. They will know which women are at risk. Customary

Fig. 2.7. Learned elders of a camp may be influential in helping implement various aspects of health care.

practices should not be denigrated unless they are really life-threatening. For example, in some societies women are most comfortable walking about during labour. They may squat rather than lie back for delivery.

Traditional midwives can perform a wide range of services such as washing soiled clothes, cooking food, minding children, and ritually washing mother and baby. They know the ceremonies for taking a woman through this period with most confidence, and reincorporating her back into society with her new status of mother.

There may also be womens' and mens' organizations, perhaps associated with puberty rites. They are usually hierarchically organized and the leaders respected; they may be suitable for implementing health programmes.

Residence patterns and self-help

The camp should be laid out to facilitate hygiene and communication. But beyond these basic considerations everything possible should be done to help people build their homes where they wish. In that way they can recreate home neighbourhoods. Some kin groups (lineages and clans) are sizeable; since all members descend from a common ancestor, all are 'children' of that ancestor or 'siblings' and there is a strong moral requirement to help each other. If kin and ethnic groups are allowed to cluster, there is more social cohesion and the potential for self-help is greater. Refugees can easily speak with each other, talking through their recent grief. Children can play safely in these neighbourhoods, and the ill and elderly are more likely to be cared for.

Fig. 2.8. Traditional midwives in a camp in Somalia.

People feel they have more privacy, even though they may live in quite restricted space. For those stratified by caste, it may be important to allow them to group themselves in accordance with ideas about pollution.

Refugees will not all have the same ability to organize themselves into groups. Some refugees may come from settled agricultural communities where there is considerable social cohesion and well-established procedures for settling disputes and looking after the weak. Others in the camp may be urban people, or nomads, who tend to be more individualistic and less amenable to settling down in restricted circumstances. Some may even have quite anarchic feelings caused by the political troubles they have suffered. However, if refugees are allowed to reconstruct home communities leaders are more likely to be near at hand to settle small disputes, assist with distribution of aid, and other self-help activities.

Community organization and the distribution of aid

The refugee population will be diverse and there may be exploitation by those who know how to 'work the system', and some groups may secure relatively more, others less, of the aid that is distributed. For historical reasons some ethnic groups have been subservient to others in the home countries. In a rural setting people in the subservient group usually have to work harder and are therefore able to provide for their own household as well as give tribute. In a refugee camp they lack access to a livelihood and may fall into the category of those medically most at risk.

When distributing aid it may be best to work through headmen or through heads of families, or to give the aid directly to women or children. However distribution is managed it is important to understand the structure of the refugee community. Otherwise, the wrong people may be chosen to carry out the programme.

Funeral rites

Funeral rites differ according to personal beliefs and different religions. Relatives often attach great importance to every detail involved in the funeral rites, when the death occurs in a place miles from the homeland. Rites may include one or a combination of some of the following; not allowing 'unbelievers' to touch the body after death; leaving the body to 'rest' for a certain period of time before touching it; ritually washing the body; dressing the body in the deceased's best clothes; wrapping the body in a simple shroud and offering homage to the deceased, through prayers, songs, wailing, the burning of incense, eating of special foods, etc. Following these rites it is usual either to bury the body in a marked grave or cremate the body in an incinerator or on a funeral pyre. If health workers or camp administrators interfere too much in these rites great resentment may result and the refugee community may become unco-operative in reporting deaths.

In a society that traditionally buries its dead, counting the number of new refugee graves in an officially designated burial site may or may not be an accurate indicator of the numbers of deaths in the refugee community. For example, it has been known for some refugees to bury their dead, at night, in places known only to them. This may be with the intention of recovering the body and taking it back across the border when they return, so they can be re-united with their ancestors. Where it is important to bury the body in a shroud, the provision of a length of suitable material has been used by administrative authorites to help record deaths. Increased demands for the material so that it can be sold at the local market is unlikely, as reporting a death means one less food ration. It is more likely that a death is not reported as it may then mean the loss of a food ration.

Relatives must be granted every reasonable wish concerned with funeral rites, but health workers should be aware of the possible transmission of some diseases such as cholera, hepatitis B, rabies, and lassa fever as a result of the close personal contact involved in the caring and washing of a person who has died from any of these diseases. Health workers must be particularly alert when funeral rites involve the preparation and eating of food.

ADMINISTRATORS AND AID REPRESENTATIVES

The administration of a refugee community is no easy matter. Administrators may be caught in a cross-fire of demands from refugees and international personnel. They will probably be representatives of the provincial authorities or may be district commissioners or military officers. The commissioners' regular duties are to maintain public works and to keep general law and order. Because their professional duties are concerned largely with maintenance of law and order they are often conservative in their approaches to problems. It is important to understand as much about the government's political ideology as possible and to work constructively with it, keeping criticism to oneself. It is essential not to become involved in factional politics.

Bureaucracies often function on favouritism, allowing short-cuts in decision making and the procurement of supplies. On the other hand, procedural channels may often be blocked by indecisive, incompetent people or those looking for personal benefit in the administration of duty. Bureaucracies are notoriously slow to respond to emergencies or unusual situations as the administrators and representatives of the aid agencies are constrained by policies decided at a higher level.

REFUGEES AND THE LOCAL PEOPLE

During the nineteenth century national boundaries were often drawn with no consideration to the distribution of ethnic groups. Refugees often flow across borders where the same group lives on both sides, and they are initially

Fig. 2.9. An administrator checking the water supply in a settlement in Ethiopia.

received sympathetically by the local population and administrators. However, as their numbers increase they may outstrip the capacity of the local population to provide basic necessities. The national government, perhaps made up of a coalition of other regional or ethnic groups, may not react so hospitably. Political strains thus arise in the host country as local people and international personnel promise refugees one thing, and national governments respond with less.

Refugees will not always be received sympathetically, however, especially if they have been powerful neighbouring groups, perhaps in the past raiding each other's area. Further stress may develop in a poor host country where what seems to be vast wealth is coming from donors for the refugees, who are after all strangers. Certainly it is not a good idea to give refugees so much aid that they are wealthier than the local host population.

If repatriation seems unlikely it is probably better to encourage refugees' absorption into local villages than to encourage them to stay in camps where they have little chance of being self-sufficient. Many of the Angolan refugees, for example, settled in farming communities in neighbouring countries, some choosing to remain after independence was attained in Angola. Other places where land is scarce, such as Hong Kong, do not see absorption as a solution for refugees.

In some communities refugees live in compounds, but in most cases they are able to mix freely with the local population. They also offer their labour to local farmers or businessmen. Sometimes there is friction. For example, women in the host population may complain about refugee women, alleging they are immoral. Middle-aged men look with grave suspicion on young refugee males, hanging around towns and markets all day, chatting with women. However, through a range of social encounters strangers may become labourers, wives, or clients. Thus some refugees are absorbed, usually as social inferiors.

Economic considerations

The economic life of a refugee community has two aspects; the economic status and activity of the refugees within the community and the impact of the community's activities on the local and national economy.

At first sight, a refugee camp might appear to be a community isolated from the ordinary world, where normal economic patterns of work, business, and trading do not exist and where a captive population is dependent on outside agencies for all resources. While the nature of refugee communities will obviously vary enormously, all will usually have some form of economic activity. There are a number of reasons why health workers should bear this in mind. One is that it may have a direct influence on the physical and, even more, the mental health of those in the community. Another is that the actions of health workers, for example the system used for the distribution of food, may affect economic relationships between refugees. More generally, if health workers are to co-ordinate their activities with other aspects of administration, they need to understand the economic problems which confront the administrators.

ECONOMIC ACTIVITIES

Refugees will usually have lost any resources that helped them to generate wealth in their homeland. Even the money that they carry with them may not be convertible into local currency. They will also have lost the network of family and community support that underlay their previous pattern of economic activity.

The longer the refugee community has been in existence, the more active may be the economic life within it. The following is a description of a camp in the Sudan:

A naive visitor to Wad el Hilayew, unaware that he was visiting a refugee camp, might be forgiven for imagining himself in some busy commercial centre. The camp supported a market where one could buy much more than the basic necessities of life; fresh fruit, vegetables and meat were for sale, restaurants and coffee shops flourished, and the number of lorries, buses and camels for transport of people and goods indicated a heavy traffic. (Johnson 1979)

Fig. 2.10. Afghan preparing wool for carpet weaving in a refugee village in Pakistan.

Such developments present both opportunities and problems. On the one hand, they can contribute to the material well-being of the refugees, to their sense of self-reliance, and to their ability to resume normal life when they leave the refugee community. On the other hand, they may create a system of economic and social roles which cuts across both the traditional patterns the refugees bring with them and the official system of the camp itself. If these roles are linked too specifically to the camp there may be groups who actually profit from the camp's existence and resist any move toward its dissolution. Such groups may even divert part of the assistance provided to the camp or control such resources as housing, water supply, or relief items. If economic activity in a refuge community boosts up one group at the expense of the others, it has to be kept in check. Clearly, health workers cannot fight against such practices. However, their unique position among relief personnel, through their close contacts with the community, gives them a responsibility to identify those refugees who are more deprived and at the mercy of this camouflaged form of dependence. Preferential distribution and allocation of commodities can then be organized to reduce the gap between various sectors of the population.

LOCAL IMPACT

The impact of a refugee camp on the local markets for food, labour, and land will be considerable. It will depend on the community's location, whether local economic activity consists primarily of subsistence farming or whether a considerable local marketable surplus is produced, and whether the camp itself is in an area affected by the circumstances that have led to the refugee problem.

In the early stages of a camp's formation, refugees with assets may have to sell them under unfavourable bargaining conditions. Thus refugees entering Bangladesh from Burma in 1978 brought cattle whose sale to the local population drove down prices locally to a level that was less than the value of the cattle as productive assets. Such situations may strain relations between refugees and the local population.

The refugee community will often be large in relation to the local population, and scope for purchasing food supplies locally may be limited. Workers in a refugee community should be aware of local food prices, of the danger that these may rise as a result of the camp's existence, and of who gains and loses in this process. However, a common feature of refugee communities is the development of a black market in food, where relief foods are bartered for local foods.

Fig. 2.11. A market in Zaire with prices well displayed; both Cabindan and Angolan refugees lived nearby and used the market frequently.

If large quantities of relief food find their way to the local market, the price of staple foods may fall below the cost of local production. In both cases, the effects are harmful to the local population. In the first instance, high prices will diminish the buying power of poor local people; in the latter, the incentive to maintain traditional activities will be reduced by the artificial economy created by the refugee influx. Frequently, after a period of settling in, the refugees may end up better off than the lower strata of local people.

Trading with local people for non-food items is also likely to develop. This will be based on the assets the refugees bring with them, or those goods they create or receive within the community such as handicrafts and donated items, and/or the maintenance of links with their own countries. Some of this trade may be illegal from the point of view of one country or the other. For instance, the Sudanese camp referred to earlier was a major outlet for goods from Eritrea, with the refugees controlling the trade. An enormous black market, supplying Kampucheans with consumer goods unobtainable on the open market, developed in 1979/80 on the Thai–Kampuchean border. Black markets raise the problems of creating economic power links within the camp and with the local community and national authorities.

Similarly, the refugee community may affect local markets for labour and land. Where working for wages outside the community is possible, the sudden influx of extra people may depress local wage rates, and provide a cheap source of labour which may displace local labourers, causing hardship. Where refugees are to be resettled in the region of the camp, this may exacerbate local scarcities of land and water.

NATIONAL RESOURCES AND DEVELOPMENT

A refugee community usually poses resource allocation problems for the host government and these problems will be particularly acute if the refugee influx is large, the resources for local resettlement are limited, and if there are special problems such as black markets. Difficulties of this kind will remain no matter how generous the international support given to the refugees. Governments will often regulate the resources so that the refugees' standard of living is neither scandalously low, nor so high as to provoke jealousy in the rest of the country, or to provide a positive incentive for those marginally affected to join the refugees. This may result in apparently callous policies and constraints within which health workers, like other refugee staff, will have to work.

At each stage the economic situation presents problems but also opportunities for improving the physical and mental health of the refugees. Initially the priority may be to secure the resources to meet the basic needs of the refugees. These may be met partly from outside and partly by using the labour and skills of the refugees themselves. Attention must also be given to the short-term effects on the local population of the refugees' needs and of the disposal of any assets they bring with them. When the community is fully established, its economic system may be increasingly dominated by the production and trading activities of the refugees themselves. At the resettlement stage, priority may have to be given to preparing the refugees to lead self-supporting lives in their new environment. They may take on different roles to those they have played in the camp.

3 Health planning

Community health care

Health workers, rather than disease staff, must organize health services for the whole community, whether healthy or sick, and not just for those who are already diseased and come asking for medical help.

Health is a difficult concept to use and so health care tends to be discussed in terms of disease. However, disease is only the final phase of an often long process of ill health, which is asymptomatic for most people. During the disease phase, the patient may treat himself, or consult traditional healers or private practitioners. There are many cultural and educational reasons why he or she may not seek help from the health centre 'disease services'.

The facilities that most medical agencies have tended to offer in refugee camps are oriented to diagnosing and treating clinical or symptomatic diseases. In the early stages there may be a great demand for curative services and setting up such services may seem professionally and politically the best

Fig. 3.1. Planning involves making the most of local knowledge, experience, and expertise.

thing to do. However, as the camp settles, the proportion of refugees requiring curative services is usually small. The proportion requiring specialized medical skills and hospital care is even less. Emphasis on clinics will lead to large queues of refugees with trivial complaints while the real problems in the community develop unnoticed.

INDIVIDUAL OR COMMUNITY CARE?

Refugees often come from either an under-developed squatter urban environment or a rural setting and have had little previous access to medical care. As they are likely to return to the same background once the crisis is over, it would be wrong to accustom them to a high standard of curative facilities that they will then miss. On the other hand, whatever they have learnt in the camp about hygiene, nutrition, and environmental health could be a great asset to them in the future.

Three major sources of diseases may be important in a refugee population:

● Diseases the refugees bring with them from their previous environment, such as tuberculosis and some specific parasitic diseases, or those that arose during their recent travels.
● Diseases present in the new environment, such as malaria, for which they lack any immunity.
● Diseases that arise in the camp itself due to the crowded and unhealthy conditions.

The most important diseases recorded in refugee camps are diarrhoeas, including gastro-enteritis and the dysenteries, broncho-pneumonias, eye and skin infections, malnutrition, anaemias, and malaria. The incidence of these diseases depends mainly on environmental conditions and food supply. Epidemics are rare in camps and contrary to popular belief they are not usually a great threat, the possible exceptions being measles and cholera. The most common complaints are symptoms such as fever, coughs, and diarrhoea. A daily or weekly record of how many people with these conditions are presenting at clinics is a biased but useful way of monitoring the diseases in the camp.

The diseases important to report are those:

● for which there are agreed diagnostic criteria and definitions and which can be diagnosed easily, e.g. diarrhoea, scabies
● which are common and severe, e.g. pneumonia
● which are potentially epidemic, e.g. measles, malaria, and meningitis

The public health importance of a disease in a refugee community can be assessed by:

● Examining its frequency in the community, its morbidity, and its contribution to mortality. A common but mild disease such as ascariasis, or a rare disease with a high mortality, are not those which should be given a high priority.

● Availability of preventive and simple curative methods. These methods must also be efficient, acceptable to the people, and technically possible within the constraints of the available programme.

Medical services have been organized traditionally around curative medicine. This kind of service offers help to sick people who come and ask for it, but does little for those who do not come because of distance, ignorance, or fear. For those people who do come, curative medicine can cure some of the diseases, alleviate some suffering, and prevent some deaths. However, these services have very little effect on the incidence of new cases of different diseases arising in the community.

Curative services are expensive to run since they usually have to rely on outside support for staff, supplies, and finance. Obviously some curative services must be provided. However, the aims and limits of such services must be well defined from the outset. Maximum effort needs to be given to keeping people healthy and to reducing the number of new cases of the important diseases. This means that health workers, rather than disease staff, must organize health services for the whole community, not just for those who are already diseased and come asking for medical help.

The demand for curative services can exhaust limited resources before anything can be done about primary or secondary prevention. The first task, therefore, is to help people remain healthy, and here preventive medicine becomes useful. However, if preventive services are used only by a few people they will be ineffectual in making the community healthier. A high coverage is very important. For example, antenatal care can only significantly reduce perinatal mortality if most of the pregnant women are seen. Similarly, a measles immunization campaign will only prevent an outbreak if a very high proportion of all susceptible children is vaccinated.

LEVELS OF HEALTH CARE

Maintaining health

Primary prevention is based on interventions that aim to maintain health and which work mainly by:

● involving healthy people in their own health care, such as

  ● an adequate and balanced diet
  ● immunization
  ● chemoprophylaxis
  ● personal hygiene

  - family spacing
  - healthy behaviour
- or through controlling their environment with
  - safe water supplies
  - good food hygiene
  - safe excreta and refuse disposal
  - control of vectors ana animals harbouring diseases;
  - adequate housing and shelter
  - safe working conditions,

These interventions can only be effective if whole communities are involved.

Screening

These methods rely on detecting a disease process after it has started but before it produces symptoms. The methods are based on the screening of individuals and to be effective a high coverage of the population must occur. However, a particular screening procedure should be carried out only if something can be done to help the affected persons, either by the medical services or by the community itself. Good examples are antenatal care, nutritional surveillance of young children, and certain laboratory investigations for infections.

Treatment of patients

These methods aim to diagnose and treat diseases in order to reduce suffering, cure diseases, and prevent disability and death. In some cases, treatment also plays a major part in interrupting the transmission chain of certain diseases such as tuberculosis and thus limiting spread in the community. Rehabilitation services may also be required for physical disabilities, blindness, or paralysis.

THE COMMUNITY HEALTH APPROACH

The first need is to gather information on:

- The refugees themselves—their various cultures, socio-economic and political processes.
- Their number and distribution—by categories such as age, sex, cultural group, and ethnic background.
- Their health problems and common diseases—as seen in the areas they have lived in, or passed through, and in the local population.
- The availability of local health care—including self-care, traditional and private practitioners, and the organized camp and government health services.

We must also look carefully at the overall relief process, since the improvement of community health cannot be achieved without good co-ordination between all parts of the programme.

Planning process

The effects of bad planning are difficult to change, so it is important that both short- and long-term objectives are agreed early on.

International health personnel are rarely present early in the life of a refugee community and it is, therefore, necessary to plan with the current situation and constraints very much in mind. The other difficulty is to maintain a long-term perspective whilst at the same time developing flexible plans that can respond to rapid changes in the size of the communities. It is all too easy to develop crisis programmes which soon become outdated. Once an expensive hospital has been built it is very difficult to close it down, even if it is no longer necessary! Health programmes must also operate within the overall development schemes and not in isolation.

The approach to the work encompasses:

• Remaining constantly aware of the political, social, cultural, and economic factors both within the host country and the refugee community.
• Giving priority to the basic needs of the refugees.
• Working 'with' rather than 'for' the refugees at all stages.
• Ensuring good co-ordination and co-operation with the national government and other agencies.
• Maintaining a flexible approach that builds upon opportunities as they arise and respects local knowledge, experience, and expertise.
• Using the six essential stages shown in Fig. 3.2 as a framework for decision making.

ASSESSMENT OF HEALTH NEEDS

Time spent discussing the situation and listening to the needs and problems as expressed at national, district, and refugee community levels is crucial. At

Fig. 3.2. The planning cycle.

national level these discussions will be mainly with government health and administrative officials and with personnel from the United Nations, the Red Cross, and non-governmental agencies. The district commissioner and medical officer are often the most important people at the district or provincial level, plus the police chief and other categories of senior health workers. In the refugee communities national staff and refugees work as administrators, health personnel, and teachers. Committees may have been established for such activities as agriculture, education, and security. Amongst the refugees there will almost certainly be traditional midwives and practitioners, health auxiliaries, nurses, and doctors. The following section on assessment of needs gives examples of the topics and questions that may need to be covered during discussions.

It is very important to obtain or make a map of the community, take impromptu walks to assess the surroundings, and hold spontaneous conversations with the refugees. They will usually be very aware of the problems. To a certain extent the needs expressed will be predictable, but they will obviously vary with each community. By listening and taking advice instead of going ahead with preconceived solutions, international health

Fig. 3.3. Among the refugees there may be health personnel such as these health auxiliaries who can be a fund of local knowledge.

workers help establish their credibility. The information may be conflicting and confusing but experience will gradually enable informed judgements to be made.

RANKING OF PRIORITY PROBLEMS

Priorities can change rapidly as the situation alters, seasons change, and unforeseen crises arise. It is still necessary to plan for the long-term, but this takes time as the refugee community and administrators must be involved. Outsiders' priorities may conflict with those of refugees, whose decisions are influenced by their culture, taboos, and community concern. A final outcome of the discussions may be:

- insufficient water
- malnutrition
- diarrhoeal diseases;
- malaria
- low level of activity
- insufficient appropriate drugs

IDENTIFYING RESOURCES

Planning should be based on the availability of local resources. Ideally, both local and national resources should be used, to prevent the programme becoming over reliant on international aid. If one or more of the problems cannot be resolved locally, they should be referred to the appropriate higher authority.

As outsiders it is all too easy to turn to aid agencies and plead urgency and shortages. However, this can often lead to bringing in inappropriate equipment which, in the long-term, may make self-sufficiency even less likely.

Before any plans are made or programmes implemented it is important to estimate their cost. The recurrent costs are often a much greater burden, especially to the national government, than the capital costs. This is why free gifts of equipment, transport, or personnel may work out to be disproportionately expensive to the host country, although looking very good for an aid agency that wants to be seen to be active. The political costs to the refugees themselves, the local people, the country concerned, and the aid agencies must also be considered.

PROJECT PLANNING

The effects of bad planning are difficult to change so it is important that both short- and long-term objectives are agreed early on. Surveys are helpful at this stage to assess the situation; they do not require much time or manpower and give reasonably reliable information. For example:

Fig. 3.4. Local technology—a weaving loom in a settlement in Ethiopia.

- Make a map of the community.
- Estimate the population by location, household, age, and sex.
- Nutritional surveys to give an indication of nutritional status.
- Household surveys to assess prevalent diseases and for information on house construction, water storage, cooking facilities, household belongings, economic status, etc.

Plans must be easily adaptable to rapid changes in circumstances such as the numbers of refugees, availability of resources, the seasons, and changing political situations. It is most important to establish the mechanisms for planning. Written plans may look good but are often inflexible and more of a hindrance than a help. Examples of objectives are to:

- Improve the nutritional status of the 'at risk' members of the community
- Improve the quantity, quality, and access to water
- Establish an effective curative service
- Improve environmental sanitation
- Train members of the refugee community to organize and run the health programmes

IMPLEMENTATION

Many of the refugees can help even if they have not had previous health training. It is important to clarify with the authorities whether the refugee health workers are on a self-help basis, a salary, or part of a food-for-work programme.

There are four things worth doing early:

• Ask which refugees have had health training in their own country and whether they are willing to co-operate or take charge of local activities.
• Establish local health committees which can supervise the refugee health workers and volunteers who are essential in organizing home care, health education, and community programmes.
• Find out who the traditional birth attendants and practitioners are and how they work.
• Hold regular meetings to discuss the progress of the health programmes. Include representatives from the community and national administration, refugees, and aid agencies.

The work is unlikely to proceed smoothly and it is probably during the implementation phase that the worst frustrations and unforeseen setbacks will arise. However, if a thorough assessment has been done and work undertaken with everyone concerned, there should not be too many insoluble problems.

EVALUATION

Evaluation is a means of assessing to what extent the health programmes are achieving their stated aim. This in turn shows the need to have some base-line information and clear aims and objectives for the programmes against which to measure progress. We need to distinguish whether it is the health status of the whole population which is to be evaluated, or whether it is just the provision of more services. For instance, are there fewer cases of malnutrition or diarrhoea? Are fewer infants dying? Improvements in the number of services such as out-patient attendances, latrines built, or surgical operations performed may say little in terms of improvement of the communities' overall health status. This is a difficulty health workers often have to face.

Evaluation is useful at three main levels:

• Overall policy decision making, forms of international aid, type of community to be developed.
• Management decisions on how the policies are to be implemented, how food aid is to be distributed, administration of the community.
• Day to day operational problems to be solved, taking into account the policy and management framework, water shortages, staff sickness, refugee complaints.

The time frame is usually longest for policy matters which cannot be changed easily and shortest for the operational issues.

The methods used must rely very heavily on informed judgements and, therefore, it is important to be aware of local political systems, culture, and traditional forms of control. The best method is to observe, listen, and ask questions. Socio-anthropological methods, sample surveys, use of sample households or informers, use of recorded data, all have their uses. However, good questions and judgements based on a broad community approach, together with up-to-date information, are the essential approaches for good evaluation. Ask yourself the following questions before undertaking any evaluation:

- What is the problem/issue?
- Why is the evaluation needed?
- For whom?
- By whom?
- How appropriate is it?
- Who has been consulted?
- Whose objectives are being used?
- What methods are being used?
- How will the findings be used?

Assessment of needs

How questions are phrased and asked is of vital importance in getting the right response, but before asking a question it is even more important to decide what information is necessary and how it will be used.

On arrival, the first task is to carry out an assessment to identify the main problems. This should take into account the refugees' need for food, water, shelter, sanitation, clothing, transport, education and health services, as well as for cultural, socio-economic, and political factors. The information gained from the assessment should give health workers a wide perspective.

The most effective way of obtaining information is by making observations and asking questions. The nationals, refugees, and aid agencies have a great deal of knowledge, but you may need to ask questions to obtain it. The dangerous health workers are those who think they have all the answers and do not allow their professional training to be adapted.

You need information on the following main areas:

- The main health and disease problems.
- The seriousness of the situation.
- The likelihood of the refugees being able to return to their own country.
- The role of international health personnel.

The following topics and questions are intended as a stimulus to the type of information it may be useful to obtain, and are not intended to be followed rigidly.

NATIONAL LEVEL

What are the main characteristics of the host country, e.g. size, population, ethnic groups, languages, religions, geographical features, seasons, etc?

What is the policy of the national government towards refugees?

What are the main political issues?

Is there a national refugee commission?

Is there a special refugee health unit within the refugee commission or ministry of health? Have any policies on health issues been formulated?

What is the extent of international aid?

Which agencies are concerned with relief work?

How much co-ordination is there between the government and agencies?

What are the main health and disease problems of the host country?

What are considered to be the main health and disease problems in the camps? How does this compare with life previously?

What are the main organizational problems?

Are there potential or actual areas of conflict with the local national population?

What proportion of funds are allocated to each of the following: water, food, logistics, sanitation, and health services?

Who has control of expenditure for these budgets?

REFUGEE COMMUNITY

What are the main geographical, transport, and communication features of the area?

What are the main health and organizational problems expressed at local-government level concerning the refugees?

What is the environment like and what is the camp layout?

Who is responsible for administration?

What local and international staff are involved in the day to day life of the community? On which programmes? What co-ordination of effort is there?

Are many refugees living outside the formal camp structure? If so, how many?

Why have the refugees come into the camp? How long have they been there?

Where have the refugees come from? What sort of environment was it? Where have they passed through?

What is the estimated total population?

What is the rate of newcomers per week? Is it increasing, decreasing, or remaining static? What are the factors involved?

What are the main ethnic groups, languages, and religions?

What is their political structure; who are the leaders?

Are the families mainly father, mother, and direct offspring (nuclear) or are they extended?

What is the average size of a family? What is the common household structure?

How many births are there thought to be per week/month? Is the number lower or higher than would normally be expected?

How many deaths are there per week/month? To what does the community attribute the deaths?

What degree of refugee community involvement is there?

How much self-sufficiency and self-reliance is there?

Cultural and socio-economic factors

What is the estimated literacy rate of the refugee community? What is considered to be the best form of communication? Are there many different languages and dialects?

Is there any evidence of any economic activities, such as farming, basket-making, weaving, wood carving, etc.?

What is the range of occupations amongst the refugees, e.g. professional training, farmers, nomads, etc.?

What resources have the refugees managed to bring with them, e.g. technical equipment, household goods, livestock?

Within the refugee community are there any particular customs, beliefs, traditions, values, or laws that will influence the type of health care provided?

For what health and disease problems is traditional medicine used?

What type of traditional practitioners are there, e.g. bone setters, traditional birth attendants, spiritual healers? Is there evidence that any of the traditional remedies may be harmful?

What are the traditional customs associated with pregnancy, birth, child rearing, and death?

Shelter

What is the most culturally acceptable form of housing for the refugees?

What is the most common form of housing in the community? What materials are used and are they adequate considering the environment?

Are there sufficient local materials for building purposes?

What is the total area of the community?

Is overcrowding an obvious problem?

How much space is there for each household or family?

How many people live in each hut or tent?

Is there a possible link between the housing conditions and the most prevalent symptoms or diseases?

If tents are used to live in and there is a cold season would ground sheets be culturally acceptable?

Clothing

Is the state of clothing amongst the community any worse than you would normally expect to find?

Do people have an adequate change of clothing?

Would material and sewing kits rather than clothes be a more acceptable form of aid?

Are blankets required?

Accidents

What are the most common accidents?

How are they treated and by whom?

Is there a strong possibility of fire? What means are available for quickly extinguishing a fire?

Transport

What transport is available for the distribution of relief supplies? To whom does it belong?

Are there logistics personnel specifically responsible for organizing the distribution of the aid?

Are there any facilities for the regular maintenance of vehicles?

What other factors contribute to the success or failure of the transport system, e.g. fuel, state of roads, seasons, cost of salaries for drivers?

Education

Is there a policy to provide primary and adult education?

How many formally trained teachers are available amongst the refugees and how many are provided by the government?

Are any particular teaching aids or educational facilities needed?

COMMUNITY HEALTH SERVICES

Is there a government policy on the provision of health services to the refugees?

What types of health services and manpower already exist?

Where and what are the nearest government health services for referral and advice?

Who has overall responsibility for the provision and supervision of the health services in the refugee community and in the local region? What is thought and expected of the services?

Is there any degree of community involvement in the organized health services? If there is a health committee, what are its expectations of, and attitude to, the existing health programme?

What are the main disease and symptom problems as determined from:

- clinic attendances
- combined symptom/nutrition surveys in children under five years of age
- household surveys
- conversations with health staff and traditional practitioners?

Is there an unusually high incidence of communicable diseases? Which ones are notifiable? Which are common in the refugees' homeland?

Is there a demand/need for more soap?

If malaria is present, which species of parasites are prevalent and is there any drug resistance? What is the seasonal pattern of transmission?

Are there many war injuries? Are special surgical and rehabilitation services needed?

Which drugs are available and in what quantities? How does this compare with what is actually needed?

Are standardized treatment schedules in use?

Is there an efficient patient flow through the clinic?

How many beds are there in the clinic? For what cases are they used?

What records are kept in the clinic? How accurate are they?

Is there a basic laboratory service? If not, would it be useful to have one and for which examinations?

What proportion of patients is referred for secondary care, for what reasons, and to where?

Is the nearest hospital experiencing any difficulties related to the care of the refugees?

Is there a home-visiting programme?

Have any disease-control programmes been implemented, e.g. for tuberculosis? Do they follow government policy?

Is oral rehydration encouraged? What methods are used?

Has there been an immunization programme? What vaccines were used? What was the coverage? How difficult was it to maintain the cold chain?

How frequently are reports needed and for whom? Are there standardized reporting forms?

Have any health education sessions been given? If so, on what topics, by whom, using what methods, and to whom?

What might help relieve the mental stress? e.g. provision of herbal teas, sports facilities, social services, etc.

How active are the private and traditional health services? Are the traditional practitioners incorporated in the programme?

Would regular informal training/discussion sessions amongst the trained staff be useful?

If there are already international health personnel present how do they perceive the state of the health programme? How good or bad do they think the overall situation is?

Is there a mechanism to co-ordinate international health action?

Vector control
What are the most common disease vectors, e.g. rodents, mosquitoes, flies, fleas, lice, etc.?

What environmental conditions affect the breeding and survival of these vectors, e.g. seasonal variations, temperature, rainfall, water, and sanitation facilities?

What vector control measures are being used?

Nutrition

What is the general state of nutrition of the refugee population and of the local people? How does it compare with previous reports and data?

Are there refugees obviously suffering from malnutrition and/or specific nutritional deficiencies, e.g. vitamin A?

What was the diet of the refugees in their homeland? Were there any particularly high vitamin or energy ingredients?

Are there any cultural taboos concerning food?

How is the food prepared, cooked, and eaten? Is there adequate fuel for cooking purposes? What are the eating habits of the families?

What factors influence the nutritional status of the refugee community, e.g. cultural acceptability of the general feeding programme, storage facilities, the frequency of food distribution?

Do newcomers seem to be in a better or worse nutritional state than those already resident?

Is any monitoring of nutritional status in progress?

What resources are available to the community for improving its nutritional status, e.g. agricultural land, seeds, livestock, fishing?

What foods are people receiving in the general feeding, in what quantities, and how often is the food distributed?

What is the average daily ration in terms of calories, fat, protein, and vitamin content?

Is there a discrepancy between the estimated total food requirements and the amount actually received?

Does the community have access to any foods other than those distributed in the feeding programme(s), e.g. at the local market?

What are the provincial and refugee community food storage facilities? Is the food stacked properly? How many days supply can be stored?

Is there policy regarding 'food for work' programmes?

Is poor lactation mentioned as a problem by the women? Are breast feeding centres/wet nurses used?

For a more specific assessment what is the nutritional status of:

- pregnant and lactating women
- children under 5 years
- schoolchildren
- old people
- special medical cases, e.g. those suffering from tuberculosis
- disabled?

With reference to infant feeding:

- Are there any cultural practices and/or taboos that affect weaning?
- At what age is weaning commenced?
- What types of foods are introduced?
- Are traditional weaning foods readily available?
- How are the foods received in the aid programme being adapted for use at this age?
- Is there any evidence of bottle feeding? Can this be controlled effectively?

If supplementary (and therapeutic) feeding programmes exist:

- What foods are used and in what quantities?
- Is the supplementary ration given as a cooked food 'on the spot' or as a dry ration to take home?
- How many feeds each day?
- Are the recipients eating normally at home?
- How many people are benefiting? How were they selected?
- How many vulnerable people are actually receiving supplementary food daily and what is the total number of vulnerable people?

Environmental health

Water supplies

Is there any one official body responsible for the water supply of the refugee community, e.g. local authority?

From where does the community get its supply, e.g. from a river, tanker, stand pipe, well, etc.?

Are all members of the community able to get a reasonable quantity of clean water close to their home?

Are the refugees involved on a community basis with any aspects of water supply?

Is the water supply adequate in quantity during all seasons?

Have bacteriological and chemical checks been carried out to determine the quality of water?

Is there any danger of contamination of the water supply from livestock, human excreta, or refugee communities upstream?

On average, how many litres of water are used per person per day? Is the amount increasing or decreasing? What factors are involved?

How is the water carried, stored, and used at home, and in the clinic?

Does the community relate certain diseases or symptoms to polluted or insufficient water?

Is there a problem with poor drainage of water?

Is there any evidence of water-related diseases, e.g. skin or eye problems, malaria, typhoid, cholera, diarrhoea, etc?

Sanitation and refuse disposal

What is the most culturally acceptable method for the disposal of human excreta?

Is indiscriminate defaecation common and is it being done too close to the water sources or homes?

What other disposal systems exist, e.g. family or communal pit latrines, bucket systems, water flush sewerage, etc.?

From a spot check are these systems:
- Culturally acceptable?
- Being used and if so by whom?
- Ensuring privacy for the users?
- Being maintained properly?
- A health hazard?
- Sufficient in number?

Are separate facilities required for each sex?

What is used for anal cleansing, e.g. sand, water, corn cobs, stones, etc?

Are materials and space available for building more latrines?

Are engineers required to help mend broken sewerage and/or water mains pipes?

Is there any evidence of a high level of disease or symptoms that may be related to poor sanitation practices, e.g. diarrhoea, helminth infections?

How are used syringes and needles and soiled dressings disposed of?

What system is there for the regular collection and disposal of refuse?

Are there regular camp clean-up campaigns?

What type of soil is the camp sited on?

How deep is the water table? Does the depth vary considerably in different seasons?

Training health workers

Are there refugee health committees and community health workers?

What categories of formally trained health staff already exist amongst the refugees?

Is there a need for a training programme for chosen members of the community? What type of training programme is envisaged?

What is the government's attitude to a proposal to commence training in the camp?

Are any similar training programmes being run in the country of asylum or in the refugees' homeland, from which lessons can be learnt?

What skills do the health workers need?

How would they be chosen?

Would basic literacy be a necessary pre-requisite?

Would they be paid a salary, be voluntary, or on a food-for-work programme?

What form would the training take, length, content, method of assessment? Single or multi purpose?

What ratio of male to female workers would there be? Would there be any tasks for which females are better suited than males and vice versa?

Would there be any formal recognition for having undertaken such a training?

To whom would the workers be directly responsible?

Who would supervise the workers?

What opportunities would there be for further in-service training?

Health management

Effective management is the key to the provision of successful health care services. Many of the day-to-day frustrations and much of the poor staff morale are often the result of poor management. They are often due to three

Ps—political expediency, professional dominance, and public apathy. Management implies promoting good relations, being observant, defining objectives, using resources such as manpower, materials, and money efficiently, getting things done, and evaluating the work in order to meet the health needs of the community.

In refugee communities the following are important in the management of health services:

• Governments and international aid agencies need to allocate funds and staff in an equitable manner between different camps and different services.
• The recurrent costs to the government of any programme must be considered before implementation.
• Only appropriate, efficient, and acceptable technologies must be chosen.
• Great emphasis should be placed on the logistics of transport supplies and other support systems.
• Available manpower must be frequently reviewed and decisions taken on efficient mixtures of different kinds of personnel.
• Effective co-ordination must be developed between the different government sectors responsible for providing services.
• Co-ordination and standardization must be effected between the government and the other national and international agencies concerned.

ADMINISTRATION

There are usually three administrative structures:

• The host government usually has overall responsibility for providing the community administrator, co-ordinating policy, general logistics, and maintaining law and order. It should also provide a central health-planning unit responsible for policy decisions on such issues as standardization of health services and nutrition programmes, training of refugees, and the deployment of health personnel, both local and international. This 'unit' is usually based in the capital, and may be responsible either to the Ministry of Health or the Government's special refugee commission. At provincial level the host government may also provide planning units and the implementation of community level health services. However, most Third World countries have insufficient staff to take on these extra responsibilities.
• The refugees themselves have their own families and social groupings. There are often key people who are accepted as leaders at each level in the social hierarchy.
• The inter-government and non-governmental agencies which are often loosely co-ordinated by UNHCR. As these agencies represent many different donor organizations it is inevitable that the type and quality of their administration will vary. Often co-ordination between them is poor and they may have different policies.

Unless positive efforts are made tensions are likely to develop between the above three groups. They may have conflicting objectives and priorities. The host government health department may be justifiably worried that the refugees are receiving better health care than the local population. The refugees will naturally push for the best they can get, while international health personnel are liable to provide a service which is too sophisticated, too costly, and orientated too much towards curative medicine. Where confusion and antagonism exist between these groups, opportunities for improving and maintaining health care are often missed. As many as 18 different factors were identified as contributing to the high mortality rate among refugees in Vietnam in 1972, most of these factors being attributable to lack of planning and organization.

Figure 3.5 shows the administrative structure organized for the health care of refugees in Somalia.

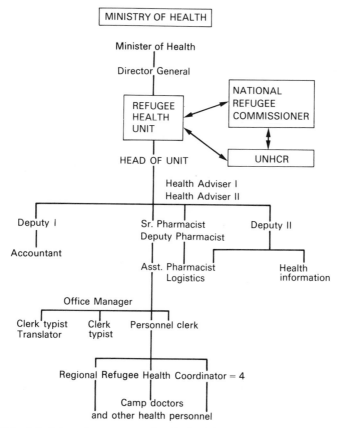

Fig. 3.5. Administrative structure for the health care of refugees in Somalia.

At community level management structures may vary and change with time, especially when the local training of refugees gets under way. There is always an administrator, sometimes committees, to deal with different aspects of the relief work, and nearly always traditional midwives and doctors. It is not helpful to try and formulate a ratio of professional health staff to number of refugees. A few experienced personnel with the right personality and a community health orientation are more important than many highly trained specialists with sophisticated skills.

Administrative procedures and techniques

Administrative procedures and techniques essential at all levels of organization are:

- Information systems, including reporting records and basic statistics.
- Budgeting and finance—especially prompt payment of bills and salaries.
- Record keeping of all financial transactions and movement of supplies.
- Regular maintenance of buildings, transport, and other equipment.
- Checking supplies, re-ordering, and ensuring logistics for regular supplies/transport.
- Adequate professional support, supervision, and guidance for the different health workers.
- Good staff management ensuring such things as a clear allocation of work, regular meetings, off duty time, and attention to personal problems.
- Ensuring good relationships between the refugee community and public/professional health services.

Four points that cannot be overemphasized are:

- The need for co-ordination and allocation of work between the government and other agencies concerned.
- Effective meetings of all the agencies concerned at least once a week.
- The development of a community layout that allows for social cohesion but which is still administratively of a manageable size.
- Regular information and reports from the camps should be submitted to the central level, who should provide a feedback of information, perhaps in the form of a newsletter.

INTERNATIONAL HEALTH TEAMS

Administration exists to serve professional and personal needs.
Professional needs:

- communication
- reporting
- supplies

- personnel—replacements and travelling arrangements
- transport

Personal needs

- feeding—housekeeping
- sleeping
- recreation
- money
- post

Ideally an administrator should accompany the team, especially if the programme is to last more than three months. Where this is not possible, administrative duties are usually divided with one person having overall responsibility and everyone else being responsible for a specific aspect. Sometimes the international doctor is in charge of health services for the whole community and he has not only to co-ordinate the various health groups but also to work alongside the administrator or commandant in overall authority. In practice this can be difficult, and tact and diplomacy are needed. Sometimes a government doctor is also present and having someone who understands local conditions and customs is a great advantage. However, such postings may be imposed on them and understandably they may be resentful of the resources and life style of international personnel, who may appear arrogant and insensitive.

Group work

Where there is a mixed professional group of doctors, nurses, nutritionists, and environmental engineers, there is a danger that the doctor will attend all outside meetings and virtually determine the health policy followed by the group. This is wrong as the nurses and other professionals may be more experienced in the day-to-day management and have a better understanding of what is practicable. Therefore discussions, teamwork, and joint decisions are needed. A leader who can act as spokesman and attend meetings will be required; if preferred, this responsibility can be rotated.

Care must be taken to ensure an adequate 'handover' period when one team is leaving and another arriving. The new team must resist the temptation to do a dramatic replanning exercise, rejecting much of what has been previously decided. A reassessment is important, but resulting changes in plans must be adequately discussed with everyone concerned, otherwise confusion and mistrust will develop. Teams working in a camp for three months should avoid the temptation to replan all the services!

Good domestic arrangements are essential. Responsibility for this should be on a rota basis unless someone positively wants to take it on. Males should not be allowed to evade their responsibilities in this field! Cooks and cleaners can be recruited locally, preferably with the help of the authorities.

One of the most common problems encountered by individuals is the very real lack of privacy. There are various ways to reduce potential conflicts and stress; this is vital if morale and the quality of work are to remain high. Some of the simplest ways are to ensure that everyone has their own tent or room to escape to, that everyone has, and takes, the opportunity to get away for a long weekend once every six to eight weeks, and that people do not make martyrs of themselves by working all hours of the day and night with too little rest.

Budget

The cost of running international health teams varies enormously. The main points to consider in any budget are:

- salaries
- drugs and medical supplies
- office equipment
- transport, vehicle fuel, repairs, and maintenance
- accommodation
- special equipment (i.e. for water, feeding)
- training
- air fares
- insurance

These can be divided into capital and recurrent costs and essential versus luxury items. In any situation it is important to allow for local inflation, especially in the price of accommodation, and the possibility of sickness among personnel.

REPORTING

Health reports are usually written to be read and acted upon by the central or provincial administration of the government refugee health unit. The purpose of reporting is:

- To give an idea of the state of health of the refugee community and highlight any changes, e.g. the nutritional status.
- To report on progress in developing health services.
- To list urgent needs, such as for drugs, food, and personnel.
- To give early warnings of epidemics or deteriorating conditions.

The contents of reports will vary, but the aim should be to keep them as simple as possible, giving basic information and requirements such as:

- Population of the community.
- Death rates and possible causes of death with an age/sex breakdown.
- Major diseases being reported and any changes in the pattern, based on clinic records and home visiting.

● Progress of feeding programmes.
● Water supply situation.
● Disposal of excreta and refuse.
● Drug and equipment supplies.
● Staff and personnel situation and the need for replacements.
● Training.
● Urgent needs.
● General points of interest—surveys that have been undertaken, with their results, climate, etc.

Reports should be standardized so that they can be compared with previous ones and those from other refugee communities. The first report will obviously be much more detailed than subsequent ones; during the early stages when the situation is changing rapidly reporting should be frequent, i.e. weekly, whereas later once a month is quite sufficient. Where possible all members of the health team should write or at least contribute to the report. Team leaders are often so involved with administration duties that they do not know what their own team is doing and may be ill-informed about what is really happening!

4 Practical epidemiology

Mapping

USE OF MAPS

Maps are essential for planning and managing any community health activities. A few of the uses of good detailed maps are as follows.

- For locating households and sick patients for follow-up and home visiting programmes.
- In epidemics they are vital for mapping the distribution of cases.
- They make the training and supervision of community health workers far easier and clearer.
- They are excellent when discussing health problems with refugee groups and administrators.
- A detailed map showing all households is necessary before a good sample can be made for a sample census.

MAP-MAKING

Does a map already exist? A search should be made to find the best and largest scale map available of the area. Unless this map is known to be

Fig. 4.1. Aerial photograph of Shatilla refugee camp, Beirut, Lebanon, August 1982. Ideally, the photograph should have been taken from a slightly higher position, to include the whole camp.

inaccurate, use it as a starting point for your own mapping. Camp administrators, military personnel, or other agencies may well have a map already. It may need updating or redrawing.

Aerial photographs can be very useful. Unfortunately most governments tend to be very secretive about such photographs and it may be difficult to get access to them. You will usually, however, have to make your map from a small-scale photograph; see p. 62 for methods of enlarging the scale. Where very dispersed communities exist in humid, forested terrain aerial photographs often provide the only satisfactory basis for map-making. From these photographs a count of all households may be made, which can then be used for a sample census.

If no suitable map exists to copy from, ask amongst the refugee community for someone with mapping skills, such as a surveyor or geographer. Government malaria control workers have often had good map-making experience. Indeed, they may have already mapped those houses that were in the area prior to establishment of the refugee community.

What scale?

It is always best to make a map on a large scale and then reduce it. For a dispersed community a scale of 1:2500 may be suitable, with a larger scale for a crowded settlement. The scale is expressed as a ratio so that one inch or centimetre on the map represents say 2500 cm on the ground in the actual camp. Remember that the larger the scale, the smaller the second number. In this case 1:2500 would be a larger scale map than 1:25 000. It is essential to be able to label each household with a legible number on the map; if this is not possible, then the scale is too small.

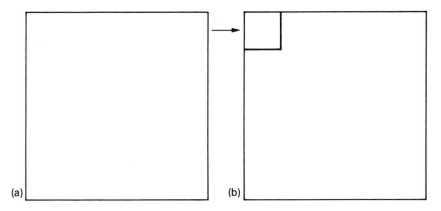

Fig. 4.2. (a) Scale of 1:2500 means one centimetre on the map = 2500 cm on the ground. (b) Scale of 1:25 000 means one centimetre = 25 000 cm on the ground.

Enlarging a map

The simplest method is to draw a series of horizontal and vertical parallel lines about 1 cm apart on the original map, or on tracing paper, or a plastic sheet which can then be laid accurately over the original map. On the sheet of paper for the new enlarged map draw the same number of lines but space them 3, 4, or 5 cm apart, depending on the enlargement required. Using the lines as a visual guide, sketch in the features from the small scale map on to the new map, as shown in Fig. 4.3.

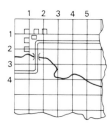
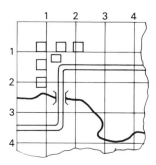

Fig. 4.3. Enlarging a map.

If a pantograph is available, it will do the enlargement more quickly and accurately. If a projector or epidiascope that can project pages from books or maps is available, a large image can be projected on to a wall on which there is a large sheet of paper. The map's main features can then be marked on and the details filled in later by hand.

Making a map

● Drawing a map by hand is usually adequate to show the relationship of a few houses and the main features such as roads, tracks, wells, and latrines. If the camp is large and laid out on a grid pattern the map can be quite easy to draw, but if the refugees have been allowed to group themselves then drawing by hand is far more difficult. The larger the land area covered by the map the more difficult it becomes to draw accurately by freehand.

● Sometimes an old 1:25 000 or 1:50 000 survey map will include the major features. This can be enlarged and the details can be sketched by hand into the enlarged framework (see above).

● If no map is available, try and borrow a level and rangefinder from a local surveyor, college, or training centre, together with some surveying poles (or use any suitable lengths of wood or metal about 2 m long).

● Take a fixed point and measure with a tape an accurate base line of several hundred metres on a defined compass bearing (Fig. 4.4).

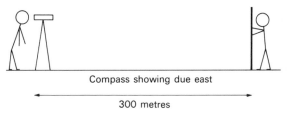

Compass showing due east

◄─────────────── 300 metres ───────────────►

Fig. 4.4. Establishing a base line.

● From this base line the rest of the map is built up, using the level to measure the angle between the baseline and the landmark for a series of prominent landmarks, and also the distance to the landmarks. If your level will not measure distances, the alternative is to measure the angle between the baseline and landmark from each end of the baseline. Provided you have measured the baseline accurately and taken good readings, the two lines from the baseline should cross at the point on the map where the landmark should be marked in.

● Using the two ends of this baseline mark on the new map all the prominent main landmarks, roads, and rivers, etc. to produce the new skeleton map. A prominent feature should be in the same spot on the skeleton map, even when its position is found by using the rangefinder at both ends of the baseline.

● Once the skeleton map has been constructed, the houses, paths, shops, water points, etc. can all be sketched in by hand. Use as much detail as is practical.

● Wherever possible, houses should be marked on or near their door with the same reference number as shown on the map. Malaria teams may have done this, and their system should then be followed. Otherwise, any logical system may be devised to identify the local area or quarter, as well as the

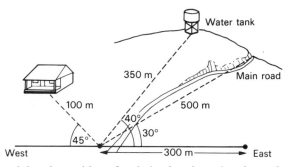

Fig. 4.5. Determining the position of main landmarks, using the angle and distance from the base line.

house itself. Numbering also gives an 'address' for health visiting and other purposes.

• Once all items are verified, the original map should be completed with a permanent marker, such as India ink or waterproof feltpens, and kept in a safe place. Copies will be needed for health workers in the field. Additions and corrections will have to be made to the master map from time to time. However, it should be clearly understood who can make these. Accurate maps of household locations, like censuses, may be politically sensitive and careful thought must be given as to who should be able to use them.

Estimating refugee populations

The aim in a census is to count everybody once and nobody twice. The reasons for conducting a census in a refugee community are to determine the size and composition of the population, for example, the proportion in different age and sex groups and in different tribes or castes. This information is necessary for planning the provision of food, shelter, and medical supplies and to organize community health programmes. The results of a census are also used in the estimation of birth, death, and disease rates. It is only possible to calculate these rates if the number of births, deaths, or disease episodes can be related to the size of the population in which these events have occurred.

Fig. 4.6. Administrators estimating the size and composition of new arrivals (returnees) to a shelter in Ethiopia.

In planning a census it must be remembered that unofficial estimates of the number of persons may differ from official ones and efforts to obtain accurate estimates may be obstructed for political reasons.

There are two strategies that may be adopted to determine the size and composition of the community. A sample census is one in which only a sample of all the refugees is enumerated; they are chosen in such a way as to be representative of the whole camp. In some circumstances, such as in more permanent camps, a full census in which every person is enumerated may be necessary.

ESTIMATING NUMBERS

If a sample census is not possible or the total number of households is unknown, an estimate of the composition of the refugee population, but not its size, is possible by surveying some randomly chosen households. The total number of inhabitants is enumerated for at least 100 households by age, sex, and the other important characteristics about which information is needed. This may form part of a household health survey as discussed on page 81. This information by itself will only provide estimates on the percentage of refugees in different groups.

A SAMPLE CENSUS

If we count the number of persons in, say, 10 per cent of the households and multiply this number by ten, an estimate of the total population is obtained. Clearly this estimate will not be as accurate as that obtained by enumerating the entire population, but for many purposes it will be sufficient. To conduct a sample census a map of all households is useful. Each household is given a number and, for example, 5 or 10 per cent are selected at random. This may be done by selecting every tenth house, or by writing each of the house numbers on a separate piece of paper, putting them in a box, and drawing out 10 per cent. The latter method is sometimes preferable as some systematic bias may exist in the way in which the houses were originally numbered. If they are available, random numbers, either from a book of tables or calculator, are likely to be quicker to use than pieces of paper in a box. See Appendix 2 for an example of random tables.

An alternative to taking a completely random sample of households is to select clusters of households evenly distributed from different parts of the camp. Start with a detailed map showing all the main sectors and preferably all the households as well. It is best to examine a cluster of not more than ten households from each of the main sectors, and at least 100 households should be interviewed in total. A larger sample gives more accurate results, but also means more work for a diminishing degree of usefulness, and takes longer to analyse. A good guide in a sample census is to include no more than about 5–

10 per cent of all households, provided that at least 100 households are included.

In a sample census it is especially important to specify clearly who should be counted as a member of a household. Neighbours of those in a 'sampled' house may try to get into the sample, if they believe, for example, that the enumeration may affect food allocation. If they succeed, an over-estimate of the total population will be obtained when the sampled population is multiplied by the assumed sampling fraction (e.g. 10).

A FULL CENSUS

When the community has settled it is important to conduct a full census so that everyone is registered. Opposition to this may be encountered for political and/or cultural reasons, but it helps in the fair distribution of food and other supplies.

INFORMATION REQUIRED AND DATA COLLECTION

Who to count and where to count them

The usual method of conducting a census is to count the number of persons in each household. A clear definition of what a household is will depend on the local organization. In some circumstances a single house will be the relevant unit, whereas in others it may be a compound consisting of several houses, all of whose inhabitants eat together. The choice of the unit will be influenced by the purposes of the census. If the aim is merely to determine the total population size, any unit that ensures that everyone is included and no one is counted twice would be appropriate. If it is desired, however, to relate subsequent events such as deaths or illnesses back to an individual's census record, it will be valuable to use a household unit with which the people themselves identify so that, for example, the census record may be traced back through the name of the head of the household.

It is important to decide before conducting a census whether record is to be made of the *de facto* or *de jure* population.

The *de facto* population of a household consists of those present at the time of the survey or, more usually, those who slept in the household on the previous night. The *de jure* population of a household is that which is 'normally resident' in the household. A census of the *de facto* population is far easier to conduct and the risks of counting a person more than once are small as few persons are likely to have slept in more than one household on the previous night. Problems may arise if it is desired to retrace some or all of the population at a later date, as there would be no record of the 'normal' place of residence. In these circumstances the *de jure* population is more useful. A census to determine this population is more difficult to conduct, as it will involve more extensive questioning of the residents of each household to determine its normal composition. Special difficulties arise if the population of a household thinks that the results of the census may be used for ration allocation. In such a situation there is likely to be a tendency to 'inflate' the size of the household by reporting non-existent members. In practice it is sometimes difficult to make a clear distinction between the *de jure* and *de facto* population, but before conducting a census it is important to specify:

● The definition of households to be used in the enumeration.
● Who should be registered and who should not be registered in each such household. Everyone should be assigned to one household and no one should be assigned to more than one.

Preliminary investigations

A satisfactory census cannot be carried out without the co-operation of the population. Gain their confidence by explaining why the census is being conducted, what information will be collected, and answering any questions. Local leaders should be consulted about any cultural or other factors that may affect the census. Local leaders will be able to advise on the best time of day to visit households, the concepts of kinships and extended families which may affect the definition of the household, and any attitudes to birth and death or to counting the population that might affect the census.

To ensure accurate counting:

● Do not inform the population in advance exactly which households are to be visited (in a sample census).
● Where feasible, all occupants of the sampled households should be seen, particularly children.
● Those counted should be identified on the census schedule in such a way that they are not counted more than once.
● Sufficient census teams should be available to complete the job quickly.

What information to collect

With only few resources likely to be available for the conduct of a census, it is imperative that only the minimum necessary information is collected. Each item about which information may be gathered should be carefully considered to determine its use. For each item the question should be asked 'Do we need this information from all members of the population or will a sample be sufficient?'.

The basic minimum information is likely to include age, sex, and place of residence, e.g. administrative sector. The amount of extra data collected will depend on the uses to which they will be put. For example, it may not be worth recording the names of each person in a house during a census. Recent birth and death rates may be estimated by asking about the occurrence of these events during the previous year, but such information may be of limited value unless the population has been stable for some time.

The refugee population should be told exactly who will have access to the information that is collected and what it will be used for. Confidentiality must be respected. It may be desired, for example, to use the census to set up a register but, in some situations, there may be strong resistance to such a scheme. These issues must be discussed with local leaders before the census is conducted. An important consideration in planning a census is that it must be carried out quickly, within a few days, or, at most, weeks. Otherwise population movements within and to and from the community may seriously affect the reliability of the data.

The record form

The record form should be easy to complete and analyse. It may be useful to record all the data about one household on a single sheet. If the population is to be resurveyed at a later date, it may be easier to record each individual on a separate card, so that these can be easily rearranged if a person changes households.

If a census or a sample census is being conducted to enumerate the age and sex composition of the camp, a form such as shown in Fig. 4.7 may be adequate. The census clerk completes one line of the form for each household and the total population of a group of households may be summarized at the bottom of the form.

Household No.	MALES						FEMALES					
	<1	1–4	5–14	15–44	45+	TOTAL	<1	1–4	5–14	15–44	45+	TOTAL
1001	1		2		1	4	1				1	2
1002		3				3				1		1
TOTAL												

Fig. 4.7. Example of a simple census form.

Figure 4.8 shows a more detailed census form that might be employed if the census is being used to set up a central system in which information about individuals may be recorded, e.g. morbidity and mortality. One such form is completed for each household. The design of the record form will depend on all the possible uses to which the census may be put.

Collecting the data

To carry out a census rapidly it may be necessary to have several teams working simultaneously in different parts of the community. The teams should consist of refugees, preferably with secondary-school education, who can speak both the local language and the language of the census supervisor. Such census clerks are more likely to be able to gather reliable information than strangers. Before the census is conducted the registration clerks should be given clear instructions on the definition of a household, who to count as its members, and how and what to record for each individual. Pilot studies should be organized to test that the instructions have been understood and that all the census clerks are using a similar approach. Spot checks should also be made to supervise and monitor the performance of the clerks during the main census itself.

Counting the refugees

The aim in a census is to count everybody once and nobody twice. Each household should be given a number, either before or during the census, by

Household No. 1007	Date: 24 Jun '82		Interviewer: P.S.			
Community Sector: E	Sector Chief: WURAPA					
Person No.	Name/father's name	Relation to head	Age	Sex	Time in camp (months)	Notes
01	OKELLO/ODOC	HEAD	39	M	13	
02	EWINA/ONGOM	WIFE	32	F	13	in hospital
03	EBONG/OKELLO	Son of 1+2	3/12	M	3	
04						
05						
06						

Fig. 4.8. A more detailed census form.

Fig. 4.9. Painting number on a house during a census in a refugee village in Baluchistan province, Pakistan.

which the household can be identified on the census forms. Ideally, the number should be painted or marked clearly on the house. Different census teams may be allocated different numerical sequences, e.g. Team one: 101, 102, ... Team two: 201, 202, ... etc., and each team may allocate its numbers sequentially to the houses it visits in the census. A team member paints the number on the house structure to show that the household has already been recorded. In the final stages of the census a check is made that every household in the sample has been visited and allocated a number. Households that are found to be unoccupied must be revisited later to register any persons who were temporarily absent. The help of local leaders may be invaluable in determining the usual residents of each household.

Completing the census forms

If the *de facto* population is being recorded it may be necessary to ask how many people slept in the household on the previous night and then to ask for them to be listed by name to ensure the counting was correct. Enumeration of the *de jure* population will require much greater care.

Be sure that newborn children are registered. In many societies there is a tendency not to declare the newborn until they are past a certain age. Questioning family members about pregnancies may overcome this problem. If any women state that they are pregnant at the time of the census, it may be useful to record this on their form

A person's sex should be requested rather than assumed, as names may be an unreliable guide to gender.

Age may be difficult to determine precisely, unless birth certificates have been in use and are available. For young children it may be important to estimate age quite accurately. This may be done by careful questioning of the mother—if possible, relating the time of birth to important local events with known dates such as seasons, floods, or the start of war. If precise indicators of age are unavailable approximate methods of estimation may be useful. For example, most children cannot reach over their head and touch the top of their ear until they are about five years and the age, in months, of a child who is between six months and 24 months can be approximated by the number of erupted teeth plus six.

ANALYSIS OF DATA

The age and sex structure of the population, together with the total number of inhabitants, can be determined by combining the information on the census schedules for each household. If forms of the kind shown in Fig. 4.7 have been used this can be done very rapidly by simply adding the columns. If an individual form has been used for each household (e.g. Fig. 4.8) the results can be summarized by a tabulation chart as discussed on p. 89. Remember to divide the totals by the sample fraction in sample surveys.

Analysis can be done manually by the census clerks themselves if they are given appropriate instructions. More complex facilities are not usually necessary, but an inexpensive calculator may be helpful. Analyses should be repeated independently by different people so that any clerical errors may be detected.

The more quickly the results can be made available the more useful they will be. A well-produced report three months after the census might look impressive to agency staff in the capital city or overseas but be almost useless in a new community which is growing fast.

FOLLOW-UP AFTER THE CENSUS

After the census has been conducted and analysed it may be possible to set up a recording system for births, deaths, and migrations by recruiting the assistance of local helpers living in different sections. Each helper should be assigned a definite area of the community or a specific number of households for which he is responsible. In this way it will be possible to maintain an up-to-date record of the population and to calculate birth and death rates, and thus monitor any changes in mortality rates.

After a time it may be desirable to re-census the population and the forms completed at the first census can be used to record births, deaths, and migrations since the first census. If it is planned to conduct a re-census in this way the design of the original forms should take this into account. A second census provides an additional method of measuring birth, death, and migration rates.

Another potential use of the census is to set up an index of the population that may be used to record, for example, visits to the dispensary or hospital. It should be stressed, however, that this kind of exercise is not likely to be worthwhile if there is a rapid turnover of persons or if there is no clearly defined and useful purpose for such recording.

Epidemiology and surveys

Epidemiological techniques help to obtain information about diseases in the refugee camp population and the extent to which the refugees are using the available health services.

Epidemiological data are vital for the effective planning, management, and evaluation of the health services and for identifying priority health problems. Usually information is obtained from an analysis of out-patient clinic attendances and from reported deaths—preferably by some indication of cause. However, both these sources can give very biased and misleading reports. To avoid this, surveys and surveillance can be organized and this section explains some of the concepts and practical techniques applicable to a defined refugee population.

DESCRIPTIVE EPIDEMIOLOGY

To understand more about why a disease is occurring or why people are not using a service or clinic, it is first necessary to describe the situation. This can be done by asking the following questions:

- Which people are involved?
- At which places?
- When?
- What is the frequency (incidence or prevalence) of the cases, episodes, or events?

People affected

People can be grouped in many different ways, but some of the more important characteristics or variables are age, sex, length and place of residence, nutritional status, occupation, socio-economic status, cultural and religious groupings, and family size. Figure 4.10 illustrates a pyramid using age and sex as variables from the Wollo famine in Ethiopia 1973/4. It demonstrates that the population in the shelters during the famine showed relatively fewer young children and old people than before the onset of the famine.

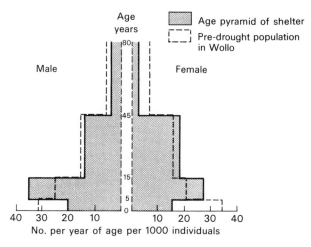

Fig. 4.10. Age pyramid (males and females) of aggregate shelter population as compared with pre-drought situation in Wollo province, Ethiopia (Belete, Gebre-Medhin, Hailemariam, Maffi, Vahlquist, and Wolde-Gebriel 1977).

It is very important to differentiate between arrivals within the last month and those residents who have been in the community longer. New arrivals are likely to bring illness and diseases with them from their original home area or from the country they have travelled through. Communicable disease arising in a resident who has been in the community for a month or more is likely to have originated from in or around the community itself. An epidemiological investigation of an outbreak of conjuctivitis amongst Vietnamese refugees on the island of Guam highlights this point (Fig. 4.11).

Places

Where people live in a community, where they work, and where they have come from may determine which diseases they suffer from. Geographical features, altitude, type of housing, and proximity to water sources may all be important factors. Also the further away a refugee lives from health facilities the less likely he is to use them and is, therefore, less likely to appear in the records.

Time

When a disease starts or the time at which someone visits the health services can also be very useful. Cases, episodes, or events can be grouped according to the number occurring per day, week, month, or year, as shown for Kampuchean refugees in Sakaeo camp Thailand (Fig. 4.12).

The incidence of diseases such as malaria, measles, and diarrhoea change with the seasons. In some countries, for example, measles is endemic throughout the year but may grow to epidemic proportions at the beginning of the rainy season as demonstrated during the Nigerian/Biafran war (Fig. 4.13). Food and water shortages also may be closely linked to seasonality.

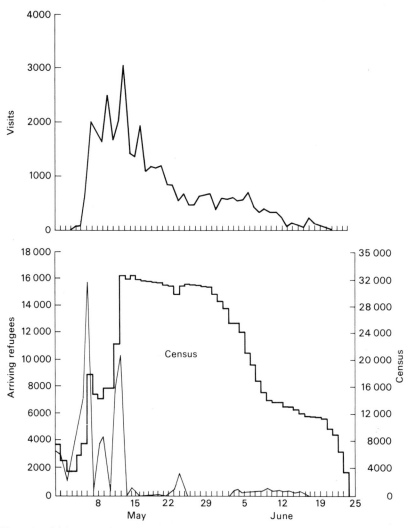

Fig. 4.11. Visits of Vietnamese refugees to camp field clinics for treatment of conjunctivitis shown in relation to the arrival of refugees on Guam and the camp census at Orote Point, Guam. May–June 1975 (Arnow, Hierholzer, Higbee, and Harris 1977).

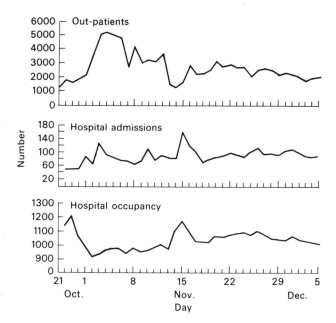

Fig. 4.12. Hospital statistics, Sakeo, 23 October and 2 December 1979 (Glass, Cates, Nieburg, Davis, Russbach, Nothdurft, Peel, and Turnbull 1980).

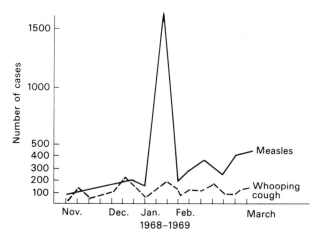

Fig. 4.13. Incidence of communicable diseases as related to seasonal changes (Nigeria/Biafra) (Aall 1972).

Measuring frequency—incidence or prevalence?

The total number of new cases, events, or episodes occurring over a specified period of time is referred to as incidence. Examples might be the number of new cases of malnourished children seen per month, the number of births or deaths per week, or the number of new children added to the feeding programme per day. Incidence is the best measure to assess what changes are occurring in the communities' disease pattern or in the use being made of health services.

The total number of persons with a case, events or episodes, at a particular point in time is referred to as prevalence. Examples are the total number of refugees or the total of children registered in the feeding programme on a particular day.

Refugee communities often grow rapidly and incidence measures can give a more accurate reflection of what is happening, especially for short duration diseases such as measles, diarrhoea, and pneumonia. However, prevalence often gives a better indication of the size of the problem, e.g. number of malnutrition cases, and is often preferred for diseases or conditions that have a long duration, such as malnutrition and tuberculosis. Table 4.1 is an example of the prevalence of malaria at two different points in time among the same community of Rwandan children in refugee settlements in Uganda and demonstrates one of the disease problems associated with migration.

Table 4.1

1961	Malaria parasites		
	No. exam.	No.	%
Infants	233	0	0
1–5 yrs	574	1	0.2
		(*P. falcip.*)	
School age	Not examined		

1967	Malaria parasites		
	No. exam.	No.	%
Infants	35	20	57
1–5 yrs old	254	145	57
School age	246	126	51

291 positive. 234 *P. falciparum*. 2 *P. malariae*. 4 *P. vivax*. 51 Mixed infections (*malariae* and *falciparum*).

(Bennett *et al.* 1968)

Two more points need to be emphasized because they can cause so much confusion when measuring frequency:

• What is the definition of a case event or episode? For instance, are cases of malaria defined as those with fever and headache or is a positive blood film also required? Agreement about how a case is defined is very important. Altering criteria can lead to an apparent change in incidence or prevalence without there being one.

• Are people or episodes being counted? One person can have several attacks of diarrhoea or malaria in one year. If it is the proportion of ill people that is required then it is obviously important to count people. A disease control scheme, however, aims to lower the incidence of attacks, or episodes, and therefore incidence of attacks is a more important measure.

What are rates?

It is usually necessary to make comparisons between different refugee communities or between what is happening in a community now as compared with previous months. For many purposes we cannot simply use total numbers as these take no account of the total population 'at risk'. Refugee communities may change rapidly in size as well as having a continuous through migration. Census techniques enable us to estimate the total population and with the total number of cases and total population we can calculate rates. By forming rates we can then make these comparisons.

The basic components of a rate are:

$$\bullet \frac{\text{No. of cases, episodes or events}}{\text{Total population at risk}} \times \text{a factor (usually 100 or 1000)}$$

Each rate has a time which must be stated, such as a date for prevalence or a time period for incidence measures.

The top figure is referred to as the numerator and the bottom one as the denominator. The factor is chosen to give a whole number for the rate, which is much easier to handle than a fraction or a decimal point.

What are mortality rates?

Mortality in a refugee community, again reported separately for recent arrivals and residents, is an obvious but very crude indicator of the severity of ill health. To be at all meaningful deaths must be expressed as a rate and preferably calculated for the main age groups, i.e. less than 1 year, 1–4, 5–14, 15–44, and 45 + years. A higher than expected number of deaths throughout all ages may well indicate famine conditions and/or an epidemic. Mortality is an incidence measure and the time period for the calculation of the rates should be stated. Comparing rates calculated using different lengths of time is not valid and can easily lead to false conclusions. Table 4.2 is an example of age-specific mortality rates in a camp for Kampuchean refugees in Thailand.

Table 4.2.   *Age-specific mortality rates at Sa Kaeo refugee camp, Oct. 28 to Dec. 5, 1979*

Age group (yr)	Estimated population	Oct. 28 to Nov. 7	Nov. 8–14	Nov. 15–21	Nov. 22–28	Nov. 29 to Dec. 5
				Deaths/10 000/day*		
<1	1200		10.7 (9)	6.0 (5)	4.8 (4)	4.8 (4)
1–4	1500		7.6 (8)	4.8 (5)	3.7 (3)	0.0 (0)
5–14	7900	(145)	2.0 (11)	2.1 (12)	0.2 (1)	0.0 (0)
15–44	19 100		2.2 (29)	1.0 (13)	0.7 (9)	0.3 (4)
45+	2200		3.2 (5)	7.1 (11)	3.9 (6)	3.2 (5)
Unknown*		(175)	(23)	(14)	(6)	(2)
Total	31 900	9.1 (320)	3.8 (85)	2.7 (60)	1.3 (29)	0.7 (15)

Actual number of deaths in parentheses.
* Out-of-hospital deaths.
(Glass *et al.* 1980)

Crude death rate (CDR):

$$\frac{\text{Total deaths in time period}}{\text{Total population existing at midpoint of time period}} \times 1000$$

CDR is a very useful but insensitive incidence measure of how serious conditions are in the community; it does not take into account the age and sex structure of the population. The CDR was used to demonstrate an inverse relationship between the supply of food and mortality in the Burmese refugee camps in Bangladesh in 1978 (see Fig. 4.14).

Infant mortality rate (IMR)

$$\frac{\text{No. of deaths in children less than 1 year old}}{\text{No. of live births in one year}} \times 1000$$

The IMR measures the effect of birth injuries, congenital abnormalities, and all serious infant illnesses such as malaria, malnutrition, diarrhoea, pneumonia, and measles among infants less than one year old. In severe situations it may rise to around 200 per 1000 live births. In refugee communities it is a difficult rate to estimate because of the problem of counting live births. The population of children under one-year-old can be used as the denominator.

Childhood mortality rate (CMR)

$$\frac{\text{No. of deaths in children 1–4 years old}}{\text{Total children 1–4 years old existing at mid-point of time period}} \times 1000$$

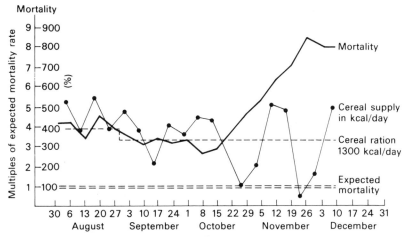

Fig. 4.14. Cereal supply rates and mortality rates in the Burmese refugee camps during August–November 1978 (Aall 1979). Note the inverse relationship between food supply and mortality: when food supply goes down mortality goes up (after an interval of one week). Once mortality reaches a high level it remains high even though supply improves; at a certain stage food does not help, it has come too late.

This rate is a good measure of the severity of malnutrition, as well as of common infectious diseases. In severe situations it can rise to over 100 per 1000.

Case fatality rate

$$\bullet \frac{\text{No. of cases who die from a disease in a given period of time}}{\text{Total No. of cases diagnosed in same period}} \times 100\%$$

This rate measures how serious or fatal a disease is, such as deaths from malnutrition or measles. A change in the rate over time can be difficult to interpret. In situations where there is severe malnutrition, a falling case

Table 4.3. *Summary of mortality from cholera and cholera-like diarrhoeas at Bongaon treatment centre, 24 June to 30 August 1971*

Patient population	Admissions	Number of deaths*	Case fatality ratio
Entire centre	3703	135	3.6%
JH-CMRT demonstration unit only	1190	12	1.0%

*Approximately half of the patients died before any rehydration therapy could be started.
(Mahalanabis *et al.* 1973)

fatality rate may indicate that the most severely affected died first, that the health services are operating more effectively, and/or that the food supply situation is improving, and/or that more mild cases are being included in the total cases diagnosed. Table 4.3 shows the case fatality rate of 3·6 per cent cholera in a camp of Bangladesh refugees in 1971 when the authorities promoted early oral rehydration in all cases of severe diarrhoea. This compared favourably with a previous estimated case-fatality rate of 30 per cent.

SURVEYS

Why carry out a survey?

The structure of refugee communities changes constantly and information on what is happening is often very inadequate, impressionistic, patchy, or out of date. Surveys (and surveillance) can provide more up-to-date information, but no survey should be carried out unless the information is really needed for policy, planning, or management decisions. Decide on what improvements are necessary, on how this could be done, and only then on the information needed.

Surveys are carried out to:

● Estimate the incidence or prevalence of some of the important diseases.
● Screen and identify people who should receive treatment or be referred to the health services.
● Provide general household information about families.
● Find out about beliefs, customs, and behaviour before organizing community programmes.
● Evaluate how the health services or distribution systems are working.

Surveys can be sensitive issues and discussions with administrators and refugee representatives must be held before detailed planning takes place.

Which kind of survey—cross-sectional or longitudinal?

Cross-sectional surveys examine a sample of the population at one point in time and, therefore, give prevalence information. Examples might be the collection of blood smears for malaria parasite examination or the screening of children for malnutrition.

Longitudinal surveys collect information about all the new cases of a disease or event over a period of time and therefore supply incidence data. For example, this might be the recording of the number of new arrivals per day, new cases of measles or tuberculosis, or new pregnant mothers attending an antenatal clinic.

Cross-sectional surveys are easier to organize and are more commonly carried out. By repeating cross-sectional surveys at regular intervals, such as monthly, fairly reliable estimates can be made of how the situation is improving or deteriorating.

Community surveys

These can be organized in two main ways:

● The investigators visit the households to gather information and screen individuals. If this is carried out on a proper sampling basis, estimates can be made for the whole community, e.g. household surveys and censuses.

● The refugees visit a centralized clinic or centre where they may be screened for various illnesses and asked questions. This approach usually requires a high proportion of refugees in the sample to attend, otherwise biased estimates will be obtained.

Household surveys

If a proper sample of households is drawn up and a high proportion subsequently visited, the survey results can usually be taken as representative of what is happening in the whole community. Information can be gathered on such items as:

● Number of persons per household, their age and sex, occupation, tribal and ethnic composition, house construction, cooking facilities, personal belongings, etc.

● Main everyday problems. These may not be so obvious to health personnel, e.g. low level of activity, or lack of cooking utensils, or education facilities.

● Fairness of distribution systems.

● Extent of malnutrition as detected by screening procedures.

● Frequency of common diseases.

● Common names for different symptoms and an estimate of the presence of common complaints.

● Proportion of children who have been immunized.

Household surveys can also be a part of a sample or full census and co-operation with other sectors can lead to the joint collection of much useful information on reasons for migration, education, literacy, income, and agriculture, etc. One of the most interesting of such studies was that undertaken during the famine in Wollo province in Ethiopia.

Screening procedures

Screening procedures are often used in out-patient clinics but they can also be very effectively incorporated into surveys. The main reason for screening is to find those individuals who are 'positive', such as children with malnutrition. The procedure should be able to differentiate clearly between the positive cases and the negatives or normals. Only a very few procedures can do this well and so there is always the problem of malnutrition cases being missed—referred to as false negatives and normals—and conversely, the problem of normals being called cases—the false positive cases.

Since it is usually more important not to miss cases, it is better to include all doubtfuls in with the cases, who, if necessary can then undergo a second, more detailed, sorting out procedure. Some common examples are using weight or height for age to detect malnutrition, haemoglobin for anaemia, and chronic cough for tuberculosis. If laboratory facilities are available, or specimens can be sent elsewhere, screening can be carried out for intestinal and malarial parasites, and bacteriological examination of diarrhoea faecal specimens.

Some important points about screening procedures:

• No procedure should be carried out if no effective treatment is known or if suitable supplies are not available, except where the information is of utmost importance for planning purposes. Staff must be prepared to treat or refer anyone found to be 'positive'.

• Screening questions and tests should differentiate clearly between cases and non-cases, i.e. the percentage of false-positive and false-negative cases should be small.

• The procedures should be simple, cheap, and reliable to use and not rely on complicated imported equipment.

• They should be acceptable to the refugees themselves, otherwise they may refuse to co-operate.

Some common faults in surveys

If certain basic principles are not followed surveys can be inaccurate and give biased results. There is then a great danger that the findings of a poor survey will be used in planning and even publicized, often with detrimental results. Some of the common faults are:

• Poorly defined objectives and a poor understanding of how the information will be used
• Trying to collect too much information.
• Poor definition of events and diagnostic criteria.
• Poor sampling procedures.
• Poor response rate.
• Inaccurate measurement techniques.
• Poorly trained interviewers.
• Badly designed questionnaires.
• Lack of pilot trials before the main survey is carried out.
• Prolonged delays in completing the analysis.
• Faulty interpretation of the findings.
• Inadequate consultation and feedback.

What are good objectives?

Objectives should be easily understood, presented in numerical terms, and it should be feasible to obtain the required data, e.g. to:

• Determine the percentage of children one to four years old below the 80 per cent level of weight-for-height using international standards.
• Screen all refugees five years or older for a history of a chronic cough lasting four weeks or more.

How much information?

It is always tempting to ask more questions than are really needed. Each added objective means more measurements, a longer questionnaire, more field time, more delays in the analysis, and more chances of error. A concise, well designed survey which is quickly analysed is much more valuable. Any survey which requires more than half an hour of an individual's time and any questionnaires asking for information on more than about 20 items is in danger of failure.

Definitions and criteria

As previously discussed on page 77 it must be clear whether people or episodes are being measured. All criteria of a case should be defined before the survey starts, and definitions should not be changed after the start of the survey or to suit the analysis. All staff must follow the agreed definitions.

What is a good sample?

It may not be feasible to survey the whole population or all the people attending the health centre or clinic. In these situations it is best to choose a sample. This must be selected in such a way that it will give roughly the same answer as if the whole population had been surveyed, i.e. an 'unbiased' sample. If the question asked is 'what is the prevalence of malnutrition in the camp population?', then it would be wrong to select a sample from people living close to the health centre, because they might have a much lower prevalence of malnutrition than people living further away. Conversely, those who have just arrived at a camp may have a higher rate. Both of these would be biased samples. By examining people in the clinics you would also have a biased sample, because these people would probably have a higher prevalence of malnutrition than people in the general population. The best way to obtain an unbiased sample is to choose a random sample, so that everyone in the population has an equal chance of being chosen or represented.

If a census has been conducted prior to the survey it will be possible to select from this a sample of persons in the age group of interest. This may be done by using random number tables. If the community is large this method of sampling may be inconvenient, especially if it is planned to conduct the investigations in the home of each person sampled and equipment must be moved to each home. In these circumstances it is common to select a cluster sample of individuals. For example, if a sample of 50 children is required a random sample of households with a child in the correct age group, say ten, is selected at random from the census list and then the child and his/her four nearest neighbours in the same age group are included in the survey. In this way there are ten clusters of five children each. Clearly it is necessary to have well defined rules for deciding who are the nearest neighbours and these rules must be adhered to strictly by those conducting the survey.

The choice of the number of clusters and the number of individuals in each cluster depends upon the variability in different parts of the community of the condition being measured. Clearly one cluster of size 50 may give a very unrepresentative sample of the total population. It is difficult to specify exact guidelines as, in general, the variability in the community of the conditions measured will be unknown. It is probably hazardous to use less than five clusters and, in most circumstances, more than 20 may be unnecessary.

If a sample survey is to be conducted without a prior census the selection of a representative sample is more difficult. If a map has been drawn it will be possible to select a random household, by giving each household a number and drawing random numbers out of a hat, or by sticking a pin 'at random' in the map. This last method is a rather unreliable way of selecting a house completely at random. The random household may then be visited and the ten (say) children of the appropriate age living in, or closest to, the selected household may be included in the survey. Again, strict definitions of 'closest' are required.

If there is no census and no map it is not possible to select a random household unless each house has been numbered, and some 'second-best' procedure must be used to determine the starting point to define a cluster. For example, select a 'random' point, toss a coin, if it is 'heads' walk 40 yards north, if 'tails' walk 40 yards south. Toss the coin again, walk 20 yards east or west depending on the coin toss. Select the house on the left or the right, again depending on the toss of the coin. Such apparently bizarre procedures help to eliminate the bias inherent in asking an individual simply to select a house 'at random', e.g. most people, when asked to select a random number between 0 and 9 select 3 or 7!

In general the larger the sample the more reliable will be the estimates obtained. Table 4.4 provides a guide to the sample sizes required to give accuracy to different prevalence rates.

For example, if the prevalence rate for a condition when measured in a large population is 50 per cent then the prevalence estimate when measured in a sample of 50 persons will probably be between 36 and 64 per cent, provided it is a random sample. If we sampled 200 persons the estimate

Table 4.4

Observed prevalence %	Sample size									
	50		100		200		500		1000	
1	—		0	5	0.1	4	0.3	3	0.5	2
5	—		2	11	2	9	3	8	4	7
10	3	22	5	18	6	15	7	13	8	12
20	10	34	13	29	15	26	16	24	18	23
30	18	45	21	40	24	37	26	35	27	33
40	26	55	30	50	33	47	35	45	37	43
50	36	64	40	60	43	57	45	55	47	53
60	45	74	50	70	53	67	55	65	57	63
70	55	82	60	79	63	76	65	74	67	73
80	66	90	71	87	74	85	76	84	77	82
90	78	97	82	95	85	94	87	93	88	92

would probably be in the range of 43–57 per cent and, for a sample of 1000 persons would be in the range 47–53 per cent. Thus, in this example, the gain in going from a sample size of 200 to one of 1000 is relatively small, but it is much larger for 200 than 50. For conditions that are relatively common, e.g. prevalence rate of 10 per cent or more, reasonable estimates of the prevalence rate can be obtained with samples of modest size and there is often little value, and considerable cost, in taking large samples. For many purposes a sample of 100 persons will be more than sufficient, but for conditions that have a low prevalence or incidence, such as around 5 per cent, much larger samples will be required.

A poor response rate?

Even if the sample is well chosen, surveys can give wrong answers when a high percentage of households or people are not contacted or do not respond. It is important to know what percentage of the people in the sample were actually seen. In surveys for leprosy, for instance, people often know they have it and may not turn up to be examined. The reverse is also true; people not in the sample may appear if they think that they are likely to get privileges, such as with malnutrition and feeding programmes.

Remember that those who are not seen are as important as those who are. As a general rule it is necessary to see at least 80 per cent of the original sample. In surveys about beliefs, customs, and behaviour the non-responders, i.e. those who did not respond or come, may not be as important as with some of the serious diseases. The problems of poor sampling and poor response rates apply just as much to surveys using questionnaires as to other kinds of surveys.

Inaccurate measurements—observers, subjects, or the instruments?

Any measurement can be inaccurate. The most common problem is with the person taking the measurement and not with the instrument or the patients. This is known as 'observer error'. There may also be problems with the instruments if they have not been checked for some time for their zero reading, particularly weighing scales. Faulty recording on the record chart is also common. These remarks apply just as much to the use of questionnaires.

The most important ways in which staff can reduce the amount of inaccuracy are to:

• Follow a standard and agreed method, such as how the infant is to be weighed, and how to ask the questions in the questionnaire.
• Be thoroughly trained and periodically checked to see that they are carrying out the method correctly.
• Sign their name against any case history, physical examination, measurement, or laboratory test so that it is clear who made it. This encourages accurate work and is also helpful when checking records for missing information.
• Check all instruments frequently, at least daily, to see that they are still accurate, e.g. put a known weight on a weighing machine, use of haemoglobin standard.

Questionnaires

Questionnaires are used to collect information about what happened to people in the recent past; what food they are getting; whether they have any illnesses: what method of child spacing they use; if any child has been born or died recently; and where they go for medical help. This information would be difficult or impossible to get in any other way. It is easier to ask where people get their domestic water supply than to observe them to find out.

Medical staff often use questions and questionnaires in their work but rarely ask themselves how accurate the information is. Questionnaires are fairly easy to prepare and use, but can often be inaccurate for the following reasons:

1. Poor questions—they may be badly worded or easily misinterpreted. General questions are different from direct ones and can give very different answers, e.g. 'Is your child under five years old?' is very different from 'How old is your child?'
2. Difficult subjects—the more private and personal the content of the question the more likely the person is to give wrong or misleading answers, e.g. it is easier to answer questions about fever or immunizations than it is about political affiliations or child spacing practices.
3. Poor memory—memories are surprisingly short and in general only major

events can be remembered more than a few days hence. As a general rule do not ask people what they did more than one week ago.

4. Observer and subject bias—people asking the questions have a tendency to interpret the questions and answers quite freely, whereas refugees also tend to answer questions in the way that they think the questioner wishes, e.g. if the health officer is asking about water usage, the people know what will probably please him!

5. Too many questions—people quickly get bored with a long questionnaire. Start with some basic questions about name, age, sex, and religion, and then go on with the particular questions that need answers. About ten more questions allow for an interview to take about ten to fifteen minutes, which means that four to six people can be interviewed in one hour.

Because of literacy and language problems it is easier to use an interviewer to complete the questionnaire than for the refugees to fill it in themselves. If this is done, interviewers must be trained to follow the wording very closely and not to introduce their own bias into the questions or answers. Choose a respected refugee, a schoolchild, or a teacher as an interviewer.

Fig. 4.15. An interviewer filling in a questionnaire during a census in the Afghan refugee villages in Baluchistan province, Pakistan.

For a questionnaire that has to be translated, one group of people can translate it into the local language and then ask another group, who have not seen the original, to translate the questions back again. Any discrepancies should then be openly discussed and a new translation agreed on.

Pilot surveys

After designing the survey methods and questionnaire always pilot test them using the interviewers and a mixed group of out-patients and healthy refugees. This is essential to discover the mistakes in the methods and questionnaire before the real survey is used. Discuss all the corrections with the interviewers and then train them thoroughly in using the agreed version. The problems of poor sampling and poor response rates apply just as much to surveys using questionnaires as to other kinds of surveys.

How to organize a survey

The following are some of the points that need to be covered when organizing a survey. They have been arranged in the order in which it is suggested they are carried out.

Planning

• Decide why the results from the survey are needed and how they will be useful.
• Consult people with the relevant experience such as refugees, local people, medical staff, camp administrators, etc.
• Visit different areas in the community to obtain information about the people, their culture, and their environment.
• Decide what observations or measurements are to be made, and standard-ize on techniques. Design and pre-test questionnaires.
• Choose an appropriate population sample.
• Make arrangements for money, staff, transport, time, accommodation, etc.

Organization

• Obtain co-operation of local leaders and refugees.
• Train survey staff.
• Arrange for laboratory facilities if needed.
• Draw up a daily work plan for the survey staff.
• Design records and forms. Pre-test them.
• Do a pilot study first to test out the organization, staff, and methods.

During the survey

• Supervise all staff to make sure they know what they are doing and that they are working accurately.
• Ask senior members of the local population to help with the survey itself, especially for checking attenders and non-attenders, and controlling crowds.

Evaluation and feedback

• Analyse the data. Unless the survey is very large analyses can be conducted manually using the 'five bar gate' method illustrated in Fig. 4.16.

• If it is desired to cross-tabulate the data in a number of different ways it may be useful to have a separate record card for each individual and to sort these cards into different piles according to the values of the variables being examined. For different analyses the cards can be re-sorted. If this method is to be used it is desirable that the survey data be collected using one card per person so that transcription is unnecessary.

Edge-punched cards can be a valuable aid in analysis of surveys of moderate size. Use of these cards is described in Appendix 2.

• Discuss the results and your interpretations with the medical staff and refugees who were surveyed, before writing a report so that you can incorporate their comments.

• Write a brief report, including recommendations and what action needs to be taken; send copies to refugee representatives and the administrators.

• Report your recommendations to relevant committees, particularly the camp committees and to the people who were surveyed or their representatives. Beware of the misuse of the results by the refugees, administrators, governments, and aid agencies.

• Follow-up surveys will be required to monitor the effects of those interventions in changing health status, community conditions, etc. In stable situations the persons included in the original sample may be re-surveyed to gather this data—provided that their inclusion in the first survey did not result in their receiving special attention and thus making them an

Age group	Males		Females		Total
<1	₥₥ ₥₥ III	13	₥₥ IIII	9	22
1–4	₥₥ ₥₥ II	12	₥₥ ₥₥ ₥₥ I	16	28
5–14	₥₥ ₥₥ ₥₥	15	₥₥ ₥₥ I	11	26
15–44	₥₥ ₥₥ ₥₥ II	17	₥₥ ₥₥ I	11	28
45+	₥₥ ₥₥ ₥₥	15	₥₥ ₥₥ ₥₥ ₥₥ II	22	37
Not known	I	1	II	2	3
Total		73		71	144

Fig. 4.16. 'Five bar gate' method of analysing data.

unrepresentative sample of the population. In less stable situations surveys can be conducted on different samples at different times to provide a semi-continuous monitor on the health status of the community.

SURVEILLANCE

Surveillance is the regular collection of information on the incidence of new cases of disease, on births and deaths, and on the use being made of health services.

For diseases information should be collected on:

Common conditions such as:

- diarrhoeas
- fevers of unknown origin
- upper and lower respiratory tract infections
- skin conditions
- injuries and fractures
- malnutrition

Potentially epidemic diseases such as:

- measles
- malaria
- typhus
- typhoid
- cholera
- meningitis

Good indicators of health services utilization are the:

- Number of new attenders per week, first attendance only.
- Total number of out-patients seen per week.
- Number of patients referred by sub-clinics to the main health centres.
- Number of patients referred outside the camp for special treatment.
- Number of home visits carried out.
- Number of new antenatal mothers registering at the clinic per week.
- Proportion of all estimated deliveries being supervised.

Each clinic should compile its own weekly figures separately for arrivals during the past month and for residents. These figures should also be aggregated to give a figure for the whole community. How accurate the figures are will depend on such factors as:

- How completely the refugees are using the services or reporting their births and deaths. There may be very serious problems of under-reporting or, more rarely, over-reporting.

- How well is the information being collected in the clinics? Is there any bias in diagnosis? Is there any falsification of the numbers?
- How well and how regularly are the figures being collated and submitted?

A change in the figures which is consistent over several weeks is more meaningful than erratic changes from week to week, provided that the surveillance system is working well. Epidemic diseases, however, may show a sudden change in incidence. The deaths amongst resident refugees, expressed as per 1000 resident refugees, should gradually decline as a community settles down, whereas the rate amongst new arrivals may stay comparatively higher. If the health services are acceptable, accessible, and appropriate to refugees they should be seeing a high proportion of the sick individuals, pregnant mothers, and young children. A surveillance system should confirm whether this is happening.

5 Nutrition

Nutrition surveys and surveillance

Malnutrition can be a major health problem in a refugee community, especially among new arrivals who have suffered from lack of food during their flight. Within the community, food shortages may be due to delayed supplies, transport difficulties, and corruption. By buying food locally, refugees and aid agencies can also create shortages among the local population.

Food shortages and malnutrition can easily become political issues and an accurate estimate of the degree of malnutrition becomes necessary. Surveys are the best way of achieving this.

Visual assessments of the nutritional status are extremely useful. Surveys, though, can indicate the extent of a problem in a given community more rigorously, and, if consistent methods are used, they allow comparison with the situation in other communities. For example, a study showed that the prevalence of severe malnutrition (Grade III) among refugees from

Fig. 5.1. Angolan administrators and Zairean refugees undertaking a nutrition survey in Angola.

Bangladesh in 1971 was twice that observed among Indian children in communities around Hyderabad (see Fig. 5.2). It may also be necessary to carry out nutrition surveys amongst the local people. This can be particularly important when there is a general food shortage during famines and droughts.

Nutrition surveys are used to:

• Estimate the extent and severity of malnutrition in the refugee population.
• Identify the individuals and families at greatest risk.
• Help plan relief activities.

The individuals in a refugee community who are most likely to be malnourished are:

• Recent arrivals.
• Poorest and under-privileged.
• Those living in the worst housing and environmental conditions.
• Pregnant and lactating mothers.
• Newborn infants and children.
• Disabled and old people.

EFFECTS OF LOW ENERGY AND NUTRIENT SUPPLY ON BODY GROWTH

The nutritional and health problems of the refugee community are often reflected by the prevalence of malnutrition in children up to five years old. A

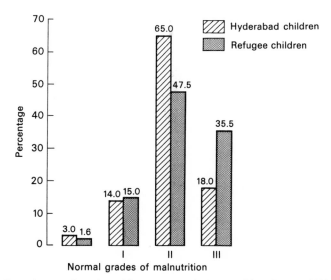

Fig. 5.2. Prevalence of malnutrition among 1–5-year-old refugee children from Bangladesh (Swaminathan, Vijayaraghavan, and Hanumantha Rao 1973).

reduction in the supply of foods to a child will lead first to a reduction of mental and physical activity. Then body maintenance is affected and fat stores and muscles start to waste away. The child loses weight and becomes thin; extreme thinness is called wasting. Finally growth will be impaired. Prolonged periods of food shortage are reflected, therefore, by a slowing down in the rate of height gain which results in the child having a height that is less than expected, that is, stunting. The rate of weight gain will also be low; this is referred to as growth faltering. Children who are wasted or stunted have a greater risk of dying than those who are not. The risk is greatest in those who are both wasted and stunted at the same time.

A child's nutritional status is affected not only by the food he or she eats but also by illness. Children who are underweight—especially those who have suffered recent weight loss—are less able to resist infection. There is, therefore, a vicious circle, with infection leading to malnutrition, and malnutrition making children more susceptible to infection.

ASSESSING NUTRITIONAL STATUS

A nutrition survey can be undertaken to estimate the extent and severity of malnutrition in the community and to help plan relief activities. Data are usually collected about the nutritional status of the children, as they are the most obviously vulnerable group. At the same time, other characteristics of the children can also be examined. In the list that follows a group of different variables is identified and the rationale for collecting data for each variable is reviewed.

Age groups

Refugees will vary in their responses to food shortage and infection:

• The birthweights of newborn children will reflect their mother's food intake and health during pregnancy.
• Since most newborn babies are breastfed only the weight gain of children under three months will reflect the adequacy of their mother's lactation.
• The weight of children between three months and three years reflects food intake—particularly of energy—during weaning. This is also a period in which children are susceptible to infectious diseases—particularly respiratory, diarrhoea, malaria, and measles, and become undernourished. They are very dependent on other family members for their nourishment. If the latter are unable to spare the time required to feed children, nutritional status may suffer. High-energy foods such as fats, oils, and sugar may reduce the volume of food that needs to be consumed in order to supply energy needs as described in the section on feeding programmes.
• In older children undernutrition probably reflects a recent lack of food for the family. A high prevalence of malnutrition in the age group three to six

years is likely to be an indicator of severe food shortage for the whole family. Measurements of weight loss, or a fall in weight-for-height in adults can also reflect a scarcity of food.

• Adults who require help to obtain food, such as the elderly and infirm, are also in great danger.

Sex

Some societies may preferentially allocate food within families to adult males and in some others, young girls may be given low priority, as seen in the Burmese refugee camps during the Bangladesh crisis in 1973. Such a tendency must be recognized as such a specific group faces higher risks of death or disability.

Length of stay

At the beginning of a refugee crisis it is useful to differentiate between children who have recently arrived and those who have been there for some time. (See section on practical epidemiology.) This differentiates between those who have suffered from hardship during their flight, and those whose malnutrition may be due to conditions in the community itself. Initially the dividing line between recent arrivals and old residents may be three months. As services become organized a limit of one month can be used to differentiate between 'old' and 'new' refugees.

Socio-economic status

In most communities the prevalence of malnutrition is highest amongst children from the poorest and most under-privileged families. Although the extreme conditions which force people to become refugees are likely to affect the whole community, the poorest families will suffer most. They may, therefore, need greater access to relief services. A rough assessment of socio-economic status, such as that given by possessions and previous occupation of the head of the household, will assist identification of extremely poor households.

Area in the community

Refugees group themselves according to cultural, religious, political, and ethnic considerations. A simple nutrition survey in a Laotian camp in Thailand demonstrated the need to relocate special feeding programmes to the most deprived areas of the camp.

Ethnic group

In some situations it may be appropriate to classify refugees according to the ethnic group to which they belong as malnutrition may appear to be predominant amongst particular ethnic groups. The specific reasons for this may be identified by looking at the relationships between ethnic group and other variables such as socio-economic status.

Season of the year

The time of year at which the survey is carried out needs to be taken into consideration when analysing results. Problems can arise if surveys which were carried out during different seasons are compared. For example, in rainy seasons food availability from the general feeding programme may be low and prices of food in the local market high. At the same time, the incidence of diseases which can affect nutritional status such as diarrhoea may be high.

Anthropometric measurements

Nutritional status should ideally be assessed by comparing weight gain over a period of time—the weight gain that would be expected over, for example, two months. This is a valuable index but, unfortunately, regular weight measurements are rarely available and difficult to do well. Nutritional indices have therefore to be calculated using weight and height measurements obtained on a single occasion. To calculate the value for an index, the child's weight or height has to be compared with a reference value and cut-off points define different degrees of malnutrition. A number of different indices can be used:

Weight-for-age (wt./age)

The child's weight can be compared with the reference weight for his age. Children with a low weight-for-age face greater risks of death than children whose weights are closer to the expected values for their age. This index is useful for discriminating those children facing high risks from those in less danger between the ages of 0 and 12 months. However, to calculate this index the child's age has to be accurately known and this information may be difficult to obtain in the field.

Weight-for-height (wt./ht.)

The child's weight can be compared with the expected weight for his or her height. One advantage of this index is that the child's age need not be known. However, the approximate age should be known when interpreting results as a deficit in any anthropometric measure, including weight, is likely to be more dangerous in very young children. The index weight-for-height can be used to identify wasted children and it is a preferred nutritional index when attempts are made to detect children in imminent danger.

Height-for-age (ht./age)

The child's height can be compared with the expected height for that age. This index assesses stunting, an index of prolonged nutritional deprivation experienced by the child. There is evidence that young children with height deficits are in much greater danger than those with the expected heights for their ages. These dangers are thought to be more a result of environmental conditions and less a direct consequence of their nutritional deprivation.

Mid-upper arm circumference (MUAC)

The mid-upper arm circumference increases in size during the first two years of a child's life, but there is relatively little increase in MUAC between the ages of two and five. In children under the age of two, MUAC can be compared with the expected value for the child's age, or when age is not known, with the child's height. The index MUAC for height can be used to identify children in immediate danger. The assessment can be made rapidly with a QUAC stick.

A number of different sets of reference values can be used to calculate these nutritional indices. Best known are the Harvard reference values though a new set of figures, presented by the United States National Academy of Sciences, is now recommended by the World Health Organization. These are listed in Appendix 2. When these reference values are used, the cut-off points that indicate an individual child to be severely malnourished facing an increased risk of death, are conventionally accepted as:

- 65 per cent of reference weight-for-age
- 70 per cent of reference weight-for-height
- 85 per cent of reference height-for-age
- a mid-upper arm circumference of 12.5 cm in children aged between 12 and 59 months

In practice, the actual choice of cut-off for identifying individuals who need help depends on the severity of the nutritional problem and the resources available to deal with it. The child's age must be taken into account when cut-offs are selected to identify children who need help. A child who is severely stunted, e.g. less than 85 per cent height-for-age, is likely to face far greater dangers if younger than two years than if older than three years of age.

A simplified method for weight-for-height assessment

Recently a new method for assessing weight-for-height has been developed which includes the use of a multi-coloured chart. This consists of a number of columns, each marked with a particular weight and colour. Children are first weighed and then placed standing (or lying) in front of the column marked with their weight. If they are wasted, the top of their head will be in front of the section of the column coloured red. If the weight-for-height is greater than 90 per cent of the international reference value, the upper end of his or her head will be opposite the green section of the column. Figure 5.3 illustrates the weight-for-height chart in use. The chart can be used to detect children who are severely wasted, e.g. less than 70 per cent weight-for-height, and to identify a target weight to be achieved after therapeutic treatment.

If this weight-for-height chart is used in conjunction with weighing scales, surveyors do not need to calculate percentage weight-for-height. They merely need to record the number of children who are in each of five different colour categories. Results can then be plotted as illustrated in Fig. 5.4. Narrow versions of the weight-for-height chart—which can easily be attached to a portable stadiometer—have been developed specifically for use in relief work, and are being evaluated. The use of this chart may cause initial confusion as a thin child appears higher on the chart than the level of a well-fed child. On the road to health chart (described in the section on Family health care) a thin child appears below the level of a well-fed child.

Physical signs in nutritional status assessment

Three physical signs can be useful indicators of nutritional status and help in identifying individuals in danger.

They are:

● Pitting ankle oedema is easily detected, though the sign is likely to be important only in helping to decide the treatment to be given to an individual child.

Fig. 5.3. Using the weight-for-height chart (Nabarro and McNab 1980).

• Signs of xerophthalmia, usually due to a combination of vitamin A deficiency and protein energy malnutrition. Night blindness is easy to detect, but signs such as dryness of the conjunctiva and Bitot's spots, or, more rarely, corneal xerosis and keratomalacia, are much harder to detect. Well-illustrated visual aids are now available and they can be used to train surveyors in the detection of these physical signs.

• Severe anaemia is most easily detected through the examination of mucous membranes in the lower eyelid or lower lip.

ORGANIZING A NUTRITIONAL SURVEY

The nutritional status of children in the community can vary rapidly. Whilst cross-sectional or prevalence surveys can give useful information, longi-tudinal monitoring of the nutritional status of a group of children over time is likely to provide more useful results for decision makers. In practice only cross-sectional surveys are undertaken. The survey should follow the principles outlined in the section on Practical epidemiology, but a number of special points relating to nutritional surveys are given here.

In any nutrition survey it is also important to diagnose and treat sick individuals. Not only does this promote co-operation and confidence but it can also provide a valuable starting point for the development of primary health care services.

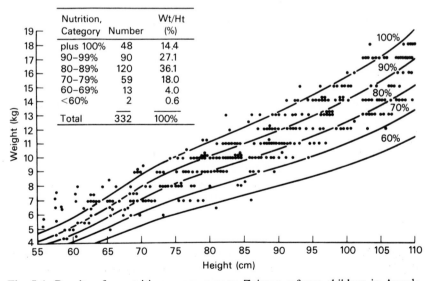

Nutrition, Category	Number	Wt/Ht (%)
plus 100%	48	14.4
90–99%	90	27.1
80–89%	120	36.1
70–79%	59	18.0
60–69%	13	4.0
<60%	2	0.6
Total	332	100%

Fig. 5.4. Results of a nutrition survey among Zairean refugee children in Angola, plotted on a scattergram (Simmonds and Brown 1979).

Design of the survey

The design of any survey must depend on the kind of information required and the use that will be made of it. For instance, administrators may need estimates of the extent and severity of malnutrition. Alternatively, data may be collected to help identify individual children who require supplementary or therapeutic feeding. Only a sample of households needs to be studied for the first kind of survey, whereas for the second all individuals—or at least those belonging to groups who are at risk of being malnourished—should be screened.

Choice of variables

This will also depend on the length of time available to carry out surveys. There may be an urgent need to compare the nutritional status of refugee children in different communities and identify which community has the higher proportion of children at risk. An important requirement may be that the technique by which nutritional status is assessed allows the rapid assessment of large numbers of children. The mid-upper arm circumference tape and the weight-for-height chart both allow rapid assessment. Only a few other variables—such as age, and length of time in the community—need to be included as well. This sort of technique demonstrated very quickly which refugee settlements needed emergency action in Biafra.

On the other hand, if an attempt is made to find out more about the pattern of malnutrition in a particular community—focusing on causes as well as consequences—a larger range of variables may need to be studied. Longitudinal survey techniques and particularly case-studies may also be required.

The sample

Severe malnutrition is likely to be encountered in only a small proportion of children in the community at any one time, say 10–20 per cent. The sample for cross-sectional study should include at least 100 individuals of each sex in each of the two main age groups—less than one year and one to three years old. The result of this kind of sample survey yields an estimate for the true prevalence of malnutrition in these particular age and sex groups among the community as a whole. Refer to the section on Epidemiology for further discussion of sampling.

Non-response rates

Ideally, these should be kept to a minimum. If no information is obtained from more than 10 per cent of the children in the whole sample, the results may be inaccurate. It is necessary to discover the reasons for the lack of response since some of them may be related to causes of child malnutrition.

Anthropometric measuring techniques

Age, weight, and height would seem to be easy measurements to obtain. In reality, they are not easy to assess accurately and precisely in children, even if the work is done by trained staff. Techniques for measurement have to be agreed in advance and training undertaken carefully and systematically. Frequent spot checks are necessary to ensure that the techniques are being followed correctly.

For example, reliable data about children's ages is more likely to be obtained if the parent is asked 'when was your child born?' rather than 'how old is the child?' Imprecise data on age can invalidate the weight-for-age and height-for-age results. A local calendar that includes rainy seasons and harvests, recent political upheavals and developments can be developed with the help of some members of the community, to assist in determining the date of birth of children. Several different approaches need to be tried in a pilot study before one approach is adopted for the survey.

Equipment

For weight and height measurements equipment that is simple to construct and maintain, but also accurate, is essential.

Stadiometers for measuring height can be constructed using local materials.

The length of children who cannot stand can be measured on a baby board. For consistency, all children below 2 years, or 85 cm in length, should be measured in the lying position (see Table 5.1).

Provided that the centimetre scales on stadiometers and length boards are correct, errors in length and height measurements are more likely to be due to the child not being properly positioned than to deficiencies in the equipment. A surveyor is often needed with the mother to help position the child correctly.

Portable spring scales, with clear markings at 0.5 kg intervals, are widely used. Before each child is weighed, the surveyor needs to check that the

Table 5.1. *Guide to approximate age according to height of the child*

Height (cm)	Age
<75	0–1 years
75–95	1–3 years
96–117	4–6 years
118–136	7–9 years
>136	10 years+

Fig. 5.5. Child being weighed on portable spring scale during a nutrition survey in a Zairean refugee village in Angola.

needle is at zero. Accuracy should be checked after every 20 weighings with the help of a known weight, e.g. a bag with stones weighing 10 kg. Always have spare scales available.

Questionnaires

If questions are being asked about the child's age, the length of the family's stay, or its ethnic group, reliable answers are likely to be obtained provided that the questions are understood by the respondent. Questions about food habits, preferences, and availability must be carefully designed and thoroughly tested beforehand. If not, answers may well be biased and could easily yield useless data. An alternative approach is that surveyors observe what foods are actually present in households and the foods that are

Sample Record for Nutrition Survey

Group area: .... Household no: ....
Child's name: .... Date: ....
Sex: .... Mother's name: ....
DOB: .... Age (months): .... Father's name: ....
Ethnic group: ....
Length of stay in camp: .... Household occupation: ....

Wt	=	.... kg	Wt/Age	....	Expressed as a
Ht/Lgth*	=	.... cm	Wt/Age	....	percentage of
MUAC	=	.... cm	Ht/Age	....	international reference
			MUAC	....	standards

		Yes	No
Oedema	pedal only	....	....
	other extremities	....	....
Vitamin A	night blindness	....	....
deficiency	Bitot spots	....	....
		....	....
Anaemia		....	....
* as applicable			

NB. Responses to these questions may be coded (each ethnic group or occupation expressed as a number, for instance) either when the form is first filled in or later when data is processed.

Fig. 5.6. Sample record for nutrition survey.

being given to children. This is likely to give a more reliable indication of feeding habits and food availability.

All questionnaires must be discussed with representatives of refugees and the administrators well in advance—not only to ensure that the information being collected is relevant to the programmes being planned, but also to check that the questions are unlikely to cause ill feeling or be misinterpreted. A simple record form for collection of nutritional data and control variables is shown in Fig. 5.6.

Logistics

The two most common problems encountered when surveys are undertaken are overcrowding and the timing of activities, i.e. to organize them so that they coincide with the time that the majority of people are in the community. Careful organization, with the help of refugee representatives, can help to overcome the former. The most appropriate time for surveying is often early morning or in the evening, but this may be difficult because of curfews, security controls, and poor light.

Calculating the results

The most common nutritional indices assessed in surveys of refugees are weight-for-height and weight-for-age. The child's weight is compared with the reference weight for his/her age or height. This is usually done by expressing the weight as a percentage of the reference. For example, a child who is 90 cm tall is found to weigh 10.2 kg. The reference weight for a 90 cm child (using the WHO reference values) is 12.8 kg. 10.2 kg is 80 per cent of 12.8 kg. The child's weight is therefore 80 per cent of the reference weight-for-height (see Appendix 2). This information is calculated for every child in the survey and these percentage values can be expressed in the following two ways.

• Data values can be plotted on a scattergram which gives an instant visual impression of their distribution. Lines drawn on the scattergram allow the surveyor to distinguish different weight-for-height percentage figures (100 per cent, 90 per cent, 80 per cent, etc.) and the number of children in these different percentage ranges can easily be counted (see Fig. 5.4).

• Alternatively, values can be tabulated by age and sex. An example table is shown in Fig. 5.7.

The table consists of a number of rows, each of which identifies a weight-for-age or weight-for-height category, with a space at the right hand end for the total in that category. A set of columns distinguish between three different age groups for males and females separately. The table thus has a total of six rows and six columns, i.e. there are 36 cells in the table. Two figures should be entered in each cell. The first figure indicates the number of individuals

Percentage values	Male			Female			Total
	Less than 1 year	1–2 years	3–5 years	Less than 1 year	1–2 years	3–5 years	
100% or more							
90–99							
80–89							
70–79							
60–69							
Less than 60%							
Totals							

Fig. 5.7. Example of a table for expressing the results by age and sex.

who, by virtue of their weight-for-age or weight-for-height value, age group, and sex, belong in that cell. The second figure is a percentage. To obtain this, the first figure (number of individuals in the cell) is divided by the total number of individuals in the same column.

This kind of table can be computed for the different variables which have already been described. Thus, for example, instead of dividing the children into groups of males and females, the surveyor could divide children into those that have been in the community for more than four weeks and those who have been present for less than four weeks. If the total sample of children was very large, the numbers of individuals in each of the cells of the above table could have been further subdivided according to their length of stay.

The same method of analysis can be used for other nutritional indices, for example, height-for-age, mid-upper arm circumference, and MUAC for height. In each case, data for children in different nutritional categories will be entered in relevant rows. Table 5.2 is an example of the comparison of data between refugee villages.

Table 5.2. *Results of the nutritional surveys from the three villages*

Village	Total examined	Weight/height No. $<80\%$	Harvard standards $\% <80\%$
Tximege	332	74	22*
Lukembo	473	68	14
Cassege	245	29	12

*The proportion of children less than 80 per cent wt./ht. was significantly higher in Tximege $(P<0.001)$ than Lukembo and Cassege (from Simmonds and Brown 1979).

Acting on the information

Surveys may be designed to help divide resources between refugee communities and results may, therefore, be used by a government or international agency to identify those communities which need attention most urgently. They may also be undertaken as part of a review of the general status of refugees in particular communities, relating nutritional studies to logistics, manpower, and supplies.

Nutritional status information may also be used to help identify individual children in need of different kinds of assistance. For example, if more than 10 per cent of the children in the sample of the community are less than 80 per cent of reference weight-for-height, a supplementary feeding programme may be implemented for a limited period, particularly if the general feeding programme needs improvement. Children who are less than 70 per cent weight-for-height should be given therapeutic feeding (see section on Feeding programmes). These children are identified by a mass screening programme to include all children in specific age groups, or in particular areas, or from particular ethnic groups which appear to have a high prevalence of malnutrition.

SURVEILLANCE

A cross-sectional prevalence survey reveals information about what is happening at a particular point in time. Even so, the results may be useful for policy decisions about the kinds of relief programmes to be implemented in the future. Information about whether or not the situation is improving can more usefully be obtained through a simple surveillance system.

Valuable early warning of impending nutritional problems may be obtained if the availability and market prices of common staple foods are watched closely. If food is scarce, market prices are likely to rise before nutritional status of individuals starts to deteriorate.

If the nutritional status of the refugee children is to be kept under surveillance, two different strategies can be used.

1. *Repeated cross-sectional surveys* can be undertaken—not necessarily on the same children—and the results compared with each other. Provided that sample sizes are sufficient and the changes in prevalence are large, and that the sampling and survey methods are the same, then repeated prevalence surveys may provide useful information.

The following approaches can provide regular prevalence data:

● Administrators can make regular visual assessments by examining children in their homes and having regular discussions with mothers, leaders, and health personnel. Careful records of these 'profiles' should be made so that they can be compared with each other. Profiles provide valuable background information against which results of prevalence surveys are interpreted.

● Cross-sectional surveys can be repeated on the youngest children every three to six months. Recent arrivals and long-term residents should be differentiated in the analysis. Comparison between surveys will show whether or not the overall situation is improving or worsening. Care has to be taken if this kind of repeated survey is used to assess the effectiveness of specific programmes. An improvement of the nutritional state of the community may be due to improved food distribution, to seasonal factors in food availability in the local markets, or to changes in the disease pattern. Specific programmes can be assessed only by longitudinal study of the children that the programme affects, comparing them with children who are not receiving the programme services. This kind of experimental investigation requires very careful planning and implementation.

2. An alternative strategy is to concentrate on *constant surveillance of a sample* of the population.

• If there are health and feeding programmes which concentrate on the regular screening of a defined population of refugee children, and if health and feeding programme records are kept, estimates can be made of the incidence of severe malnutrition among the population being screened. Data can be obtained that indicate the number of children who present to feeding programmes and clinics as new cases of malnutrition. If, at any time, the number of malnourished children detected is seen to rise, care must be taken before the data is used as evidence of a worsening situation to make sure that this is not the result of increased coverage of the health services.

• All infant and child deaths occurring in the sample should be recorded and the death rates calculated at regular intervals be assessed separately for new arrivals and for those who have been resident for some time. Again, provided that the reporting system is consistently maintained and covers a defined population section this data will provide valuable information about health and nutritional trends in the community as a whole.

• If children are being weighed regularly, records should be kept of the proportion that are losing weight. Ideally, all children would be expected to gain weight. For example a sample of, say, a hundred children selected randomly from throughout the community can be followed monthly on a longitudinal basis. The proportion of children who are losing weight can provide a sensitive indicator of the nutritional trends.

Feeding programmes

The foods need to be culturally acceptable and to maintain the traditional food habits of the refugees as far as possible.

Refugees are usually cut off from their normal food supply and find themselves totally reliant on the international community to supply them with foods that are culturally acceptable and meet their nutritional needs. Refugee communities self-sufficient in food, such as those in Zambia for Angolan and Zimbabwean refugees and in Tanzania for refugees from Burundi, are rare. They have evolved only over a number of years and their development was particularly dependent on the host government giving sufficient fertile land to the refugees.

Three types of feeding programmes—general, supplementary and therapeutic—are commonly used in refugee camps. These all rely on a regular, adequate supply of appropriate foods and an equitable, efficient distribution system.

General: every refugee is given a certain amount of food.

Supplementary: the most vulnerable are given an additional ration.

Therapeutic: The severely malnourished receive a specially formulated diet.

Factors which determine whether any type of feeding programme is effective include the following:

- *Availability*—whether the food can be purchased locally in the host country, has to be imported from neighbouring countries or, more typically, imported from outside the region by purchase or donation.
- *Appropriateness*—the foods should be culturally acceptable and should maintain the traditional food habits of the refugees as far as possible. Other foods may be inappropriate, e.g. because of difficulties in preparing them safely in the camp conditions. For example, milk products in powdered, condensed, or evaporated form, if distributed indiscriminately, will create health problems associated with incorrect dilution, reconstitution with contaminated water, and substitution for breast-feeding.
- *Transportation*—speed and regularity of supply depending on land, sea, or air freight; the local transportation costs, including cost of vehicles, fuel, salaries for drivers; the availability of maintenance facilities, fuel, and drivers, and the type of transportation used may also include camels, donkeys, and oxen (see Table 5.3). Irregular supplies or missing commodities will lead to severe hardship.

Table 5.3. *Average weight of sacks of commonly used foods and estimates of load capacity of different forms of transport*

Average weight of sacks		Estimates of load capacity	
		Average	
Cereal	25 or 50 kg	long 6-wheeler lorry	7000 kg
DSM*	25 kg	4-wheel lorry	3000 kg
CSM†	23 kg	4-wheel landrover vehicle	500 kg
Sugar	45 kg	Camel	200 kg
Oil	1 litre (= 1 kg)	Donkey	100 kg
		Bicycle	50 kg

* Dried skimmed milk.
† Corn soy milk.

- *Storage*—the warehouse capacity at national, regional, and camp levels; the amount of loss from corruption, inadequate record keeping and poor stock control. Losses also occur from poor protection from pests, such as mice and rats. Stacking the food on a raised platform can improve storage.
- *Limited variety*—too many different food items will unnecessarily complicate transportation and distribution. The packaging should be low weight, low bulk, and be able to withstand rough handling and changes in temperature.

Fig. 5.8. Example of a community store with raised platform inside.

• *Manpower*—sufficient trained refugees to manage the programmes must be a high priority. The training and supervision of such workers must be standardized between communities and organizations.

• *Infant feeding*—breast-feeding should be encouraged for as long as possible. This offers considerable protection against irregularities in alternative food supplies and against some of the environmental hazards created by overcrowding and poor sanitation. Feeding bottles should NOT be used in refugee communities since they present too great a risk in such unhygienic conditions. It has been shown that adequate lactation can be stimulated even among sick or malnourished mothers if positive steps are taken to help them, by, for example, organizing breast-feeding centres and giving encouragement during home visits.

GENERAL FEEDING PROGRAMME

Diet

The first priority is to satisfy the energy and protein requirements of the refugees. The following figures give some guidance:

• 1800 calories (7.5 MJ) per person per day for 'Temporary maintenance', which can be only for a period of a few months.

• 2000 calories (8.4 MJ) or more per person per day plus 50 g of protein per day for long-term maintenance.

Table 5.4. *Guide to approximate quantities of general food supplies required*

Food	Per person per day (g)	Per person for 14 days (kg)	Per person for 30 days (kg)	10 000 persons for 14 days (kg)	10 000 persons for 30 days (kg)
Cereal	400	5.6	12.0	56 000	120 000
Oil*	40	0.6	1.2	5600	12 000
Protein	50	0.7	1.5	7000	15 000

* 1 kg = 1 litre.

A typical ration per person for one day might be as follows:

a staple food, e.g. cereal 350–400 g,
an energy rich food, e.g. oil 20–40 g,
a protein rich food, e.g. beans 50 g,
with other such items as:

tea 3 g, sugar 40 g, salt 2 g, fruits 10 g, vegetables and spices provided according to cultural and nutritional needs. Table 5.4 is a guide to the possible quantities of the essential general food rations required for individuals and a community of 10 000. The practice of giving half rations to children less than five years of age is not recommended, as by the time a child is one year old he or she needs at least 1360 calories, and 1800 calories by age four.

Attention should also be paid to providing adequate vitamins and minerals through the diet. The effects of a change in diet may particularly affect the intake of certain vitamins. For example, a sudden change from local brown, unpolished rice to imported white, polished rice during the war in Kampuchea contributed to an epidemic of both wet and dry Beri-beri

Table 5.5. *Vitamins A and B—preventive and treatment doses*

Vitamins	Preventive dose	Treatment dose
Vitamin A	4500 units/day in diet, 0–12 years 7500 units/day in diet, adult Mass distribution of capsules 100 000 IU, 0–1 years 200 000 IU, 1–5 years 200 000 IU, women post-delivery	Immediately on diagnosis, 200 000 IU orally. Second day 200 000 IU orally, followed possibly 2–4 weeks later by 200 000 IU orally
Vitamin B (Beri-beri)	1 mg/day in diet	50 mg at once then 10 mg daily until recovery
Vitamin B_6 (pellagra)	15–20 mg/day in diet	300 mg niacin daily until recovery

among the soldiers. The change from a diet including camel's milk which has a high vitamin C content, to a ration with almost no vitamin C may have been one of the factors that contributed to the outbreak of scurvy among refugees in Somalia in 1982.

Two of the most common deficiencies are of vitamins A and B (see Table 5.5). The distribution of multivitamin tablets is not recommended. They are a waste of time and money as they contain insufficient quantities of individual vitamins to replace deficiencies, and moreover create a false sense of security.

Distribution systems

A fair and efficient distribution system is heavily dependent on an accurate estimation of numbers of people in the camp (see section on Estimating refugee populations). A full census with the registration of every individual will help to minimize exploitation and corruption. When registering, refugees should be handed food distribution cards, either individual or family cards, which should be presented and marked every time food is collected. The food can be distributed to each individual or to a representative from each family or group.

There are two major patterns of food distribution; either as dry or as cooked food. Both require sufficient quantities of cooking pots, utensils, and fuel. It is also essential to ensure that those who are doing the distribution have exact instructions regarding the quantity of each food to which each individual is entitled. Standard measuring utensils should be used.

Distributing food in its dry form is the favoured method. It has the major advantage of allowing the refugees to retain a certain degree of independence because they can take the food home, prepare it as they wish, eat together as a family, and when they want to. It also means that distribution needs to take place only at fortnightly or at the most weekly, intervals. Distribution of more than two weeks' supply is not to be recommended as storage in the home becomes a problem, and it can be difficult to ensure that sufficient food is left for consumption towards the end of a longer period. Provision must be made for adequate containers and storage sacks.

Cooked food distribution usually needs a centralized kitchen with suitably trained personnel preparing at least two meals a day. It necessitates an efficient cooking and distribution system to avoid delays for the refugees who sit in a compound to eat the food 'on the spot' or perhaps carry it home. Cooked food distribution is undesirable. There are problems of hygiene in the centralized kitchen, with the risk of food poisoning on a mass scale. This was reported among Vietnamese refugees on the Island of Guam, where a local food-borne outbreak of diarrhoea was traced to millet prepared in one of the common kitchens. The negative cultural and social implications of such dependence are two other considerations that usually make such centralized cooked-food distribution schemes undesirable.

Fig. 5.9. Distributing food in its dry form to a Cabindan refugee in Zaire.

Monitoring effectiveness

The general feeding programme must be monitored for its effectiveness, since refugees should not gradually lose weight and end up less healthy than when they arrived. The suggestions on how to organize surveillance in the section on Nutrition surveys should be followed.

SUPPLEMENTARY FEEDING PROGRAMMES

The decision to implement supplementary programmes will ultimately depend on the health and nutritional status of the population, the existing environmental health hazards, the effectiveness of the general feeding programme, and the resources available.

Aim and diet

A supplementary feeding programme is intended for refugees who, for social or cultural reasons and/or because of their age or physical state, are at 'higher risk' or more vulnerable to developing malnutrition. It is also intended in some cases to treat malnutrition. The aim is to provide extra high-energy (350–500 kcal), high protein (about 15 g), low bulk food once or twice a day as a supplement to the general feeding programme, but not as a substitute for it.

For this purpose cereal mixtures are very helpful and are often more culturally acceptable than the commonly used dried skimmed milk. They need preparation with safe water, sugar, and spices according to tastes. Oil can be added to increase the calorie intake (see Table 5.6). Some organizations are now developing protein concentrates such as egg powder or fish protein; these products should be tried in pilot projects before large consignments are sent. Some Third World countries are also developing their own preparations, e.g. Faffa in Ethiopia, which should be used if at all possible. Tables of the quantities of each food to be mixed according to the numbers of people to be fed should be developed, once it is known what foods are available.

Selection

The number of people included in a supplementary feeding programme will depend on need and the resources available. There may also be a policy laid down by the central authorities limiting the coverage. Nutrition surveys and surveillance will provide information for planning the most appropriate programme.

The criteria for admission to a full-scale supplementary feeding programme are as follows:

• Any person discharged from a therapeutic feeding programme.
• All children less than five years of age or less than 115 cm in height.
• Any malnourished person of any age.
• Pregnant and lactating women.
• Medical referrals.
• The elderly, unaccompanied minors, disabled, and others with particular social problems.

Where resources are limited, selective feeding may be necessary whereby those admitted are:

• Children and adults less than 80 per cent of standard weight-for-height.
• Pregnant women in the last trimester of pregnancy and lactating women during the first year of lactation.
• Medical referrals.
• The elderly and others based on clinical judgement.
• Those discharged from therapeutic feeding programmes.

To ensure that all those most in need are registered it is necessary to do a systematic house to house assessment. Following selection, details such as each child's name, age, sex, weight and height, and actual and expected percentage of the standard weight-for-height should be recorded in a register. For others, such as pregnant and lactating women, the total number of all due to attend is usually the only information needed. Everyone should be issued with a card, identity bracelet, or some other durable means of identification to facilitate follow-up, and a rapid clinical assessment made with referral for medical care as necessary.

Table 5.6. *Foods commonly used for supplementary feeding*

Food	Average nutritional value per100 g		Preparation of food	Special points
	Kilocalories	Protein (g)		
Corn soy milk (CSM)	370	20	Mix 1 part CSM to 2–3 parts cold water. Boil. Cook 5–10 minutes	Add 1/10 part extra sugar for taste and 1/10 part oil for extra kcalories if desired. Can be used as dry ingredient added to other foods
Instant corn soy milk (ICSM)	380	20	Mix 1 part ICSM to 1 part cold boiled or hot water. Pre-cooked	Sweetened. Add extra sugar and oil if desired
Wheat-soy blend (WSB)	360	20	Mix 1 part WSB to small amount of 10 parts water. Add rest of water. Boil. Cook for 5–10 minutes	Add sugar for taste
Dried skimmed milk (DSM)	350	35	Mix 1 part DSM to 4–6 parts cold boiled or hot water	Ensure vitamin A enriched. Always add extra oil and/or sugar. Add sugar previously dissolved in hot water. Can be used as a dry ingredient added to other foods
Dried full cream milk (DFCM)	500	25	Mix 1 part DFCM to 8 parts water. (Check instructions on tin)	
Fish protein concentrate (FPC)	360	75	Add to other foods in dry form	Type A does not smell or taste of fish
Type A	360	75		
Type B	340	65		

Fig. 5.10. Children waiting to walk under a height arch of 115 cm. All those who are too tall to walk through are taken to be five years of age or more.

Distribution systems

The same systems apply here as for general feeding but in this case 'on the spot' feeding is often preferable to the 'take home' system as it is the only way of ensuring that the person actually eats the food intended for him or her. It also enables quick regular visual assessments of everyone. There may be a demand for the 'take home' system, especially from pregnant and lactating women, and the system of distribution must be flexible enough to respond to cultural and other factors.

'On the spot' feeding requires the organization of feeding centres. One centre per 300–500 registered refugees is needed, with facilities for everyone to sit down and consume the food.

Criteria for discharge

No child should be discharged from a supplementary feeding programme

Fig. 5.11. Zairean refugee women in Angola running an 'on the spot' supplementary feeding programme.

until a 90 per cent weight-for-height standard has been attained and maintained for at least two consecutive weighings at least two weeks apart. All other beneficiaries should be judged on a clinical basis.

Success or failure

Several factors may affect the success or failure of 'on the spot' supplementary feeding:

• The distance from home to feeding centre must be as short as possible.

• Arrangements must be made to adapt the programme to cultural needs and demands.

• The food must be readily acceptable, if necessary using local spices and sugar to improve the flavour, but not provided in such portions as to detract from the quantity eaten at home.

• As far as possible the style of eating should follow normal social and cultural practices.

• The serving procedure must be rapid and efficient to avoid long periods of waiting.

• The staff should maintain discipline in a calm, cheerful manner without creating a regimented atmosphere.

• Mothers should be encouraged to maintain breast-feeding habits.

● The schedule for supplementary feeding should not interfere with food distribution for the general feeding supplies or any other equally important activity—including the traditional meal pattern of the refugees.

● An effective system of 'scouts' should encourage attendance and follow-up of those who have not attended for two consecutive days.

● Successful lactation can be restored and maintained if a positive and reassuring approach is taken.

Monitoring effectiveness

It is important to monitor effectiveness in order to make changes as and when necessary. This can be done without a great effort if the initial registration system was carried out well. Results from the monitoring of the general feeding programme should be considered alongside data specific for supplementary programmes such as:

● The numbers attending daily and the regularity of attendance.

● The percentage of those attending compared to the total considered 'vulnerable' in the whole community.

● Re-weighing the children at regular intervals to monitor their individual progress.

● The proportion losing or failing to gain weight.

Associated activities

As supplementary feeding centres concentrate on vulnerable groups in the community, they are an ideal place for specific preventive activities such as malaria chemoprophylaxis, deworming, immunizations, and health education.

THERAPEUTIC FEEDING PROGRAMMES

Therapeutic feeding is intended for the severely malnourished who are unlikely to survive on the general and supplementary foods alone. It is likely to be needed following prolonged food shortages resulting from drought or conflict, and is a feasible and effective intervention in relief.

In an emergency, severely malnourished children are obvious and tend to be the focus of attention. However, no therapeutic feeding centre should be set up unless steps are being taken simultaneously to establish supplementary feeding programmes for the many others who are in immediate danger of becoming severely malnourished unless helped. In a settled community a therapeutic programme should be only a short- to mid-term requirement, e.g. three to six months if proper case finding has occurred, where the other feeding programmes are adequate, and where there are disease control and surveillance programmes.

Aim and diet

Therapeutic feeding is intended to treat those with severe protein energy malnutrition using a high energy and protein diet combined with medical care. Specially formulated foods are used.

Individual daily needs are calculated as follows:

(at least) 150 kcal/kg body weight/day

3 g protein/kg body weight/day

plus 4 mmol of potassium/kg body weight/day

for two weeks (see Table 5.7).

Table 5.7. *Stock solution for potassium supplement*

7.5 g of potassium chloride
plus
100 ml of water, previously boiled
contains
1 mmol of potassium to 1 ml of solution

The volume of food required is calculated as:

150 ml/kg body weight/day divided into 2–3 hourly feeds (see Table 5.8).

Table 5.8. *Volume of food according to weight of child and frequency of feeding*

Weight of child	Volume of food (ml)	Energy require-ment (Kcal)	Volume required for each feed at 4 feeds/day (ml)	Volume required for each feed at 5 feeds/day (ml)	Volume required for each feed at 6 feeds/day (ml)
less than 5 kg	750	750	200	150	150
5.0– 7.5 kg	1125	1125	300	250	200
7.5–10.0 kg	1500	1500	400	300	250
10.0–12.5 kg	1876	1876	500	400	300

Over 12.5 kg give at least 500 ml at each feed.
(From Peel 1977).

Foods commonly used include a combination of dried skimmed milk, sugar, oil, and water (see Table 5.9).

Table 5.9. *How to prepare high energy foods*

(a) *Measured by volume*

	Milk or milk preparation (ml or cm^3)	Oil (ml or cm^3)	Sugar (ml or cm^3)	Approximate energy (MJ)	Cooking requirements
Cow's milk/goat's milk	900	60	80	5.7*	
Buffalo's milk/ewe's milk	800	35	75	5.6†	
Skimmed milk powder‡	180	95	75	5.6†	Heat oil,
Full cream milk powder‡	270	60	75	5.7*	sugar, and
Evaporated milk	430	55	80	5.7*	milk slowly
K-MIX2†	130	95	40	5.7*	
Yogurt§	900	70	80	5.7*	

* Approximately 1360 kcal$_{th}$. ‡ Unreconstituted.
† Approximately 1350 kcal$_{th}$. § Energy value of milk with half the carbohydrates.

(b) *Measured in cups and level tablespoons*

	Milk or milk preparation	Oil (tbsp*)	Sugar (tbsp*)	Approximate energy (MJ)
Cow's milk/goat's milk	$3\frac{3}{5}$ cups†	5	7	5.7‡
Buffalo's milk/ewe's milk	$3\frac{1}{5}$ cups†	3	6	5.7‡
Skimmed milk powder§	13 tbsp*	8	7	5.7‡
Full cream milk powder§	15 tbsp*	5	7	5.6‖
Evaporated milk	$1\frac{3}{4}$ cups†	5	6	5.7‡
K-MIX2§	10 tbsp*	8	4	5.7‡
Yogurt¶	$3\frac{3}{5}$ cups†	6	7	5.7‡

* One tablespoon = 15 ml, or 12.5 g (sugar). § Unreconstituted.
† One cup = 250 ml, or 208 g (sugar). ‖ Approximately 1350 kcal$_{th}$.
‡ Approximately 1360 kcal$_{th}$. ¶ Energy value of milk with half the carbohydrates.

(c) *Measured by weight*

	Ingredients				Energy or protein provided			
	Milk or milk preparation (g)	Oil (g)	Sugar (g)	Approximate total energy	Approximate energy per 100 ml	Protein g/l	g/100 ml	Mixing
Cow's/goat's milk	900	55	70	5.6 MJ*	0.56 MJ†	0.030	3.0	
Buffalo's/ewe's milk	800	30	65	5.6 MJ*	0.56 MJ†	0.030	3.0	After mixing
Skimmed milk powder‡	90	85	65	5.6 MJ*	0.56 MJ†	0.032	3.2	with oil and sugar make up
Full-cream milk powder‡	120	55	65	5.7 MJ§	0.57 MJ‖	0.030	3.0	to 1000 ml with water
Evaporated milk	450	50	70	5.7 MJ§	0.57 MJ‖	0.031	3.1	
K-MIX2‡	120	85	35	5.7 MJ§	0.57 MJ‖	0.030	3.0	
Yogurt¶	900	65	70	5.7 MJ§	0.57 MJ‖	0.030	3.0	

* Approximately 1350 kcal$_{th}$. ‖ Approximately 136 kcal$_{th}$ per 100 ml.
† Approximately 135 kcal$_{th}$ per 100 ml. ¶ Energy value of milk with half the carbohydrates.
‡ Unreconstituted. (From WHO 1981)
§ Approximately 1360 kcal$_{th}$.

Selection

Admission is always based on clinical judgement supported by anthropometric measurements. In practical terms this is usually:

- Children less than 70 per cent weight for height.
- Children with kwashiorkor or marasmic kwashiorkor.
- Children and adults with poor nutritional status and a complicating disease, e.g. measles or tuberculosis.

On admission patients should be registered, the nutritional status measured, a medical history taken, and dietary requirements calculated. All this information should be carefully recorded on a card kept in a safe place at the bedside. Every child should be accompanied by a guardian, preferably the mother, who should be responsible for feeding and caring for the child.

Distribution system

Therapeutic feeding should take place on an in-patient basis to ensure adequate supervision and care. In the early stages of treatment small amounts of food need to be given regularly every three to four hours. This allows for six to seven feeds in the 24 hour period and a recovery period of about 30 days. Recovery and weight gain seem to take longer in marasmus than kwashiorkor; though children with kwashiorkor may, after about ten days of treatment and an encouraging loss of oedema, suddenly die for no obvious reason. On an out-patient basis it is impossible to guarantee more than four feeds a day, and the rate of recovery becomes correspondingly slower.

In-patient feeding requires a centre or ward with suitable accommodation for not more than 50 patients and their guardians, kitchen facilities for both the patients and the guardians; a suitable store for food and medical supplies; water and sanitation facilities, and medical and nursing staff. Considering the comparatively low number of beneficiaries, therapeutic feeding is expensive in terms of facilities, effort, time and personnel.

Special care

Half-strength feeds should be given for the first 24–48 hours of starting treatment. Progress from half to full strength feeds, to semi-solid, and finally solid foods should take no longer than 10–12 days. All volumes of food given at each feeding time should be carefully recorded on a card for each patient. Table 5.8 gives the volume of food required according to weight of the child and the frequency of feeding.

Naso-gastric feeding is sometimes required where anorexia persists for more than 24 hours or for children in a state of collapse. It should be discontinued as soon as possible. Most children with severe malnutrition will have a complicating disease or condition, and medical treatment therefore is an essential aspect of their care.

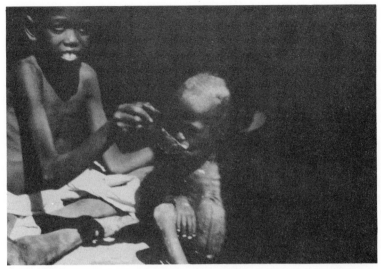

Fig. 5.12. Older brother feeding younger sister. Many such feeding scenes took place in therapeutic feeding programmes during the Ogaden famine in Ethiopia in 1975.

Medical conditions of particular importance

Anaemia

This is commonly associated with low intakes of iron and/or folic acid during pregnancy, malaria, or helminth infections. Where appropriate, the cause should be treated and then oral iron and folic acid tablets given daily for one month. Blood transfusion should be considered only in very severe anaemia or when anaemia has been caused by a large acute blood loss.

Anorexia

A very common problem that requires patience and firm handling. The parent or guardian in particular needs to understand that regular feeding must be carried out whether or not the patient seems to want it.

Diarrhoea

This is associated with poor absorption of food through the damaged mucosa of the gut. Staff should advise parents and patient that this is normal for the first few days of treatment and does not require medication. Persistent diarrhoea of more than three to four days, may, however, be associated with infection or, less commonly with lactose intolerance. Rehydration should be done with oral fluids and monitored carefully due to the possibility of overloading and congestive cardiac failure (see section on Diarrhoea and the community). In marasmus children are usually extremely hungry once the diarrhoea has settled.

Hypoglycaemia

This occurs most frequently at night between the last feed of the evening and the first feed next morning. The risk of this complication can, therefore, be reduced by keeping this time period as short as possible.

Hypothermia

Severely malnourished children have difficulty maintaining their body temperature. It is vital that they are kept as warm as possible, especially at night. One of the simplest measures is to ensure that mothers hold their children close to their own bodies.

Intestinal infections

Giardiasis, trichuriasis, and ascariasis, and to a lesser extent ancylostomiasis and strongyloidiasis may occur. Treatment should be withheld until about day 5 when the child will be better able to tolerate the drug treatment.

Measles

This is associated with a very high mortality among the malnourished, and is itself also an important cause of malnutrition. As stated in the section on immunization, priority should be given to an immunization campaign against measles. Those children admitted to a therapeutic feeding programme should be given special priority. There is a common association of measles, keratoconjunctivitis with xerophthalmia and bronchopneumonia.

Potassium deficiency

Most severely malnourished children are deficient in potassium and should be given the solution as in Table 5.7 in divided doses with the feeds for two weeks; the amount of solution to be given each day is calculated according to the weight of the child, as described on p. 118.

Respiratory infections

May be a major cause of malnutrition especially in the cold, wet season. Overcrowding may help the rapid spread of infections such as influenza, pneumonia, and bronchopneumonia.

Skin infections

Pustules, impetigo, fissures, ulcers, scabies, and thrush are commonly seen among the malnourished, and should be treated appropriately.

Tuberculosis

Anybody not responding to the therapeutic diet after 10–14 days should be investigated for tuberculosis; it is a common cause of marasmus. Treatment of the tuberculosis should be commenced only if it can be guaranteed for the full period required.

Urinary tract infection

Frequently associated with severe malnutrition. Confirm where possible by microscopic examination and treat appropriately.

Vitamin A deficiency

This complication can lead to xerophthalmia and blindness. The condition may not be immediately noticed and it can be brought on by a sudden increase in food intake. It is, therefore, advisable to give all patients 100 000 or 200 000 IU if they have not already received it as part of a mass vitamin A distribution programme. See Table 5.5 for the treatment doses.

Criteria for discharge

Before discharging any patient he or she should be:

● Active and alert.
● Gaining weight without oedema.
● Free from obvious illness.
● Have a good appetite and taking a mixed diet, using the food provided in the general and supplementary feeding programme.
● More than 80 per cent of standard weight-for-height.

On discharge, immediate referral to continue with supplementary feeding is essential.

Success or failure

Many of the factors referred to in the success or failure of a supplementary feeding programme also apply here, but in addition:

● The 'in-patient' building should follow traditional design and facilities rather than a 'hospital-like' setting.
● Trust, confidence, and full participation of the patients, parents, and other staff are vital.
● All the activities must be arranged around a strict feeding schedule.
● Playing and talking with malnourished children is essential to their full recovery.
● Effective referral and follow-up in the supplementary feeding programme to prevent deterioration after discharge.

Fig. 5.13. Malnourished children participating in a game in a shelter in Ethiopia.

Monitoring effectiveness

The very nature of the programme means that monitoring is aimed specifically at the individual patient. It usually takes the form of:

● Re-weighing regularly, e.g. every three to five days, to ensure that the child is neither losing weight nor failing to gain weight. Adequate feeding should ensure a weight gain of 10–20 g/kg per day.
● Recording daily the presence of oedema and the general condition.
● Admissions, discharges, medical transfers, and deaths must be recorded daily to give an indication of the effectiveness of case-finding and care given.

6 Communicable diseases

Control of communicable diseases

Communicable diseases are likely to be more of a hazard to camp populations than to the same people before they migrated. This is due to various factors such as overcrowding, low levels of nutrition, and the possibility of increased severity of infectious diseases in malnourished people leading to higher transmission rates. However, in some respects the crowded conditions make the implementation of control measures easier than when people are scattered over large areas. International and national relief staff are also exposed to communicable diseases and often lack the acquired immunity that the refugees may have to the same infections (see Chapter 10).

The communicable diseases that refugees suffer from may have originated from:

1. The country of origin or the areas the refugees travelled through before arriving at the camp.
2. The camp itself.
3. The local area and population.

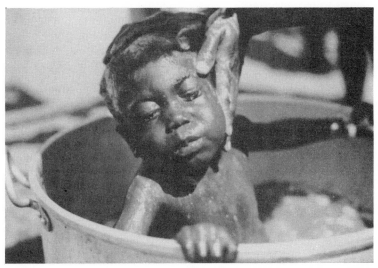

Fig. 6.1. Personal hygiene is an important factor in the prevention of disease.

Fig. 6.2. Overcrowding in Sakaeo camp for the Kampuchean refugees in Thailand in 1979 (UNHCR, Gangler).

Malaria is a good example of a communicable disease where transmission may occur in any one, two, or all three of these situations. The greatest danger is for refugees coming from non-malarious areas, who are therefore not relatively immune, into areas where *falciparum* malaria is endemic.

Refugees with 'infections' who have been in the camp for more than four weeks are most likely to have caught the disease in the camp itself or in the surrounding area, because most communicable diseases have incubation periods of less than four weeks. This does not apply to the parasitic and helminthic infections (such as malaria, schistosomiasis, trypanosomiasis, filariasis, and intestinal helminths) or to tuberculosis or leprosy, all of which have long incubation periods.

GENERAL PREVENTIVE MEASURES

The spread of communicable diseases can be controlled by attacking the source of infection, interrupting the spread or transmission, or by protecting the susceptible individuals in the general population. The main methods are summarized in Table 6.1. For the majority of communicable diseases the best general preventive measures are adequate supplies of safe water, hygienic disposal of both refuse and excreta, good personal hygiene, adequate shelter from extremes of climate, and sufficient food fairly distributed. There are also many communicable diseases which are not easily preventable, but for which prompt treatment of cases may prevent further spread.

Table 6.1. *Summary of the main methods for controlling communicable diseases*

Attacking the source of infection	Interrupting transmission	Protecting susceptible individuals
Treatment of cases and carriers	Environmental health: Water supplies	Immunization
	Excreta disposal	Chemoprophylaxis
Isolation of cases	Food hygiene	
		Personal protection
Surveillance of suspects	Personal hygiene	Better nutrition
Notification of cases to authorities	Vector control	
	Disinfection and sterilization of surroundings	
Control of animal reservoirs of disease	Reduce population movements and migration	

Immunization is often an important and effective method of control. However, for vector borne diseases like malaria, trypanosomiasis, and dengue, controlling the particular vector can be the most important method.

Terrifying epidemics are not usual in refugee camps. However, rumours of epidemics are a common problem and an early task is to set up a simple disease surveillance system. A few diseases may produce large outbreaks shortly after a camp is established and measures against them must take priority. The most important are malaria in endemic areas, cholera, typhoid, diarrhoeas, and typhus.

The next most important group are those diseases that are more likely to become a problem, and may give rise to epidemics when the camp has been established for some months, such as dengue, hepatitis, influenza, measles, meningitis, sleeping sickness, whooping cough, and yellow fever.

Finally, some communicable diseases need long-term control measures but are unlikely to produce epidemics, for example, Chagas' disease, hookworm, leprosy, loiasis, onchocerciasis, and tuberculosis.

Immunization procedures can protect against the following diseases: cholera, diphtheria, measles, meningococcal meningitis, poliomyelitis, tetanus, tuberculosis, typhoid, typhus, whooping cough, and yellow fever. See below and pages 137 to 146 for further details.

MAJOR PROBLEMS

Malaria

This is a common early problem, especially where refugees migrate from an upland area or one free from malaria, to a highly malarious zone.

Transmission may already be brisk among the local population and anopheline mosquitoes can transmit malaria to the refugees. Outbreaks should be prevented but if they occur prompt control measures are necessary. For adequate control measures against malaria, information is needed on:

● Which species of parasites are prevalent locally and the spectrum of drug resistance? In particular, is *Plasmodium falciparum* a major problem and is it resistant to chloroquine?

● Breeding habitats of the principal anopheline mosquito vectors.

● Resting habits of the vectors, whether indoors (endophilic) or outside (exophilic) and their susceptibility to the available insecticides.

There are four main ways of controlling malaria in a refugee camp:

1. *Reduction of mosquito breeding*—This can be achieved both by getting rid of unnecessary collections of water and by making those that remain unsuitable for the particular local vectors. Mosquitoes tend to be highly specific in their choice of habitat. Some prefer shaded flowing water, others flourish in temporary, muddy, sunlit ponds. In most places public health officials will already know about local vectors. With this information it is often possible to reduce greatly the numbers of malaria vectors by altering specific sites—an approach known as species sanitation. This approach is particularly cost-effective in overcrowded conditions.

2. *Spraying with insecticides*—Where vector mosquitoes mainly bite and rest indoors (endophilic vectors) control of malaria transmission is most readily achieved by spraying the inside walls and roof of the houses with DDT, malathion, or other residual insecticides. Depending on the building materials, a spray may remain effective for up to six months. The mosquitoes resting on the sprayed surface take up the insecticide on contact. However, spraying may not be the answer in refugee camps; the vector may bite outdoors, and shelters may lack walls or surfaces for spraying. It is obviously necessary to ensure that the vector is susceptible to the insecticides used. Simple kits are available for such tests, though usually the local health authorities will be aware of the resistance pattern. Sometimes, in the face of an epidemic, volume aerial spraying of the camp may be needed to combat exophilic and other vectors, but this is a specialized procedure and there is little reason to consider it in most circumstances.

3. *Use of mosquito nets*—Where the predominant biting by vector mosquitoes takes place indoors at night, the use of nets will reduce exposure to infection. The success of introducing nets will depend largely on previous customs of the refugees and on the level of nuisance biting. It cannot be the only measure used.

4. *Chemotherapy*—In all malarious camps it is necessary to have ample supplies of the most useful drugs and to treat those with fever, using

chloroquine, except where there is resistance to it, in which case Fansidar or a combination of other drugs may be needed (see p. 221). Where a highly susceptible refugee population is moving into an endemic area, mass chemoprophylaxis may be considered. In other circumstances it is usually confined to young children and pregnant women.

As with other diseases, it will often be necessary to control the disease in the neighbouring population around the refugee camp, and liaison with the national malaria programme is essential. If spraying is to be undertaken, trained workers are needed, preferably from the refugee population but, failing that, from the national programme.

The intensity of malaria transmission varies greatly between different parts of the world. It is highest in sub-Saharan Africa where measures against the vectors on their own are unlikely to stop transmission. Where seasonal transmission occurs, chemotherapy and chemoprophylaxis, particularly in children, will be most important (see section on Clinical care, especially Table 8.5, p. 220). Elsewhere in the world, apart from Papua New Guinea, transmission is less intense and vector control may be relatively effective.

Evaluating the prevalence of malaria

In a refugee camp where malaria is a problem it is necessary to know the frequency and age distribution of the people infected and the details of the mosquitoes transmitting the disease if control measures are to be properly planned. It is essential to consult with the host countries' national malaria service. They can possibly provide data or an accurate guess on the vectors causing transmission. The malaria service is less likely to know the clinical and epidemiological pattern amongst the refugees.

Malaria transmission is often seasonal. If there is a marked wet season, malaria incidence will usually peak during the latter part of it. A survey in the dry season should not be allowed to create a false sense of security.

There are three ways in which the prevalence of malaria may be estimated in the population sample:

- parasite rate
- spleen rate
- malaria seropositivity rate

The choice will depend on available facilities and so also will the sample of refugees examined. Ideally, that should be a random sample of the camp population, stratified to cover subgroups of the refugees who have come from places of possibly different malaria endemicity, and chosen to have comparable numbers of children and adults. This should eventually be done anyway for a long-standing camp. As a first step, however, it will be important to assess the situation among patients presenting at the various clinics, especially those with fever, and among children at feeding centres. This will help to decide if all such patients and malnourished children should be given antimalarials routinely until more elaborate control arrangements are made.

Parasite rate: The use of blood smears to establish the percentage with parasites is the most direct and unequivocal way to diagnose malaria and determine its frequency in the sample. It requires a microscope with an oil immersion objective and the appropriate stains (see Appendix 2), and someone who is familiar with the identification of malaria parasites under the microscope. It may be possible to borrow a technician from the malaria service or a hospital. Thick films (see p. 226) are more useful than thin films because a larger blood sample is scanned for the malaria parasites, but thick films are harder to read and more subject to artefacts. It is useful to know the species of parasite and their relative frequencies. The main division will be between *P. falciparum* and the three other species, since *falciparum* is the one that causes the most deaths. Anti-malarials should not be indiscriminately available immediately before and at the time of survey if the results are to give meaningful epidemiological results.

The main questions that can be answered by a parasite survey are: how important is malaria as a cause of fever, how common is it, and what is the likely pattern of human immunity?

Very odd infection patterns with some groups heavily infected and others not at all should first rouse suspicions of access to antimalarials on a large scale; more complex explanations require an expert in malaria. The main patterns of prevalence likely to be seen are:

● a high prevalence at all ages, indicating high transmission in a newly exposed community
● a high prevalence in children but low in adults, suggesting heavy transmission in a community exposed previously to malaria
● a low prevalence at all ages, suggesting either low transmission or an early stage in an epidemic

Spleen rate: This is the percentage of the various age-groups who have their spleen sufficiently enlarged to be palpable through the abdominal wall. There are many causes of splenomegaly but few that occur on such a large scale as with malaria, so that the spleen rate may be used as a measure of malaria prevalence in the community, though it is not as reliable as parasite rates. Other diseases such as intestinal schistosomiasis and kala-azar may give high prevalences of splenomegaly locally, and where they are common it is unreliable to assess malaria in this way.

While the disadvantage of spleen rates is the lack of specificity, an advantage is that the enlarged spleen represents the cumulative effect of malaria infection over weeks, months, or years and is less sensitive than the parasite rate to erratic use of chemotherapy.

Seropositivity rate: This is calculated as the percentage with detectable antibodies to malaria parasites in finger-prick blood samples collected in capillary tubes or as spots on filter paper. This technique requires a good laboratory with skilled technical help using fluorescent microscopes. It is therefore less applicable than the preceding methods. There are two advantages: the antibodies remain for years after malaria infection and so are not affected by erratic chemotherapy, and it is possible to do a rapid survey by collecting blood samples on filter paper. These can be sent to a distant laboratory, thus removing one task from the field area where pressures are greatest. It is clearly impractical for clinical diagnosis in the field.

The results of spleen and parasite surveys of the refugee community may give very high rates. In sub-Saharan Africa it is common for parasite and spleen rates to exceed 75 per cent in the 2–9 year age group and in some places over 80 per cent are infected by 1 year. Sub-Saharan Africa is thus characterized by very highly endemic (holoendemic) malaria. Under these conditions the spleen rate in adults is low, although very high in children. Parasite rates are lower in adults than children in many areas of endemic high transmission, because of the induced partial immunity.

Cholera

The risk of cholera should be realistically assessed and will depend on the camp location and whether the infection is endemic there or in the home area of the refugees. The main control measures are good environmental sanitation and adequate safe water supplies, and these must be given priority. The vaccine available at present gives limited protection (about 60 per cent for up to six months). It is more often demanded than needed. Its chief value is when an epidemic is expected but has not yet reached the camp. In the face of an actual outbreak the prophylactic use of tetracycline may be considered, unless there is a resistant strain of *Vibrio* organism. However the main emphasis during an epidemic must be to keep the death rate as low as possible by prompt and adequate rehydration of patients using oral rehydration methods wherever possible, as outlined in the section on the Management of diarrhoea. Other control methods are aimed at reducing transmission through good environmental health (water, excreta, and food hygiene) and safe burial procedures.

Typhoid

This is also feared, but dramatic outbreaks are unusual. The monovalent vaccine gives unequivocal but incomplete protection to susceptible in-dividuals. Sound environmental hygiene and isolation of cases are the best means of interrupting transmission. Typhoid and cholera vaccinations are partly useful, but they also give an unrealistic sense of protection while general measures will have a much wider impact. See p. 149 for further details.

Diarrhoeas

Early promotion of environmental health, health education, and simple rehydration are the principal control measures against the far more common, and often lethal, diarrhoeal diseases due to other infective agents. (See section Diarrhoea and the Community.)

Typhus

The other greatly feared vector-borne disease in refugee camps is louse-borne typhus. However, this is only a major hazard in mountainous and cold areas where clothes are kept on for prolonged periods and where washing is difficult, such as occurred in the Wollo shelters in Northern Ethiopia in 1973/4. Lice are controlled by dusting people with a suitable insecticide such as DDT or malathion. A vaccine is available for those persons at special risk (see p. 243).

Fig. 6.3. Recovery from malnutrition for these children in shelters in Wollo province, Ethiopia, in 1973/74, was often complicated by diseases such as typhus, typhoid, meningitis, hepatitis, or tuberculosis.

Other diseases

Dengue

Outbreaks of dengue are best tackled by vector control. The *Aedes* mosquito vector is a day-biting species that breeds in small containers and closed collections of clean water, and is thus not accessible to residual spraying and individual protective measures. In well organized camps it should be reasonably easy to resort to health education and community action to control the breeding sites. In disorganized camps, in case of outbreaks, insecticide spread by aerial fogging of the camp with ultra low volume preparations may be necessary.

Hepatitis

Although hepatitis may be a problem, it is only possible to protect against the form transmitted by needles and serum, hepatitis B, by specific action such as careful sterilization of injection needles. For hepatitis type A and type non-A–non-B general hygienic measures are all that is feasible. Immuno-globulin is not available in adequate quantities for routine use amongst refugees and, in any case, many will already have acquired immunity. However, international health staff are at high risk (see p. 243).

Influenza

This can cause severe epidemics with a high death rate from complicating respiratory infections, amongst the weak and old, but it is not usual to vaccinate against it in refugee camps.

Intestinal worms

These provide a different challenge. The intestinal worms are not difficult to treat, but re-infection is often rapid. Therefore a useful community campaign against worms by chemotherapy should await the completion of adequate water and sanitation facilities. However, if in the emergency phase surveys have shown that some specific helminths are highly prevalent, and cause infections severe enough to interfere with nutritional status, repeated treatment of groups at risk such as those at feeding centres, may be a necessary temporary measure (see p. 222).

Meningitis

In the sub-Saharan meningitis zone, particularly, meningococcal immuniza-tion may be of importance for the whole camp population. In view of the cyclic nature of epidemics of meningitis it is possible to predict when immunization is most needed rather than making it a regular activity. The cycle of meningitis epidemics usually occurs every few years. If the vaccine is in short supply, its administration should be reserved for household contacts of cases. The administration of chemoprophylaxis to contacts has lost some value since there is evidence of widespread resistance to sulfonamides in the African meningitis zone, but it should be considered as a cheaper alternative to immunization. Antibiotic sensitivity can be determined on a few specimens of spinal fluid from meningitis cases in a central laboratory. Immunization offers individual protection; the antigenic type of the vaccine must be appropriate for the strain of meningococcus circulating locally.

Skin and eye infections

Infections of the skin and eyes are major causes for concern. Scabies is often a major problem but it is easily treated with benzyl benzoate. Effective treatment on a large scale is by diluting the benzyl benzoate in a large tank and dipping everyone in it, rather than painting it on each individual's skin. Secondary infection of scabies then clears up also.

Eye infections are often troublesome. Viral conjunctivitis epidemics are hard to control, but antibiotic eye ointment can be used against trachoma and other microbial infections.

Tuberculosis

This is frequently a major problem and it may be the most serious long-term communicable disease problem in a camp. The control of tuberculosis is a question of feasibility. Control rests on two main measures. The first is a reduction of the susceptible population by BCG immunization of children and adequate nutrition; and the second by a reduction of the source of infection by treating all patients who are coughing up live tubercle bacilli.

Finding patients with a positive sputum is based on collecting specimens from all cases of chronic cough for over four weeks and examining by microscopy and bacterial culture techniques. There is hardly any place in refugee camps for tuberculin skin surveys or the mass use of chest X-rays.

All cases proved by bacterioscopy must be started on an adequate treatment scheme (see section on Clinical care). Such programmes are difficult to implement during an emergency phase and should only be started when there is some reasonable guarantee that patients will receive long-term treatment. A similar approach may be taken to leprosy and other chronic infections.

Yellow fever

This usually presents as an outbreak of jaundice and may be easily confused with hepatitis. The virus is a natural infection of monkeys in parts of Africa and South America and is spread to man by mosquitoes. Vector control measures are important, but mass immunization is very effective in stopping transmission.

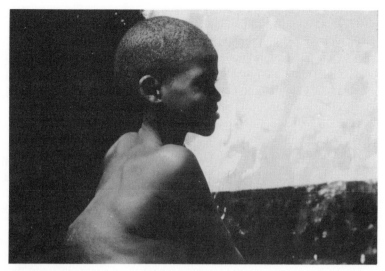

Fig. 6.4. TB of the spine. A permanent disability that emphasizes the importance of the control of tuberculosis.

INVESTIGATING EPIDEMICS

Epidemics may be caused by infectious diseases such as measles, gastro-enteritis, meningitis, typhoid or typhus, or toxic substances like agricultural sprays and poisons in food. An epidemic is said to be present when an excessive number of new cases is being reported. This means that you need to know what the expected incidence for the disease is at that time of year in the host country. Epidemics are frightening, so be careful of calling any outbreak an epidemic. The medical staff will probably first come to know about the 'epidemic' by hearsay or because cases come to the clinics or hospital. The following steps are useful in tackling the problem.

Is it a real epidemic?

Some diseases like measles show considerable variation from month to month in the number of cases that occur, and it has to be decided if there is an excessive number. It can be difficult to decide whether there is an epidemic or not, and sometimes reasons for saying whether there is or not may be more political than epidemiological. The task is made much easier if a regular surveillance system exists so that the usual frequency of cases is known already.

Defining the cases

Often the disease people are suffering from can be easily diagnosed but, if not, take good clinical histories and examine the patients. Pay particular attention to where the patients live and what they have been doing and eating over the past few days or weeks. Decide if any laboratory tests are necessary to confirm the diagnosis. Are sub-clinical cases a possibility? The district medical officer should be informed and his help requested. Decide on the diagnostic criteria to follow for categorizing patients as definite, probable, and possible cases. A special effort should be made to find sub-clinical and mild cases and those ill people who have not reported to any clinic. Collect any blood, faecal, urine, or particular specimens that need further laboratory investigation.

Describing the epidemic

Use the technique of 'Who, Where and When' to describe the epidemic (see p. 72). The first step is to show on a map where the patients live and then to construct an incidence graph showing the day of onset of the illness for all cases diagnosed; this is called an epidemic curve. Then analyse the known cases to see how many males or females, and how many there are in each main age group, i.e. 0–4 years, 5–14 years, 15–44 years, and 45 years and over. Work out the percentage cases in each age group. Are the percentages similar to what might be expected for the percentage in each age group of the whole population or is there an excess in one particular age group or in one sex? Also examine other relevant 'Who' characteristics.

How can the epidemic be explained?

Where there is sufficient information about the clinical cases and about 'Who, Where and When' try and answer the following crucial questions:

How do the cases differ from the normal population?
What do all the cases have in common?

Then go on to:

What is the diagnosis?
What is the organism or agent?
What is the source of the epidemic?
How is the organism or agent being transmitted?
Why did the epidemic occur?

It may be necessary to carry out small surveys, visits, or laboratory tests to see if you can confirm your ideas on what is happening. Remember to collect and save samples that may be analysed later in laboratories.

How can the epidemic be controlled?

The implementation of control measures often cannot wait until the epidemic is fully understood. It may be necessary to start an immunization campaign (e.g. measles), to isolate cases, or to close a water supply. Before taking any action you must consult with camp administrators, medical officers, and health inspectors. Epidemic control measures can cause panic and may have political repercussions.

The aim is to lower the incidence of the disease to a number that is no longer a problem to the community and preferably even further, so that the disease is eradicated altogether. Control measures may have to be continued indefinitely, since the incidence of new cases of the disease may start to rise again if they are stopped.

The main control methods for communicable diseases have been summarized in Table 6.1.

Immunization

The priority given to immunization programmes which are aimed at reducing morbidity and mortality from important communicable diseases, depends on their feasibility.

IMPORTANCE OF IMMUNIZATION

In nearly all refugee situations measles epidemics are, at some time, a major cause of death. To a lesser extent the same is true of whooping cough and poliomyelitis, though with the latter, the younger the age of onset the less likely is paralysis to be a complication. Immunization, particularly against measles, should have priority together with the provision of basic clinical services, although immunization is probably less important than the supply of adequate food and water.

The priority given to immunization programmes depends on their feasibility. You must decide whether it is possible to obtain a high immunization rate amongst the susceptible refugees (target population) using a viable and effective vaccine.

This depends on two main issues:

• Is the cold chain (see p. 139) adequate; if not can it be set up quickly and at low cost? Vaccines must be kept properly refrigerated at all times. Unless and until this is possible, immunization programmes should not be undertaken and vaccines should certainly not be ordered.
• Can a high percentage of the target population be covered? The cost of establishing a cold chain and delivering the vaccines to remote places is only justified if high coverage is possible. Although gathering people in a well defined area should facilitate good coverage, this is often seriously limited by cultural and organizational problems.

ORGANIZATION

An immunization programme should ideally be co-ordinated by the host government. Where this is not possible, the programme should still be discussed with and approved by the local health authorities. Most countries have programmes for their own population and wherever possible plans for immunizing refugees should be in line with these. However, the need of the refugee population may be greater due to crowding and poor nutrition. Immunization may also be more feasible amongst large densely packed refugee communities than amongst a more scattered local population.

In addition to the local government, the advice and co-operation of WHO should be sought. WHO has an Expanded Programme on Immunization (EPI) which helps countries implement immunization programmes against diphtheria, measles, poliomyelitis, tetanus, tuberculosis, and whooping cough.

As well as involving the national health authorities and WHO, the refugee community itself should take an active part in the planning and execution of the programme. Refugee health staff can quickly be trained to give the immunizations and maintain records. Generally, the more vaccines that are included in an immunization programme the less costly it is per person, as transport and labour costs remain virtually constant. Therefore, with the possible exception of measles, an immunization campaign which only includes one or two vaccines should be given low priority.

Types of programme

There are three main ways of obtaining a high immunization coverage. By immunization of:

● Refugees on arrival.
● The target population within the community by mass campaigns.
● Susceptible individuals attending health centres and as part of mother and child health services.

These approaches can either be used singly or together. Different methods are more appropriate at different stages of the camp's development. Factors influencing which methods to adopt include the level of organization, the stability of the population, the type of vaccine, the number of doses required, and seasonal incidence of the diseases to be prevented.

Immunization on arrival is best so long as it does not take precedence over more urgent needs and provided that some orderly processing of refugees is possible.

Immunization requiring more than one vaccine dose needs more organization as it is difficult to ensure a high coverage for the second and third doses. A study in a Kampuchean camp showed a steep decrease in attendance for a three-dose programme for typhoid vaccination (see Table 6.2).

Table 6.2. *Percentage of target population receiving inoculations*

	Age 2–5 years			Age 6–14 years			Adults		
	Total	M	F	Total	M	F	Total	M	F
Target population:	172	97	75	362	175	187	455	144	311
% of target receiving									
1st inoculation	80.8	80.4	81.3	76.2	76.0	76.5	69.2	69.4	69.1
2nd inoculation	57.6	57.7	57.3	51.1	41.1	60.4	41.5	40.3	42.1
3rd inoculation	29.7	27.8	32.0	26.5	18.9	33.7	28.4	17.4	33.4
4th inoculation	21.5	17.5	26.7	18.5	14.9	21.9			

From Bollag (1980)

Nevertheless, vaccinations given in MCH clinics will only ensure a good coverage if the clinics draw in a high proportion of mothers and children from the various sectors of the community. In a new community this is unlikely, and such an approach will only be reliable when a good system of home visiting has been implemented (see p. 207).

THE COLD CHAIN AND VACCINE STORAGE

The cold chain is the process by which a vaccine is kept cold from the time it leaves the factory until it is given to an individual. If at any point the chain breaks down the vaccine is likely to become overheated and rendered useless. It is, therefore, essential to ensure an adequate cold chain before implementing any immunization programme.

The main links in the cold chain are:

Manufacturer
↓
Airport
↓
Central store
↓
Regional store
↓
District store
↓
Health centre (national)
↓
Refugee camp
↓
Refugee

One member of the health team must take full responsibility for the whole immunization programme and ensure that all requirements are fulfilled. This will involve checking the capacity and condition of freezers and refrigerators at all the relay points, and ensuring a sufficient supply of cold packs, cold boxes, and vacuum flasks.

There are several critical points in the chain, but the problems associated with maintaining small refrigerators make the final link the most problematical. It is often very difficult to maintain refrigerators in the field, and this may necessitate a mass immunization approach as against integrating immunization into routine work. Generally, during the early stages of relief it is advisable to use mobile immunization units working from central or district stores. In this case it is imperative that unused vaccine is not returned to the cold store if there is any likelihood that it has been overheated. If there is any chance that the vaccine has been spoilt it should be thrown away. Wherever vaccines are stored the stock should be rotated so that oldest vaccines are used first. Vaccines deteriorate at a rate determined by time and temperature (see Table 6.4).

Some particular points:

● The use of time–temperature tags permits the monitoring of vaccines during shipment. A good system along the cold chain helps to guarantee that vaccines arrive at their various relay points on time and without being spoilt.
● Special dial thermometers with maximum/minimum pointers are now available and should be used at all levels of the chain.

● Travel documents should state maximum/minimum temperatures for the vaccine at each stage in its travel and at relay points.

● Where possible top-opening refrigerators should be used, as they will give better storage and allow much less loss of cold air. Petrol and gas-operated refrigerators are usually less efficient than electric ones, especially when the surrounding air temperature rises above 43 °C. However the availability of electric power is a problem in camps. Solar refrigerators are being developed, as are cold boxes that will retain the correct temperature for one week, if unopened.
● When a diluent is required it should be kept together with the vaccine in the refrigerator, so that its higher temperature compared to the cold vaccine does not inactivate the vaccine during the mixing. Adequate storage space must, therefore, be planned in advance to prevent wastage.

COMMON VACCINES

The following vaccines are usually included in immunization programmes:

Diphtheria, pertussis (whooping cough) and tetanus, measles, poliomyelitis, and BCG.

There are differing views about the use of typhoid and cholera vaccines. Vaccines against meningitis and yellow fever may sometimes also be needed. See also pp. 125–34.

Measles

For refugee communities this is probably the most useful immunization, but it is also expensive and the most sensitive to any failure in the cold chain. New measles vaccines that are more heat stable are being developed. Measles usually occurs during the dry season in most countries and so epidemics can be predicted to some extent and immunization campaigns planned in advance. A single intra-muscular injection of 0.5 ml can provide good immunity. Sub-cutaneous injections seem to be less effective. The vaccine should not be given to children under six months of age as maternal antibodies block the effect. However, as the disease is most dangerous in young children, the vaccine should be given as soon as possible after six months. Children immunized between 6 and 12 months of age should ideally be given a second dose at 15 months. In most tropical countries there is usually no point in giving the vaccine to children older than three years, since by this age most children will have had a natural infection already.

Measles vaccine contains a live attenuated virus which induces, after approximately one week, a rise in antibodies and it is thus useful in controlling an epidemic. If mass campaigns are feasible they are extremely effective in stopping an epidemic once the first cases have been reported. During immunization sessions the vaccine must be protected from sunlight and kept cool, as heat rapidly inactivates it.

There is debate about the usefulness of providing measles immunization to malnourished children. Although studies have shown that the vaccine is effective in stimulating a rise in antibodies in malnourished children, in severely malnourished children this rise may be delayed.

Side effects of the vaccine are usually mild, even in severely malnourished children. They may include febrile attacks and temporary weight loss, but these potential dangers must be weighed against the high risks of leaving malnourished children unprotected. Case fatality rates in nutrition centres in some tropical communities are known to range from 1 per cent to 50 per cent. The overall positive response of malnourished children to measles vaccine argues for immunization whenever feasible.

Diphtheria–pertussis–tetanus (DPT)

After measles this is probably the most important vaccine because it affords young children protection against whooping cough. This disease is usually under-diagnosed and under-estimated.

The pertussis component of the vaccine is at present the object of considerable debate concerning its toxicity. There is no doubt that it has a higher complication risk than many other vaccines. Cases of neurological complications have been estimated to be about 1 per 10 000 immunized children. However, as with measles this must be weighed against the heavy mortality and morbidity caused by the disease, especially in many developing countries.

The vaccine is maximally effective from three months of age, but it can be given from one month old. Three doses of 0.5 ml given at intervals in the lateral aspect of the thigh are needed, although two provide considerable protection. Give the vaccine only to children less than five years old.

Tetanus toxoid (TT)

This is often given on its own to pregnant women in order to protect the newborn child from neonatal tetanus. It is usual for two doses of 0.5 ml to be given at a month's interval between the sixth to seventh month of pregnancy. One booster dose need only be given during subsequent pregnancies. Tetanus toxoid and DPT vaccines are destroyed if they are frozen.

Polio vaccine

Two types of polio vaccine are available. The Sabin vaccine is a live attenuated preparation of three different polio viruses. It is cheap, easy to

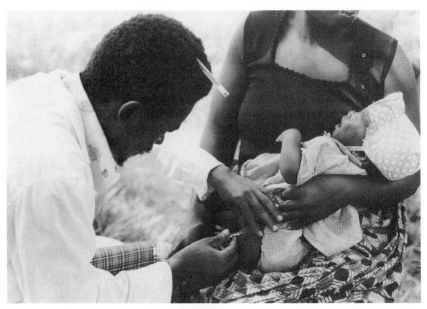

Fig. 6.5. Health worker giving a subcutaneous dose of DPT in the lateral aspect of the thigh.

administer, and it is currently utilized by the EPI worldwide. Three doses of one drop are given orally at intervals of not less than four weeks. It induces both humoral and gut cell-mediated immunity, competes with the wild polio viruses, and prevents the carrier state. The rise in antibodies is very rapid, but three doses should be provided to ensure adequate protection.

The Salk vaccine is a killed preparation and has to be administered subcutaneously by injection. Three injections one month apart are necessary to induce adequate protection, which is only humoral. In most populations in developing countries it is only necessary to give booster doses to children over five years old.

BCG (Bacille Calmette–Guerin)

Despite some doubts reported from India about the effectiveness of BCG vaccination in protecting adults from pulmonary tuberculosis, there is no evidence at present that it fails to give protection to children, particularly from the most lethal forms of tuberculosis, such as the miliary form or meningitis. WHO guidelines are that in developing countries where tuberculosis incidence is high BCG should be given as soon as possible after birth.

In mass campaigns, it is recommended for all children up to 12 years of age that BCG be administered together with other live and killed vaccines. In this case the BCG scar will act as a useful 'marker' for refugees who have received vaccines. Care should be taken to apply it to a standard place on each individual, such as below the right shoulder. The vaccine is extremely sensitive to sunlight and is easily killed by a few moments of exposure. The vaccine must be kept well covered and out of direct sunlight. Where the BCG vaccination is to be given in a mass campaign and to children over the age of six months, it may be better to give it at the same time as the third dose of polio and DPT. If the BCG is given at the time of the first doses of all the vaccines, the cold abscess that develops may discourage mothers from bringing their child for further vaccinations.

Cholera

Immunization is not usually recommended as the protection it provides is short lived, e.g. three to six months, and only about 60 per cent effective. Moreover, the vaccine does not stop the carrier state and only induces a rise in antibodies after a week. Therefore cholera vaccine can only be justified when it is known that a cholera epidemic is moving towards the refugee community. If cholera has already reached the community it is too late. The organization of a cholera immunization campaign is difficult, as two 0.5 ml doses are given one to two weeks apart (half that amount for children 1–10 years). Ensuring that all those vaccinated in the first round get a second dose requires very careful organization. If such organization is not feasible such a campaign will be pointless.

Typhoid

This vaccine is not commonly included in immunization programmes. As with cholera, more emphasis should be placed on environmental health factors for controlling transmission and potential epidemics. Immunization is not particularly useful once an epidemic has begun, as immunity takes about two weeks to build up. The main justification for typhoid vaccination is in large unorganized communities where sanitation is extremely poor and where the presence of typhoid has been proven, by laboratory services, to be endemic. Two doses of the single monovalent Typhoid vaccine are preferable to the old Triple Typhoid–Paratyphoid A and B vaccine.

Meningitis

This vaccine requires only one dose to be effective and acts against meningococcal biotypes A and C. It may be useful where regular epidemics occur, particularly when the pattern of outbreaks is well established. It is, however, an expensive vaccine. When supplies are limited only contacts of cases in an epidemic should be vaccinated. This will not stop the epidemic but it will limit the high secondary attack rate, particularly in areas where meningococcus has become resistant to sulfonamides, the traditional chemo-prophylactic agent. The vaccine is a stable polysaccharide but there is evidence that the immunity provided is temporarily reduced if the patient has malaria. There is, therefore, a good case for giving malarial prophylaxis before, or at the same time as, the vaccine is administered.

Yellow fever

This vaccine contains a live attenuated virus and it should be available in yellow fever endemic areas, especially to cover populations which may not have benefited from its protection for many years due to civil disturbances. It is rarely an urgent requirement. One injection of 0.5 ml given subcutaneously is the usual dose.

Table 6.3. *Immunization timetable*

For immunizations performed in maternal and child health clinics the EPI schedule is as follows:

- BCG—newborn or as soon after as possible up to 12 years
- DPT and Polio (oral) at 2, 3, and 4 months (with the possibility of starting at one month if one of the diseases, e.g. whooping cough, is highly endemic)
- Measles—6–9 months of age
- Tetanus toxoid: for pregnant women two doses one month apart in last trimester of pregnancy. One booster dose in subsequent pregnancies

In mass campaigns, and to all children presenting after six months of age:

- 1st contact: Measles, DPT, Polio
- 2nd contact 1 month later: DPT, Polio
- 3rd contact 1 month later: DPT, Polio, BCG
- tetanus toxoid to pregnant women during last trimester of pregnancy

EQUIPMENT

Apart from transport, storage, and refrigeration, the main requirement is for syringes and needles plus some means of cleaning the skin. Care should be taken to ensure sterilization of instruments, and a new sterile needle must be used on each patient to reduce the risk of hepatitis B and abscesses. One person can give 300–500 injections in a day using syringes and needles. Injector guns like the Pedojet or Portojet are capable of immunizing, by sub-cutaneous or intradermal injection, 500 people in an hour. However, they need professional maintenance and are really only effective when large numbers, such as 2000 or more per day, are involved. Such injectors frequently go wrong and require considerable maintenance. In Appendix 2, two possible kits are suggested for a complete cold chain and comprehensive immunization campaign.

RECORDS

Both clinic and home records must be maintained to ensure that the programme can be monitored. Road to health charts, if already used in MCH clinics can be used to record immunizations. If these cards are not yet in use, a mass campaign is a good opportunity to distribute them as an incentive to attend MCH clinics later on and to facilitate follow up of those children who have been immunized. Such a process is preferable to the distribution of loose vaccination certificates that tend to be lost.

Fig. 6.6. Mothers awaiting immunization session with their children and home-based record cards.

Table 6.4. *Summary of vaccines discussed in the text*

| Vaccine | Type | Storage | | | | Method of administration and No. of injections | Dose | Age | Contraindication | Reactions |
| | | Undiluted | | Diluted | | | | | | |
		Refrigerator (not freezer)	Room temperature	Refrigerator (not freezer)	Room temperature					
Measles	Live attenuated virus freeze-dried	6 months May be frozen	1–2 days	7–8 hours	5–6 hours	Intramuscular injection in thigh × 1	Usually 0.5 ml	6 months to 3 years	None	Mild fever, slight rash after 6–10 days
DPT (triple vaccine)	Diphtheria toxoid; pertussis—dead bacteria : tetanus—toxoid	Do not freeze*		2–3 years	2–3 days	Subcutaneous or intra-muscular injection in thigh × 3 at least one month apart	Usually 0.5 ml	1 month to 5 years	High fever	Pain at injection site for 24 hours
Tetanus	Toxoid may be alum absorbed	Do not freeze*		2–3 years Do not freeze	2–3 days	Subcutaneous or intra-muscular injection × 3 for primary course. At least 6–8 weeks between 1st and 2nd dose and 1 year between 2nd and 3rd dose. One booster dose during subsequent pregnancies or serious injury	Usually 0.5 ml	Any age or antenatal	None	Pain at injection site, for 12–24 hours

Polio-myelitis (Sabin)	Live attenuated virus, contains three strains	**May be frozen −15° to −25°C**		6 months	2 days	Oral × 3 at least one month apart	1 drop	1 month to 5 years	Diarrhoea or vomiting	None
BCG (for Tuberculosis)	Live attenuated bacteria, freeze-dried	1-2 years*	1 month cold room	2-3 hours	1-2 hours	Intradermal injection on right shoulder × 1	Varies according to manufacturer	Birth to 12 years	Known tuberculosis	Papule-ulcer scar after 6-12 weeks
Cholera	Dead bacteria, contains several strains	2 years Do not freeze	1-2 days	6-8 hours Do not freeze	1 hour	Subcutaneous injection × 2 for primary course, 1-2 weeks apart. One booster dose every 4-6 months	Varies but usually 1-10 years. 0.5 ml. Older children and adults, 1.0 ml	1 year to any age	Acute illness, chronic heart, liver or kidney disease	Pain at injection site for 24 hours
Monovalent Typhoid	Dead bacteria			2 years Do not freeze	2 days	Deep subcutaneous injection × 2 for primary course at an interval of 6 weeks. One booster dose every 12 months	Varies with manufacturer	1 year to any age	Acute infections, tuberculosis, heart or kidney disease	Pain at injection site, mild fever for 24 hours
Yellow Fever	Live attenuated virus, freeze-dried	1 year May be frozen	1-2 days	1 hour	1 hour	Subcutaneous injection × 1	Usually 0.5 ml	1 year to any age	Under 1 year of age; acute illness; 1st trimester of pregnancy	Mild fever, malaise for 24 hours
Meningitis	Acts against meningococcal Types A and C	1-2 years	1-2 days	2-3 hours	1-2 hours	Usually subcutaneous injection × 1, but check instructions on label	Usually 0.5 ml but depends on manufacturer	2-15 years	None. N.B. Immunity reduced if patient has malaria. Therefore give malaria prophylaxis before, or at same time as vaccine	Mild at injection site

* +4°C to +8°C maximum storage temperature.

EVALUATION OF COVERAGE

All immunization programmes must be evaluated in terms of coverage, which can be estimated by calculating the number of doses of each vaccine effectively given and then dividing this total by the estimated number of refugees who were eligible for immunization. The figure should be at least 75 per cent. For those vaccines that are given in two or three doses coverage can be calculated by:

$$\frac{\text{Number of persons in the target population who received a total of two or three doses}}{\text{Total number of persons in target population}} \times 100 \ (\%)$$

Coverage can also be estimated by random household surveys or more simply, by random questioning or evaluation of documents during a general food distribution where all families attend. BCG scar counts can also be used. A disease surveillance system should pick up whether immunization has reduced the incidence of the relevant disease. These are not, strictly speaking, measures of effectiveness of the vaccine as there is no control group, but they assist in monitoring the programme and in changing policies when necessary. Table 6.4 presents a summary of the cold chain requirements, methods of administration, and problems linked to each vaccine discussed in the text.

Diarrhoea and the community

Only with the co-operation and participation of the refugees will it be possible to organize an effective management scheme for diarrhoea. The people, especially mothers, need to understand that diarrhoea is not normal for their children, even though it may be common.

CAUSES OF DIARRHOEA AND THEIR CONTROL

Diarrhoeas are very common in refugee communities and one of the main causes of death, particularly in young children. Death is usually caused by dehydration, especially if vomiting also occurs. Diarrhoea can lead to malnutrition as nourishment is lost, children are reluctant to eat, and many mothers do not feed their children when they have diarrhoea, and even for some days after the diarrhoea has improved. Diarrhoea is worse and more common in malnourished people. It may be acute, lasting for hours or days, or chronic lasting for several weeks or months. The management described here is mostly for acute diarrhoea. A stable and very effective treatment to prevent dehydration is available and can be given at home or by health workers. Since most diarrhoea episodes last for one to three days rehydration by oral fluids is often all that is needed. However, severely dehydrated cases that require intravenous fluids are difficult to care for and require more highly trained personnel. Diarrhoea that lasts for more than a week may also need more careful investigation. The various causes of diarrhoea and their clinical features are summarized in Table 6.5. Most diarrhoea episodes, especially in children, fall into the acute watery diarrhoea category and for these, rehydration fluids are the essential treatment. Antibiotics are required only for a small proportion of cases.

All the main diarrhoea-causing pathogens are transmitted from the faeces of one person to the mouth of someone else, i.e. the faecal–oral route of transmission. There are obviously many opportunities for such transmission in the overcrowded conditions of a refugee camp.

Only with the co-operation and participation of the refugees will it be possible to organize an effective management scheme for diarrhoea. The people, especially mothers, need to understand that diarrhoea is not normal for their children, even though it may be common. They also need to know that an effective treatment, rehydration therapy, is available and that for mild cases they can treat their own children. If treatment is given early it can be simple and safe, but if it is delayed until a child's condition is severe, it may be difficult and dangerous. Honduran authorities established a successful oral rehydration programme among Nicaraguan refugee children that relied almost entirely on mothers themselves giving a suitable fluid by mouth to their own children. Diarrhoea can be critical for malnourished children as it causes the appetite to drop and after some time the gut becomes less able to absorb nutrients. Feeding and diarrhoea can be discussed with parents as part of the camp's feeding programme.

Rehydration therapy alone, however, will not reduce the incidence of diarrhoeal diseases in the camp. The other major factors that need stressing are:

• Continued breast-feeding and improved nutrition.
• Reducing the transmission of diarrhoeal diseases by:
improved water supplies and better excreta disposal systems,
improved domestic hygiene, especially food and personal hygiene.

Feeding

Breast-feeding is crucial, and should continue until the child is at least one year old. When breast-feeding is not possible and other milk formulas have to be given to small babies, they should be given with a cup and spoon and not from a feeding bottle.

By three months (and certainly not later than six months) all babies should start to have weaning foods. By one year of age a child should receive between four and six meals per day in addition to breast milk.

During diarrhoea episodes foods which contain a lot of fibre (e.g. coarse fruits and vegetables, vegetable and fruit peel, and whole-grain cereals) and

Table 6.5. *This chart provides basic information on the most common agents of diarrhoea. It is greatly simplified. For example, some agents produce a variety of clinical features. Only agents of major importance worldwide have been included. Remember*

Presenting complaint	Possible aetiology	Incubation period	Other possible signs and symptoms	Therapy Rehydration see code 4
Acute watery diarrhoea (the stool takes the shape of the container)	Rotavirus	1 to 3 days	**Vomiting** Fever Severe dehydration	✓
	Enterotoxigenic *Escherichia coli* (ETEC)	6 hours to 3 days	Vomiting Abdominal pain Fever Severe dehydration	✓
	Vibrio cholerae	6 hours to 5 days	Vomiting Rapid dehydration	✓
	Salmonellae (non typhoid) **see code 2**	6 hours to 3 days	Vomiting Abdominal pain Fever Malaise	✓
Acute dysentery (the stool is soft or watery with blood and/or mucus)	*Campylobacter jejuni* **see code 3**	2 to 7 days	**Abdominal pain** Fever Malaise	✓
	Shigellae **see code 3**	1 to 3 days	Abdominal pain Fever Malaise Urgency to defecate Painful defecation	✓
Prolonged diarrhoea or dysentery (for at least 10 days) the stools have been more frequent or of softer consistency (with or without blood and/or mucus) **see code 1**	*Giardia lamblia* **see code 3**	1 to 3 weeks	Foul-smelling stools Abdominal pain Bloating Weight loss or failure to thrive	✓
	Entamoeba histolytica **see code 2**	2 to 4 weeks	Abdominal pain Irregular bowel habits Urgency to defecate Painful defecation	✓

Code 1: some persistent diarrhoeas are due to bacterial overgrowth of the small bowel and may respond to tetracycline therapy.

Code 2: may also present as acute dysentery.

Code 3: may also present as acute watery diarrhoea.

Code 4: oral rehydration is usually effective. However, intravenous rehydration may be indicated in cases of severe dehydration or persistent vomiting.

Code 5: decision on selection of antibiotic for treatment should take into account frequency of resistance to antibiotics in the area.

Code 6: these derivatives include metronidazole, tinidazole, ornidazole, and nimorazole.

Code 7: a faecal-oral pathogen is one that leaves an infected person or animal in the faeces and enters another person through the mouth.

that there are other enteric agents that may cause diarrhoea. In certain areas, at certain times, the picture may therefore be very different

First choice	Second choice	Faecal–oral	Other epidemiological features	Control see code 9
Widely advocated drugs		*Dominant transmission routes*		
None indicated		see codes 7 and 8		
		Man to man Direct Sometimes via water, food, air	Infants and young children Colder season Common world-wide in all socioeconomic groups	?
		Man to man Via food and water Direct	Infants and young children Warmer seasons Diarrhoea in travellers (all ages)	A/B/C/D
Tetracycline	Furazolidone Erythromycin Trimethoprim-sulphamethoxazole	**Man to man** Via food and water Direct	Children in endemic areas Adults in newly affected areas Crowding	A/B/C/D plus epidemiological surveillance (immunization **not** helpful)
Antibiotics not essential but shorten duration of illness and excretion of organisms **see code 5**				
None indicated		**Animals to man** **Man to man** Via food and water Direct	Infants and young children Warmer seasons Foodborne outbreaks Hospital outbreaks	A/B Control of infection in animals Hygienic slaughtering and food distribution systems Known carriers discouraged from handling foods
Erythromycin in **severe** cases		**Animals to man** **Man to man** Via food and water	Children and young adults Warmer seasons	A/B Adequate cooking of animal products Care in handling animals
Ampicillin Trimethoprim-sulphamethoxazole	Tetracycline	**Man to man** Direct Via food, water, ?flies	Young children Malnutrition Warmer seasons Crowding Institutions such as schools and orphanages May occur in outbreaks	A/B/C/D plus fly control
Antibiotic therapy required especially in infants with persistent high fever **see code 5**				
5-nitroimidazole derivatives **see code 6**	Furazolidone Mepacrine	**Man to man** Direct Via food and water **Animals to man** possible	Young children Malnutrition Schools/orphanages, etc. Diarrhoea in travellers (all ages) Some waterborne outbreaks	A/B/C/D
5-nitroimidazole derivatives **(see code 6)** in combination with diloxanide furoate		**Man to man** Direct Via food and water	Older children and adults Malnutrition Some waterborne outbreaks	A/B/C/D

Code 8: the reservoirs of a pathogen are indicated by describing them as *man to man* or *animals to man*. The routes by which this transmission takes place are described as *via food* (when food is contaminated and subsequently eaten), *via water* (when water is contaminated and subsequently drunk), *via flies* (when flies play a role in moving faecal particles), *via air* (when the pathogen is inhaled) or *direct* (embracing many transmission routes among persons in close contact—such as via unclean hands, via contaminated objects or bed linen, or via dirt which is ingested).

Code 9:
A Personal and domestic cleanliness;
B Hygienic food preparation and storage;
C Clean and plentiful water supply;
D Hygienic excreta disposal;
? Uncertain.

Ross Institute (1982).

Fig. 6.7. Patient encouragement may be needed to encourage a mother to breastfeed her malnourished, dehydrated child.

spicy foods should be avoided. *Energy-rich foods* are important such as edible oils, fats, and sugar added to or cooked with cereals and other foods, and so are foods containing potassium (e.g. pineapple and citrus fruits and their juices, bananas and coconut milk).

Especially if there is a fuel shortage in the camp, mothers may cook large quantities of food and store it for long periods before giving it to children. This can be a particular problem with weaning foods, which may become heavily contaminated with bacteria. Distribution of food supplies every two weeks or less, as well as attempts to improve supplies of fuel, may help prevent this problem (see chapter on Environmental health).

Water supplies

Water-borne transmission of diarrhoeal diseases is reduced by improving water quality. Replacing water sources such as open wells, ponds, or streams in the camp by piped or protected wells (see section on Water supplies) can increase water quality and decrease the incidence of diarrhoeal diseases. The quantity of water available for washing is important for better personal hygiene.

Excreta disposal

This is discussed fully in the section on Environmental health. The most important point is that each family must have access to a latrine nearby. These must be kept clean and well maintained, otherwise it will not be used and will have little impact in reducing the faecal–oral transmission of the viruses and bacteria causing diarrhoea.

Improved domestic and personal hygiene

Since diarrhoea-causing pathogens are also transmitted by non-waterborne routes (e.g. on hands, clothes, and food) it is important to improve personal and domestic hygiene. This is obviously difficult if the nearest water source is far from the house and only small containers are available for carrying water. It is also difficult if there is only an intermittent supply of water. Improved hygiene depends very much on the correct use of water once it is available. Personal hygiene, such as regular washing of hands after defaecation and before preparing and eating food, can have a substantial impact on the incidence of diarrhoeal disease (see chapter on Environmental health).

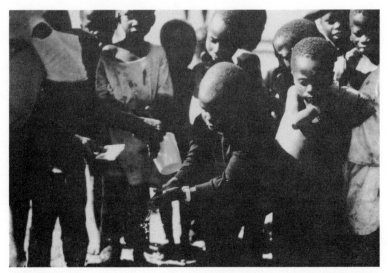

Fig. 6.8. Children washing their hands before a meal in a refugee village in Angola.

Health education

Many refugees may never have had access to plentiful supplies of clean water or to latrines before. Provision of these facilities will have little impact on the incidence of diarrhoeal disease unless people understand them, like them, use them, and maintain them. Community health education is vital if this is to happen. In particular, education programmes should explain to the whole family the role of children. They are not only the main sufferers from diarrhoea but also the main source of infection. It is their faeces that are most likely to spread infection to the rest of the family and to neighbouring households. The defaecation and hygienic behaviour of children is the vital but neglected component of many diarrhoeal disease control programmes. If health workers are only successful in getting just one message across through health education, i.e. that the stools of small children are dangerous, and people really understand and act on this, a substantial effect on the amount of diarrhoea will have been achieved.

Oral rehydration mixtures

All members of a family should be taught that as soon as they start passing more faeces than normal they should drink extra fluids, whether it be tea, coffee, Coca cola, etc. Young children should be given one of the following

Fig. 6.9. This child has diarrhoea. His stools are dangerous.

rehydration mixtures. These can be made with ingredients as shown in Tables 6.6 and 6.7. The ingredients should be completely dissolved, and when correctly prepared and administered, the solutions replace salts and water lost in the liquid faeces. Unfortunately supplies of sugar and salt in many refugee communities are often insufficient for the mixtures in Table 6.6 (to which can also be added the juice of an orange or of half a grapefruit) to be made up in the home. Wherever possible, families should be encouraged to make these mixtures at home rather than relying on packets supplied by the Health Centre.

Table 6.6. *Oral rehydration mixtures*

Salt	Sugar	Water
Pinch (two fingers and thumb method)	Scoop (in palm of hand)	1 glassful
Tip of teaspoon (less than $\frac{1}{4}$ level teaspoonful)	1–2 teaspoons	1 glassful
1 level teaspoon	8 level teaspoons	1 litre

Table 6.7. *Oral rehydration mixture*

Salts and sugars	Amount required for *one litre* of solution	Note
Sodium chloride (common salt)	3.5 g	Rehydration solution cannot be made without salt
Glucose or Sucrose (common sugar)	20 g 40 g	Rehydration solution cannot be made without one of these
Sodium bicarbonate Potassium chloride	2.5 g 1.5 g	Rehydration solution can be made without these but it is much better if one or both of them are added

Table 6.8. *Molar concentration of components of ORS solution*

Component	mmol/litre of water
Sodium	90
Potassium	20
Chloride	80
Bicarbonate	30
Glucose	110

Ingredients in Table 6.7 are usually made up in sachets (sealed packets). Potassium is important because it is easily lost from the body, especially in infants, in tropical climates. The bicarbonate helps to correct any acidosis, and glucose increases the ability of the small bowel to rapidly absorb the salts and water. (Such sachets distributed by UNICEF and WHO may be called ORS or 'Oralyte'.) The contents of one packet should be dissolved in one litre of clean drinking water. During the 1971 Bangladesh refugee crisis where cholera was a problem, different size packets were produced and packaged locally and delivered to field centres with labels indicating the volume of water for dilution (see section on Epidemiology, p. 80). If packets are not available, the salts and sugars can be measured by any one of the following methods:

- Scales may be available, for example in a local pharmacy.
- Small volume measures, e.g. 5 or 10 ml syringes can be used to give approximate weights as follows:

  3 ml = approximately 3.5 g sodium chloride;
  3 ml = approximately 2.5 g sodium bicarbonate;
  1.5 ml = approximately 1.5 g potassium chloride;
  30 ml = approximately 20 g glucose;
  50 ml = approximately 40 g sucrose (i.e. common sugar).

- For a simple salt–sugar solution:

  salt = 1 volume; sugar 10 volumes; water 200 volumes.

- If the salts and sugars are measured or weighed out and mixed together in bulk, it is essential to mix them very well before dividing them into smaller amounts.

The following points about the use of ORS are important:

- *Families* should be taught not to rely on packets of ORS being supplied by the health centre but encouraged to make simple salt–sugar solutions in the home.
- *Drinking* is the essential element in oral rehydration therapy—even if the only water available is contaminated. Advise everyone to use the cleanest water available, to boil it if possible, and not to keep the oral rehydration solution more than 24 hours.
- *Helpers and mothers should be shown how to mix ORS.* Everyone should taste the solution so they know what the correct concentration tastes like.
- *For small children* ORS can best be given with a cup and spoon. If the child vomits, wait five to ten minutes and then give more ORS solution. Vomiting is not a reason to stop oral rehydration unless it is very severe and frequent. Give children one cupful of solution for each watery stool passed and two

cupfuls each stool in an adult. For more detailed calculations see pp. 161–2 and Table 6.10).

● *Additional fluids when giving ORS solution.* In a breast-fed baby, the infant should be given breast milk as often as it wants four to six hours after starting ORS solution. This should be in addition to the ORS solution which is being given to correct fluid losses. In non-breast-fed infants and older children plain drinking water and other fluids should also be given, as long as ORS solution is being given. This is a maintenance volume and is in addition to ORS solution.

ASSESSMENT OF SEVERITY AND TREATMENT

Because dehydration is the main cause of death its rapid assessment is of vital importance. This assessment includes taking a history of the disease, examining the patient, and weighing him or her if possible. In summary, ASK, LOOK, and FEEL for the signs and symptoms of dehydration (summarized in Table 6.9). Particular attention should be given to the 'danger signs' in the right-hand column of this table. A person, especially a child, with any of these signs can die if not treated quickly.

Fig. 6.10. Drinking more, whether breast milk or other fluids is one of the main factors in preventing dehydration in diarrhoea.

Table 6.9. *The signs and symptoms of dehydration*

				DANGER SIGNS
1. ASK	DIARRHOEA	Less than 4 liquid stools per day	4–10 liquid stools per day	More than 10 liquid stools per day or Much blood and mucus
	VOMITING	None or small amount	Some	Very frequent
	THIRST	Normal	More than normal	Unable to drink
2. LOOK	URINE	Normal	Small amount, dark	No urine for 6 hours
	CONDITION	Well, alert	Unwell, sleepy, or irritable	Very sleepy, floppy, unconscious, having fits or seizures
	EYES	Normal	Sunken	Very dry and sunken
	MOUTH and TONGUE	Wet	Dry	Very dry
	BREATHING	Normal	Faster than normal	Very fast and deep
3. FEEL	SKIN	Pinch goes back quickly	Pinch goes back slowly	Pinch goes back very slowly
	PULSE	Normal	Faster than normal	Very fast, weak, or cannot be felt
	FONTANELLE (in infants)	Normal	Sunken	Very sunken
4. WEIGH	*if possible*	No weight loss during diarrhoea illness	Weight loss of 25–100 g for each kilogram of weight	Weight loss of more than 100 g for each kilogram of weight
5. TAKE TEMPERATURE	*if possible*	—	—	High fever: more than 39°C (102°F)
6. DECIDE		If the child or adult with *diarrhoea* is like this there is *NO DEHYDRATION* **Use plan A**	If the child or adult with *diarrhoea* has one or more of these signs there is *DEHYDRATION* **Use plan B**	If the child or adult with *diarrhoea* has 2 or more of these *DANGER SIGNS* there is *SEVERE DEHYDRATION* **Use plan C**

Treatment plans

The treatment adopted depends initially on whether there is some dehydration. If there is no dehydration then giving extra simple home-made fluids or ORS will probably be sufficient (Plan A). If there is dehydration more intensive efforts are needed to replace the lost fluids and to rehydrate the patient (Plan B). If severe dehydration is present or develops, the life of the patient is in danger and immediate help is required (Plan C). These treatment plans are summarized in Fig. 6.11.

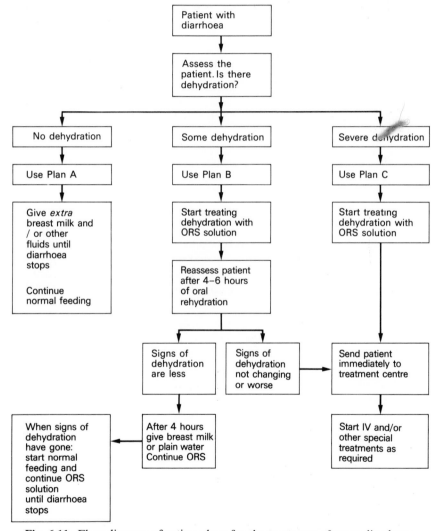

Fig. 6.11. Flow diagram of action plans for the treatment of acute diarrhoea.

Treatment Plan A: diarrhoea with no signs of dehydration

This involves giving extra drinks of ordinary fluids, continuing the normal diet, and keeping the situation under review. The aims are to prevent dehydration, maintain nutrition, and be ready in case dehydration appears. Home treatment is very effective.

• Extra drinks of locally available fluids. These include breast milk and other drinks like plain water, soups, fruit juices, barley or rice water, herbal tea, according to what the family have and what is culturally acceptable. Home prepared sugar–salt solutions can also be given (see p. 155). If infants are not breast-fed, until the diarrhoea stops the artificial or dried milk they receive should be half strength, e.g. mixed with an equal volume of clean or boiled water.

• Children with diarrhoea must not be starved as this may cause malnutrition or make it worse. Locally available and easily digestible foods should be given four to six times per day.

• While diarrhoea continues, give ORS solution by mouth in the same volume as the fluid lost in stools.

• It is important to watch for the signs of dehydration (Table 6.9). Review the situation after some time, preferably after four to six hours.

Treatment Plan B: diarrhoea with some dehydration

The aim is to replace the fluid lost by using oral rehydration salts (ORS, for formula see Table 6.7) available, or a simple sugar–salt solution. Breast-feeding should be stopped only for about four to six hours during active rehydration and other foods can be given as soon as the signs of dehydration disappear. The aims of Plan B are to treat dehydration by mouth, prevent it from recurring, and to maintain nutrition. This can be done in the home or as an outpatient.

Estimate the volume of fluid needed by the individual. Two methods are given for calculating this volume. The first is a more detailed method of replacing the lost fluids and electrolytes, together with those required for bodily functions. The second is a rough approximation. The first is obviously best, but may be too complicated or take too long to calculate in some circumstances.

Table 6.10. *Method of calculating the volume of treatment fluid required*

Degree of dehydration and rehydration	
No visible dehydration	Extra fluids + +
Mild dehydration	50 ml ORS solution/kg in 4–6 hours
Moderate dehydration	75 ml ORS solution/kg in 4–6 hours
Severe dehydration	100 ml ORS solution/kg in 4–6 hours. May need IV fluids

(a) *Detailed calculation.* There are three volumes to consider:

• The volume of fluid to *replace* what has already been lost by diarrhoea and vomiting and which has caused the dehydration.
• The volume for *continuing* losses during the treatment phase.
• The volume required for *maintenance* of normal bodily functions.

The volume for *correcting the dehydration* is found in Appendix 2, p. 328. For mild or moderate dehydration this is 50 or 75 ml /kg of the child's body weight, and for severe dehydration 100 ml/kg of body weight.

The volume for *continuing losses* is the amount needed to replace any diarrhoea or vomiting which occurs during treatment. The best way of estimating this is to measure the volume of diarrhoea stool or vomit. Often this is not possible in a camp situation; therefore a set amount may be given for every diarrhoea stool passed. For small infants this can be 50 ml or a quarter of a glass of fluid, for older infants 100 ml or half a glass, for older children 200 ml or one glassful, and for adults 400 ml or two glasses per diarrhoea stool.

The *maintenance volume* for 24 hours should be 150 ml/kg for small infants, 120 ml/kg for older infants, 100 ml/kg for toddlers, and 80 ml/kg for older children and adults. This amount may need to be doubled if the weather is very hot or if the patient has a fever.

The volumes for replacement and continuing losses should be of oral rehydration solution, and the maintenance volume should be given as water, fruit juice, half strength milk, and similar normal drinks. The replacement volume of oral rehydration solution should be given over 4–6 hours, and the continuing loss and maintenance volumes over the subsequent 20 hours. An example of how this calculation can be made is given in Appendix 2, p. 328.

(b) *Approximation volume.* This is the total intake for a moderately dehydrated child. It includes fluid for replacement, continuing losses, and maintenance. The volume will depend on the child's weight or age. If possible weigh the child and find out his/her approximate age.

	Weight	Age	Fluid required per kg	Fluid required per 24 hours
Infant	5–10 kg	6–12 months	200 ml	1–2 litres
Toddler	15 kg	2–6 years	175 ml	2.6 litres
Child	25 kg	8–10 years	150 ml	3.8 litres

Give about half the total volume estimated for 24 hours in the first 4–6 hours, and the other half volume over the remaining 18–20 hours.

With this regime give only *one type of fluid*;

Either   ORS solution diluted, e.g. 2 volumes of ORS solution to 1 volume of drinking water.
Or   simplified sugar–salt solution, e.g. 1 level 5 ml teaspoon of salt and 8 level teaspoons of sugar to 1 litre of drinking water.

Reassess the child 4–6 hours after starting oral rehydration and decide about further treatment.

ASK, LOOK, and FEEL for the signs of dehydration (see Table 6.9). If the signs are persisting or getting worse, the patient should be changed to Plan C and given special treatment. If the signs are still present but improving, give the same volume of ORS solution in the next four to six hours as was given in the first period. This can be repeated again if necessary. If the child is no longer dehydrated but still has some diarrhoea, continue to give ORS solution to replace the continuing losses along with other fluids and food.

Food and dietary advice during and after diarrhoea: During the four to six hours of rehydration, food and milk should not be given as all efforts are concentrated on rehydration by mouth. During the maintenance phase, the fluid and dietary advice given under Plan A should be used. After an episode of acute diarrhoea, a child should ideally receive one extra meal per day for a week. This can be encouraged at home or provided through a supplementary feeding programme.

Treatment Plan C: Diarrhoea with severe dehydration and 'danger signs'

These patients need special treatment in addition to oral rehydration which should be started while they are being transferred for special care. The aims of Plan C are to start rehydration and get the patient to the camp health centre or if there is no doctor or senior nurse available then to the nearest

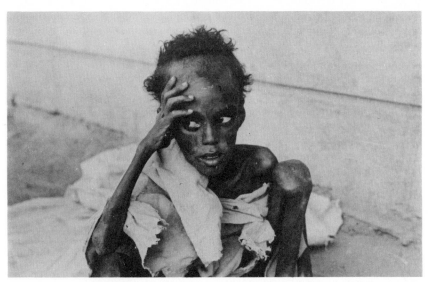

Fig. 6.12. Oral rehydration is crucial for a dehydrated and malnourished child such as this boy in a shelter in Ethiopia.

national hospital as quickly as possible. A summary of the action plans for a patient with diarrhoea is shown in Fig. 6.11. Intravenous (IV) therapy is indicated where dehydration is getting worse, vomiting is uncontrollable, shock is present, or complications prevent ORS being used.

Once circulation has been restored by IV fluids, which is usually within one to four hours, the patient should be conscious and rehydration by mouth may be started using ORS solution. Diarrhoea may continue for some hours or days, but if the signs of dehydration are decreasing or absent, the volume of losses can be replaced by oral rehydration and electrolyte losses of acute diarrhoea are shown in Appendix 2, p. 329.

A nasogastric tube is useful to administer ORS solution to babies who cannot drink because they are exhausted or drowsy, but babies unconscious due to shock require intravenous fluid. If intravenous fluid is not available, intragastric fluid can be given as an emergency measure.

Medical complications of diarrhoea

Protein-energy malnutrition (PEM)

This may be caused or aggravated by episodes of diarrhoea. The signs of dehydration may be more difficult to detect in a child with kwashiorkor or marasmus. Dehydration should be managed as described above, but ORS solution should be given for a longer period than in well-nourished children in order to replace chronic losses of sodium and potassium. Rehydration therapy may increase the oedema in children with kwashiorkor and there is particular risk of congestive heart failure when IV fluids are given. Therapeutic feeding as outlined in the section on Special feeding programmes should be given.

Fever

Fever often accompanies diarrhoea.

It may be due to dehydration, to the infection directly causing the diarrhoea, or another underlying infection. Treat the dehydration and also bring down the temperature by bathing or sponging with tepid water. Underlying infections which occur in patients with diarrhoea and fever include malaria, respiratory and urinary infections, otitis media, skin sepsis, and meningitis. Review the patient for these conditions; if suspected they should be treated accordingly.

Convulsions

These may occur in a patient with diarrhoea. The following causes and treatments should be considered.

• Febrile convulsion: Treat the fever as described above.
• Severe dehydration: Assess hydration and manage as described.

• Hypoglycaemia (low blood glucose level): This may result from inadequate food intake and/or malabsorption. If the patient is unconscious, give 20 per cent glucose injection intravenously (2.5 ml/kg). If hypoglycaemia is the cause, consciousness will improve rapidly.

• Hypernatraemia (sodium overload): This may result from milk feeds and other fluids containing too much sodium. It is rarely a complication of therapy with ORS unless the solution has been incorrectly mixed, or given in excessive amounts, or continued after diarrhoea has stopped. Thirst in a fully hydrated patient may be a symptom of hypernatraemia. Stop giving ORS solution and give more plain water.

Drug therapy and diarrhoea

Drug therapy

Many medicines are available for treating acute diarrhoea. Most of them are not useful and some can prolong the condition or have bad side effects. Rehydration is more important and medicines may distract attention from this essential treatment.

Table 6.11. *Antimicrobials used in the treatment of specific causes of acute diarrhoea*

Cause	Drug(s) of choice*
Cholera†,‡	Tetracycline *Children*—50 mg/kg per day in 4 divided doses × 3 days *Adults*—500 mg 4 times a day × 3 days
Shigella†,§ dysentery	Ampicillin—100 mg/kg per day in 4 divided doses × 5 days Trimethoprim (TMP)—Sulfamethoxazole (SMX) *Children*—TMP 10 mg/kg per day and SMX 50 mg/kg per day in two divided doses × 5 days *Adults*—TMP 160 mg and SMX 800 mg twice daily × 5 days Tetracycline—50 mg/kg per day in 4 divided doses × 5 days (all ages)
Acute intestinal amoebiasis	Metronidazole *Children*—30 mg/kg per day × 5–10 days *Adults*—750 mg 3 times a day × 5–10 days
Acute giardiasis	Metronidazole *Children*—15 mg/kg per day × 5 days *Adults*—250 mg 3 times a day × 5 days

* All doses given are for oral administration unless otherwise indicated.

† Decision on selection of antibiotics for treatment should take into account frequency of resistance to antibiotics in the area.

‡ Antibiotic therapy not essential for successful therapy but shortens duration of illness and excretion of organisms in severe cases.

§ Antibiotic therapy especially required in infants with persistent high fever.

Antibiotics and antimicrobial drugs

These should NOT be used routinely for acute diarrhoea. They are of specific value only for the following conditions:

cholera;
severe Shigella dysentery, particularly due to *Sh. dysenteriae*;
amoebic dysentery;
giardiasis.

The recommended medicines for the treatment of these diseases are given in Table 6.11. Other drugs should be used for the treatment of underlying infections such as malaria, otitis media, etc.

Other drugs

Antimotility drugs and absorbents to 'stop diarrhoea' do not treat the causes of diarrhoea but may give some temporary relief. They include kaolin mixtures, opium and codeine compounds. These drugs should not be used in the routine treatment of acute diarrhoea, and so have not been supplied in the standard drug list. They should not be used for children.

The anti-secretory drugs may be important in the future, but they are not recommended at present for refugee camps.

Stimulants and steroids should not be used in acute diarrhoea.

7 Environmental health

Water- and excreta-related infections, and hygiene

The control of environmental conditions in a refugee camp is very important for several reasons:

- It minimizes the spread of faecal-borne pathogens.
- It prevents the breeding of insect and rodent vectors of disease.
- Psychologically, sufficient water, washing facilities, and a clean environment all boost morale.
- Practically, a clean and tidy community area is easier to run.

Refugees may have differing ideas on health and what constitutes a healthy environment. Adequate food and access to health facilities and water are likely to be seen by refugees as high priorities, whereas the need for improved water quality or the need for excreta-disposal facilities may not be recognized. It is essential to understand the refugees' approach to water and sanitation and to ensure that facilities are provided that will be optimally

Fig. 7.1. All members of a community can help keep the camp clean.

used. Efforts must be made to identify in the community 'facilitators' who understand both the refugees' point of view and the need for environmental improvements.

The activities described in this section are all important, if not essential, to the well-being of the refugees and, to achieve maximum effect, they should have priority over many of the medical services during the early stages of setting up camps. An adequate share of the budget must be allocated for environmental health with provision for running and maintenance costs. This financial planning requires a precise survey of the local conditions and the refugees' needs. Planning must allow for an increase in population and for changes related to different seasons.

To predict which diseases can be limited through improvements in domestic water supply, drainage, or sanitation, it is necessary to understand the exact links between water and excreta and the transmission of specific infections. Infections related to water are called water-related infections (not water-borne infections) and infections related to excreta are called excreta-related infections.

WATER-RELATED INFECTIONS

All water-related infections are transmitted by one or more of four mechanisms:

Water-borne transmission

Transmission occurring when the pathogen is contained in water which is drunk or used in the food, e.g. cholera.

Water-scarce or water-washed transmission

Transmission from person-to-person in the domestic environment which might be reduced if more water was available and if it was used to improve personal and domestic cleanliness, e.g. scabies.

Water-based transmission

Transmission of a pathogen which needs an aquatic intermediate host or hosts to maintain its life cycle, e.g. schistosomiasis.

Water-related insect vector transmission

Transmission by insects which breed in water or which live and bite near water, e.g. malaria.

All water-related infections which may be transmitted by the water-borne mechanism may also be transmitted by the water-scarce or water-washed mechanism.

EXCRETA-RELATED INFECTIONS

An excreta-related infection is one related to human urine and faeces. Only two transmission mechanisms are excreta-related:

Transmission via infected excreta

The pathogen is released into the environment in the faeces or urine of an individual.

Transmission by an excreta-related insect vector

An insect which visits excreta to breed or feed may mechanically carry excreted pathogens to food. An insect vector of a non-excreted pathogen may preferentially breed in faecally polluted sites.

All excreta-related infections are also water-related, except for two types of helminth which are excreted and reinfect through the skin without requiring an intermediate host—namely the hookworms and *Strongyloides*. By contrast, many water-related infections are not excreta-related, for instance, skin infections, trachoma, guinea worm, and malaria.

HYGIENE

This and other chapters particularly emphasize the importance of personal and domestic hygiene in the control and prevention of disease.

The importance of young children in transmitting infections must be emphasized. Young children are not only the main sufferers from diarrhoeal diseases, for instance, but also the main excretors of the pathogens that cause diarrhoeas. They are often the least hygienic members of the family and the least likely to use a latrine. The importance of child hygiene and the disposal of children's faeces must be vigorously communicated in education programmes. Without improvements in child hygiene and excreta-disposal, other environmental improvements in the camp may have little impact on illness rates.

For all infections (except Guinea worm) improving water quality alone is not sufficient. For many infections, especially for diarrhoeal diseases, improving the quality of the water available and encouraging personal and domestic cleanliness are more important control strategies than improving water quality by itself. Improved personal and domestic cleanliness and food hygiene are crucial in the control of diarrhoeas, enteric fevers, poliomyelitis, hepatitis A, skin infections, and eye infections.

Environmental health programmes in refugee communities must therefore emphasize the following:

• Improving water availability to bring 20–30 litres daily per person to within a short distance (e.g. 100 m) of every dwelling.

● Improving water quality to remove gross faecal contamination.
● Provision of adequate latrines that are used by everybody, especially children, and kept clean.
● Health education to promote personal, domestic, food, and camp hygiene.
● Drainage of rain and waste water.

Living in a refugee community is a new experience and new attitudes towards hygiene must be learnt from the start. The installation of the water system or latrines can be used as a focus for this activity as the interest they create draws people together. The preventive work carried out by the health personnel should also include instruction on hygiene, the importance of hygienic water storage, use of latrines, washing, and general cleanliness.

Provision of soap

A very strong case can be made for a possible link in refugee camps between the poor supplies of water and soap and the excessive numbers of diarrhoeal diseases, scabies, conjunctivitis, and typhus. Encouraging the washing of hands after defaecation and before preparing and eating food, may significantly reduce the spread of diarrhoeal diseases.

If the regular supply of adequate quantities of soap cannot be guaranteed to a camp, then the manufacture of soap within the community as a village industry should be considered.

Production of soap

There are three types of processes for the production of soap: cold, semi-boiled, and full boiled. Only the cold and semi-boiled processes are described here as the full boiled method requires a level of technology that is neither available nor appropriate to most refugee communities.

Raw materials for soap making

Soap is produced by the action of caustic soda on fat and/or oil. Water is also used and perfumes and dyes can be added as desired. Table 7.1, which is not exhaustive, shows some of the fatty materials used in the manufacture of soap and the resulting characteristics of the soap. Coconut, palm-kernel oil, palm oil, groundnut oil, and soyabean oil are particularly good for the cold process. Other possibilities include olive oil, beeswax, curd, and chicken fat.

Caustic soda (sodium hydroxide), which is often manufactured from common salt, should be of high quality. It absorbs water from the atmosphere and should therefore be stored in sealed containers. Caustic soda is a dangerous, corrosive poison and can cause serious burns. Protective gloves should always be worn when dealing with the crystals or solution. If the skin accidentally comes in contact with caustic soda wash the area with water followed by a vinegar solution. Too much caustic soda in the soap will

Table 7.1. *Fatty materials used in the manufacture of soap and the resulting characteristics of the soap*

Oil or fat	Used alone or in conjunction with other fats	Consistency of soap	Odour	Foam	Detergent quality	Skin reaction	Use
Coconut oil	Can be used alone	Very hard, brittle	Slight odour of nut	Quick big bubbles, short-lasting	Good. Also in cold water	Makes skin rough	All kinds of soap, especially toilet
Palm kernel oil	Can be used alone	Very hard, brittle	Slight odour of nut	Quick big bubbles, short-lasting	Good. Also in cold water	Makes skin rough	Household and toilet soap, soap powder
Palm oil	Can be used alone but often combined with palm kernel oil	Very hard	Original oil	Slow, small bubbles	Very good	Very mild	Household and toilet soap, soap powder
Ground nut oil	Usually used in combination	Firm	Original oil	Fairly good	Fairly good	Very mild	Household, textile and toilet soap
Soya bean oil	Blended with other oils, especially coconut	Soft	Original oil	Mediocre	Mediocre	Very mild	Household, textile and toilet soap
Cotton seed oil	Use in combination with coconut oil and/or tallow	Fairly soft	Original oil	Mediocre but lasting	Good	Mild	Household soap
Tallow* or lard†	Generally used in combination with other oils	Very hard	Neutral	Slow, small bubbles lasting	Good	Very mild	Household, textile, toilet, shaving soap
Fish oil	Can be used alone	Fairly soft	Fishy	Greasy	Fairly good	Mild	Soft soap

* Tallow is fat obtained from the tissues of beef and mutton by heat treatment.
† Lard is similar to tallow and obtained in the same way from the fat tissues of pigs.

have an irritating effect on the skin. Caustic soda solutions dissolve tin, zinc, aluminium, and alloys such as brass. For the methods described iron and steel are little affected.

Water should preferably be soft water, but hardness is not regarded as a major disadvantage. Rain water is ideal.

Perfume added during the cold process should be resistant to alkali. Crude oils such as citronella, oil of cloves, and oil of lemon and a number of refined chemicals such as geraniol and citronellol are suitable. Oil-soluble dyes are recommended for the cold process. A list of the equipment needed can be found in Appendix 2.

Recipes

Advice should be sought from local commercial manufacturers of soap where possible, as they will often have experimented with all the locally available materials. Experiment with small quantities before attempting to make sufficient for the whole community.

As a general guideline the following quantities can be used:

To make one bar of soap:

Oil or clean hard fat	230 ml
Caustic soda	23.5 gm
Water	115 ml
Perfume	a few drops

To make 4 kg of soap:

Oil and/or fat	3 litres or 2.75 kg
Caustic soda	370 g
Water	1.2 litres
Perfume	20 ml, oil of sassafras
	10 ml, oil of citronella and oil of lavender
	5 ml, oil of cloves or oil of lemon

Manufacturing processes

Cold water—fat of a better quality is required than when the boiled process is used, and exact proportions are crucial.

- Dissolve caustic soda crystals by adding them to the water.
- Pour oil into separate container.
- Pour caustic soda solution on to oil very slowly stirring continuously in one direction.
- Continue stirring, if not mixed properly free fat could lead to rancidity later.
- If a combination of oil and fat is being used, add melted fat to oil/caustic solution now.

● Add perfume and dye as desired.
● When soap mixture is of very thick consistency transfer to moulds or cooling frames lined with cloth or waxed paper, for about two days. Do not move or hit the mould otherwise the ingredients may separate.

Once cooled the treatment is common to the semi-boiled process. The first stage of the latter method is now described.

Semi-boiled process—(Optional—clarify fat by putting equal amounts of fat and water in a pot, boil, strain mixture through sieve or piece of cheese-cloth. Add 1 part cold water to 4 parts hot liquid. Allow to stand until cool. Clarified fat can then be removed from top and used as required in the recipe.)

● Add caustic soda to water. Allow to cool to body temperature.
● Melt fat to body temperature. Allow to cool.
● Add caustic solution to fat. Stir slowly and evenly in one direction for about 30 minutes.
● Add dye and perfume as desired.
● Allow to stand then stir once or twice every 15–20 minutes for several hours.
● When very thick pour into moulds or cooling frames and allow to set for about two days. Do not move or hit the moulds.

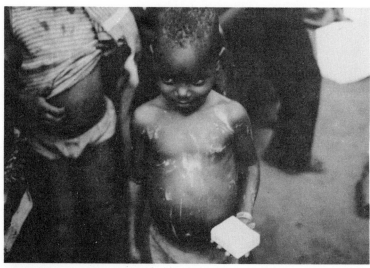

Fig. 7.2. Zairean refugee in Angola supplied with soap as part of a control programme for scabies.

Finishing stages—for both cold and semi-boiled processes:

- Cut cooled soap into slabs and then into smaller bars.
- Stack bars on trays and allow to dry thoroughly for four–six weeks.
- When dry cover bars if desired with wrapping to prevent loss of moisture.

FOOD HYGIENE

Food can be spoiled by bacteria, parasites, insects, rodents, warm temperatures, and too little or too much moisture. Bacterial contamination of foods and milk by *Escherichia coli* in particular, may play a significant role in the incidence of diarrhoea (see section on Family health care). The hygienic preparation, storage and handling of food, especially in warehouses, supplementary and therapeutic feeding programmes, tea bars, and in the home are, therefore, important. It may be useful to appoint 'health inspectors' to monitor standards of cleanliness (see School health).

Fig. 7.3. Food hygiene can play a significant role in diarrhoea.

Animal slaughter

When a certain amount of slaughter is carried out in the community it will be worth building a small slaughter house with a cement floor, drainage pit, incinerator, and adequate water supply for cleaning. It will form a centralized place for the inspection of animal meat before it can be sold in the community.

Water supplies

The provision of an adequate quantity of reasonably pure water is absolutely essential and, along with food and shelter, must be the first priority.

CONTROL OF WATER DISTRIBUTION

Water should be available and free to all the refugees. If the camp layout has not allowed a distribution system following community sub-sections problems may arise at the stand pipes for priorities and rights. Unscrupulous persons may even establish a whole network of control over water points and sell it to other refugees through water carriers. There is no standard answer to such practices, but they highlight the necessity to discuss with refugee communities the siting of distribution points and to allocate responsibile persons for their supervision, maintenance, and reporting of problems.

Water for special purposes

International personnel and medical facilities will also require water of a higher standard of purity. For their purposes, small-scale purification for drinking water using silver-impregnated ceramic filters is appropriate. Purification tablets can be used for water for domestic purposes, e.g. rinsing food.

Supplies

Household containers for carrying and storing water will be required. Refugees may have their own traditional water containers. In many cases, an additional supply of oil drums cut in half will be very useful for storage. Oil drums should be well washed and the bungs removed before cutting to avoid explosions. To limit domestic pollution lids must be provided for drinking water. Other suitable local ways of storing water should also be encouraged.

SOURCES OF WATER

There are three main types of water sources and the initial survey must find the most suitable long-term source. It is essential to bear in mind that conditions may change dramatically between wet and dry seasons of the year, so local advice should be sought.

Fig. 7.4. Afghan refugee filling an animal skin with water.

Fig. 7.5. Traditional baskets lined with cement are used for water storage in settlements in Ethiopia.

Rain water

Rain water is not polluted and is easily caught. It can be very seasonal but worth using, particularly at the beginning of the crisis. This leaves time to plan permanent solutions for the next dry season.

Surface water

This may be flowing (streams and rivers) or standing (ponds and lakes). It varies in amount according to the season and it is often grossly polluted. These water sources also expose the refugees to all the diseases related to insect vectors and intermediate hosts. They appeal to people, however, because water is easily available and in many instances will be similar to what they have been used to.

Ground water

This may appear at the surface through springs. In this case it must be assessed as to whether it is a superficial spring, and therefore likely to be polluted, or whether it comes from deep down. Wells may be shallow (5–10 m) and again susceptible to pollution and seasonal variations, or they may be deep and more constant in yield and quality, but requiring more complex techniques to build.

Table 7.2 gives useful information about each source.

The most important of these parameters is the quantity of water available. Typical yields for various types of wells are given in Table 7.3.

Fig. 7.6. Collecting rain water off a corrugated tin roof in a settlement in Ethiopia.

Table 7.2. *Baseline data for water supply planning*

General data
- Total no. of people likely to need water eventually
- Nature of the terrain
- Geological conditions and hydrology (in general terms)
- List of potential sources (including groundwater)

For each source
- Distance from camp and/or depth underground
- Quantity available in the driest season
- Type of river beds
- Highest likely level (for rivers)
- General appearance of water (including estimate of contaminating solids)
- Existence of odours, algae, or other problems
- Potential for faecal and chemical pollution
- Legal or traditional water rights
- Acceptability of taste to refugees

Tests on the water
- Faecal coliforms (see Chapter 12)
- Salinity (if the water is palatable, the salinity is not too high and the source is acceptable)
- pH (should be between 6 and 9)

Table 7.3. *Typical well yield in different geological formations*

Sand and gravel
General yield of about 10 000 l/min, but may yield less depending on pump, well construction, and development

Sand, gravel, and clay (Intermixed or Interbedded)
General yield between 2000 and 4000 l/min, but can yield up to 10 000 l/min, depending on the percentage of clay

Sand and clay
General yield about 2000 l/min, but may yield up to 4000 l/min

Fractured sandstone
General yield about 2000 l/min, but may yield more than 4000 l/min depending on the thickness of sandstone and the degree and extent of fracturing

Limestone
General yield between 40 and 200 l/min, but may yield more

Granite and/or hard rock
General yield about 40 l/min, but may yield less

WATER QUALITY

Bacteriological and chemical checks should, where possible, be carried out on the quality of the potential water source. If permanently used, this source should then be regularly monitored for further pollution and/or to check the efficacy of the treatment system.

Bacteriology

Faecal coliforms (f.c.) can easily be counted. Although no rigorous cut-off point can be given, the following indications are provided as orders of magnitude:

- Less than 10 f.c./100 ml, water is acceptable.
- 10–100 f.c./100 ml, mild pollution. Calls for better protection of the source and simple treatment (p. 182).
- 100–1000 f.c./100 ml, serious pollution. Still clearable by treatment, but calls for a review of alternative sources.
- More than 1000 f.c./100 ml, major pollution. Source to be avoided.

However, no source should ever be condemned, especially if it means that other more polluted sources would then be utilized. Ground water, if available, should not be rejected as it can be protected and improved.

Chemistry

Palatability is the main test for acceptable chemical levels in the water. However at the beginning of the crisis, when a permanent source is being considered, it is worth requesting measures of:

- Iron; maximum acceptable is 1 mg/l.
- Fluoride; maximum acceptable is 5 mg/l; higher levels can lead to skeletal fluorosis.

INITIAL ACTIVITIES

- If the community is close to an existing source of water immediate protection measures must be taken against pollution. This may be especially difficult in the case of a river or other open water, and more so if there is vegetation along the banks providing cover for defaecation. A strip of land of about 500 m wide should be left clear between the camp and the river and people firmly instructed not to use this area or the river bank for defaecation or bathing. It may be worth clearing dense vegetation along the river banks to discourage defaecation.
- Existing wells can be protected by sealing the ground around the top of the well to a depth of two to three metres with puddled clay and covering with concrete. Around this an outward-draining concrete apron one to two metres wide should be built, with a drainage channel to catch spillages and finally a

pump installed (see Fig. 7.7). Depending on the yield obtainable (see below) this may be a handpump or a motorized pump. In the latter case a storage tank will be required.

• Although handpumps are generally most suitable for rural settlements, a motorized system may be better suited to camp conditions. Handpumps will be appropriate only if there are major problems in obtaining fuel, or if none of the refugees have even basic mechanical skills. Refugees will often start hand-dug wells by themselves. Guidance must be given on siting and provisions made to provide them with adequate material. Care should be taken to put a cover on the wells and to disinfect them after they have been dug. In the early phases, pumps are unlikely to be available and buckets will be used. It is important to devise a system by which the buckets thrown in the wells are fixed and not deposited on the ground or carried through the camp. Pollution can also be reduced by constructing a parapet wall around the well.

• A spring may be protected as in Fig. 7.8 by building a spring box and a drainage ditch on the uphill side to prevent contamination by surface water, and fencing off or otherwise barring access to the area for 30 m above the spring.

Few of these techniques may be relevant when faced with a community of refugees on a small island such as occurred with the Vietnamese refugees on Pilau Bidong, off the coast of Malaya in 1979. In these circumstances specialist advice is required.

• Initially, there may be little alternative except to transport water into the

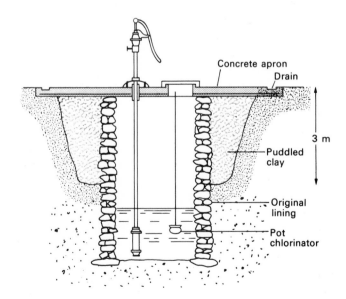

Fig. 7.7. Improving an existing well.

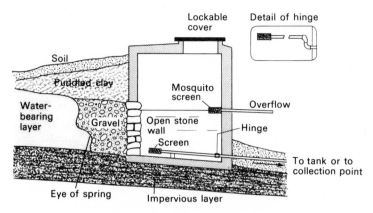

Fig. 7.8. A protected spring.

camp by truck. 'Pillow' tanks, large bags made of fabric reinforced rubber mounted on any available lorry, are ideal for this purpose and can be re-used later on if a piped water system is installed. A portable pump will be needed to fill them; suitable machines are easily available either as small irrigation pumps or those used by building contractors for de-watering excavations. Alternatively, purpose-bought units stocked by the relief agencies may be used.

Permanent solutions

Some of the solutions set up in the emergency phase will only need to be improved. In other cases, for example, if rain or surface water was used, some permanent solutions will need to be sought. These are discussed below depending on the source.

Abstraction

The least attractive but often only available water source is a river. A sandy bed is the most advantageous, as it can be used for a river-bed filter abstraction point.

Methods of constructing protected wells and springs are shown in Figs 7.7 and 7.8. For well-drilling it may be possible to obtain a drilling rig from the government or international organization's water-supply department, but this may take some time.

In relatively soft soils, wells can be jetted or hand-augered. For harder or rocky soils a power auger may be necessary and can be driven by an agricultural tractor. In all cases a well screen and PVC casing for the borehole will be required.

Hand-dug wells should be sited around the camp. Bore holes will be few, even in large camps, depending on their yield.

Fig. 7.9. Protected well in an Afghan refugee village in Pakistan.

PUMPING AND DISTRIBUTION OF WATER

Suitable pumps and engines should be mounted on a base and be small enough to be fitted into a long wheelbase Landrover or similar vehicle. A second, identical stand-by pump-set should always be provided. The water main should be of 75 mm polythene pipe, which is available in 50 metre coils, thus minimizing the number of joints required. They can be laid initially on the surface and later buried in a trench. It is important to ensure that the pipeline is not washed away during heavy rains and so they should preferably be laid on the spur of a hill and the trench backfilled to leave a slight mound over the pipe. Pipes should never be laid in a gulley.

The water should be pumped to a storage tank, equivalent in volume to half a day's total consumption, allowing pumps to be turned off at night. Where the supply is by gravity, storage of about a quarter to a third of a day's requirement should be provided. Liquid drum tanks are the most suitable, being easy to erect and cheaper than pillow tanks. The drums consist of a cylinder made of preformed corrugated steel sections with a butyl rubber liner. A ball valve or overflow pipe should be provided. If possible the tank(s) should be situated to provide a head of 10–20 m for distribution in the camp. If this is not possible, a second pump is required for distribution. This pump can also be used as a spare for the main pump, although water will then have to be collected from the main storage tank.

Fig. 7.10. Storage tank with taps in a camp in Somalia.

For distribution within the camp 50 millimetre polythene pipe is suitable. Every branch to a standpipe manifold should have an isolating valve, as should the outlet from the tank. Taps should be provided at the rate of one per 200–300 people and can be conveniently mounted on a manifold of four to eight taps, made of galvanized iron pipe.

At the end of the manifold a 50 millimetre valve should be provided for attaching fire-fighting hoses. The manifold can be supported initially on a timber frame over a soakaway filled with rocks which can subsequently be replaced by a more permanent concrete structure. Taps should be 0.6–1 m above the ground to allow for filling containers. Other facilities such as showers and washing areas can be added later. A simple shower is shown in Fig. 7.11.

Before the distribution system is used it should be disinfected with a 100 mg/l chlorine solution (see below). This is left to stand in the pipes for four to six hours, and then pumped out with appropriately treated clean water until no chlorine smell is detectable.

WATER TREATMENT

The objective is to reduce bacterial contamination. Packaged water treatment plants are available from many manufacturers but are expensive and in many instances unsuitable. A suggested schedule for treating different types of water is given in Table 7.4.

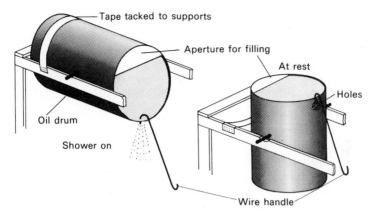

Fig. 7.11. A simple shower.

Table 7.4. *Summary of water treatment methods*

Class	Source	Abstraction	Settlement	Filtration	Disinfection
1	Borehole	Strainer	—	—	—
	Deep wells	Strainer	—	—	Install pot chlorinators
	Springs	Strainer	—	—	—
	Underground rivers	Bed-filtration unit	—	—	Marginal chlorination*
2	Silty rivers	Bed-filtration unit properly sited	—	—	Low free residual chlorination†
	Unsilted rivers, lakes, streams	Bed-filtration unit properly sited	—	—	Low free residual chlorination†
3	Lakes, rivers, ponds/sumps, shallow wells	Bed-filtration unit	—	Diatomite filtration	Free residual chlorination‡
4	Slow moving rivers with chemical pollution	Strainer	Coagulation settlement	Diatomite filtration	High free residual chlorination§
	Other rivers, ponds, with very high faecal pollution	Bed-filtration unit	—	Diatomite filtration	High free residual chlorination§

* Marginal chlorination—applied dosage 0.5 mg/litre.
† Low free residual chlorination—to leave a residual of 0.1–0.2 mg/litre.
‡ Free residual chlorination—to leave residual of 0.2–0.3 mg/litre.
§ High free residual chlorination—to leave a residual of 0.5 mg/litre. This would typically require a dosage of up to 10 mg/litre of chlorine.

Chlorination can be carried out by using calcium hypochlorite, chloride of lime, or high test hypochlorite (HTH). These are all available as drums of powder which can be stored for long periods if kept cool and unopened. The chlorine can be applied in pot chlorinators (see Ross Bulletin No. 10) for wells, or by a drip feeder in the main storage tank. The rate of flow of chlorine solution from the drip feeder depends on the type of chemical used, its concentration and the dosage of chlorine required, but in general a capacity of about 200 litres per day per 10 000 people is adequate, and adjustment of the flow-rate and disinfectant concentration will give the required level of disinfection. A comparator and tablets of DPD will be required to check the residual chlorine level in the water from the taps furthest from the storage tank.

Chlorine-containing powder will be needed at the rate of 1–2 kg per day per 10 000 people. To calculate the applied dosage it can be assumed that high test hypochlorite (HTH) contains 70 per cent by weight of available chlorine, and tropical chloride of lime about 30 per cent. Unfortunately, many people not used to chlorinated water may find even a slight chlorine taste unacceptable, and the dosage will have to be reduced.

Diatomite filters can be installed, when necessary, immediately downstream of the main water pump. Manufacturers will be able to advise on a model with suitable capacity. They require some care to operate, but with supervision from someone with basic technical understanding they are reliable.

For heavily polluted water, coagulation with alum is required. A drip feeder similar to that used for chlorination is satisfactory, provided the concentrated solution is fed into the turbulent zone where water falls into the storage tank. The dosage is determined by trial and error, observing the formation of flocculated particles, and their settlement. Five to 10 milligrams per litre is a typical dose. The alum is obtainable in solid form, packaged in sacks. To achieve adequate settlement, two tanks in series should be used, the alum being added to the first and the chlorine to the second.

Sanitation and waste disposal

In very hot and dry desert climates defaecation in the open, provided it is well away from the community, is not a serious hazard as the sunlight and heat will quickly render the faeces harmless. In general however, efforts should be made right from the beginning to ensure adequate excreta disposal.

It is important to take into account traditional sanitation practices of the refugees when planning the provision of latrines. For example, are they sitters or squatters? People not accustomed to using latrines will generally prefer a large enclosure with no roof, with a squatting slab over the pit. The provision of appropriate anal cleaning materials will be necessary. In some societies the same latrine cannot be used by both sexes, or by certain members of the family group. Nor must the latrine face Mecca in a Muslim country. If these factors are not investigated at the planning stage, time will be wasted and if inappropriate latrines are installed, resistance to the whole idea of using latrines may well evolve.

Even before basic facilities are constructed, a significant improvement can be made by designating certain areas for defaecation only, away from the community and water sources. A vigorous campaign should be organized to encourage people to use these areas and not to defaecate indiscriminately within the camp. The siting of these areas is a matter for compromise; ideally they should be far from the camp, but they will not be used unless they are sufficiently near.

At the same time the soil should be investigated to assess its infiltrative capacity and stability. A highly impervious soil precludes the use of pit latrines. In unstable sandy soils, thought must be given to the availability of materials for lining the pits—such as open-ended oil drums with holes punched in the sides, or vertical wooden posts with palm fronds or creepers woven into them horizontally.

LATRINES

There is no doubt that 'private' household latrines are better kept and used than communal ones. Dirty and smelly latrines will not be used. Families or small groups should be encouraged to build their own with some assistance from the authorities. One latrine per 10–15 people is suitable. Latrines should not be built within 50 m of wells for fear of contamination, or within six metres of dwellings, mainly because of the possible smell factor. Latrines should not be constructed in low lying areas which are prone to flooding or which have a high groundwater level during some seasons. If latrines are built in these areas they will fill with water and provide ideal mosquito breeding sites and the excreta will contaminate the environment. For other systems, see p. 190. Once a suitable design has been evolved, in consultation with the community, construction should begin as soon as possible. The most difficult item to make is the squatting slab (Figs. 7.12 and 7.13).

Construction of squatting slabs

Fibreglass slabs may be imported at first, but it is preferable to make them at the camp using cement. To do this, steel or wooden moulds are required. One mould is sufficient for up to 15 slabs per day, if the cement used is mixed with 2–3 per cent calcium chloride to promote quick setting, and if the slabs are turned out onto pieces of plywood before they are completely set.

A rich mix should be used for the concrete, with a sand–cement ratio of 1:3. This can be used on its own with two layers of chicken wire

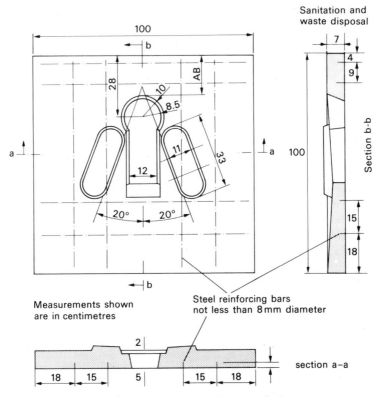

Fig. 7.12. Typical squatting plate design.

reinforcement to make a ferrocement slab 40–50 mm thick. Alternatively, a 1:3 concrete can be used, with 8 mm reinforcing bar at 200 mm centres, with a thickness of 70–80 mm. In either case about 25 kg of cement is required per slab.

To make the slabs, the mould should first be oiled with used engine oil or similar lubricant; an unlubricated mould will stick. A suitable design is shown in Fig. 7.14. The reinforcement must be adequately buried in the interior of the slab. With ferrocement this is achieved by partially filling the mould and then putting in the chicken wire prior to complete filling. If reinforced concrete is used, the bars should be rested on spacer blocks. These are small precast blocks 30 mm thick with a wire for tying on the rods cast into them. They are placed in the mould and the bars tied in place before pouring the concrete which should then be packed in place by repeatedly prodding with a stick perpendicular to the plane of the slab.

If neither chicken wire nor reinforcing bar is available, unreinforced slabs

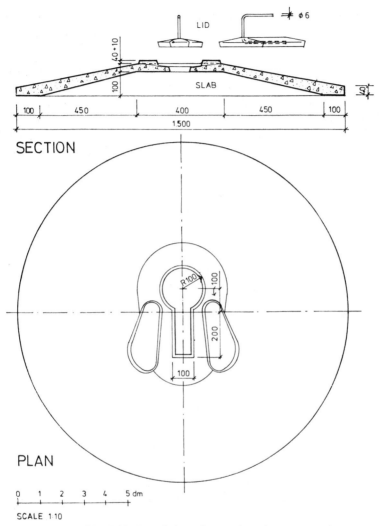

Fig. 7.13. Unreinforced squatting plate.

can be made using a 1:1.5:2 cement:sand:aggregate mix. They should be 40–50 mm thick and formed in a shallow dome shape for extra strength (Fig. 7.13).

● Where cement is in short supply, poles can be placed across the pit and then covered with termite hill earth, earth/cowdung mixtures, or similar building materials, and rendered with a 5–10 mm layer of cement mortar. In this case the pit should be long and narrow, rather than circular (Fig. 7.14).

Latrine superstructures can be improvised according to what is available. They should have a roof and offer privacy. A cover for the drop-hole should be provided, but it is not essential.

As the camp settles down, it is a good idea to improve the latrines by installing insect-proofed ventilation pipes. These should be of 150 mm diameter or more, about 2 m high and can be of any rigid piping, rolled sheets of galvanized iron, or of local materials in wattle and daub. They should be placed on the sunny side of the latrine and painted black to promote solar heating and the inducement of an up-draught. The top of each

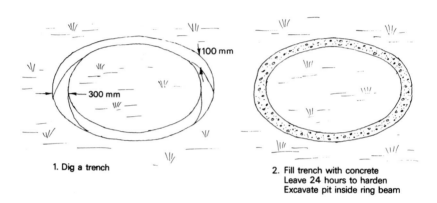

1. Dig a trench

2. Fill trench with concrete
Leave 24 hours to harden
Excavate pit inside ring beam

Concrete reinforcement

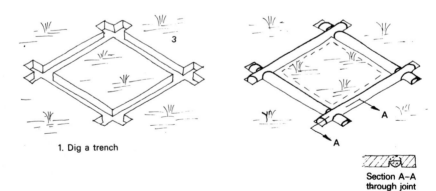

1. Dig a trench

Section A–A
through joint

2. Make timber frame
Put in trench
Excavate pit about 100 mm inside frame

Timber reinforcement

Fig. 7.14. Reinforcing the top of a pit.

pipe should be covered with a corrosion-resistant gauze with apertures not larger than 1.3 mm. This action will reduce insect breeding in the latrines, but if the pits are generally wet, and a major mosquito breeding problem occurs, about one litre of kerosene or used motor oil can be poured into the pits every two to four weeks to further reduce the problem.

The pit wall should be strengthened on the inside, if necessary, as described above. The rim of the pit should always be reinforced, either by pouring concrete into a 100 mm square cross-section trench, prior to digging, or using oiled or creosoted timber (see Fig. 7.15). Digging equipment should be

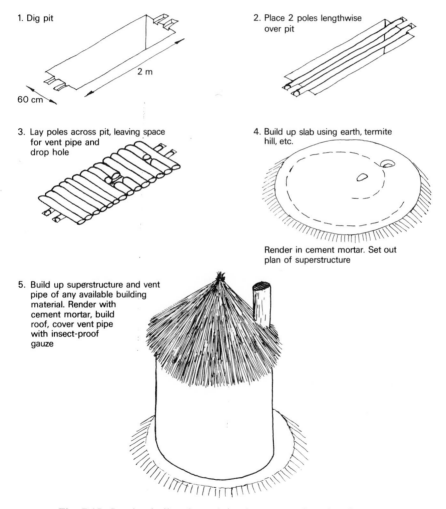

1. Dig pit

2 m

60 cm

2. Place 2 poles lengthwise over pit

3. Lay poles across pit, leaving space for vent pipe and drop hole

4. Build up slab using earth, termite hill, etc.

Render in cement mortar. Set out plan of superstructure

5. Build up superstructure and vent pipe of any available building material. Render with cement mortar, build roof, cover vent pipe with insect-proof gauze

Fig. 7.15. Latrine built using minimal amount of steel and cement.

chosen based on the initial survey. Shovels may be adequate in softer soils, but in harder areas picks will also be required.

As the latrines become full, e.g. to within about 300 mm of the surface, they should be filled in with earth and others reconstructed elsewhere, using the original components. A pit latrine should be left for a minimum of one year after filling in to allow degradation of contents and loss of pathogenicity by infective agents.

There is often not enough space or budget to construct latrines for individual households so communal latrines will have to be set up. One can limit their 'publicity' by allocating a latrine for a group of households who agree to share and will take responsibility for its cleanliness and maintenance. If this is not possible, a special team must be recruited to maintain communal latrines as they will not be kept in good condition by individual users. This means equipping the team with clothes, boots, gloves, and material to carry out this unpleasant job. Communal latrines must be situated close to shelters, on an accessible path and lit at night, to be effectively used.

Other systems

If the ground is too hard to allow digging, is highly impervious, or if the water table is extremely high, more sophisticated systems will have to be considered. As they are more expensive, it is useful to carry out a pilot project to assess their effectiveness. Depending on water availability, the two main options will be aqua privies, as set up in camps in Thailand, or septic tanks. A unit based on the septic tank principle, the Oxfam sanitation unit, was appropriate for the conditions in the Bangladeshi camps in India, 1971–72, where the water table was very high, but it may not necessarily be a solution for other situations as it requires a large volume of water. In many circumstances the immediate surroundings of camps will remain saturated with openly deposited excreta. At the beginning of the rainy season they become really dangerous, being washed by the rains into water-sources, drains, and houses if flooding occurs. If the problem persists, the best solution may be to clean the open ground with mini-bulldozers and bury the whole amount before flies can lay their eggs.

WASTE WATER

This must be disposed of to avoid insect breeding. If the ground is permeable, a large pit should be dug, with sidewall area of around 1 m^2 per 200 litres per day of sullage produced. This is filled with rocks to 300 mm below ground level and covered with sacking, cement bags, plastic sheeting, or similar material, prior to backfilling with soil, in order to prevent the soil filling up the spaces between the rocks. To avoid blocking the pores in the soil, a grease trap should be provided for waste water containing grease and fat. This consists of a box or trench about 1 m long and 500–700 mm square, with two baffles, one near either end, extending from above the water surface to 100 mm above the bottom (see Fig. 7.16).

Where the soil is too impermeable or waterlogged, the sullage will have to be piped away, using 75 mm polythene pipe, to the nearest stream or lake, taking care not to pollute any water source used by the camp or by local inhabitants.

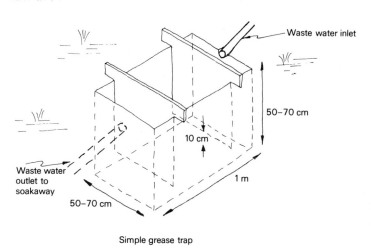

Simple grease trap

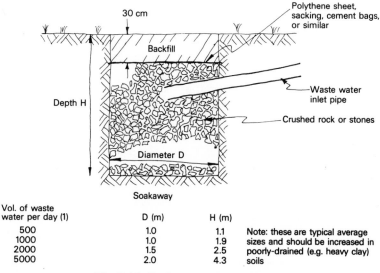

Soakaway

Vol. of waste water per day (1)	D (m)	H (m)	
500	1.0	1.1	Note: these are typical average
1000	1.0	1.9	sizes and should be increased in
2000	1.5	2.5	poorly-drained (e.g. heavy clay)
5000	2.0	4.3	soils

Fig. 7.16. Soakaway and grease trap.

REFUSE DISPOSAL

Some camps may generate little refuse, requiring no more than a few pits in strategic areas. In other camps refuse may be produced at the rate of about 2–4 cubic metres per 1000 people per day.

In these circumstances receptacles for the refuse should be placed at regular intervals, and supported a little way off the ground. If there is a lot of rain, the bottoms should be pierced with small holes to allow drainage. An oil drum cut in half may be sufficient for 20–40 people's daily refuse production. Daily collection is advisable, and certainly at least once every three days to minimize insect breeding. One five-ton truck is probably sufficient for 10 000 people. Handcarts can, of course, also be used. If the carts have side-walls, the refuse can be collected in bulk. Alternatively, spare refuse cans can be used to replace the full ones which are then loaded onto the truck.

Final disposal should be by incineration or burial. The latter is the simplest solution. The refuse should be placed in pits or trenches about 1–2 m deep. At the end of every day's collections, it should be covered with soil which may be taken from a parallel trench for later use. The soil should be crushed well down to prevent maggots burrowing through. The disposal site should be well-drained and at least 2 km from the community. A gently-sloping site on the downwind side would be ideal.

Hospital wastes such as used syringes and dressings and other pathogenic wastes should be treated separately, and the construction of a small incerator for them is justified.

Fire and flooding

FIRE

In the densely populated areas of the community where the dwellings themselves are often highly inflammable (e.g. thatched huts or tents) there is a high risk of fires starting and spreading. An obvious way of preventing the spread of a fire is to space the dwellings further apart, but this can be self-defeating as subsequent arrivals may build their homes in the space left. It is worth siting dwellings just close enough to prevent in-filling and overcrowding by later arrivals.

Roadways through the camp can operate as fire-breaks and should preferably be about 10 m wide. It is also worth investigating the refugees' cooking habits. In many cultures simple stoves made of mud are traditional, and refugees can show others how to make and use them. This will diminish the risks of cooking on open fires which are subject to winds. Simple stoves are also more economical on fuel by decreasing heat loss.

Little can be done to fire-proof a camp, so planning should enable speedy action in the event of a fire. If the community is divided into blocks rather than rows, these would form suitable subdivisions for fire-watchers. Otherwise the camp should be subdivided into areas with two or three people, possibly older children, responsible for immediate reporting of any fires and for raising the alarm.

It is useful to have about ten oil drums constantly ready and full of water, with buckets available nearby for small fires. These again should be under someone's direct responsibility or the water and buckets will tend to disappear!

Beaters made from old tyres or a similar material attached to timber handles may be useful for fighting nearby bush fires and these should be the responsibility of the fire-watchers. When fighting a large fire it is wisest (though not immediately obvious) first to contain the fire and then to put it out. Total destruction over a small area will cause less damage in the long run than partial destruction over a wider area. The fire must, therefore, be contained and controlled on all sides as quickly as possible, before extinguishing it from the edges towards the centre.

For large fires, running water will be required. Where a water distribution system has been installed with 50 mm fire-fighting valves on the distribution manifolds, these can be coupled to lengths of hose and turned on. It is, of course, necessary that the hose and appropriate couplings be available! All other taps in the system should be turned off to maximize the available pressure. If isolating valves have been installed on the branches to the standpipes these can be turned off to prevent people using the taps. In the absence of a pressurized water supply, all available vehicles will have to be loaded with water in any suitable containers and rushed to the fire.

FLOODING

Virtually nothing can be done about flooding beyond careful siting in the first place. If the site is near a river then the river should have been assessed as a water source in any case, but the value of this information is re-emphasized here.

Dry riverbeds and wadis are certain to carry large quantities of water at some time during the year and should be avoided. In some parts of the world flash floods are common, sometimes at unlikely times and places. Here again local knowledge must be consulted.

Sensitive installations such as the food stores, hospital and water supply, camps administration headquarters, etc., must be protected with drainage trenches. A sensible size would be about 0.5 m wide at the bottom, 1 m at the top and about 500 mm deep. The trench should have an arm leading away on the downhill side to somewhere where the water will do less harm. Trenches around all dwellings and along roadways are on balance not a good idea unless the area is prone to very high rainfall. During the dry parts of the year they will inevitably become full of dirty water and refuse and start to constitute a general health hazard. In areas where the onset of the rains can be predicted, trench digging should be carried out for dwellings and roadways in the week or fortnight prior to the rains.

Vector control

Insects and pests are likely to be a hazard in refugee camps, where there is overcrowding, poor refuse disposal and sanitation, inadequate domestic and food hygiene, and a lack of personal hygiene.

It is essential to consult the local government authorities on the main disease vectors common to the environment, as the control measures will vary according to such factors as government policy, the vegetation, and patterns of resistance to insecticides.

General preventive measures include:

● Adequate planning on the siting and layout of the camp including spacing and type of shelter (see section on Physical environment).
● Enforcing administrative rules and regulations covering camp hygiene.
● Improving latrines by installing insect-proofed ventilation pipes (see p. 188).

Direct control of the most commonly encountered vectors is now briefly discussed.

HOUSEFLIES

Houseflies are often a major problem and apart from the nuisance element may play a significant role in the transmission of diarrhoeal diseases, conjunctivitis and trachoma, and in infecting wounds.

To help reduce the fly population:

● Keep the camp area free of indiscriminate human and animal faeces.
● Install insect-proof ventilation pipes in latrines.
● Until ventilation can be added to existing latrines:

   ● pour about one litre of used motor oil or kerosene down a latrine every two/four weeks.
   ● cover the upper side and top surround of the latrine with the empty sacks the food is supplied in, previously soaked in oil.

● Bury or burn all refuse.
● In areas where the fly population is already a problem and excreta and refuse disposal are a hazard, use insecticides in the form of ultra-low volume sprays.
● Where a major hazard exists, it may be necessary to cover the area with an insecticide fog, but this is an expensive procedure and potentially dangerous.

Emphasis should be placed on trying to clean up the environment as quickly and as effectively as possible.

• Do not use insecticide in latrines as it destroys the ecological balance and may result in an increase in the fly population.

• Do not allow animal slaughter and dissection to take place within the camp area.

MOSQUITOES AND LICE

These have previously been discussed in the section on Control of communicable diseases (see pp. 128, 129, and 132).

BED-BUGS, REDOVIDAE, AND FLEAS

In most circumstances these can all be controlled by spraying the appropriate insecticide on to walls, bed frames, and into cracks, crevices etc. where it can persist for several months. The insecticides, unless marked otherwise, should not be applied to people, animals, clothing, or bedding.

MICE AND RATS

• Store all food on a raised platform.

• Bury or burn refuse.

• Use poison only if it can be guaranteed that humans, especially children, will not be harmed by its presence.

8 Health centre activities

Family health care

In a refugee community the physical and mental well-being of all individuals is at risk but women and children, especially those from the poorest families, are amongst the most vulnerable. Families should be encouraged to take an active part in developing family health care programmes. The self-reliance generated by this approach will help offset the dependency which can so easily develop in communities exposed to mass relief programmes for long periods.

MATERNAL AND CHILD HEALTH

Probably the best known of the family services is maternal and child health care (MCH). In general MCH services aim to provide comprehensive, ongoing care and supervision to women and children throughout the particularly vulnerable periods of pregnancy, birth, lactation, early infancy, and childhood. Activities carried out by MCH staff at clinics and in the home should contain as much curative care as is necessary, but every opportunity should be taken to include a strong preventive and educational element.

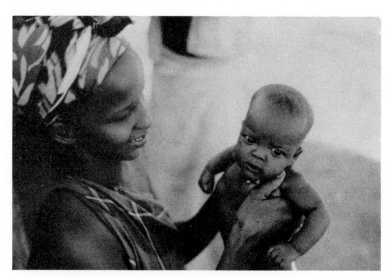

Fig. 8.1. Healthy children depend on healthy parents.

Activities should also be integrated so that the needs of a mother and her child are met on the same day at the same place. Indeed, one of the major criticisms of MCH services is that too much attention is paid to the child to the neglect of the mother.

Care should be taken to site MCH clinics where they are readily accessible to the population. An additional home visiting service will allow for greater coverage and provide:

• a means of reaching high risk families and individuals who fail to attend clinics
• a means of treating patients in their own homes

A supplementary feeding programme, if implemented, often forms the logical starting point for MCH care. As with any of the other activities, plans can only be developed appropriately if they are based on information about local circumstances and on the main health and disease problems.

Staff

Amongst the refugees there are often trained professional health workers who may have had MCH experience. If possible they should be brought in to help run the services. In many situations deliveries are undertaken by local midwives or traditional birth attendants. Where possible links should be established with them, so that antenatal and delivery care can be extended and improved by supervision, training, and co-operation. Interested refugees with no previous training can also become valuable members of the health team. They will provide an important bridge between relief personnel and the community as they will be familiar with the language and with any cultural factors which may have a bearing on MCH activities, e.g. in some cultures women do not like publicly to admit to being pregnant by attending antenatal clinics, and some are confined to the home for 40 days after delivery.

With adequate training and supervision health workers from amongst the refugees can undertake a variety of tasks (see section on Training refugees). Regular meetings for all levels of MCH staff are very important as they provide an opportunity for learning and discussion. Local staff may be more able to provide reasons for problems which may be hindering the MCH programme, such as the under-utilization of services. The overall responsibility for running MCH services usually rests with the senior health staff.

Summary of main MCH activities

Care during pregnancy

• Supervision and regular examination of women during pregnancy. Examinations should be related to the obstetric pattern of the area. If severe anaemia is more common than toxaemia it may be more important to estimate haemoglobin at a particular visit than to measure the blood pressure.

● Health education on what is normal and what is abnormal during pregnancy.

● Advice and treatment of common diseases and nutritional problems during pregnancy, e.g. malaria, anaemia, malnutrition.

● Course of tetanus toxoid vaccination to the mother during the last trimester of pregnancy, to prevent neonatal tetanus.

● Possible malaria chemoprophylaxis.

● Identification of the 'at risk' mother who will require skilled help during labour and delivery, e.g. abnormal presentations, fifth or more pregnancy, anaemia, toxaemia, short height of mother.

● Recording all the above information on a simple antenatal record card kept by the mother.

● Antenatal women should be enrolled on supplementary feeding programmes where these are in existence.

● Co-operation with local midwives and traditional birth attendants.

Care during labour and delivery

● Most normal deliveries will take place in the home, supervised by a local midwife or family member. Clean delivery packs for each imminent house delivery should be provided.

● Where possible complicated maternity cases should be referred or transferred to local hospitals.

● Some women will need care at the health centre with supervision during labour and delivery. A clean room equipped with bed, linen, and simple apparatus (e.g. for resuscitation of the newborn) should be set aside for this purpose.

● With the co-operation of local midwives or maternity aides it should be possible to provide a 24 hour service with two midwives providing supervision at any one time.

● Women should deliver in their traditional positions, be it squatting, sitting, or lying.

● A close relative should stay with the mother during delivery for support and reassurance.

Neglect of the last two points may lead to resentment and under-utilization of the services.

Supervision of labour

● Supervision of labour must be done by the most competent staff.

● Vaginal examinations must be kept to an absolute minimum and only performed by a senior person.

- Regular checks are needed on foetal heart, but other recordings should be kept to a minimum.
- It is essential to provide sterile delivery packs containing:

  pair of scissors or razor blades
  bowl
  swabs
  tape, string, or elastic bands for tying the cord
  small bar of soap

- Equipment for sucking mucous from the infant's nose and mouth.
- 1 per cent aqueous solution of gentian violet for painting cord.
- A supply of Ergometrine or Symtometrine should be available.

Care after delivery

- Mothers delivering in the clinic will often be accompanied by another woman from the 'family' who will provide support during and after delivery.
- It should be possible for the mother to be washed after delivery and for the baby to be bathed and clothed.
- A preventive dose of vitamin A, 200 000 IU should possibly be given to the mother (see p. 110).
- Regular home visits should be made by local midwives to the mother and new baby, e.g. daily or every other day until cord has dropped off, then once every 2–4 days until the tenth day.
- During home visits particular care should be taken to detect and deal with any complications or problems such as sores, engorged breasts, a smelly vaginal discharge, 'sticky eyes', or an infected 'sticky' cord in the baby.

Staff should be aware of local customs associated with childbirth and care of the newborn. For example, in some Far East countries women lie on a bamboo bed over a bed of charcoal embers for four to five days after delivery. In some instances a baby may not be given breast milk for the first three days of life but be fed sticky rice instead. These customs should be discussed with local midwives and clinic staff so that appropriate teaching can be agreed upon.

Some customs are very strongly upheld and should not be disregarded.

Breast-feeding and weaning

The importance of breast-feeding has already been emphasized in the sections on Feeding programmes and Diarrhoea. It cannot be over-emphasized.

Weaning practices may vary within each community. Mothers often need help in adapting the relief foods to weaning foods. There may be a particular association between weaning foods and diarrhoea in refugee communities due to contamination with high levels of *Escherichia coli* for one or a combination of the following reasons:

● Because of inadequate fuel supplies, large quantities of food may be cooked inadequately and then stored for long periods.
● Insufficient food storage containers.
● Poor water supplies.
● An environment where the temperature is higher than the refugees are used to.
● Poor personal and domestic hygiene.

In some societies the traditional method to stop breast-feeding is for the mother to use a bitter substance applied to the nipples. In Tigray, northern Ethiopia, for example, a broken surface of the fleshy leaf of the aloe which exudes bitter juice is used. Some of these mothers, when refugees in Eastern Sudan where the plant is not available, used bitter drugs such as chloroquine and tetracycline in its place. Such indiscriminate use of antibiotics, in particular, may increase the chance of bacterial resistance and should be discouraged.

Child spacing

Mothers and fathers, and where possible also other men and women need to learn about the advantages of maintaining an adequate birth interval by spacing their children (Table 8.1). Traditional methods of birth spacing should be examined and encouraged where appropriate. Family planning activities should conform to government policies except perhaps where it can be seen that certain groups of people are being positively discriminated against, e.g. traditional enemies. As with many other activities, provision must be made for follow-up. Ensure adequate and frequent supplies. It may be necessary to have a separate clinic or the family planning may be a part of the MCH services.

Some women may complain of secondary amenorrhoea, due in part perhaps to the high levels of stress common to war situations and/or weight loss associated with drought/famine conditions.

Supervision and promotion of growth in children

● Regular weighing and use of weight charts for monitoring growth (see p. 204).
● Early identification of children who are failing to grow well.
● Provision of adequate support and advice to the mothers of these children.
● Special recording of 'at risk' children for follow-up (see p. 207).
● Precise and practical nutrition advice with emphasis on breast-feeding and the best use of locally available food as infant food.
● Any aid food should be culturally acceptable and simple instruction for preparation should be given.

Table 8.1. *Summary of contraceptive methods*

	Effectiveness	Acceptability	Availability	Side effects	Reversibility
Rhythm method	fair	fair	nothing required	none	complete
Withdrawal	good	fair	nothing required	none	complete
Traditional abstinence	very good	fair	nothing required	none	complete
IUCD	very good	good	hospital health centre	moderate local only	complete
Condom	good	good	hospital health centre, dispensary, shops	none	complete
Diaphragm	fair	fair	hospitals	none	complete
Pills	very good	very good	hospital, health centre dispensary, chemists	minimal on low dose variety	complete after 1–3 months
Injections	very good	good	hospital health centre	moderate	complete 3–14 months
Spermicides	fair	fair	hospital health centre	minimal and local	complete
Tubal ligation	very good	fair	hospital	during procedure only	irreversible
Vasectomy	very good	fair	hospital	during procedure only	irreversible

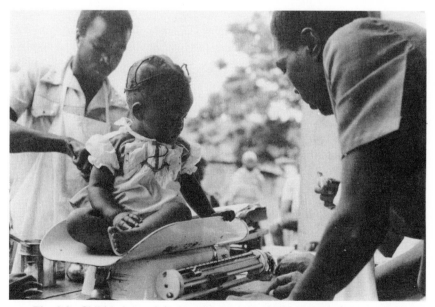

Fig. 8.2. Child being weighed on beam scales during a young child clinic.

Care of sick children

● Early diagnosis and treatment of common childhood conditions such as: diarrhoea, respiratory infections, measles and whooping cough, malnutrition, tuberculosis, malaria (where present), skin conditions, anaemia, and accidents.

● Recognition of the need for supplementary feeding, where applicable, e.g. to child recovering from measles or tuberculosis.

● Referral of the seriously ill for more skilled care if possible.

● Teaching and demonstrating treatments that can be carried out in the home, e.g. giving a sugar–salt solution to child with diarrhoea, or feeding malnourished children in the home. Health workers should be aware of local practices which may conflict with the advice they are giving, e.g. it is often common practice to withhold fluids and foods from children with diarrhoea.

● Children handicapped owing to war injuries will need special care including psychological support, physiotherapy, and perhaps prosthetic equipment.

Immunization

Protection against measles, tuberculosis, diphtheria, tetanus, whooping cough, and poliomyelitis as described in the section on Immunization. Immunizations given should be entered on a home-based record card as explained on p. 145.

Organizing MCH clinics

Sequence of clinic activities

Antenatal clinic	Registration
	Weighing (height at first visit to identify women below 151 cm or $59\frac{1}{2}$ inches)
	Physical examination
	Treatment and advice for common problems
	Investigations (urine, blood pressure, haemoglobin etc., depending on laboratory facilities and cause for concern)
	Tetanus toxoid injection
	Dispensing (iron, vitamins, folic acid, and malaria prophylaxis)
	Health and nutrition education, e.g. demonstration of choice and preparation of the donated food and any locally available foods especially good for antenatal mothers
Child spacing clinic	Registration
	Examination and advice
	Dispensing medicines
	Health and nutrition education
Young child clinic	Registration
	Weighing and charting weight
	Examination and advice
	Advice and treatment of common problems
	Immunization
	Dispensing medicines and food supplement if there is no 'on the spot' supplementary feeding
	Health and nutrition education, e.g. practical demonstration of how to use cup and spoon for the available foods for a 5–6 month old baby

General suggestions for clinic organization

● Establish 'lines of flow' so that large numbers can be seen as quickly as possible.

● Teach all staff to recognize dangerously ill children attending clinic, e.g. dehydrated children, so that prompt treatment can be given.

● Arrange for routine tasks, e.g. registration and weighing, to be undertaken by local health workers, but check them now and again for accuracy.

● Arrange for referral of complicated and serious cases, e.g. children with suspected tuberculosis.

● Arrange for follow-up in the home and at the clinic of 'at risk' attenders.

● Arrange for short teaching sessions at clinics.

● Provide daily clinics with special arrangements to cover the weekend period.

● Use 'quieter' times in the afternoon for spending time with parents of 'at risk' children, or in teaching/discussion sessions with staff.

● Encourage and allow parents to participate in clinic work, e.g. mothers who have been attending for some time can often be supportive to 'new' mothers, or help with cleaning premises, etc.

Fig. 8.3. Father and child watching a nutrition demonstration.

• Encourage fathers to bring their children if the women are busy elsewhere, e.g. at the market or in the fields. Fathers can be very influential in child rearing practices and family planning.

Home-based records

Weight chart

Where government policy allows, the introduction of weight charts of the type shown in Fig. 8.4 and 8.5 has been found to be useful. The front of the weight chart (Fig. 8.4) has sections for recording details of the child and his family, immunizations, and clinical details. The reverse side contains the weight record for the first five years of the child's life (Fig. 8.5). These can also be used as scattergrams to plot the results of a weight-for-age survey or to record the weights of all children who attend an MCH clinic. The chart shown is from Ethiopia and was used to monitor the individual and community weights of children in shelters during the Ogaden famine, 1975. This and charts in other countries are continually being revised as comments are received from field workers.

With adequate training local health workers can use these charts to supervise the growth of individual children and detect early signs of growth failure. As well as providing a complete medical and nutritional history there are areas on the chart for recording reasons for special care, child-spacing details, malaria prophylaxis, immunization, and essential family details. Parents rarely lose the cards and soon remember to bring them to every session.

Antenatal record chart

A simple chart, kept by the pregnant woman, which provides a record of previous obstetric history and details of the current pregnancy, such as reasons for special care, illnesses, routine examinations, and investigations, etc., can enable staff to provide improved antenatal care, especially to those at risk, and is useful at delivery and afterwards.

Clinic based records

Tally sheet

One way to make decisions about how to improve the MCH services is to use statistics collected on a regular basis at clinics. It is important, therefore, to have a simple record system whereby useful information can be collected with reasonable accuracy. Tally sheets of the type shown in Fig. 8.6 provide a quick means of recording information and can be designed to meet local needs and government requirement for certain statistics. For each attendance a line is put through one circle, then grouped in fives for easy counting.

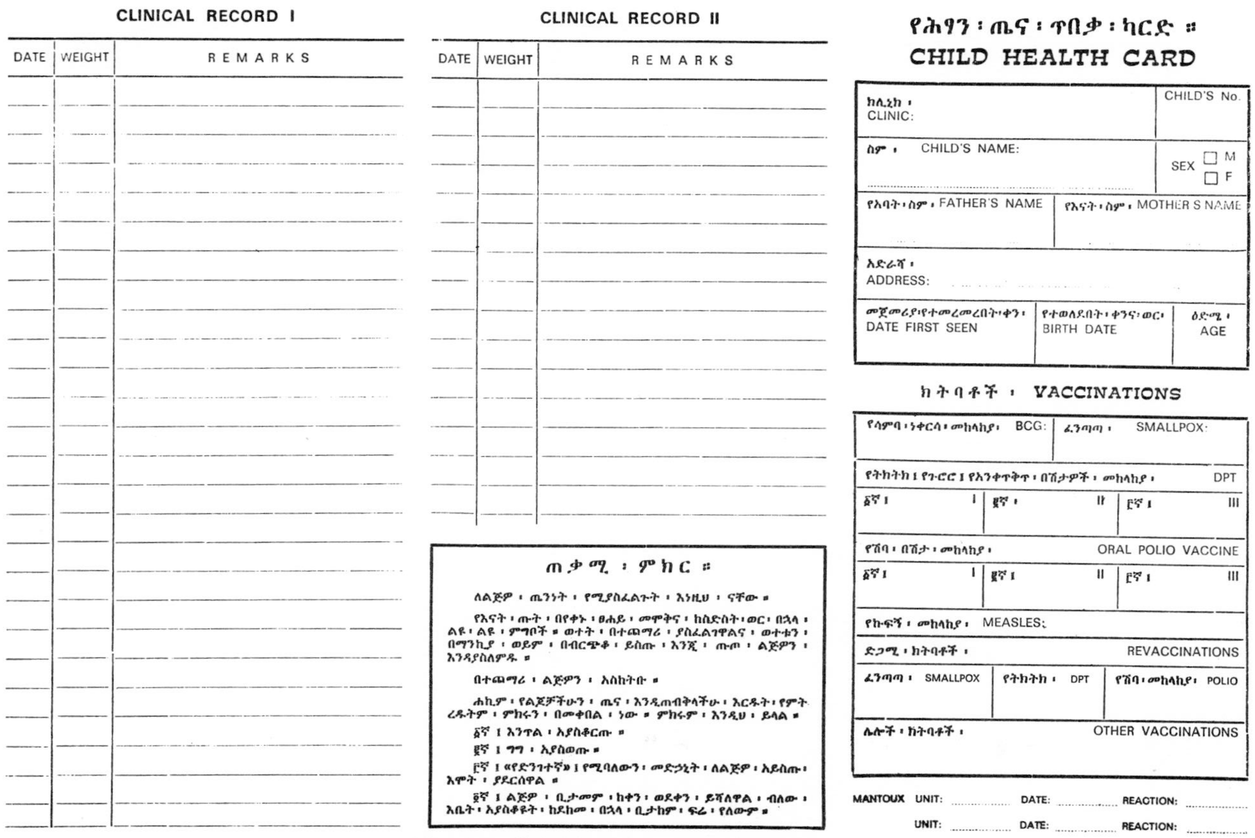

የልጆች ፡ ጤና ፡ ጥበቃ ፡ ካርድ ፡፡
CHILD HEALTH CARD

ክሊኒክ ፡
CLINIC:

CHILD'S No.

ስም ፡ CHILD'S NAME:

SEX ☐ M ☐ F

የአባት ፡ ስም ፡ FATHER'S NAME   የእናት ፡ ስም ፡ MOTHER'S NAME

አድራሻ ፡
ADDRESS:

መጀመሪያየተመረመረበት ቀን ፡   የተወለደበት ቀን ፡ ፀሐፊ ፡ ወር ፡   ዕድሜ ፡
DATE FIRST SEEN   BIRTH DATE   AGE

ክትባቶች ፡ VACCINATIONS

የፈንጣጣ ፡ ክትባት ፡ መከላከያ ፡ BCG: SMALLPOX: ፈንጣጣ ፡

የትክትክ ፡ ተ፡ርር ፡ የአንገት፡ተት ፡ በሽታዎች ፡ መከላከያ ፡   DPT

፩ኛ ፡   I   ፪ኛ ፡   II   ፫ኛ ፡   III

የሽቦ ፡ በሽታ ፡ መከላከያ ፡   ORAL POLIO VACCINE

፩ኛ ፡   I   ፪ኛ ፡   II   ፫ኛ ፡   III

የኩፍኝ ፡ መከላከያ ፡ MEASLES:

ድጋሚ ፡ ክትባቶች ፡   REVACCINATIONS

ፈንጣጣ ፡ SMALLPOX   የትክትክ ፡ DPT   የሽቦ ፡ መከላከያ ፡ POLIO

ሌሎች ፡ ክትባቶች ፡   OTHER VACCINATIONS

MANTOUX   UNIT: ....   DATE: ....   REACTION: ....

UNIT: ....   DATE: ....   REACTION: ....

CLINICAL RECORD I

DATE	WEIGHT	R E M A R K S

CLINICAL RECORD II

DATE	WEIGHT	R E M A R K S

ጠቃሚ ፡ ምክር ፡፡

ለልጅዎ ፡ ጡንነት ፡ የሚደስቱለት ፡ እነዚህ ፡ ናቸው ፡፡

የእናት ፡ ጡት ፡ በየጊዜ ፡ ያለዲ ፡ መሥጠት፡ ከሕፃናት ፡ ወር ፡ በኋላ ፡
ለፍ ፡ ልጅ ፡ ምግብ ፡ ወተት ፡ በተጨማሪ ፡ ያስፈልጋቸዋና ፡ ወተቱን ፡
በማንኪያ ፡ ወይም ፡ በብርጭቆ ፡ ይስጡ ፡ እንጂ ፡ ጠጠ ፡ አይሥጡ ፡
እንዳይበላሡ ፡፡

በተጨማሪ ፡ ልጅዎን ፡ አስኩተ ፡፡

ሕክሙ ፡ የአጃፃችሁን ፡ ጡና ፡ እንዳጠበቃችሁ ፡ እርሷት ፡ ፀም
ሩጪ ፡ ምክር ፡ በመቀበል ፡ ነው ፡ ምክሩ ፡ እነዲህ ፡ ይሆላ ፡፡
፩ኛ ፡ እንጎል ፡ አያሰጡ ፡፡
፪ኛ ፡ ቀደንጎተኛን ፡ የሚበሉወን ፡ መድኃን ፡ ያስያዙ ፡ ይፈልፈ ፡ ብሐ ፡
አለት ፡ አያሳዩት ፡ ከሕክሙ ፡ በጊ ፡ ቢያከም ፡ ፈሬ ፡ ያለውም ፡፡

Fig. 8.4. Child health care card, Ethiopia.

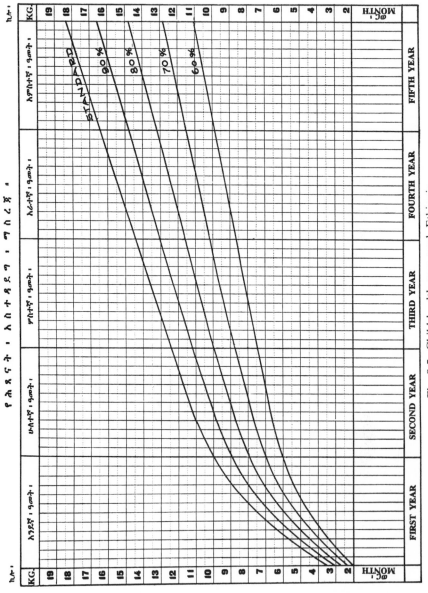

Fig. 8.5. Child health care card, Ethiopia.

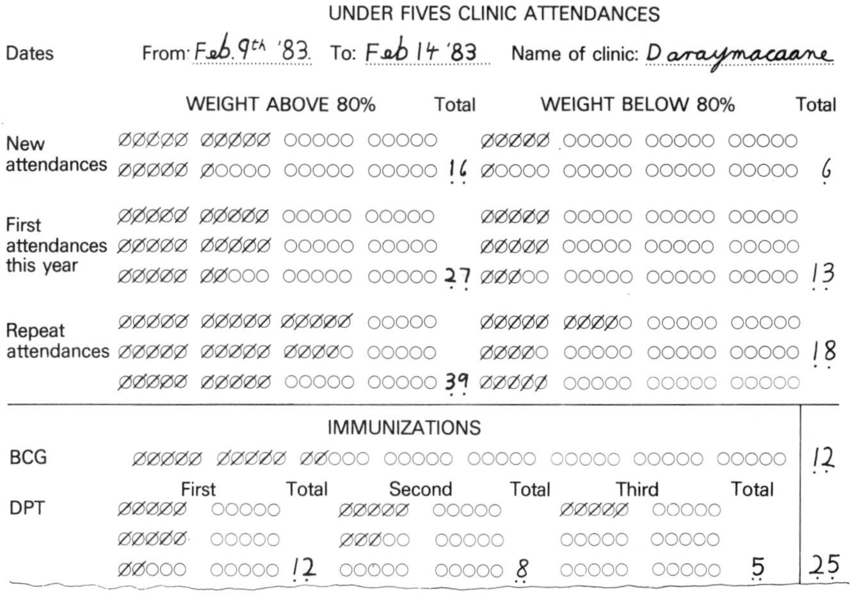
UNDER FIVES CLINIC ATTENDANCES
Dates
From: Feb. 9th '83
To: Feb 14 '83
Name of clinic: Daraymacaane
WEIGHT ABOVE 80%
Total
WEIGHT BELOW 80%
Total
New attendances
16
6
First attendances this year
27
13
Repeat attendances
39
18
IMMUNIZATIONS
BCG
12
DPT
First
Total
Second
Total
Third
Total
12
8
5
25

Fig. 8.6. A simple tally system for recording clinic statistics.

'At risk' register

A special care register or card system should be compiled of all 'at risk' children who require careful supervision and follow-up. The following are some reasons for special care:

- Premature and low birth weight babies.
- Twins.
- Babies with breast-feeding difficulties.
- Lastborn children of large families.
- Children recovering from acute illnesses, e.g. measles.
- Malnourished children.
- Children of malnourished/ill/inadequate mothers.
- Children with tuberculosis or family history of tuberculosis.
- Children in families where several siblings have died.
- Orphans or infants separated from their parents. It is wise to resist any suggestion to open an orphanage as this often creates even more of a problem.

HOME VISITING

This is an essential part of the health programme and is quite possible in most refugee communities where people live close together. In a large community with reasonable roads the service may be extended by equipping staff with bicycles.

Home visiting is an area in which local or refugee community health workers have a particularly important role to play. A home visiting programme provides health workers with a valuable opportunity to:

- Follow up and support families and individuals who are particularly at risk, e.g. malnourished children, dehydration cases.
- Follow up clinic defaulters and supervise those with chronic conditions such as tuberculosis.
- Teach and encourage families to take responsibility for their own health by improving standards of hygiene in the home and being aware of the special needs of vulnerable members.
- Randomly visit homes to ensure that there is neither a high number of ill people that has not come to the attention of the clinic staff, nor that there are individuals in dark corners of their homes such as those too sick to move or severely disabled.

Families are more likely to respond to advice and health education which is sympathetic to many of the difficulties and constraints of their daily life. This sympathy and necessary knowledge can only be gained by visiting and talking to people in their homes.

Home visiting is an important part of the care of the newborn. It provides the health worker with an opportunity to check that all is well with the mother, both physically and mentally, and that she has successfully established breastfeeding. The baby can be examined and appropriate steps taken if any abnormality or problem is detected. This is also a good time to tell families about available health services and encourage regular attendance at clinics, especially during the first two years. A record of the home visit should be entered on the weight chart, antenatal card, or at risk card. Local health workers may want to discuss with medical and nursing staff their findings and observations during visits and a regular time should be set aside for this.

SCHOOL HEALTH

There is often a high proportion of school age children amongst refugees. Despite a lack of formal facilities schools are often a prominent feature and provide a measure of stability for children. MCH staff should normally undertake responsibility for the supervision of school health. During routine inspections attention should be focused on identifying children with signs of common health problems which can be treated. Conditions will vary in importance but the following are common:

malnutrition
anaemia

skin and eye infections
ear discharge
intestinal parasites
head lice

● Some diseases like malaria, schistosomiasis, or pellagra may be of local significance and should be looked for where appropriate.
● Eye testing and dental checks should also be undertaken.
● Teachers should be helped to recognize common problems so they can refer children with medical or social problems to the clinic.
● Older children and teachers can learn about simple first-aid measures, and a limited supply of medicines and skin dressings can safely be left at the school for this purpose.
● Previous BCG immunization status can quickly be assessed in schools and vaccinations can be safely carried out without prior tuberculin skin testing.
● A large number of children may not attend school. This may be for reasons of extreme poverty. More often it is because they represent a valuable source of labour and are expected to look after younger siblings or undertake household or agricultural work, such as going out to search for firewood. The health needs of these children should not be overlooked by the clinics or during home visiting.

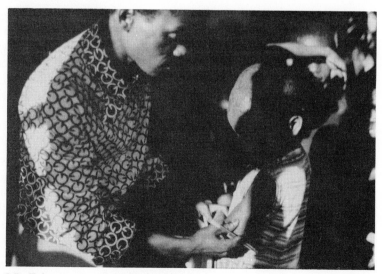

Fig. 8.7. Zairean nurse checking immunization status of school children in a refugee village in Angola.

Schools are an important place for health education. School-age children are generally receptive to new ideas and may adopt attitudes which result in improved health for themselves and their families.

Examples of topics to teach school children are:

- The building, use, and maintenance of latrines.
- The safe disposal of the faeces of younger brothers and sisters and why this is necessary.
- Food hygiene. Children can be taught to act as 'health inspectors' in the feeding programmes, camp markets, tea houses, and in the home, checking that hands are clean, floors swept, food protected from flies etc.
- The preventive and therapeutic aspects of the diarrhoeal disease control programme.

Recreation facilities also promote mental health among the school children. Signs of stress are most likely to be seen amongst children temporarily separated from their parents and among orphans.

Clinical care

The exact nature and emphasis of curative services needed in a refugee camp will depend upon the information provided during the initial assessment. It is crucial that services complement the host government's health policies and particularly the services provided for the local population.

Fig. 8.8. Encouraging traditional craft activities such as wood carving, basket work, knitting, and painting may help promote mental health.

In the past much criticism has been directed by national doctors and others towards international medical teams over the latter's tendency to create services far superior to those available to the local population. In relief operations in Somalia the Ministry of Health produced a set of health guidelines in an effort to standardize much of the care given—especially in clinical medicine and drug supplies. A similar approach was taken in Thailand for the Kampuchean refugees.

WHAT SERVICES MIGHT BE ORGANIZED?

Depending on resources, the following primary services, which include both curative and preventive elements, represent the minimum that should be organized from the health centre:

- Regular general out-patient sessions.
- Regular clinics for the treatment and control of communicable diseases, such as tuberculosis and leprosy.
- Provision of day beds and emergency overnight inpatient care.
- Pharmaceutical store and drug dispensing.
- Basic laboratory investigations.
- Home visiting and referral systems.
- Health education to individuals and through community organizations.
- Family health care, including immunizations, family planning, school health, and maternal and child care.
- Oral rehydration for diarrhoeas.
- Regular formal and informal health staff training sessions and meetings.
- Administration, including the compilation of statistics based on births and deaths, symptoms and diseases, and disease and nutrition surveillance systems.

Other services that it may be possible to develop are:

- Collaboration with traditional healers and practitioners, particularly traditional birth attendants.
- Dental care.
- Optical services.
- Prosthetic and other care for the physically disabled.

THE HEALTH CENTRE

The building

It is difficult to lay down precise guidelines, but one health centre per 30 000 people, with a maximum of ten beds for in-patient or day care may be adequate. With communities over 10 000 people it is advisable also to have, in strategic locations, smaller sub-centres, without beds, from which decentralized services can be organized. The main health centre can then act as the referral point for the sub-centres. The temptation to build a hospital should be resisted unless there is overwhelming evidence for the need of an emergency and temporary field hospital. The primary health care system developed in Ubon refugee camp in Thailand obtained lower morbidity levels than similar camps with hospital facilities were able to achieve in the same time.

The design of the building should be simple, preferably using local materials. The layout and internal organization should ensure a logical flow of patients. A simplified layout of a health centre building is shown in Fig. 8.9.

The specific dimensions are not crucial and will vary from place to place. An important practical issue is that sufficient space is given for a waiting area adjacent to the clinic. In the layout illustrated it is assumed that males and females will be dealt with by the same health workers in the same rooms. In certain societies this will not be culturally acceptable and other solutions must be found.

Equipment

The basic equipment required in the health centre is quite limited and a possible list is given in Appendix 2. Not included but also usually required, are items such as lockable cupboards to store drugs and supplies, and furnishings such as tables and chairs.

General out-patient sessions

The number of people demanding care will vary greatly. In most refugee communities the demand will be especially large in the first few weeks, when the available resources are probably most limited. Outpatients might be seen for four to five hours each morning, five days a week, with the afternoons devoted to specialist clinics and community health visiting. 'On call' rotas need to be organized for night and weekend work to cover emergencies and inpatients.

Clinic records

A simple card index filing system using census/house number, location in community and name, for each refugee or for each family may be the easiest method of retaining records in the clinic. This system is usually used in conjunction with a special 'at risk' register and home based 'Road to Health' and/or 'Family Health' cards as described in the section on Family health care. Figure 8.10 is an example of the Family Health Card presently undergoing trial, supplied with the WHO/UNHCR 'Emergency Health Kit' (see Appendix 2). It is A4 size with treatment headings continued overleaf, and comes in a plastic wallet.

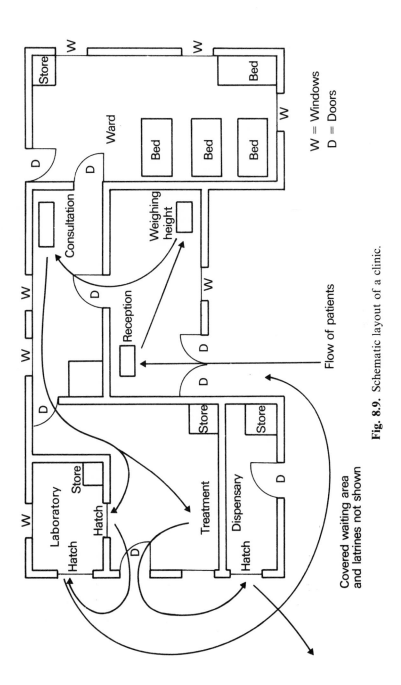

Fig. 8.9. Schematic layout of a clinic.

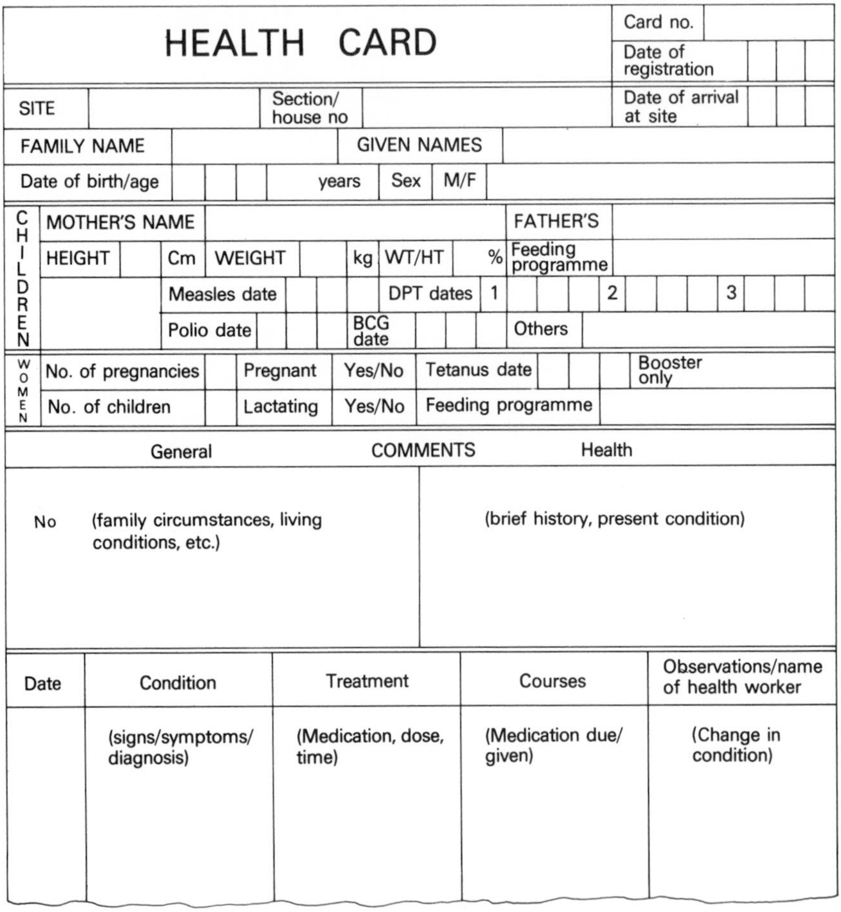

HEALTH CARD							Card no.		
							Date of registration		
SITE			Section/ house no				Date of arrival at site		
FAMILY NAME				GIVEN NAMES					
Date of birth/age				years	Sex	M/F			

CHILDREN

MOTHER'S NAME							FATHER'S		
HEIGHT		Cm	WEIGHT		kg	WT/HT	%	Feeding programme	
		Measles date			DPT dates	1		2	3
		Polio date		BCG date			Others		

WOMEN

No. of pregnancies		Pregnant		Yes/No	Tetanus date			Booster only	
No. of children		Lactating		Yes/No	Feeding programme				

General	COMMENTS	Health
No (family circumstances, living conditions, etc.)		(brief history, present condition)

Date	Condition	Treatment	Courses	Observations/name of health worker
	(signs/symptoms/ diagnosis)	(Medication, dose, time)	(Medication due/ given)	(Change in condition)

Fig. 8.10. Health card.

Personnel

Much of the day to day work in a health centre can be done by national and refugee health assistants or nurses, with a regular referral session attended by a doctor.

The health worker with the appropriate level of training should be providing care to those patients with conditions that require no more than his or her particular skills, at the same time identifying or screening those people with conditions which do not fall within his or her level of competence and referring them to other senior staff with the necessary skills. There are sometimes problems with patients whose demands are only satisfied when they are treated by a person of a certain professional status, even though clinically their condition does not justify this.

The establishment and organization of such a system of screening and treatment will help to ensure that a larger number of people can receive effective care. It is also more equitable and efficient than one that relies upon queuing to health professionals.

Triage, which is the selection and sorting of the sick and potential patients for medical attention in the face of overwhelming needs and insufficient resources, is most likely to be needed immediately after severe natural disasters rather than in refugee communities. Civil or aggressive border wars may necessitate such action. In triage there are usually three categories of patients:

● Those who cannot benefit from the treatment available under the emergency conditions and are, therefore, not treated.
● The seriously ill or injured who might respond to life-saving emergency treatment and should, therefore, be attended to first.
● Those who after initial first aid, can wait for medical attention until those more seriously ill have been attended to.

MANAGEMENT OF PATIENTS

Detailed medical care will, of course, depend on the particular circumstances of the refugees. However, certain diseases are particularly common.

In children aged less than 15 years old the most important diseases are:

respiratory infections
gastro-enteritis
malnutrition
intestinal helminths
skin infections
eye and ear infections
specific infectious diseases
trauma and fractures
malaria, in endemic areas

In older children and adults:

respiratory infections
symptoms associated with the digestive system, including intestinal helminth
    infestations and gastro-enteritis
symptoms associated with the musculo-skeletal system
skin infections
nutritional deficiencies, including anaemia
genito-urinary tract infections

ear and eye infections
specific infectious diseases
mental disorders
trauma and fractures
malaria, in endemic areas

The number of new cases of some symptoms or diseases may hardly vary from month to month, e.g. parasitic infections, whereas others such as malaria or malnutrition may fluctuate due to seasonal changes. In particular circumstances some refugees present with symptoms that are probably psychosomatic. For example, some mothers in the Somali camps took their children to the clinics insisting that both they and the children had severe stomach pain. Close questioning revealed that the pain was attributed to the deprivation of milk, an important element of their normal diet. It is important to be aware of these problems, react sensitively, and resist the use of placebos.

During the Thai/Kampuchean operation from 1979 onwards, traditional medicine was well integrated in the formal health service. An effective two-way referral system meant that many of those presenting at out-patient sessions with symptoms, thought to be of psychological or psychiatric origin, were given time and attention by the traditional doctors. These doctors meanwhile referred to the curative health personnel those diseases recognized to have a known cause.

If traditional medicine is promoted as part of the health programme, the traditional midwives and doctors may need help in getting the plants and herbs they most commonly use, especially where the vegetation is markedly different from that of their homeland. In societies where a stick is used as a toothbrush, supplies may also need to be brought into the camp. When supplies are low it is probably more appropriate to encourage using a finger to clean the teeth than promote buying a toothbrush and toothpaste!

Standard treatment schedules

For efficient use of staff time and drugs, standard treatments should be agreed on. This is crucial when international health personnel are present and especially vital when more than one organization is working in the same refugee community. The standardization should also be co-ordinated between different camps. An example of possible standardized treatments can be found in Appendix 2. It is useful to consider standard schedules for common symptoms such as fever of unknown cause, cough, fits, diarrhoea, abdominal pain, and chest pain.

Diagnostic flow charts

Standardized diagnostic flow charts are helpful as aids in caring for patients with certain presenting symptoms and signs. The main aims are to:

- Identify those conditions which can be easily treated and are not generally severe.
- Identify people with complaints that require more complicated investigation and/or treatment.
- Enable these decisions to be made more quickly.
- Make more efficient use of various categories of health staff.

The following example is concerned with the differential diagnosis of patients presenting with a cough by a person with limited training. The intention is that by the use of a few discriminating criteria, such as presence of fever, length of time the person has had the cough, etc., the health worker will be able to identify those patients he can treat and those requiring referral to more highly trained health workers (Fig. 8.11).

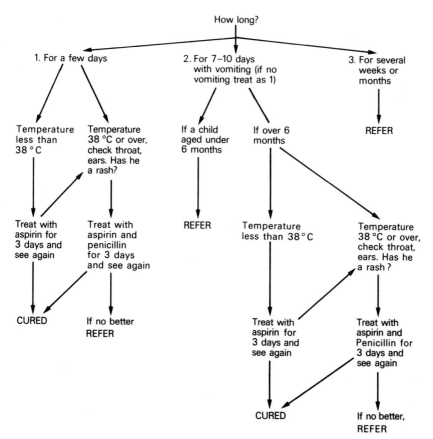

Fig. 8.11. Person with a cough—an example of a flow chart for a health worker with little training.

Treatment of three important diseases is now briefly discussed.

Tuberculosis

Where it is reasonably certain that there is some chance of continuing anti-tuberculosis treatment, then case finding by sputum examination should be instituted for all people with a chronic productive cough of over four weeks duration. Every effort should be made to adhere to the locally agreed standard treatment regimens. These are largely determined by the availability of drugs and the capacity of the health system to provide drugs on a continuing basis. The drugs in standard regimens are isoniazid, thiacetazone, and streptomycin. The minimum duration of treatment is one year, which should not be interrupted, including the initial intensive phase of daily chemotherapy for one to three months. The alternative regimes are shown in Table 8.2.

Table 8.2. *Standard treatments for tuberculosis*

Initial intensive 1–3 months		Continuation up to 12 months	
Drugs	Administration	Drugs	Administration
Isoniazid + streptomycin + thiacetazone	daily	(i) Isoniazid and streptomycin *or*	twice weekly
		(ii) Isoniazid and thiacetazone	daily

Drug	Daily dose for body weight		Twice weekly dose
	less than 50 kg	more than 50 kg	
Isoniazid	300 mg	450 mg	600–900 mg
Streptomycin by intramuscular injection	0.75 g	1.0 g	1.0 g
Thiacetazone	150 mg	150 mg	—

In refugee situations where the chances of achieving regular treatment of patients with tuberculosis for at least one year are unlikely, consideration should be given to short-term chemotherapy with rifampicin, which has special sterilizing properties. Trials have shown that rifampicin with isoniazid alone or together with streptomycin for a period of six months can produce a cure without relapse in about 95 per cent of cases.

The major problem with rifampicin is its cost. Regimens including it, even if only lasting half as long as usual standard courses, cost about ten times more per course. However, a high proportion of patients are cured within the first three months of treatment, which makes it an attractive alternative treatment for refugees.

Table 8.3. *Short-course   tuberculosis   chemotherapy   regimens   including*
rifampicin

Regimen	Drugs	Administration	Duration (months)
1.	Streptomycin plus isoniazid plus rifampicin	daily	6
2.	Isoniazid plus rifampicin	daily	6
Dosage:	Streptomycin 1 g daily intramuscularly, isoniazid 300 mg daily, rifampicin 450 mg daily for patients weighing 50 kg and less, 600 mg to those weighing more than 50 kg		

Ensuring continuous drug taking is the most common management problem. Practical as well as cultural and social factors play a role in this. For example, a programme in the Sudan designed to promote self-sufficiency in food particularly affected patients with tuberculosis. If they stayed in the camp to receive treatment they were unable to work for local farmers and, therefore, had no alternative method of feeding themselves, as food was given only on a 'food for work' basis.

Malaria

It is difficult to recommend a standard treatment for malaria because:

● In some countries there is resistance to certain drugs, particularly chloroquine (see Table 8.4).
● In people who are partially immune to malaria, an attack can be controlled by a shortened treatment regimen.

Wherever possible treatment schedules should be in line with those advocated by the local authorities, but modified to take account of malaria infections common in the area from which the refugees have come.

Table 8.4. *Areas with chloroquine-resistand* Plasmodium falciparum, *1985*

Central and South America	Bolivia, Brazil, Colombia, Ecuador, French Guiana, Guyana, Panama, Peru, Surinam, Venezuela
Asia	Bangladesh (north and east), Burma, China (Hainan Island and southern provinces), India (NE especially Assam), Indonesia (Kalimantan, Irian Jaya), Java, Sumatra, Sulawesi, Kampuchea, Laos, Malaysia (peninsular, and Sabah and Sarawak), Nepal, Pakistan, Philippines, Thailand, Vietnam
Oceania	Papua New Guinea, Solomon Islands (West)
Africa	Burundi, Kenya, Madagascar, Rwanda, Sudan, Tanzania, Uganda, Zaire, Zambia, Zanzibar, and isolated reports in Angola, Gabon, Malawi, and Namibia (Ovamboland and Caprivi Strip)

Ross Institute (1981).

Treatment in areas with chloroquine-sensitive P. falciparum malaria—The most commonly advocated oral treatment of moderately severe infections in adults of average weight (70 kg) is as follows:

Day 1: chloroquine base, 600 mg immediately, followed six hours later by chloroquine base, 300 mg.
Day 2: chloroquine base, 300 mg.
Day 3: chloroquine base, 300 mg.
1 tablet of chloroquine normally contains 150 mg of chloroquine.

Table 8.5. *Doses of anti-malarials for children (when weight and age are both available, weight is preferable)*

Dose in relation to adult dose	Age range (years)	Weight range (kg)
One-quarter	<1	<5
One-half	1–5	5–20
Three-quarters	6–12	20–40
Adult dose	>12	>40

This may be applied to all anti-malarials for prophylaxis.

P. falciparum infection can usually be prevented from recurring by taking 300 mg of chloroquine once a week for four weeks. This is not true for the other three forms of malaria.

In severe infections where patients have such complications as involvement of the central nervous system, anaemia, very high fever, dehydration, or cardiovascular, gastro-intestinal, renal, or liver symptoms, treatment must be started rapidly. In such cases anti-malarial drugs should be given by intra-muscular or intravenous injection, chloroquine or quinine being the best for this purpose. If they are given by intravenous injection great caution should be exercised and they should be given in very diluted form by a doctor or senior nurse. For intra-muscular injections, chloroquine 2.5 mg/kg per dose in two injections separated by six to twelve hours and a total dose of 20 mg/kg should be used. If a pregnant woman has malaria she should receive chloroquine treatment, as malaria will do more harm to both the woman and foetus than the drug.

In children oral treatment is preferable as intra-muscular and intravenous injections of anti-malarial drugs can be fatal. Chloroquine syrup and tablets do not have a pleasant taste. Some cases of poor response to treatment may be attributed to poor drug taking.

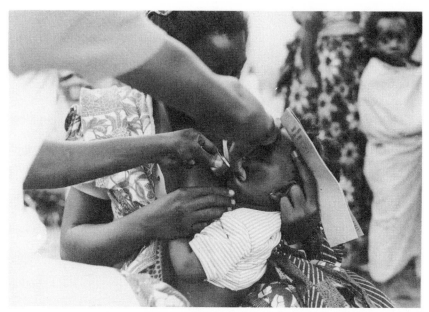

Fig. 8.12. Care must be taken to ensure that children take the full amount of the oral dose required. Firm handling may be necessary.

Shortened treatment regimen—Give one dose of chloroquine by mouth:

- adults, 4 tablets (600 mg base)
- children over 22 kg, 3 tablets (450 mg base)
- children between 15 and 22 kg, 2 tablets (300 mg of base)
- children between 10 and 15 kg, $1\frac{1}{2}$ tablets (225 mg of base)
- babies between 7 and 10 kg, 1 tablet (150 mg of base)
- babies under 7 kg, $\frac{1}{2}$ a tablet (75 mg of base)

Treatment in areas with chloroquine-resistant P. falciparum *malaria*—The combination of pyrimethamine (25 mg) and sulfadoxine (500 mg) in a single tablet (Fansidar) has been the treatment of choice for uncomplicated infections where *P. falciparum* is resistant to chloroquine. Two to three tablets in a single dose have been reported to cure 80–90 per cent of such adult cases. However, more recently Fansidar resistance has also been reported in certain places, including refugee camps in Thailand. Here the addition of quinine to Fansidar treatment did not improve the overall cure rate. Tetracycline given for ten days in combination with quinine cured all patients (quinine sulphate given orally three times daily and tetracycline 250 mg four times a day for ten days).

Treatment of intestinal helminths

Intestinal helminth infestations, particularly ascaris (roundworm) and hookworm, are likely to be common causes of morbidity in refugee camps, especially among children. Ascaris infestation in young children can be severe enough to cause secondary malnutrition. In view of the usual high prevalence of ascariasis it is often considered reasonable to treat all under-nourished children with piperazine, 2 g immediately, and on a regular monthly or three monthly basis. When infestation with other helminths is clinically suspected, it is usual to give a broad-spectrum anthelmentic, such as mebendazole. This is effective against *Trichuris trichura*, *Ancylostoma duodenale*, and *Necator americanus* in addition to ascariasis. The usual paediatric dose is 500 mg twice a day for two days and for adults 1.5 g twice daily for two days. Where other intestinal helminths are suspected or the patient has not responded to treatment with mebendazole, it is suggested that laboratory examination of a stool specimen be carried out.

PROVISION OF DRUGS

If efficient use is to be made of a hierarchy of treatment levels decisions must be taken on the provision of a continuous supply of drugs for each level. When the disease pattern has been obtained from analysing outpatient attendances and decisions taken over their appropriate treatment, standard drug regimens should be agreed upon.

The World Health Organization has prepared a list of 200 essential drugs. This listing should be used as a basis to decide which drugs should be available; large quantities of a few varieties are far more useful than a wide variety of drugs in small quantities. A standardized re-ordering form is also useful. Guidelines are given in Appendix 2 for the types and quantities of drugs likely to be required for a community of 10 000 refugees over a three month period, or 30 000 refugees for one month, at two levels:

• Community health centre.
• Senior nurse or doctor.

Figure 8.13 is an example of a possible visual aid to explain to patients when to take drugs. The symbols may have to be changed to suit the particular community.

PATIENT REFERRAL

A frequent complaint from doctors working at national hospitals within reach of a refugee community is that they are inundated daily with large numbers of refugees suffering from common symptoms and diseases that do not require hospital attention. Their own limited resources are stretched and local people have to compete for a place in long queues. A common reason

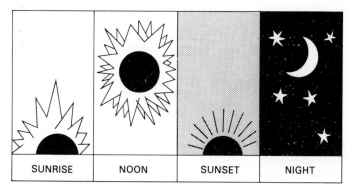

Fig. 8.13. Visual explanation of when to take drugs.

for refugees seeking help outside their own community is that the services provided at the refugees' clinic are not acceptable to the community. This may be due to insufficient appropriate drugs, lack of qualified staff, or poor quality of care. If the situation is reversed so that the majority of refugees are treated in the community for the most common problems, then only a small proportion will need referral for most specialist attention.

One way to further limit the number of refugees who may continue to turn up at the hospital is to come to an arrangement with the hospital authorities whereby only those patients with a signed letter of referral from the refugee clinic staff will be seen; the hospital for their part agreeing that those patients who do arrive with such a letter will be seen promptly. This helps to make the system reasonably efficient, effective, and reassuring for the clinic staff who have recognized that the patient needs more sophisticated care, and for the patient who knows that having made the journey he is not going to have to sit for hours awaiting attention. All this can only be resolved following discussions with the community chief and administrators, so that they fully understand the need for such restrictive action and can explain the need for it to the rest of the community.

The other main problems associated with referral systems from a refugee community are:

- transport
- distance and time
- cost
- communication

Transport

Often the question here is not 'which' vehicle to use as an ambulance but whether the community has even one vehicle which can be used at any time for emergencies. If not, then some arrangement will need to be reached with local government or a commercial company. Transport of patients back from a stay in hospital may also present problems. For non-emergency cases, consider using public transport, commercial vehicles, or horses, mules, camels, or rickshaws. Air transport is expensive and can rarely be justified.

Time and distance

Never underestimate the time needed to transport a sick patient. It is far better to send an 'at risk' pregnant woman to hospital a few days before her expected date of delivery than risk waiting until the onset of labour. Damage to roads and tracks may be permanent due to pot-holes, sand dunes, or mines etc., or temporary, due to flooding in the rainy season. Curfews also need to be remembered, for in some countries these may be strictly enforced for as long as 12 hours.

Cost

Cost can be considered in terms of the costs of the referral to the patient, to the relatives, and to the hospital. If public or commercial transport is to be used, can the patient afford the fare? How will the relatives afford to live in the urban environment in which hospitals are invariably found? Will it be necessary to build self-care huts in the hospital compound in which both patients and relatives can live? How much will it cost the relatives to travel to and from the refugee community to collect their rations of food and other supplies? Is the extra number of refugees being treated in the hospital causing an unprecedented rise in the cost of running the hospital, due to the use of drugs, dressings, and operating facilities.

It may be necessary to consider separate grants to cover some or all of these costs. Instead of attempting, for example, to supply a hospital with all the drugs and equipment that are being used in the care of refugees, it may be simpler to give a grant to the hospital authorities to cover these expenses, or consider donating the kit of drugs described in Appendix 2.

Communication

The system is liable to break down if at any time the hospital feels that the refugee clinic staff are sending insufficient information with each patient or too many patients, or if the refugee community staff feel their patients are not receiving prompt attention at the hospital. As a policy, drugs prescribed outside the refugee camp should be available from the refugee standard drug supply if continued treatment is required, or they must be supplied with the initial prescription in sufficient quantity.

Referral between different levels and types of health workers in a refugee community is equally important. For example, refugees trained as community health workers should be able to refer health and disease problems outside their level of competence and be confident that their request for assistance will receive prompt attention.

LABORATORY SERVICE

Communicable disease surveillance and control are probably the most important community health measures that benefit from a laboratory service. It is also useful for improving the quality of differential diagnosis. Why not use the nearest national laboratory facilities? This is the best approach if the refugee community is small (e.g. 2–3000), the nearest accessible facilities are efficient and can cope with the extra demand from the refugees. Unfortunately this is rarely possible. Refugee communities are often anywhere between 10 and 50 000 and the nearest national facilities may have barely enough personnel and resources for the local needs. Nevertheless, arrangements should be made whereby 'problem' patients can be referred for more accurate and precise investigations than may be possible within the limits of a basic service.

Investigations

In the early life of a community it is very helpful to be able to confirm or discount the presence of malaria and anaemia through laboratory techniques, since appropriate interventions can then be quickly implemented. As the community becomes established, the facilities needed will depend on the capabilities of the technical staff, the resources available, the incidence of symptoms and diseases and, most importantly, the possible interventions. The minimum investigations required are usually:

- Examination of blood-slides for malaria infection.
- Estimation of haemoglobin level.
- Zeihl–Neelsen staining of sputa for tuberculosis bacilli.

Other possible laboratory investigations include those for leprosy, schistosomiasis, trypanosomiasis, leishmaniasis, filariasis, onchocerciasis, intestinal parasites, urine specimens, urethral smear, and blood white cell count. Blood grouping and cross-matching may be an urgent requirement where war injuries are serious and have to be dealt within the refugee community.

Facilities and equipment

A quiet corner in the clinic or health centre, with a table or bench and a good source of light are the main facilities required. In some circumstances it may even be more convenient to do the work outside. Minimum equipment should include a simple but robust microscope, a hand centrifuge, and adequate quantities of slides, overslips, stains, and specimen containers (Appendix 2). The availability of electricity (rare) will determine the type of

Fig. 8.14. Health worker doing stool microscopy during an MCH clinic.

equipment needed. Other requirements will depend on the specific techniques used.

A record book should be routinely kept of the names of the refugees, where they live, the investigations, and results. The results should be compiled weekly and compared with previous weeks. Staff should question and discuss with the senior nurse or doctor any increases in diseases. Local governments may routinely require to be informed of certain communicable diseases. A monthly standard form for re-ordering equipment may also be useful. The handling and transportation of specimens both within the health centre and to the nearest national laboratory should be undertaken with due care and attention, to minimize the risk of spread of infections such as hepatitis B., cholera, and Lassa fever.

Some essential points

Malaria and other blood parasites

• Thick and thin blood smears are prepared from patients suspected of having malaria, thick films for establishing the presence of parasites, thin films for parasite morphology and species identification.

• Capillary blood is obtained from a finger or an ear lobe, except in an infant, when preference is for the heel or big toe.

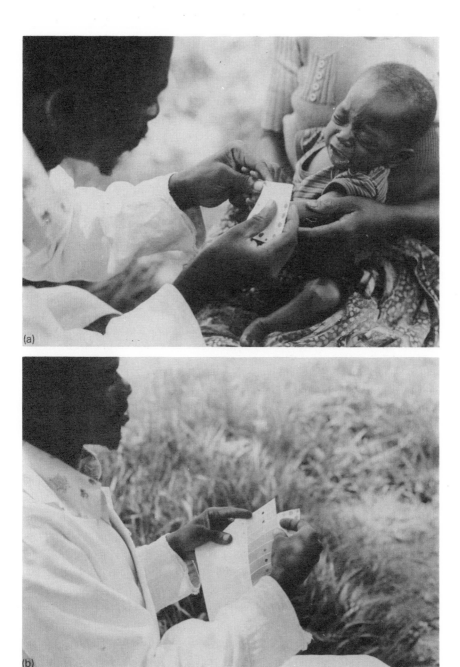

Fig. 8.15. (a and b) A pin prick of blood is absorbed on to blotting paper and the colour visually compared with a chart showing levels of anaemia. This technique is only useful for detecting severe anaemia.

• All smears should be labelled with the patient's name and/or number using a diamond marker or a wax crayon, or in the case of a thin smear, the name can be written on the slide with a lead pencil.

Intestinal parasites

• To identify parasites in faeces, one of two methods can be used: direct examination or a concentration technique. Usually, concentration methods are preferred because low numbers of parasite eggs or cysts may not be seen when using the direct method. Eggs of parasitic worms are relatively large and are usually easily recognized. Protozoa cysts are smaller and require much more skill to find and identify.

Tubercle and other acid-fast bacilli

• Make sure that the specimen is sputum and not saliva.
• Specimens can travel days in sterile containers and they can then be cultured for tubercle bacilli by laboratories at the main centres.

Haemoglobin estimation

• For routine haemoglobin estimations consideration should be given to using indirect techniques, such as colorimetry or visual comparison.
• For blood transfusions look for donors among the refugee's relatives. If the patient is in a national hospital do not assume the local authority has access to a plentiful blood bank!

9 Education

Training of refugee health workers

A training programme for refugee community health workers is an essential part of the community health approach advocated by this book. Such a programme would have the following advantages:

- Trained refugees can become invaluable members of the health team, acting as intermediaries between the people and the health services.
- Being from the community itself these trained refugees are far more likely to understand the cultural and behavioural circumstances contributing to ill health in the camps.
- They can help the health care programme be less dependent on national and international health staff, and thereby promote the refugees' capacity for self-care.
- They can ease the workload of the professional health workers.
- By being responsible for a defined number of households, or sections in the camp, they are invaluable for community-based health activities.

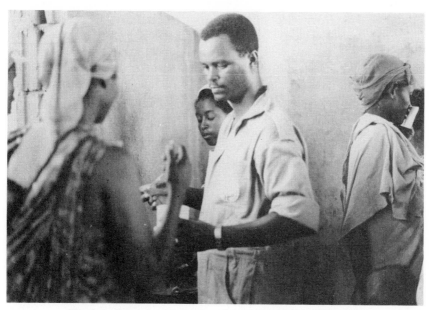

Fig. 9.1. Every health worker should be a health educator.

• The programme can provide some refugees with health skills they can utilize if they are repatriated or resettled.
• It will help alleviate the low level of activity and resulting boredom encountered in camps.

ISSUES INVOLVED

Much has been written on the training of auxiliary health personnel for national programmes, including village and community health workers. Many of the issues in the literature are relevant to refugee camps and are extremely useful background reading. The following points cover some of the issues that make training programmes in camps particularly different from national programmes.

The government's attitude

The host government's attitude to the refugees will greatly influence how easy or difficult it will be to implement such a training programme. Many governments will welcome the idea as a positive means to restore refugee dignity and self-respect, because it lessens the dependency on external agencies.

Some governments may only allow a programme that trains the refugees in a few basic skills, because fewer international health teams may mean less international publicity and less foreign currency. A few governments may be against training as it can imply some sort of permanence, when they want the refugees to be repatriated to a country of asylum as soon as possible. Training refugees may also imply that they will become more political and voice their dissatisfaction as they recognize their needs, inequalities, and exploitation. Governments may see this social change as a possible threat.

In Asia another factor to consider is the possibility of repatriation to a third country of asylum. Few refugees in Africa ask for such repatriation and so the people trained are likely to stay, although there may be pressure (from families) to set up in private practice. Recent experience from Thailand showed that Kampucheans and Laotians who received training in the health sector were more acceptable to the third country immigration officials.

What type of training programme?

This will depend on the level(s) of health worker to be trained. There are usually only two types of training programmes that it is possible to undertake in a camp:

• In-service training of those refugees already qualified as health workers, to meet the new circumstances.
• Training refugees with no previous experience in the health sector as primary health care workers.

In-service training for qualified staff requires little formal organization and is probably best done through regular discussions and by each national or international health worker working with one or two refugee counterparts. The training of traditional midwives may also fall into this category.

Organizing a community health worker training scheme will take a lot more thought, preparation, and effort. It will need at least one, maybe two, persons to give it their full-time attention, at a time when there will be great demand for their professional skills. Training programmes need to be standardized between different staff and also between camps.

How will the unskilled refugees be chosen?

There may be no shortage of refugees offering to be trained, as they are keen to get additional training and language skills. How to choose the best ones? In national development programmes it is common for the community to choose the candidates. Unfortunately many 'communities' may have been broken up by their flight to freedom and are therefore unable to decide who should sit on a health committee or how to select the trainees. Outsiders to the community find it all too easy to choose the wrong people for the wrong reasons.

The ratio of male to female workers will depend on the local factors, as some tasks need more females than males and vice versa. One worker for evey 50–100 families is a ratio for community programmes such as health visiting.

Literate or not?

Illiterate people can provide a useful service to their community. Older more mature people may not have had the opportunity to go to school, but if they are respected by the community, they are far more likely to be accepted as a health worker and stay with their community than someone who is young and educated. This is particularly so among refugees, as the young tend to seek higher educational opportunities, employment outside the camp, or are favoured for resettlement. However, different training is needed for illiterate trainees; it should be based on oral and visual methods and practical situations.

Incentives

Remuneration is one of the most controversial issues. Many governments feel that since refugees already receive substantial amounts of aid they should not expect to receive any payment for their work. Moreover, who will guarantee the money required for all the camps? Practical experience shows that few refugees will continue to work on a regular basis without some sort of financial incentive.

Sometimes the workers are given extra food from the general feeding programme supplies. A community decision is needed though it may be difficult to obtain for reasons already mentioned. Also the food supplies may not always be sufficient. Special supplies of food may be earmarked for 'food for work' programmes by governments or agencies.

What skills?

The workers may lose credibility with the community if they have no special skills but only a superficial knowledge of a variety of topics. In a camp this may result in the refugees placing increased demands on the curative health facilities whilst the environmental health and nutrition problems go unresolved. There are three possible areas to consider:

• What the health workers need to know.
• What it would be useful to know.
• What it would be nice to know.

One of the most important skills to teach is how to communicate.

OUTLINE OF A POSSIBLE PROGRAMME

The national doctor at district level with overall responsibility for the health programme in the camp should assume ultimate responsibility for the training course.

Fig. 9.2. Working with the refugees on all aspects of the activities is an essential part of training.

The emphasis should be on learning by doing, and opportunity should be given for:

• Regular meetings to discuss problems encountered, whether these are technical, administrative, or personal.
• A continuous educational process.
• Regular guidance on all professional matters.

Areas and division of work

The responsibility of a refugee trained as a community health worker in a camp is for the individual and community health of a well defined area of the camp. The health worker is usually under the direct supervision of the qualified refugee or national nurses.

There are at least three main areas of work:

• Health centre.
• Feeding programmes.
• Environmental health.

The total number of refugees to be trained should, therefore, be divided by the number of main areas of work and the relevant training given to each group of refugees. The workers should be responsible for the area of the camp in which they live. This area should have about 50, but not more than 100, families.

Place and type of training

The refugees should be trained in the camp and become proficient in one main area of work before perhaps rotating to the next. The emphasis should be on a very practical training.

Period of training

Two weeks, intensive practical with some theoretical work, followed by at least six weeks, possibly as long as three months, 'learning by doing', for each main area of work.

Recognition of training

A certificate may be given, endorsed by the host government, but it should not guarantee employment outside the camp. Sometimes having a uniform and/or name badge helps establish credibility.

Responsibilities, duties, and limitations

These will vary according to the area of work in which the refugee is involved and circumstances peculiar to each camp, but must be clearly defined. Limitations might include such things as being forbidden to prescribe drugs and give intravenous injections. Whether refugee health workers prescribe drugs or not can cause a lot of debate. The workers' capability is not usually in question, but it has been recognized that there are, or will be, undue pressures on them to sell the drugs and/or set up in private practice.

Possible tasks and, therefore, objectives

At the end of the training period in each area of work the health worker should be capable of performing tasks such as the following, which are examples of the possible priority tasks in a refugee community. They should know how to refer all other problems to a more qualified auxiliary nurse or doctor.

Health centre activities

● Direct an orderly flow of patients through a clinic, help the nurse/doctor examine a patient, and ensure that all treatments are given.
● Assist in the administration of drugs, the maintenance of clean equipment, and the safe disposal of used syringes and needles.
● Undertake basic first aid for burns and accidents.
● Clean a wound, apply a clean dressing, and dispose of infected material.
● Prepare for and assist at a normal delivery. Know what to recognize as normal and abnormal.
● Help where necessary on disease control and other special programmes based at the clinic, especially the follow-up of defaulters.
● Collect and transport laboratory specimens.
● Encourage families to use all available facilities, especially the preventive ones like MCH and immunization.
● Promote personal domestic and food hygiene.
● Teach about oral rehydration therapy and the use of oral rehydration solutions.
● Report births and deaths in a defined area of the camp.
● Help collect and interpret information collected.
● Follow up through a home visiting programme 'at risk' children and adults who attend the clinic with malnutrition and diarrhoea.

Nutrition

● Assist in the equitable distribution of general food supplies.
● Teach families in the community how to make best use of the relief foods, and how to store and prepare the food hygienically.
● Identify those members of the community nutritionally 'at risk'.
● Act as nutritional 'scouts' in the community, ensuring that no cases of marasmus or kwashiorkor go undetected.
● Help the other members of the health team plan and implement nutrition surveys.

- Organize and run a supplementary feeding programme.
- Help run a therapeutic feeding programme.
- Help collect and interpret nutrition information collected.

Environmental health

- Ensure a high day to day standard of general hygiene in the camp.
- Promote personal, domestic, and food hygiene.
- Know where the safest areas for indiscriminate defaecation are and ensure the community uses those areas.
- Teach mothers and older children how to safely dispose of the faeces of young children.
- Know the safest distance from water to build latrines and refuse pits.
- Be able to teach the community about latrine siting, design, hygiene, and maintenance.
- Be able to dig a refuse pit and advise the community how to use it.
- Ensure the source of water is not being excessively polluted.
- Ensure there are no potential or actual mosquito breeding sites in the area.
- Ensure no undue risks exist and maintain simple means for extinguishing fires.
- Help organize and run a simple soap-making industry.
- Help collect and interpret information.

Assessment

In order to check that health workers can do the task they have been taught reasonably well, it is necessary to assess their ability. This assessment acts as:

- A guide to the refugee health workers about which topics or skills they need to learn more.
- A guide to the teacher about which parts of the training course have been successful and which parts need to be improved.

It is necessary to decide who will do the assessing, when it will be done, what method(s) will be used, and what kinds of questions will be asked. Ensure that the assessment tests the most important skills and abilities. Frequent in-course practical assessments may be a more reliable test than one final exam, especially for those refugees who are illiterate. Self-assessment, where the health worker can compare his own work with a correct answer, is extremely useful for literate people.

Health education

Health workers in refugee communities may not see immediate results from health education. It needs time to encourage members of the refugee community and local staff to change certain harmful practices and to convey the message to the rest of the community.

During the initial assessment and subsequent discussions and work you will gradually learn about:

- Health beliefs and practices in the community.
- Important health and disease problems.
- Possible links between the main problems and the way in which people live and any local customs or practices which may be harmful.
- Personal and community measures that could help reduce sickness rates.
- At risk groups within the community.
- Which refugees to talk to about health care issues.

With this knowledge members of the health team and community leaders can decide on the important topics for health education and the most effective ways of communicating the information.

WHAT TOPICS?

These should be based on the priority health and disease problems in the community and, to a lesser extent, taking into consideration the health education priorities of the host government. Some problems may be more difficult to deal with than others because of cultural factors. Initially it may be best to start by dealing with those problems most amenable to change. The following are a few examples of topics important in camps:

Information

- What supplies and services are available, from where, how often etc?

Community hygiene

- The value of camp clean-up campaigns.

Personal hygiene

- The need for regular bathing and hand washing.

Nutrition

- How best to use the relief foods.
- The promotion of breast-feeding.

Health services

- The value of immunization and the need to attend for all doses despite possible side effects.
- The need to continue drinking and eating when ill.
- The need to take all tablets prescribed.
- The need to report births and deaths.

Sanitation

How to dispose of faeces and wastes safely and why this is necessary.

Accidents

• Why cars and lorries are dangerous and why children should not chase them or play near roads.

It is important to remember that community health education can be an essential component in support of administrative rules and regulations covering camp hygiene and environmental health. Opportunities to explain why these rules and regulations are necessary should be taken at public meetings and at discussion groups.

TO WHOM?

Some topics, such as immunization campaigns or safe areas for defaecation, may be of concern to the whole community. Other topics may be of particular relevance to certain 'at risk' members of the community, e.g. the use of feeding bottles or the feeding practices of mothers whose children are suffering from diarrhoea.

HOW?

In many societies the best method of carrying out health education is by talking with individuals in small groups for a short period of time. This requires no teaching materials, encourages an informal two-way exchange of knowledge, and allows for caring, respect, and concern. Other very effective means of communication are story telling, role-playing demonstrations, and 'learning by doing'. Methods requiring a higher level of technology such as posters, flip charts, and slide shows are dependent on regular supplies of chalk, pens, paper, batteries, electricity, etc. They can also be confusing. A picture of a mosquito enlarged ten times may mean nothing to an audience as they claim never to have seen such a large insect! Equally, a picture of a woman in a short dress standing outside a western-style house will cause many women to 'switch off', as the message is irrelevant to their own circumstances. Appropriate visual aids depend on a clear understanding of the social and psychological environment. Agricultural techniques and the value and use of nutritious foods can often be taught by encouraging families and schools to grow gardens. Some of the foods grown can be stored for use as supplementary food during the wet season, e.g. a handful of peanuts would provide about 300 kcal (see also School health in section on Family health care).

WHERE AND HOW MUCH?

Every opportunity should be taken to put across health education messages both informally—when walking around the community, at water collection

Fig. 9.3. Teaching and learning about new foods.

Fig. 9.4. Health education session using a flip chart.

Fig. 9.5. Educating parents about the Road to Health chart.

points—or during the more formal atmosphere of a clinic, special feeding centre, or general aid distribution point—or during local and administrative meetings. Each culture will also have meeting places such as churches, temples, or Koranic schools, and perhaps agricultural, health, and women's development committees. As long as the place is easily accessible and acceptable to the community almost anywhere will be suitable.

Short sessions held regularly will be more acceptable than long sessions at irregular intervals. Health education sessions should not last longer than ten to fifteen minutes. One of the main complaints from women attending nutrition demonstrations is that the sessions usually take far too long. In a refugee community women have many competing demands on their time so health messages should be concise and relevant.

BY WHOM?

Members of the refugee community such as the traditional doctors and midwives, tribal chiefs, elders, political and religious leaders, interpreters, and professionally trained people such as teachers, or health staff, usually make the best health educators. Local political leaders are helpful for reinforcing messages such as environmental health, or the danger of road accidents, or security near the border. If you can speak the local language do not make the mistake of over-simplifying a message and treating your audience as if they were children.

10 International health workers

Personal health care for international staff

Disaster situations, especially in the tropics and subtropics, are obviously potential personal health hazards. There is no way in which the maintenance of health can be guaranteed, but certain steps can be taken to minimize the risks. The commonest illnesses are probably hepatitis and diarrhoea. The commonest cause of death is road traffic accidents.

Measures before departure
- Immunization schedule.
- Dental check.
- Start malaria prophylaxis.

Measures on site
- Continue malaria prophylaxis.
- Reinforcement of immunizations, if residence is long-term.
- Attention to personal hygiene.

Measures after return
- Continue malaria prophylaxis.
- Monitor personal health and report untoward symptoms immediately.

IMMUNIZATION SCHEDULE

The following immunizations may be considered routine, though not all are required for any given location. Smallpox vaccination is no longer necessary. (See also Immunization, p. 148–9.)

- Yellow fever
- Cholera
- Typhoid
- Tetanus
- Poliomyelitis
- Hepatitis A
- Rabies

Acute illness, pregnancy, and immuno-suppressive drugs should be regarded as potential contra-indications to immunization procedures.

Yellow fever

This is required for most of sub-Saharan Africa and for Central and South America, including parts of the Caribbean. One injection only is required. The international certificate becomes valid after ten days and lasts for ten years. A reinforcing dose is required every ten years. Side effects are few, but the usual contra-indications apply. People sensitive to egg protein should not have this vaccine.

Typhoid

Two injections of the monovalent vaccine should be taken at an interval of six weeks. Immunity is acquired six days after the first injection. Reinforcement should be by a single dose yearly. This vaccine is not 100 per cent effective, but if vaccinated persons become ill with typhoid they are likely to have a milder illness.

Cholera

This vaccine only gives around 50 per cent protection and only for about four months. It should be taken, however, as some protection is better than none. It is unnecessary for Central and South America but recommended for Africa and Asia. Two doses should be taken at an interval of six weeks for the primary course. Thereafter it should be reinforced by single doses at intervals of four-to-five months. Side effects are few. Validity of the international certificate commences six days after the first injection and lasts for six months.

Tetanus

Two injections of tetanus toxoid should be taken at an interval of six weeks, and a third dose after six to twelve months. Immunity commences a few days after the second injection and lasts one year. After the third injection immunity lasts for five years. Reinforcement should be by a single dose every five years. If a seriously contaminated wound or a deep puncture wound be sustained, it is appropriate to have a reinforcing dose of toxoid. The immunized person should never have anti-tetanus serum (ATS), which often gives rise to serious reactions.

Poliomyelitis

Three doses of the oral (Sabin) vaccine are required for primary inoculation—two at an interval of six to eight weeks and a third six to twelve months later. For those who have had a primary course, a reinforcing dose is advised at five yearly intervals.

Hepatitis A

This is the common hepatitis virus and a major cause of ill-health among international workers. Considerable passive protection can be had by having an injection of human immune globulin (gammaglobulin). This gives protection for four to six months. If possible, the injection should be repeated at six monthly intervals. It may also be possible to arrange to have a blood test to determine whether you have hepatitis A antibodies and if you have, then this inoculation is unnecessary. The inoculation should not be given within three weeks of any other, to avoid its neutralizing effect (a hepatitis B vaccine may become available in the near future).

Rabies

Two doses of the prophylactic rabies vaccine are given at an interval of four weeks, followed by another dose 12 months later. Reinforcing doses are given at intervals of two to three years, depending on the degree of exposure.

Bubonic plague

In areas where plague is known to be endemic, e.g. Vietnam, and for people at special risk, e.g. zoologists on field expeditions, plague vaccine exists and may be used. It gives rise to considerable, though temporary, side effects. Two injections at an interval of six weeks should be given, and then reinforcing single doses every six months while the individual is at risk.

Typhus

There is only a vaccine for louse-borne or epidemic typhus. This is now a rare disease, except in Ethiopia and Zaire, but might appear in refugee situations where people are crowded in unsanitary conditions. Two injections are given at an interval of four months. A single annual reinforcing dose is advised as long as the individual is at risk.

MALARIA PROPHYLAXIS

In countries where malaria is endemic, it is mandatory to take a prophylactic drug (see Table 10.1). It is not always easy to decide which prophylactic to take, because of the development of drug resistance by the malaria parasite in various areas. It is best to seek expert advice about the particular area to which you are going.

In the absence of expert advice, consider whether the area concerned is an area of known chloroquine-resistant strains of *Plasmodium falciparum* or not (see Chapter 8, Table 8.4).

If the area is one in which chloroquine resistance is known, Maloprim or Fansidar are the drugs of choice. If the area is not known to be chloroquine-resistant, proguanil or chloroquine may be used (Table 10.2).

Table 10.1. *Countries with a malaria risk in some part*

Afghanistan	Guinea	Papua New Guinea
Algeria	Guinea-Bissau	Paraguay
Angola	Guyana	Peru
Argentina	Haiti	Philippines
Bahrain	Honduras	Qatar
Bangladesh	India	Rwanda
Belize	Indonesia	Sao Tome and Principe
Benin	Iran	Saudi Arabia
Bhutan	Iraq	Senegal
Bolivia	Ivory Coast	Sierra Leone
Botswana	Jordan	Solomon Islands
Brazil	Kampuchea	Somalia
Burma	Kenya	South Africa
Burundi	Korea, Republic of (South)	Sri Lanka
Cameroon	Lao People's Democratic	Sudan
Cape Verde	Republic	Surinam
Central African Republic	Liberia	Swaziland
Chad	Libyan Arab Jamahiriya	Syrian Arab Republic
China, People's Republic of	Madagascar	Tanzania, United Republic of
Colombia	Malawi	Thailand
Comoros	Malaysia	Togo
Congo	Maldives	Tunisia
Costa Rica	Mali	Turkey
Djibouti	Mauritania	Uganda
Dominican Republic	Mauritius	United Arab Emirates
East Timor	Mexico	Upper Volta
Ecuador	Morocco	Vanuatu (formerly New
Egypt	Mozambique	Hebrides)
El Salvador	Namibia	Venezuela
Equatorial Guinea	Nepal	Vietnam
Ethiopia	Nicaragua	Yemen
French Guiana	Niger	Yemen, Democratic
Gabon	Nigeria	Zaire
Gambia	Oman	Zambia
Ghana	Pakistan	Zimbabwe
Guatemala	Panama	

Ross Institute (1981).

Maloprim and Fansidar are not recommended for children under five years, or during pregnancy. The other drugs are safe in doses recommended in pregnancy, and in infancy at suitable reduced dosage. Fansidar should not be given to persons allergic to sulphonamides.

It is important to realize that there is no regimen of malaria prophylaxis which can guarantee freedom from malaria. With every regimen there is the possibility of 'break-throughs', usually due to drug-resistant strains. It cannot, therefore, be stressed strongly enough that fever occurring during a period of residence overseas, or in the months following such a period, must be considered as potentially malarial until proved otherwise. It is very important to take some prophylactic and to take it before departing,

Table 10.2. *Recommended anti-malarials*

Name (non-proprietary where available)	Formulation of tablet	Adult prophylactic dose	Comments
(A) In areas of chloroquine-resistant P. falciparum			
Fansidar or	Pyrimethamine 25 mg Sulphadoxine 500 mg	One tablet weekly	In areas of high *P. vivax* exposure chloroquine as in (B) may be added
Maloprim	Pyrimethamine 12.5 mg Dapsone 100 mg	Usually one tablet weekly	
(B) In areas without chloroquine-resistance			
Chloroquine or	100 mg, 150 mg, or 300 mg of base	300 mg base weekly	Change drug after a few years. Alternative regimen: 100 mg daily, except Sunday.
Proguanil or	100 mg	100–200 mg daily	Resistance occurs. Otherwise very safe.
Pyrimethamine	25 mg	25 mg weekly	Resistance occurs. Tasteless.

From Ross Institute (1981).

continue with complete regularity in the field, and for at least four weeks on return to non-malaria countries.

Now that drug prophylaxis has become uncertain, it is very important to observe the rules of personal protection against malaria:

- Sleep under a mosquito net, if not in a screened room.
- Check the net frequently for holes.
- Wear long clothes and roll down sleeves at sunset.
- Use 'knock-down' insecticides in living rooms and bedrooms.
- Have residual insecticides sprayed on interior walls every six months.
- Use insect repellants if it is necessary to be out at night.
- Keep vegetation well trimmed down in the vicinity of where you are living.
- Keep the area around houses free from casual collections of water, e.g. in pots, tins, old tyres, etc.

PERSONAL DRUG KIT

It may be helpful to take small supplies of the following with you:

Anti-malarial:	Choice dependent on factors outlined above.
Analgesic:	Paracetamol 500 mg, tablets × 100, or Asprin.
Anti-allergic:	Chlorpheniramine 4 mg, tablets × 20.
Anti-infective:	Albucid 10% drops × 5 ml.
	Tetracycline hydrochloride 250 mg, capsules × 50.
	Metronidazole 200 mg tablets × 30.

Dental:	Oil of cloves.
Dermatological:	Autan (insect repellant) stick.
	Tineafax (anti-fungal) 25 g, tube.
	Sun screening lotion, e.g. Aquasun.
Disinfectant:	Savlon 60 g tube.
Gastro-intestinal:	Lomotil, 2.5 mg, tablets × 20, or Streptotriad.
Sedative:	Nitrazepan, 5 mg, tablets × 20.

Plus:
Water purifying tablets e.g. Puritabs.
Collapsible water carrier.
Lip salve.
Medium and small size pre-sterilized gauze squares.
Roll of adhesive tape.
Plasters, assorted sizes.
Packet of steri-strip (skin closures) 3 in. × 0.5 in.

Practical considerations for international staff

Working with a refugee community means a rare opportunity of being in circumstances quite different from anything at home or what the average tourist in the country will ever experience. Following perhaps a few days in the capital city you will usually be transported away from the well worn paths of other travellers.

In order to ensure that personal frustration, irritation, or disillusionment is kept to a minimum you must prepare yourself professionally and personally.

PROFESSIONAL PREPARATION

Professional standards must be maintained. There is no place or excuse for amateur work. This does not mean that you should not adapt your professional skills to suit the circumstances.

● Keep abreast of overseas news in the newspapers.
● Read some of the relevant standard textbooks on health care in developing countries and papers that have been written about health in refugee communities.
● Attend a training course on health care in the Third World and/or one specifically orientated towards demonstrating the usefulness of community health care in refugee communities.
● Once you know which country you are going to, try and obtain as much relevant information about that country and the one the refugees have fled from.
● Ensure that the employing organization gives a full briefing covering political, cultural, and social factors, the state of the refugees, and what the agency expects your role to be.
● Make sure you understand the policies and administrative procedures of the organization you will be working for.

• Check that the organization has made all the arrangements necessary for your work in the country, e.g. visa, accommodation, transport, work permits if necessary, essential equipment plus spares, and most importantly, that the organization has a support system that will ensure that your stay in the country goes as smoothly as possible.

• Ensure that the organization provides the necessary insurance to cover you in the event of illness, injury, or death. Make a will; it could save your relatives much distress.

• Ensure that your bank and account number is recorded for salary payments. Also details of your next of kin.

• Enquire if the organization will provide a clothing and book allowance, a personal drug kit, and pay for a reasonable amount of excess baggage on the outward journey.

• Confirm that your rent or mortgage payment is covered by standing order.

• Arrange for a friend to check your home regularly.

PERSONAL EQUIPMENT KIT

You can survive with little more than a change of clothes, a few basic toiletries and drugs, and some good books! To maintain standards however, it is worth taking more than you may need, including a few luxuries!

The following check-list is by no means exhaustive but is probably the minimum needed. Changes should be made according to personal preferences, climate, and cultural demands. Keep a list of everything packed. It may come in useful for customs, insurance, or your next trip.

• Tough, hard-framed suitcase preferably with wheels.
• Overnight bag with change of clothing, personal drugs, books, camera, films etc., maximum size 21 × 36 × 46 cm.
• Shoulder-bag with documents.
• Sleeping bag weighing about one kilogram.
• Cotton sleeping bag liner.
• Perhaps a small pillow and closed-cell sleeping pad.
• Personal drugs as outlined in 'Personal health care'.
• Passport plus at least ten spare passport photos.
• International driving licence.
• Money in travellers cheques plus some cash if possible.
• Camera and spare battery.
• Films in lead protection bag.
• Pocket calculator, solar powered or take spare batteries.
• Airmail letters, writing paper, envelopes, and a few stamps in case someone offers to post your mail when back in your own country.

- Map, guidebook, dictionary, phrasebook.
- Paperback books, textbooks.
- Loose-leaf notebook, ball point pens, pencils.
- Torch plus spare batteries and bulbs.
- Flat, squat candle, matches.
- Short-wave radio with or without cassette recorder/cassettes plus spare batteries.
- If electricity available, travelling iron and hairdryer plus adapters.
- Sewing kit.
- Pocket knife, e.g. Swiss army traveller.
- Teaspoon, tea-infuser.
- Two litre metal water flask, small water filter.
- Games, e.g. playing cards, scrabble, backgammon.
- Alarm clock.
- Sun glasses plus spare.
- Spare reading glasses and/or contact lenses plus fluid.
- Plastic bags for wet towel, dirty underwear, etc.

Toiletries

- Toothbrush, toothpaste, soap, shampoo, talcum powder, body lotion, deodorant, perfume, hand razor plus blades, shaving brush/soap/cream, tampons and/or sanitary pads.
- Tube of cream detergent.
- Face cleanser pads.
- Mirror.

Clothes

None of the clothes should, in any way, resemble military uniform. Cotton is preferable to artificial fibres for comfort.

- T-shirts, blouses, shirts.
- Underwear and socks.
- Dressing-gown/nightdress/pyjamas.
- Skirts, dresses, jeans, trousers.
- One smart dress or lightweight suit.
- Swimming suit or trunks.
- Scarf, sun hat.
- Light anorak plus thin wool sweater.
- Cheap thin towel.
- Tough sandals and walking shoes.

Appendix 1: References and bibliography

References

C. Aall (1970). Relief, nutrition and health problems in the Nigerian/Biafran War. *Journal of Tropical Paediatrics and Environmental Child Health* **16**, 70–90.

C. Aall (1979). Disastrous international relief failure: a report on Burmese refugees in Bangladesh from May to December 1978. *Disasters* **3**, 429–34.

P. M. Arnow, J. C. Hierholzer, J. Higbee, and D. H. Harris (1977). Acute hemorrhagic conjunctivitis: a mixed virus outbreak among Vietnamese refugees on Guam. *American Journal of Epidemiology* **105**, 68–73.

S. Belete, M. Gebre-Medhin, B. Hailemariam, M. Maffi, B. Vahlquist, and Z. Wolde-Gebriel (1977). Study of shelter population in the Wollo region. *Journal of Tropical Pediatrics and Environmental Child Health* **23**, 15–36.

F. J. Bennett, D. B. Jelliffe, E. F. P. Jelliffe, and M. Moffat (1968). The nutrition and disease pattern of children in a refugee settlement. *East African Medical Journal* **45**, 229–46.

U. Bollag (1980). Practical evaluation of a pilot immunization campaign against typhoid fever in a Cambodian refugee camp. *International Journal of Epidemiology* **9**, 121–2.

R. I. Glass, W. Cates, P. Nieburg, C. Davis, R. Russbach, H. Nothdurft, S. Peel, and R. Turnbull (1980). Rapid assessment of health status and preventive medicine needs of newly arrived Kampuchean refugees Sa-Kaeo, Thailand. *The Lancet* **1**, 868–72.

T. Johnson (1979). Eritrea refugees in Sudan. *Disasters* **3**, 417–21.

D. Mahalanabis, A. B. Choudhuri, N. G. Bacchi, A. K. Bhattacharya, and T. W. Simpson (1973). Oral fluid therapy of cholera among Bangladesh refugees. *The Johns Hopkins Medical Journal* **132**, 197–205.

D. Nabarro and S. McNabb (1980). A simple new technique for identifying thin children. *Journal of Tropical Medicine and Hygiene* **83**, 21–3.

Pakistan, Government of (1981). *Official Handbook on Refugee Management in Pakistan*. States and Frontier Regions Division, Government of Pakistan, Islamabad, 89 pp.

S. Peel (1977). Practical relief and preventive methods. *Disasters*, **1**, 179–97; also published as *Selective Feeding Procedures* (1977). OXFAM Working Paper, No. 1, OXFAM, Oxford, UK, 33 pp.

Ross Institute (1981). Malaria prevention in travellers from the United Kingdom. *British Medical Journal* **283**, 214–18.

Ross Institute (1982). *Diarrhoeal diseases: what is causing diarrhoea in your area?* Ross Institute Publications, London School of Hygiene and Tropical Medicine.

S. P. Simmonds and H. Brown (1979). Angola: meeting health and health related needs with refugees. *Disasters* **3**, 403–11.

M. C. Swaminathan, K. Vijayaraghavan, and D. Hanumantha Rao (1973). Nutritional status of refugees from Bangla Desh. *Indian Journal of Medical Research* **61**, 278–84.

UNHCR (1979). *Collection of international instruments concerning refugees.* Office of the United Nations High Commissioner for Refugees, Geneva.

UNHCR (1982). *Handbook for emergencies.* United Nations High Commissioner for Refugees, Geneva.

WHO (1981). *The treatment and management of severe protein-energy malnutrtion.* World Health Organization, Geneva, 47 pp.

WHO (1982). *The work of WHO 1980–1981, Biennial Report of the Director-General.* World Health Organization, Geneva, 241 pp.

Bibliography

The bibliography was first published in 1982 (and is still obtainable) as Ross Institute Publication No. 14, edited by Stephanie Simmonds and Michel Gabaudan.

During our search for published papers a definite bias towards the English language developed. For future editions we welcome our attention being brought to papers in other languages, but stress that a summary in English will widen the audience of readers. The sources of literature are medical and other relevant journals easily available in medical libraries, and books published internationally. We deliberately restricted ourselves to published literature and the period covered is mainly from 1968 onwards.

The first section is an annotated bibliography, arranged by author's name in alphabetical order of some of the papers published about health work in refugee and displaced communities. The papers vary from anecdotal personal accounts to the more scientifically documented reports often based on standard epidemiological procedures. Very few answer all the technical issues that they raise.

Therefore a second, more technical section follows, classified by subjects, based on experiences on development programmes or during acute disasters. We consider these papers and books to be relevant to refugee communities and they are given as a basis for reflection. It is not possible to cover all the literature, and we have quite deliberately kept this list short according to priority health and disease problems common, in our experience, to most refugee communities.

The third and final section is a bibliography of relevant material by countries where refugee or displaced person problems have occurred. This section is not annotated, but attempts to serve as a reference for health workers assigned to a country and who want to obtain insight into what has previously happened there.

> Please send suggestions of
> useful material to be included
> in future editions to:
>
> The Refugee Health Group,
> London School of Hygiene and
> Tropical Medicine,
> Keppel Street (Gower Street)
> London WC1E 7HT.

SELECTED ANNOTATED REFERENCES

C. Aall (1970). Relief, nutrition and health problems in the Nigerian/Biafran war. *Journal of Tropical Paediatrics and Environmental Child Health* **16**, 70–90.

Every disaster is the consequence of multiple factors that contribute to its shaping. This comprehensive paper analyses the various elements that contributed to the large loss of life in Biafra during the war; elements such as overpopulation, very low protein and carbohydrate food supplies, poor soil, low resistance to disease, high child mortality rates, and dependence on trade and remittances from outside Biafra. The main difficulties are categorized as political, with particular suspicion directed towards outside assistance which was regarded by some as outside intervention; problems due to local conditions such as a weak infrastructure, inadequate transport and storage, and difficulties arising from the organization and structure of the international relief work, due in part to lack of professionalism. From the experience gained five priorities for future programmes are given, the first being the need for the establishment of policies, priorities, and planning on the basis of continuous nutrition surveillance, and the second, general food distribution and vulnerable group feeding. General preventive and medical measures are ranked third and fourth priorities and continuous assessment or evaluation the fifth priority. The author concludes with some general remarks directed to international relief agencies on how to improve their response through a more systematic approach using the five priorities mentioned.

C. Aall (1979). Disastrous international relief failure: a report on Burmese refugees in Bangladesh from May to December 1978. *Disasters* **3**, 429–34.

This extremely disturbing paper shows how a fundamental error in the initial planning of the food ration led to widespread malnutrition and an estimated 10 000 deaths within a period of eight months. It highlights a rise in mortality over time, proof that the camps were generating ill-health. The mortality was inversely related to food supply, e.g. when the food supply decreased, mortality increased (after an interval of one week). The worst feature was the poor response by the relief officials to the author's repeated suggestions as to why such a situation was developing and how to remedy it. The basic ration amounted to an average of 1300 kcal per person per day, which falls short of the minimum recommended figure of 1800 kcal. Basic recommendations included the provision of extra rations for two months for all refugees and better identification of nutritionally vulnerable groups. This is a reminder to the health profession of the political and bureaucratic battles that may have to be fought if refugees are not to die unnecessarily. A letter to the Editor by M. D. Thompson seriously criticizes the demographic and mortality figures reported by Aall, arguing that the inflated number of refugees initially recorded were adjusted by 'creating' artificial mortality rates when precise figures were needed for the repatriation programme in Burma (Reliability of recorded death rates among Burmese refugees in Bangladesh. *Disasters* **4**, 1980, 355–6). Cato Aall replies to these showing that the increase in death rate was significant because even a gross error of 50 per cent over-reporting would have shown an unacceptable increased mortality (Reply. *Disasters* **4**, 1980, 356–9). This exchange of views serves as a good illustration of the difficulties of obtaining reliable data during refugee crises, partly because of political considerations and poor administrative control.

A. S. Ahmed (1980). Afghan refugees, aid and anthropologists. *Overseas Development Institute Review* **2**, 1–13.

One of the few papers written by an anthropologist on the subject of anthropology as applied to refugee communities. The author takes an interesting perspective on the problems of the distribution of aid to refugees, using the Afghan refugees in the North-West Frontier Region of Pakistan as a case-study. He maintains that there are three parties to the problem, and conceptualizes them as 'A' the aid-giving countries and institutions (notably the UN); 'B' the host country; and 'C' the refugees themselves. Personnel for 'A' tend to ignore the sociological aspects crucial to the understanding of the role of the government and special problems of the refugees. While the role of 'B' is that of someone, often an administrator, caught as an interpreter between 'A' with its more advanced aspects of the twentieth century including high technology and 'C' whose problems of migration, a tent and camel economy, and code of behaviour date back to the middle ages. While certain aspects of refugee relief can and must be standardized, the special needs of each community of 'C' must be identified. The author concludes with the main recommendation that an anthropologist be attached to every major administrative unit of 'A' in order to help bring 'some understanding, imagination and compassion to a problem that is essentially a human one'.

P. Anton, K. Arnold, G. K. Trnong, and W. T. Wong (1981). Bacterial enteric pathogens in Vietnamese refugees in Hong Kong. *Southeast Asian Journal of Tropical Medical Public Health* **12**, 151–6.

An epidemic of enteric fever or gastroenteritis was considered a possibility among Vietnamese refugees in camps in Hong Kong due to a combination of factors such as overcrowding, inadequate water supply and sewage systems, and the 'open camp' policy. A screening survey was therefore undertaken to detect the carrier rate of bacterial enteric pathogens. Three consecutive stools were examined from 228 'arbitrarily' selected, asymptomatic refugees, all of whom were over 40 years of age. A prevalence rate of 13.5 per cent of *Salmonella* was found but no *Vibrio cholerae*. As the highest infection rates of most of the bacteria being sought occur in young children, the usefulness of the study was limited.

P. M. Arnow, J. C. Hierholzer, J. Higbee, and D. H. Harris (1977). Acute hemorrhagic conjunctivitis: a mixed virus outbreak among Vietnamese refugees on Guam. *American Journal of Epidemiology* **105**, 68–73.

A well documented epidemiological investigation of an outbreak of disease among a refugee community. The conjunctivitis caused concern not only because of extensive morbidity in the community but also because of the possibility of the refugees importing it to their third country of asylum. Overcrowding, scarcity of water, and poor hygiene, including the sharing of towels on the boats that ensured evacuation from Vietnam, were factors responsible for the outbreak of this 'water-washed' disease. The illness, however, was short-lived mainly due to the rapid exhaustion of the pool of susceptible hosts.

G. Barnabas (1982). Popcorn and fairies in the management of measles in Ethiopia (letter). *The Lancet* **1**, 450.

A brief insight into the local beliefs about causation and local customs in care of children with measles, among refugee mothers from Tigre, Ethiopia. The author interviewed 34 mothers in a camp in eastern Sudan. They mentioned the need for an appeasement ceremony for fairies and foods, including popcorn, are prepared as a gift. Asked why they give popcorn, the mothers said that it behaves like the spots and that 'it helps the rash to come out'. Asked whether they wash a child sick with measles the mothers replied 'wash after 12 days for mild measles; wash after 40 days for severe measles'. The author advocates that we may be able to improve our teaching of home care in the management of certain diseases if we understand better the cultural practices involved.

S. Belete, M. Gebre-Medhin, B. Hailemariam, M. Maffi, B. Vahlquist and Z. Wolde-Gebriel (1977). Study of shelter population in the Wollo region. *Journal of Tropical Paediatrics and Environmental Child Health* **23**, 15–36.

The paper is the first in a series of three (see M. Gebre-Medhin 1976 and 1977) and is the result of a cross sectional study of the complex factors that affected the Wollo community in Ethiopia, mainly during the famine years of 1973 and 1974. The results of the household and nutrition surveys undertaken in the 13 shelters with a total population of about 29 000, the climatic and agricultural factors, and the reasons for migration are well documented. Mortality and morbidity results are compared with what would normally be expected from the area; these highlight an important point in evaluation, that is, the necessity to have base-line information on which to discuss developments. The shelter population was under-represented at the extremes of the age pyramid, probably because the very young and the very old had already died, and also among the 15–44 age group of men, who travelled around looking for possible employment. A nutrition survey showed a very high rate of malnutrition with 47.7 per cent of children 0–4 years of age, and 38 per cent 5–14 years of age less than 70 per cent standard weight for height. Crop failure and lack of seeds were responsible for over 80 per cent of migrations and 42 per cent of the people had either sold or mortgaged their land. From the responses by the Relief and Rehabilitation and Settlement Commission and the Ethiopian Nutrition Institute to subsequent drought conditions it is obvious that much was learnt from that disastrous famine, partly thanks to documentation such as this. One of the most interesting and comprehensive studies of a population displaced due to famine.

F. J. Bennett, D. B. Jelliffe, E. F. P. Jelliffe and M. Moffat (1968). The nutrition and disease pattern of children in a refugee settlement. *East African Medical Journal* **45**, 229–46.

This study describes the changes occurring in the disease pattern of Rwandan children in refugee settlements in Uganda, as determined by two prevalence surveys six years apart. It examines how changes in diet and socio-economic status, exposure to a new environment, and political factors influenced the health of the children. Some of the results of the surveys, such as fewer cases of nutritional marasmus, conjunctivitis, and skin disease may be considered beneficial, but a change in the malaria parasite rate from 0.2 per cent in 1961 to 57 per cent in 1967 demonstrates just one of the disease problems associated with migration. Interesting reading on the modification of disease patterns linked to migration.

M. Bizuneh (1980). An Ethiopian refugee camp in Sudan—the problem of tuberculosis. *Disasters* **4**, 167–70.

Repercussions from food-supply policies can have unperceived effects. So claims the author who explains how an interruption of food distribution designed to promote self-sufficiency particularly affected patients with tuberculosis. If the refugees stayed in the camp to receive treatment they were unable to work for local farmers, and therefore had no alternative method of feeding themselves, as food was only given on a 'food for work' basis.

U. Bollag (1980). Practical evaluation of a pilot immunization campaign against typhoid fever in a Cambodian refugee camp. *International Journal of Epidemiology* **9**, 121–22 (also reported in *Disasters* **3**, 1979, 413–15).

One of the few published papers on the evaluation of an immunization programme in a camp. Using attendance rates as an indicator of the quality of a campaign against typhoid and paratyphoid, a conclusion is drawn that it would have been useless to try to control those diseases by immunization alone. Attendance rates fell from 80 to 29 per cent in children and from 69 to 28 per cent among adults, from the 1st to the 3rd injection, despite health education and the offer of curative care at the time of the injection. These low rates are partly ascribed to side effects of the vaccination and to the fact that the camp population was always changing. Because of these and other factors, the promotion of personal hygiene and improvement of environmental sanitation are the control measures most strongly advocated.

R. E. Brown (1969). Mission to Biafra: a study and survey of a population under stress. *Clinical Pediatrics* **8**, 313–21.

A clearly written summary of the main health problems at one time during the Biafran war. It discusses nutritional and demographic features, and makes particular reference to psychological disturbances. The population within the war-locked area is estimated to have risen from 4.5 to 7 million people, and the increased number of cases of malnutrition among older children and adults is used as an indicator of the severity of the famine. Possible solutions to some of the problems are outlined, including mobile units to reach distant villages and camps, a tuberculosis control programme, and increasing the coverage of both preventive and curative activities through standardization of procedures and delegation to para-medical staff, who would be trained on the spot.

R. E. Brown (1972). Some nutritional considerations in times of major catastrophe. *Clinical Pediatrics* **11**, 334–42.

The title of this paper does not do justice to its scope. The author's brief was to observe the nutritional and general health status of children in the Bangladesh refugee camps in Northeastern India during a short period in

1971. The author recalls the determinants of nutritional status in refugee situations and then lists a series of recommendations to deal with the associated problems. Strong emphasis is placed on mass treatment for malaria, anaemia, intestinal parasites, and skin diseases, and for vitamin A supplementation. The general organization needed, including training programmes, is discussed. Epidemiological data, according to the author, is important to help assess needs and evaluate programmes but is difficult to record due to lack of adequate census records. Objective measurements can be made though on selected groups of refugees in order to develop a longitudinal profile of disease behaviour in the camps. Attention is also given to the methods of promoting breast feeding, a much neglected aspect of nutrition programmes. A paper well worth reading as it summarizes most of the crucial points to be considered for appropriate health care in refugee communities.

R. E. Brown, D. Carroll, G. Mulvihill, M. Mulvihill, S. Silberstein, and S. Thacker (1974). Field nutrition survey of Nigerian children in Ivory Coast refugee camps. *Tropical and Geographical Medicine* **26**, 152–6.

An example of how not to do a nutrition survey on refugee children. The survey, on 888 children aged from two to nineteen years and evacuated two years previously to the Ivory Coast from Nigeria, included at least 12 physical signs, nine laboratory examinations, technical procedures such as fingernail clipping for mineral analysis, and finally anthropometric measurements. Few conclusions were drawn and standard indicators were not used for the data collection.

N. R. M. Buist (1980). Perspectives from Khao-I-Dang refugee camp. *British Medical Journal* **281**, 36–7.

This is a somewhat emotional account of an American physician's experience in the largest of the Cambodian refugee camps in Thailand. It summarizes the refugees' ordeal, the strained relations with the national authorities, and the lack of inter-agency co-ordination. All are recurring problems in a community that has probably received the most international attention in the last ten years, and a prime example of how little we seem to have learnt from past experiences. D. B. Jelliffe and E. F. P. Jelliffe comment to this effect in a letter to the *British Medical Journal*, blaming much of the problem on the poor training given to international health workers prior to working in refugee camps (Refugee health programme. *British Medical Journal* **281**, 1980, 677).

M. P. Chisholm (1978). Lessons from a school building project, and refugee relief operations—Bangladesh 1975–77. *Disasters* **2**, 148–51.

The author became involved, in 1976, in the provision of emergency shelters for people who moved from the border area with India. From his experience he raises a series of provoking issues which can be applied to the general philosophy of relief work. Is the technology employed efficient and does it meet the cultural needs? What are its mid- and long-term consequences for the refugees and the country? Deliberately critical in its attack on international relief work, the paper concludes with some basic recommendations to western agencies on what to teach relief workers, how to evaluate programmes and record data, and how to use the information to plan future programmes.

H. Christensen (1982). *Survival strategies for and by refugees.* United Nations Research Institute for Social Development, Geneva. 48 pp.

This is one of the few publications which examines in depth the long-term problems of refugees. One camp in each of the three regions in Somalia most heavily populated by refugees was selected, and the study was based on interviews with key informants and refugees from the camps and on information obtained by following the food distribution process. Apart from providing an overview of the camps, a number of interesting issues are raised. These include the various economic systems which are generated, based on food aid and local environmental resources, the social stratification that develops based on the differential access to food and the changing role definitions in the refugee society, with the work being highly biased to women who subsequently gain strength and status in the community. Clearly all of these social changes have implications for the future.

Overall the impression is that far from being spoon-fed and dependent the refugees show much initiative and are active in improving the camps despite the unsettling effects of an uncertain future. The recommendations which are made are likely to be applicable in many long-term refugee settlements and this booklet is recommended to all health workers likely to be involved in such situations.

F. C. Cuny (1977). Refugee camps and camp planning: the state of the art. *Disasters* **1**, 125–43.

This paper analyses the crucial factors that must be considered before a camp is born, so that it develops an infrastructure that contributes to social cohesion and greater efficiency of the relief work. Problems may ensue if refugees start building their homes without first planning the camp layout. The work is based on a wide review of refugee camps created following civil disorders (India) and natural disasters (Managua and Honduras) and in the final discussion looks at systematic camp layout, emphasizing the community unit approach as more successful and manageable than the grid layout which is easier to set up. The author also outlines three different types of camp that require different planning. The emergency camp requires immediate relief supplies. Planning is made difficult because of the suddenness of the situation and the mobility of the population. These camps serve as processing centres to semi-permanent camps, where more long-term planning can be undertaken. Permanent camps are planned from the beginning in order to maximize the delivery of services, develop long term programmes, and keep ahead of the settlement of any new arrivals in the camp. Though this classification presents a useful framework for camp planning, in reality these three types of camp often intermingle at the same place.

K. Dahlberg (1980). Medical care of Cambodian refugees. *Journal of the American Medical Association* **243**, 1062–5.

Aimed at those international health workers intending to work with the Kampuchean communities in Thailand from 1980 onwards, the paper reviews the most common nutritional and disease problems encountered, mainly marasmus, kwashiorkor, beriberi, anaemia, and vitamin A deficiency. It goes on to explain how to deal with the problems in the light of locally available drugs and the authors' personal experience. The paper is concise and aims at a standardized approach to treatment, an essential element if quality of care is to be implemented and maintained.

L. E. Davis (1971). Epidemiology of famine in the Nigerian crisis: rapid evaluation of malnutrition by height and arm circumference in large populations. *American Journal of Clinical Nutrition* **24**, 358–64.

A rapid nutrition survey using height and arm circumference was undertaken in 60 villages in Biafra, and comparisons made according to broad classifications, for example, villages close to or far from the war front, had or had not recieved food aid. The results permitted redistribution of aid to the most needy areas, as they demonstrated a very marked increase in malnutrition as one went inland from the coast to the war front. Nowadays there is mounting concern regarding the use of such a measurement as an individual screening index; however, it is a simple and rapid method that can be undertaken by volunteers trained rapidly on the spot, and has proven effective in helping to identify major differences between communities in different geographical areas.

C. de Ville de Goyet and M. F. Lechat (1977). Les activités de santé prioritairés dans les camps de réfugiés. *Revue d'Epidemiologie et de Santé Publique* **25**, 99–106.

This paper attempts to standardize the health approach to refugee camps. The difficulties, while recognizing the very real need, in establishing a surveillance system are stressed. From the experience of such surveillance systems in the past, identical priorities such as nutrition assessment, sanitation, and other general preventive measures have become evident.

Curative medicine, often the main tool of foreign agencies, needs to be kept to a minimum level and integrated within the local system as far as possible. Quality must be sacrificed for coverage and one must avoid creating a need for curative services that cannot be guaranteed once the emergency crisis is over. The paper concludes on the danger of the ease with which it is possible to give assistance to refugees in excess of that available for the local host population.

P. Gardener, J. E. Rohde, and M. B. Majumdar (1972). Health priorities among Bangladesh refugees. *The Lancet* **1**, 834–6.

The authors examine the results of a quantitative prevalence survey of all members of randomly chosen families, in a camp at Barosat, India. The camp was typical in size of the 1000 camps dispersed throughout Eastern India, sheltering an estimated 10 million refugees, and the survey was undertaken just prior to the refugees' repatriation to Bangladesh. All the major disease problems identified concern community health, e.g. malnutrition, diarrhoea, vitamin A deficiency, and tuberculosis, with a constantly higher prevalence in the 1–5 age group. These problems are discussed, with their implications for health care, not only while the refugees remain in the camp but also on their return to Bangladesh. An example of a disease prevalence survey providing a basis for health planning.

J. C. Gaydos, T. A. Mino, L. E. Ashmore, M. L. Bertsch, T. J. McNeil, and B. Eisen (1978). A preventive medicine team in a refugee relief operation— Fort Chaffee Indochina refugee camp (April–July 1975). *Military Medicine* **143**, 318–21.

This paper describes the organization of a preventive health team in a processing centre for Vietnamese refugees in the USA. A preliminary survey identified factors overlooked in the hasty preparation of the camp and enabled workers to define priority areas such as environmental sanitation, entomological surveys, epidemiological surveillance, and community health. Interesting reading for those who might be involved in the reception of refugees in the West.

R. I. Glass, W. Cates, P. Nieburg, C. Davis, R. Russbach, H. Nothdurft, S. Peel, and R. Turnbull (1980). Rapid assessment of health status and preventive medicine needs of newly arrived Kampuchean refugees, Sa Keo, Thailand. *The Lancet* **1**, 868–72.

The use of epidemiological techniques to help plan an effective health programme in a refugee camp from inception is the main theme of this paper. Malnutrition and malaria prevalence surveys and surveillance systems, including mortality data by age and cause in hospital and in the community, hospital admissions, outpatient attendance, and the monitoring of laboratory log-books are described. The paper is a good example of the method required to develop prospective epidemiological information, but it tends to reach rather far-fetched conclusions. The most striking is the assumption that the reduction in mortality was due to the 'timely health intervention measures'. S. Ebrahims' arguments on the limitations and drawbacks of epidemiological techniques as applied to the changing situation of a camp, expressed in a letter to the author in reply to this paper, serve as a reminder as to how careful we must be over our interpretation of the data obtained (Health needs of refugees. *The Lancet* **1**, 1980, 1139). Nevertheless, put together, this paper and Ebrahims' letter should be influential in trying to get health workers to produce such work in order to evaluate the changing needs of a refugee community.

R. E. Gribbin (1973). Two relief crises: Biafra and Sudan. *Africa Today* **20**, 47–59.

Health is a political issue, and there is no greater reminder of this than when confronted with the reality of how to get aid to those suffering from the effects of a war. This paper is a reminder of the types of relations that relief agencies may have with recipient governments, and how the political stance of the donor and receiving bodies can affect the destitute populations regardless of their real needs. During the Biafran war, for example, the voluntary agencies found their humanitarian goals frustrated by the political–military goals of the Nigerian government and the means used to achieve them such as applying strict conditions to the provision of food and other relief supplies. Even following peace the government banned certain countries and agencies from involvement in the massive relief programme as they were regarded as hostile to Nigeria.

A. H. I. Guinena (1977). Protein–calorie malnutrition in young refugee children in the Gaza Strip. *Journal of Tropical Paediatrics and Environmental Child Health* **23**, 38–57.

After establishing local anthropometric standards based on a combination of transverse and longitudinal surveys of children showing weight gain, the author proceeds to analyse the pattern of malnutrition among the refugee children according to several variables: age, sex, feeding practices, disease, and maternal factors are each correlated to anthropometric assessment. This is an interesting paper, but complex and aimed at those well conversed with nutritional terminology and far beyond the requirements of adequate standard relief work.

R. K. Harding and J. G. Looney (1977). Problems of Southeast Asian children in a refugee camp. *American Journal of Psychiatry* **134**, 407–11.

The authors review some of the psychiatric problems expressed by Vietnamese refugee children following their resettlement in the USA and conclude that they usually adapted very well to the difficult transition. Only those children who had either temporarily or permanently lost their parents or who had been separated by bureaucracy from their unofficial foster families, developed psychiatric problems such as depression, manifesting itself in such symptoms as sleep disturbances, tantrums, violent anti-social behaviour, marked withdrawal, and attempted suicide. Recommendations are directed towards administrative authorities on how to deal with such 'at risk' groups.

R. Hickman (1971). Deteriorating health of refugee children in India. *The Lancet* **2**, 917–18.

An anecdotal account of work in a camp in West Bengal in 1971 that emphasizes how important it is to do a house to house survey to ensure that all cases of malnutrition are found, and not to rely on first visual impressions of those healthy children who inevitably crowd around one on arrival. The survey revealed that 10 per cent of the children had moderate to severe malnutrition, and more important that the worst cases were to be found among those who had arrived a few months earlier, whereas the recent arrivals appeared fairly healthy. This finding suggested that the basic food ration was inadequate, and on further investigation a serious lack of protein became apparent. The problem was complicated by the presence of diseases such as gastro-enteritis, typhoid fever, chest infection, measles, tuberculosis, and vitamin A deficiency. Supplementary feeding programmes were implemented to try and treat the widespread malnutrition but they were not as successful as they might have been as there was no corresponding improvement to the general diet.

A. G. Hill (1983). The Palestinian population of the Middle East. *Population and Development Review* **9**, 85–103.

Amongst other things, this paper looks at the child survivorship of Palestinian refugees in camps in Jordan, Syria, Gaza, the East and West Banks of Jordan, and Lebanon, and compares the rates with those for the national population or for Palestinians who do not live in camps. The results show that the basic health-care system developed by the Palestinian Red Crescent Society and UNRWA has been extraordinarily effective in reducing infant and child mortality in the camp communities, despite indications of the lower socio-economic status of the camp residents. In Lebanon, infant mortality rates in the camps are as low as in the host population (40 per 1000 in the 1970s), whilst in Syria the camp infant mortality rate may be as much as 40 points lower than for the rest of the country. On the East bank of Jordan, the differences are intermediate between these two extremes. In general, the good mortality of the camps is attributed to the emphasis on public and community health care and to the focus on the welfare of mothers and babies in particular.

J. Howard (1979). Survey on water supply and sanitation for Pulau Bidong. *Disasters* **3**, 461–7.

At one point in 1979, almost 42 000 refugees from Vietnam were living on the previously uninhabited island of Pulau Bidong. The area of the island is approximately 3 km² with a central elevation of 320 m and the nearest port on the mainland of Malaya, approximately 26 km away. The author describes a systematic approach of examining local possibilities regarding water resources and sanitation facilities, including alternative solutions and cost estimates. A thorough evaluation that makes recommendations such as the construction of additional water-storage facilities before the monsoon season starts so that there would be at least 7 days water supply on the island; a sanitation/sewerage plan to ensure the safe disposal of human excreta; the provision of incinerators to dispose of human excreta; the provision of incinerators to dispose of rubbish; the means to provide burial at sea, and the need for the organization of fire-fighting teams.

E. S. Hurwitz, D. Johnson, and C. C. Campbell (1981). Resistance of *plasmodium falciparum* malaria to sulfadoxine-pyrimethamine (Fansidar) in a refugee camp in Thailand. *The Lancet* **1**, 1068–70.

The observation that many patients in Boen Kaeng refugee camp, with uncomplicated chloroquine-resistant *Plasmodium falciparum* were not responding to treatment with 'Fansidar' prompted the follow-up of nine patients with serial parasite counts. The patients were all Khmer refugees who had arrived in Thailand via southwestern Kampuchea where malaria is hyperendemic. The results of the study suggested that Fansidar-resistant strains were prevalent among refugees with *Plasmodium falciparum* malaria. Possible explanations for this finding are given, including the repeated and widespread use of the drug in 'an attempt to treat the camp's population en masse' and the availability of the drug on the camp's black market combined with the importation of an already highly resistant strain from Kampuchea.

P. Isaza, Z. T. de Quinteros, E. Pineda, C. Parchment, E. Aguilar, and M. J. McQuestion (1980). A diarrhoeal disease control programme among Nicaraguan refugee children in Campo Luna, Honduras. *Bulletin of the Pan American Health Organization* **14**, 337–42.

Concerned about the incidence of diarrhoea in the camps for Nicaraguan refugees in Southern Honduras, the Honduran authorities decided to test the feasibility of establishing a diarrhoeal disease-control programme that could be administered by trained auxiliaries at the health centre level using oral rehydration therapy. The oralyte was successfully given to mothers for administration to 71 children, of whom 35 had mild, 33 moderate, and 1 child severe dehydration. Only this latter case had to be transferred to hospital. The success of the method is put into perspective by some statistical analysis showing that the length of treatment was related to the severity of dehydration and length of time suffered from diarrhoea before admission. Malnutrition was significantly associated with the extent of dehydration.

D. B. Jelliffe and E. F. P. Jelliffe (1981). Refugee medicine. *The Sciences* **21**, 14–15 and 18–19.

Following a brief review of the present world refugee crisis, this paper examines what the various refugee communities throughout the world have in common and how they differ. Common to most, for example, is the pattern of disease which is usually an exacerbation of the major problems frequently found in developing countries. Cultural needs differ, as do the political responses. Even so, the authors state that the general similarity of most camps must encourage efforts by the international community to develop a standardized emergency response to future crises. Based on the theory that refugee situations move from country-wide confusion to the development of collection camps, to stable camps, and thereafter either to relocation camps leading to resettlement, or least desirably, to 'chronic' camps, the standardized response would emphasize the provision of simple emergency life-savings measures for the collection camps; the organization of camp health services in stable camps, with particular attention on disease surveillance, health education, immunization, environmental sanitation, and maternal and child care. Educational activities become a priority in relocation camps. The different needs of each community will gradually emerge from thoughtful planning and should be met accordingly. Crucial to all this is the need to plan to have trained workers available, a sadly neglected aspect of relief work according to the authors. A well written paper that summarizes the main issues in health care planning for refugee communities.

T. Lusty (1979). Notes on health care in refugee camps. *Disasters* **3**, 352–4.

A brief analysis of the main factors affecting health in refugee camp communities—which according to the author are crowding and poor nutrition with uncertainty of supplies—is followed by a review of the environmental, preventive, and administrative measures that may be implemented in order to limit the ill effects generated by large populations dependent on international aid. Environmental measures such as planning for an adequate quantity of clean water, a culturally sensitive excreta disposal system, and a housing system that protects the refugees from the elements, provides privacy, and allows for social cohesion, are discussed. The preventive measures include the provision of an adequate diet, immunization with particular emphasis on measles, control of communicable diseases, health education, and simple curative treatment. The administrative measures entail ensuring logistics, appropriate technology, participation with the refugees, and co-ordination with the government and other agencies concerned. A useful checklist of the main topics to be analysed in any refugee community.

D. Mahalanabis, A. B. Choudhuri, N. G. Bacchi, A. K. Bhattacharya, and T. W. Simpson (1973). Oral fluid therapy of cholera among Bangladesh refugees. *The Johns Hopkins Medical Journal* **132**, 197–205.

Among the six million refugees from East Bengal who moved to West Bengal in 1971, diarrhoeal diseases carried a case fatality rate of almost 30 per cent. When a cholera epidemic erupted during the summer months the health authorities were faced with a large population to care for, with limited treatment facilities and an extreme shortage of intravenous fluids and trained personnel. This prompted the authorities to promote early oral rehydration in all cases of severe diarrhoea. The powder, containing 22 g of glucose, 3.5 g of sodium chloride, and 2.5 g of sodium bicarbonate, but no potassium salts as they were unavailable, was produced and packaged locally. Packets were delivered to the field centres with labels indicating the volume of water with which to dilute them (4 and 16 litre packets were prepared) and patients were served directly from a drum close to where nursing care was undertaken. Some 3700 patients were treated in eight weeks with a case–fatality ratio of 3.6 per cent. Severely dehydrated patients, with hypo-volaemic shock, needed only an average of three litres of intravenous fluids, if oral therapy was initiated as soon as the patient could tolerate fluids. No complications due to overhydration were observed, despite the majority of patients being children who are usually more difficult to rehydrate accurately. The simplicity of the method, and the local production of all ingredients and equipment were major factors contributing to the large coverage realized.

J. B. Mason, R. W. Hay, J. Leresche, S. Peel, and S. Darley (1974). Treatment of severe malnutrition in relief. *The Lancet* **1**, 332–5.

Conditions resulting from famine, drought, and/or war tend to result in an increase in the incidence of severe protein–energy malnutrition, especially amongst young children. Although the treatment of this problem using a therapeutic feeding programme had been shown before 1974 to be effective in a hospital environment, it had rarely, apart from a few reports from Biafra and India, been demonstrated as a feasible and effective intervention in relief.

In this paper the authors describe very convincingly how it was possible to implement such a programme in a shelter in Dessie, Ethiopia. Of the 44 children admitted to the programme, 20 had kwashiorkor and 21 were 70 per cent of the standard weight for height or less. Based on their weight and height on admission, each childs' energy and protein requirements were calculated and small feeds were given at regular intervals using milk and other foods locally available. Medical treatment for any existing infection was also given. This resulted in rapid rates of recovery, at low cost, with a mortality rate no worse than under hospital conditions. One of the best documented examples of a programme that has now been accepted as mandatory where nutritional rehabilitation is needed for members of a camp community suffering from marasmus or kwashiorkor.

Ministry of Health (1982). *Health guidelines for refugee camps*. Refugee Health Unit, Ministry of Health, Mogadishu, Somalia, 51 pp.

When as many as 30 refugee/displaced person camps are dotted all over a country and almost as many different international agencies have health personnel 'doing their own thing' in the camps, there is a danger that the types of health services implemented will be inappropriate and far more sophisticated and expensive than those provided by the host government in 'normal' times. These guidelines are an example of an effort to standardize much of the care given in the fields of clinical medicine, feeding programmes, disease and nutrition surveillance, and drug supplies. A similar approach was taken in Thailand for the Kampuchean refugee problem and it is to be hoped that more countries will take a similar stand very soon after a refugee problem becomes evident.

J. G. Morris, G. R. West, S. E. Holck, P. A. Blake, P. D. Scheverria, and M. Karaulnik (1982). Cholera among refugees in Rangsit, Thailand. *The Journal of Infectious Diseases* **1**, 131–4.

Approximately two thirds of Indochinese refugees accepted to enter the United States from Thailand passed through a transit centre at Rangsit Zokm, north of Bangkok. The first outbreak of cholera was linked to drinking beverages with ice bought from local Thai vendors. In the second outbreak it was impossible to implicate any one mechanism but overcrowding, poor sanitation, and inadequate chlorination of unprotected water supplies may have contributed to the transmission of the disease.

M. J. Murray, A. B. Murray, M. B. Murray, and C. J. Murray (1976). Somali food shelters in the Ogaden famine and their impact on health. *The Lancet* **1**, 1283–5.

The authors argue in this paper that the provision of aid to the nomads in the Ogaden desert in Ethiopia caused two major complications. Firstly the re-emergence of diseases due to re-feeding and, secondly, the development of psychosomatic symptoms due to sudden idleness. The arguments about the association between malaria and re-feeding are unconvincing, although interesting. Mention is also made of an association with brucellosis and tuberculosis.

B. W. Neldner (1979). Settlement of rural refugees in Africa. *Disasters* **3**, 393–402.

There are often three phases in the process of assistance to rural refugees, especially if their length of stay in the country of asylum is likely to be protracted. These are the emergency phase, the self-support phase, and the intending to work in refugee communities. This article is a brief resume of is not all about emergency relief, but should, from the onset of the crisis include elements of rehabilitation. The various steps of such development planning are analysed in relation to the flexibility required from the administrative level.

H. Nelson (1981). Health care for refugees stirs resentment among Thais. *Los Angeles Times* 29 January.

This article has been included because it is such an excellent example of the resentment that may be felt by the local people as hosts to a refugee population. It relates the excessive attention provided by relief agencies to the Cambodian refugees as viewed by a Thai physician; attention that far exceeds what the government can provide for its own people. A reminder of one of the most crucial aspects of relief philosophy, that of setting targets according to local patterns of health care!

P. Nuttall (1980). Light years away from the NHS: a recent course on refugee camps gave invaluable insights to volunteer helpers. *Nursing Times* **76**, 1206.

There are remarkably few training courses for international field workers intending to work in refugee communities. This article is a brief resume of one such course organized by the Ross Institute at the London School of Hygiene and Tropical Medicine. The aim of the annual one week course is to demonstrate the usefulness of community health care so that potential workers will have an appreciation for the activities in which they will need to become involved.

T. C. Okeahialam (1972). Children with protein–calorie malnutrition evacuated to Gabon during the Nigerian Civil War. *Journal of Tropical Paediatrics and Environmental Child Health* **18**, 169–84.

A detailed account of the possible complications such as hypothermia, convulsions, coma, cardiac failure, infections, and fractures of long bones of what is now termed protein–energy malnutrition and the systematic approach to their treatment. The experience was gained whilst caring for nearly 2000 children evacuated by plane to the Gabon. Whilst the medical aspect of their care makes interesting reading, one's interest is marred by the realization that many of the children were evacuated without their mother or some other close realtive. The very concept of transporting the most seriously ill to another country in such circumstances must be questioned, a serious omission of the paper.

M. Reacher, C. C. Campbell, J. Freeman, E. B. Doberstyn, and A. D. Brandling-Bennett (1981). Drug therapy for *Plasmodium falciparum* malaria resistant to pyrimethamine-sulfadoxine (Fansidar): a study of alternative regimens in Eastern Thailand, 1980. *The Lancet* **2**, 1066–9.

The widespread resistance to 'Fansidar' in the treatment of chloroquine-resistant *Plasmodium falciparum* among Khmer refugees in Thailand (see E. S. Hurwitz *et al.* 1981, annotated in this section) created a serious problem in malaria chemotherapy. A trial of five drug regimens was therefore conducted in a camp in an area of tropical rain forest where malaria is transmitted all year round. All the regimens included quinine sulphate given three times daily as 300 mg (salt) tablets for three to ten days, used either alone or with the addition of either Fansidar or tetracycline. Quinine alone and quinine plus Fansidar did not significantly improve the overall cure rate. Tetracycline given for ten days in combination with quinine cured all patients, suggesting that this was the regimen to be used.

G. O'Sullivan, S. Ebrahim, J. O'Sullivan, and C. Tafts (1980). Nutritional status of Laotian refugee children in Ubon camp, Thailand. *Journal of Epidemiology and Community Health* **34**, 83–6.

An interesting paper that demonstrates how a nutrition survey can assist a health team to determine whether its activities meet the needs in the community. The survey revealed, for example, that all severely malnourished children were known to the infant welfare clinic, but that children attending the supplementary feeding centres were more healthy than would be expected given the prevalence of malnutrition in the community. This finding prompted the team to relocate the supplementary feeding centres to the poorer areas of the camp. The paper also argues for the use of arm circumference as a screening test for the measurement of nutritional status amongst one to five-year-olds in refugee camps.

J. O'Sullivan, G. O'Sullivan, and S. Ebrahim (1980). Primary health care in Ubon refugee camp. *British Medical Journal* **280**, 779–81.

The authors describe how, in a refugee camp for Laotian refugees in Thailand, they took a deliberate stand against developing a medical unit with in-patient facilities and instead concentrated on a community approach to the health problems. The primary health-care system they developed with its emphasis on infant welfare, midwifery, public health, home visiting, and outpatient clinics especially for paediatrics, tuberculosis treatment, and gynaecology and family planning, relied heavily on volunteer refugee health workers, contributed to a reduction in morbidity that camps with hospital facilities were never able to achieve, and despite an increasing population, costs were lowered. As the medical assistants and community gradually realized that they not only had a responsibility, but also the ability to improve their own health, their natural suspicions about the primary health-care approach were overcome and the programme proved efficient and raised much interest.

J. O'Sullivan (1981). *Thailand: medical care for Lao refugees in Ubon camp 1978–1979.* International Disaster Institute, London, 55 pp.

Many agencies fail to learn from the experiences of their field staff, partly due to the fact that de-briefing sessions tend to be unstructured and end as unproductive chat sessions supplemented perhaps with a few written words. This publication is a good example of how interesting and informative an end of mission debriefing report can be. The report is divided into four sections; the first two dealing with 'soft' data, analysing social and administrative factors of the relief work and the remaining two sections review in detail the health services including epidemiological and disease control aspects that were implemented.

R. H. Rahe, J. G. Looney, H. W. Ward, T. M. Tung, and W. T. Liu (1978). Psychiatric consultation in a Vietnamese refugee camp. *American Journal of Psychiatry* **135**, 185–90.

This paper is one of the few examples of how useful it might be to have the services of psychiatrists available, especially where refugees are received in a camp in a third country of asylum. In this case the authors analyse how migration to the United States of America, and confinement to a refugee camp in California affected Vietnamese refugees fleeing from the fall of the South Vietnam government. The evaluation comprised both informal discussions with the refugees and camp staff, and the use of standardized questionnaires to a random sample of refugees. Findings included poorly organized social activities, lack of educational facilities, absence of meaningful and useful jobs, and excessively long waits in food lines resulting in a growing incidence of cases of anxiety, depression, and suicide attempts. These findings and the recommendations made helped administrators respond better to the cultural, socio-economic, physical, and health needs of the refugees and so prevent possible psychiatric problems.

E. M. Ressler (1979). Evaluation of CMU/INTERTECT A-frames as emergency shelter in Bangladesh, March 1979. *Disasters* **3**, 457–9.

There has been much criticism directed towards the many different types of emergency housing flown in to disaster areas. Here the author interestingly documents how he evaluated a special form of housing two years after it was set up in some of the Bihari refugee camps in Bangladesh. The method of evaluation included observing how the housing was used and cared for, its acceptability to the user, looking at details of the construction such as bindings, roofing, floor, and frame, and taking into account an evaluation by other voluntary agencies involved in housing in the camps. Conclusions made from the study were that conventionally-built houses with their lower costs, more usable floor space, and more traditional style had advantages over the A-Frame shelter. This rare example of an agency evaluating its work and publishing the results, despite the evidence weighing against it in favour of traditional housing, is to be commended.

B. Ryan (1975). General factors in the mortality among refugees in Vietnam. *The Medical Journal of Australia* **1**, 625–9.

A list of 18 factors, all of which were identified as contributing to the high mortality rate among the refugees in 1972, are explained in detail. Factors such as insufficient preparation of the site, inadequate water supply, poor environmental sanitation, rampant corruption, lack of standardization of aid, and no co-ordination between the various agencies involved in relief. They serve to remind the reader that almost ten years later some of those very same problems are still occurring in camps all over the world, due to lack of planning and organization. Fascinating reading that presents at its worst the fundamental failures in the organization of refugee relief.

B. Ryan (1976). Severe measles in Vietnam. *The Medical Journal of Australia* **1**, 353–5.

Measles is an important disease in developing countries because of the development of the vicious circle of malnutrition and diarrhoea. This report illustrates this interrelation with the added factors of poor housing and an inadequate general diet, in two camps for Cambodian refugees. The author relates how, over a period of three months, a considerable influx of refugees leading to overcrowding, poor camp hygiene, and insufficient food supplies combined with the start of the rainy season contributed to a high incidence of both diarrhoea and malnutrition following measles, resulting in an unacceptably high number of deaths among the children.

J. A. Seaman (1972). Relief work in a refugee camp for Bangladesh refugees in India. *The Lancet* **2**, 866–70.

An assessment of the work in progress in the Salt Lake camp, including environmental factors, nutritional status, and medical work combined with a house to house survey, caused the author to conclude that the death rate, especially amongst small children, was much higher in the camp than might be expected, even considering the high infant mortality of the population in 'normal' times. This was despite considerable relief effort, and is attributed to lack of planning to meet the special needs of the 'vulnerable' members of the community, delay in the provision of adequate sanitation and the poor coverage and inappropriateness of care in the medical programmes. The paper ends with a list of four lessons that can be learnt from the experience; efficient refugee relief work must be based on a proper appraisal of the nature of the society involved, a centralized surveillance system is required, good co-ordination of the voluntary agencies is essential, and a firm commitment from those agencies to build an evaluation process into their programmes is needed, so as to build up experience for future relief operations. Dr. Seaman's paper is criticized in a letter to *The Lancet* by B. Pastakia (Relief for Bangladesh refugees in India. *The Lancet* **2**, 1972, 1139). Pastakia argues that Seaman gives a very biased picture of the situation and ignores much of the valuable planning and actual work that was going on, including nutrition surveys and nutrition therapy centres which contributed to a 'big improvement in the nutritional status of the vulnerable "under fives"'.

R. Shaw (1977). Preventive medicine in the Vietnamese refugee camps on Guam. *Military Medicine* **142**, 19–28.

This paper presents in some detail many of the different aspects of health care provided for the 120 000 refugees from Vietnam. Subjects such as environmental health, mass feeding, recreation, entomological considerations, medical and preventive health, communicable diseases, and inpatient and outpatient care are covered. This is followed by a review of the most common problems encountered, such as communication, information systems, transport, the role of the refugees and the foreign health personnel, and cultural differences. One of the most stimulating and comprehensive papers, stressing the wider perspective that should be developed when working with a refugee community.

R. Shaw (1979). Health services in a disaster: lessons from the 1975 Vietnamese evacuation. *Military Medicine* **144**, 307–11.

Following the collapse of South Vietnam in 1975, many of the most healthy Vietnamese refugees were evacuated to the island of Guam in the Pacific. A United States of America military health team assigned to work in the camps found that their training was well suited to developing efficient environmental health control, but it did not prepare them to meet the needs of a civilian community who did not require acute medical or surgical care. The paper comprises a few useful comments on some aspects of the control of communicable diseases, such as the value of screening all the refugees on arrival, responding rapidly to any reports of unusual or important illnesses, and the methods employed to control the fly and mosquito populations. The paper also emphasizes the need to ensure that the most appropriately skilled health personnel are sent to each type of disaster.

S. P. Simmonds and H. Brown (1979). Angola: meeting health and health related needs with refugees. *Disasters* **3**, 403–11.

The authors describe the method they applied to plan, implement, and evaluate a health-development programme in three Zairian refugee villages in North Eastern Angola. The approach was community based and reviewed not only the disease pattern of the community but equally all their basic needs, the community structure, and the available resources. This facilitated the establishment of a primary health-care programme directly geared to the refugees' needs and priority problems. Refugee participation in the planning process was important and guaranteed acceptability and support by the community.

S. P. Simmonds (1980). Seminar on health and health-related needs of refugees. National Office of the Commissioner for Refugees, Somalia. *Disasters* **4**, 129–32.

This conference report is one of the few documented examples of the crucial aspect of co-operation between a host government and the relief agencies. In an effort to determine a standardized approach to health-development programmes in the refugee communities, working groups comprised of both national and international health personnel, decided upon basic guidelines in the priority problem areas of nutrition, training of interested refugees, health education, information reporting system, sanitation and water, and drugs, immunizations, and diagnosis and treatment of common diseases, based on information and experience from the field. These guidelines determined a common policy in an attempt to improve the delivery of health care, essential where large numbers of refugees/displaced persons and different agencies are involved.

S. P. Simmonds (1980). Curative medicine or community health? Appropriate health services with refugees. *Journal of Tropical Medicine and Hygiene* **83**, 49–52.

A general policy paper on the organization of health services in refugee communities. Following an analysis of the various determinants of health in any community—health not being merely a consequence of good medical care but rather the meeting of the basic needs in life ranging from adequate housing, nutrition, transport, education, water and sanitation facilities, and access to 'appropriate' medical care—the paper goes on to describe the essential stages that must be taken in the planning process. Each community needs a proper assessment of each of the factors mentioned previously and of the available resources, the ranking of the problems in terms of priorities, the implementation of the problem solving activities, and continuous evaluation. All of this must be undertaken 'with' the refugees so that a system is not set up 'for' them which will then collapse as soon as international personnel depart. International agencies and recipient governments are asked to consider the need for 'health' advisers who can approach a refugee community with a wider perspective than most medical personnel.

S. P. Simmonds (1981). From bedside nursing to digging latrines. *Nursing Times* **77**, 57–62.

Health workers wanting to work on refugee relief programmes in the field should abandon some of their preconceived western attitudes towards medical care and develop a comprehensive approach to health. This paper, one of six in a special edition of the journal devoted to refugee nursing, looks particularly at the role of nurses and also repeats some of the philosophy to the approach in the planning of a health programme as described in the preceding abstract of Simmonds (1980).

R. N. Srivastava (1973). Nutrition therapy centre: experience at a West Bengal refugee camp. *Indian Pediatrics* **10**, 503–6.

As a result of the nutrition survey undertaken by the All India Institute of Medical Sciences, Hyderabad (M. C. Swaminathan *et al.* 1973, annotated in this review), nutrition therapy centres were established in some of the West Bengal refugee camps. This paper is one of the first and most interesting documentations of therapeutic feeding in camps. The reader, however, is asked not to become involved in the process of intensive care that therapeutic feeding demands, to the detriment of those older children who may need preventive supplementary feeding to prevent them from falling into a lower nutritional status.

E. A. Sumpter (1980). Teach a man to fish. *American Journal of Diseases of Children* **134**, 1025–7.

This is a thought-provoking reflection on the role of the expatriate health worker in a refugee programme, based on the author's experience in Kamput camp in Thailand. Reference is made to such practices as 'placebo-giving', to the attitude of going in as 'saviours', to the role of Western medicine, and to the attitude of the host country having to harbour an ancient foe. Finally, the worker is asked to consider establishing the means whereby the skills and attitudes of both expatriate and refugee combine to establish an effective programme.

M. C. Swaminathan, K. Vijayaraghavan, and D. Hanumantha Rao (1973). Nutritional status of refugees from Bangla Desh. *Indian Journal of Medical Research* **61**, 278–84.

The All India Institute of Medical Sciences, Hyderabad, was asked to undertake a nutrition survey amongst the refugees in North Eastern India at the onset of the Bangladeshi crisis in 1971, to establish the nature and magnitude of the nutrition problem. The well-planned and organized nutrition survey showed a very high prevalence of malnutrition among those children younger than five years of age (35 per cent severe protein calorie malnutrition according to the Gomez classification), twice that observed in Indian children under normal conditions. Further investigation demonstrated that contributory factors included a diet of only 1000 calories per child less than ten years of age per day, cultural practices and taboos, and the presence of infections.

A. J. Taylor (1979). Emergency sanitation for refugees: experiences in the Bangladesh refugee relief camps, India, 1971–1972. *Disasters* **3**, 435–42.

Based on experience in the Bangladeshi camps in India, where during the monsoon season especially refugees could be seen wading knee high in a putrid slurry of mud and excrement, the author reviews the different excreta-based technologies that were employed. The very high water-table during the rainy season meant that the life of a pit latrine was very short as it had to be shallow, and so a unit based on septic tank principles was developed and became known as the OXFAM sanitation unit. It is appropriate for those conditions, but not necessarily a recommended solution for other situations as it requires a large volume of water. The author concludes with ten recommendations to be considered when deciding what type of sanitation system to implement in any future camp. These cover cultural acceptability, siting, local adaption to physical and climatic conditions, maintenance, and simplicity of operation. One of the few good references on the planning of adequate excreta disposal in refugee camps.

P. Temcharoen, J. Viboolyavatana, B. Tongkoom, P. Sumethanurugkul, B. Keittivuti, and L. Wanaratana (1979). A survey on intestinal parasitic infections in Laotian refugees at Ubon Province, North Eastern Thailand, with special reference to schistosomiasis. *South East Asian Journal of Tropical Medical Public Health* **10**, 552–4.

The importation of new diseases into a country by refugees is an ever present problem, more so when they come from areas in their home country which have not previously reported the presence of the disease. On the basis of finding a prevalence rate of 0.22 per cent of *Schistosoma mekongi* among a sample of Laotian refugees, concern is expressed by the authors over the possible transmission of Schistosomiasis *japonica* to the local Thai population, especially as the intermediate snail host, *Lithoglyphopsis aperta*, resides in the nearby river. Adequate control measures are deemed necessary if the health and economic status of the Thai community is not to suffer.

M. van der Westhuizen (1980). Kampuchean refugees—an encounter with grief. *The Australian Nurses Journal* **10**, 53–6.

This paper deals with the psychological stress of the Cambodian population and how it was expressed. A point very often underestimated in refugee/displaced person situations, as it is less obvious than physical needs and tends to be treated by traditional practitioners. As Westerners we have few answers to psychological problems, but we should be aware of stress and traditional ways of dealing with it.

F. Vertongen and M. Carael (1981). Refugee camps in Somalia: a micro survey—March 1980. *Disasters* **5**, 18–23.

The authors review the 1980/1981 refugee problem in Somalia and then document the results of a clinical and nutritional survey they undertook in Jalalaski camp, in the Hiran region. Acknowledging that they cannot compare their results with any longitudinal data, the authors conclude that the high rate of malnutrition in children one to six years of age, 27 per cent of whom had moderate malnutrition and 5 per cent severe malnutrition, was consistent with the prevailing condition of crowding, poor sanitation, and a low level of food supplies. These were all problems in a camp within reasonably close access to the provincial capital, thus causing the authors to question what conditions must be like in camps in the more remote northern and south-western areas of Somalia.

WHO (1983). *WHO emergency health kit. Standard drugs and clinic equipment for 10 000 persons for 3 months.* World Health Organization Emergency Relief Operations, Geneva, 10 pp.

Refugee camps have tended to be used as a dumping ground for a variety of commodities, one of them being drugs. The problem is magnified when each agency sends its own personnel with a supply of drugs that it thinks will be needed. This results in a wide variety of inappropriate, often dangerous drugs in small quantities being available, when what is generally required is a few basic drugs in large quantities. These lists were based on the practical, research, and administrative aspects of work with refugees and went through several drafts receiving world-wide criticism and comment in the process. The end result is three much needed lists which attempt to standardize the supply of basic drugs and equipment for clinics. A general explanation of the concept is given, together with a more detailed explanation of how the lists were drawn up, including a possible standardized treatment schedule. A limited number of sets of the drugs and equipment are made up in emergency health kits and held ready for despatch by UNHCR. Some voluntary agencies are now following the same list and kit example.

S. York and K. Grant (1980). *Afghan refugees in Pakistan: a report on current conditions.* International Disaster Institute, London, 83 pp.

The various elements of the relief programme are analysed in the context of the demographic pattern of the Afghan refugee community and the administrative constraints of the Pakistani government. Among the recommendations is a call for more operational involvement from the United Nations High Commissioner for Regugees, more community involvement with the refugees in the design of the health programmes, more emphasis on longer term plans, and a monitoring of the voluntary agency projects.

RELEVANT PAPERS AND BOOKS

Diseases

A. S. Benenson (ed.) (1981). *Control of communicable diseases in man.* American Public Health Association, New York, 444 pp.

Communicable diseases are likely to be more of a hazard to refugees than to the same people before they migrated. It is, therefore, important both to prevent epidemics and to control endemic diseases in refugee communities. Many of the diseases are ones with which Western nurses and doctors have had no previous personal contact and perhaps even no instruction. This valuable manual presents the basic facts on recognition, diagnosis, and mechanisms of spread and control in an attempt to help the health worker recognize and manage the situation. Essential in the field.

L. J. Bruce-Chwatt (1980). *Essential malariology.* William Heinemann Medical Books, London, 354 pp.

One of the most common early disease problems among refugees is malaria, especially where they have migrated from an upland area or one cleared of malaria, to a highly malarious area. Malaria cannot be controlled by applying a patchwork of randomly selected control measures, but needs an integrated approach specific to the environment, the type of vectors and parasites predominant in the area, the immunological status of the community, and the host countries' policies. This book is the most recent and comprehensive document on all aspects of malaria, and a useful source of information when attempting to establish a rational control approach.

W. A. M. Cutting (1979). Management of diarrhoea in children at the primary care or peripheral level. *Annales de la Societe Belge de Medicine Tropicale*. **59**, 221–39.

Given that refugee camps are often overcrowded, that the water supply is commonly inadequate in both quantity and quality, that environmental sanitation problems exist, that there is often moderate malnutrition, a shortage of food and fuel supplies, and severe social disruption, it is not surprising that diarrhoeal disease is often stated as being one of the major causes of morbidity and mortality. One of the most important treatments of diarrhoea is oral rehydration. This paper examines the scientific rationale for oral rehydration, provides guidelines on how to practise the method according to various criteria, and reviews the clinical assessment of dehydration, composition of oral fluids, treatment schedule, and the relevance of drugs. The author concludes by looking at the prerequisites for the organization of a diarrhoea disease service, such as a standardized schedule, a referral system, adequate supplies, health education, and community involvement.

W. D. Everett (1979). Malaria and beriberi: unresolved military medical problems contributing to the fall of Cambodia. *Military Medicine* **144**, 158–61.

Many health activities such as disease control programmes can be seriously disrupted in war time. The two main points of interest in this paper are firstly, that there was strong evidence that as a result of civil war and disruption of the malaria control programme, vivax malaria reappeared. Secondly, that international food aid in the form of polished white rice, to a nation used to eating brown, unpolished, thiamin-rich rice, contributed to an unnecessarily high number of cases of both wet and dry beriberi. Good examples of the medical consequence of civil disorders that may add to the plight of those remaining in, as well as those fleeing from, a country.

R. Feachem (1981). Oral rehydration with dirty water? *Diarrhoea Dialogue* **4**, 7.

Clean water for every member of a refugee community is not always available in adequate quantity. More commonly refugees can be seen drawing water from highly polluted rivers, wells, or hand-dug shallow holes. Medical personnel have been heard to advise refugees to boil contaminated water before drinking it. This is totally impracticable advice given that there is usually little or no fuel available. In this brief paper the author, in answer to the question 'does it matter if oral rehydration fluid is made up with water containing pathogens of faecal origin?', reviews the information available to date and concludes that where clean water is unobtainable, the advantages of early oral rehydration far outweigh the possible risk of using dirty water.

N. M. Foege (1971). Famine, infections and epidemics. *Famine: A Symposium Dealing with Nutrition and Relief Operations in Times of Disaster* (ed. Blix) Nutrition Foundations, Uppsala, 200 pp.

Since as early as 700 BC an association between famines and outbreaks of infectious diseases has been noted. This paper documents how famines lead to increased severity and transmission of infectious diseases and contribute to mortality rates. The consequences of this interrelation are analysed regarding the overall planning of famine relief. Thus, in the opinion of the author, the prevention and control of infectious disease epidemics must receive the same priority as food distribution. An effective epidemiological surveillance system and the enforcement of environmental control measures must also be standard procedures.

J. Murray and A. Murray (1977). Suppression of infection by famine and its activation by refeeding—a paradox?. *Perspectives in Biology and Medicine* **20**, 471–83.

The hypothesis that malnutrition enhances infection rates and severity of illness is criticized in this paper, in the light of the authors' historical, clinical, and laboratory observations. It is during the refeeding period, according to the authors, that severe intercurrent disease outbursts may occur. Some possible explanations for the apparent paradox are suggested, but no convincing scientific evidence is available to date. The implications of this concept are that in famine, a thorough evaluation of potential outbreaks must be made before refeeding starts, and attempts to eradicate quiescent diseases and protect against infections by immunization should precede any nutritional relief programme.

K. Toman (1979). Tuberculosis. *Case-Finding and Chemotherapy*. World Health Organization, Geneva, 239 pp.

Tuberculosis control is often a much neglected aspect of health activities when refugee camps are set up, because tuberculosis does not appear as a potentially explosive disease. Yet given the crowding factor common to many refugee communities, the disease is in the ideal milieu for transmission. This book reviews two major aspects of tuberculosis control that must be considered before embarking on long-term therapeutic schemes, those of active case-finding and choice of chemotherapy. Among the various treatment protocols reviewed, particular attention is paid to short course regimens. These are relevant to refugee communities as it is often difficult to plan on sufficient time to approach the disease according to classical steps.

Drugs

C. de Ville de Goyet and M. F. Lechat (1976). Drugs and supplies for disaster relief. *Tropical Doctor* **6**, 168–70.

Much time and energy can be wasted having to sort through unsolicited gifts of drugs and supplies, at a time when attention should be on the priority health problems in the community. This paper reviews the major factors to be considered at the co-ordinating level to ensure that an adequate quantity and quality of drugs reach the field. Factors such as the type of disaster, duration of the problem, the qualifications of the users, the operational constraints, and the epidemiological profile. Although this is discussed in the context of acute disaster situations, it very much applies to refugee camps.

WHO (1979). *The selection of essential drugs.* Technical Report Series No. 641, World Health Organization, Geneva, 44 pp.

Spending on preventive health measures frequently suffers because a large proportion of many national and international budgets is used for buying a wide variety of drugs, many of which are expensive proprietary preparations. Bearing this, and the promotional activities of the pharmaceutical companies in mind, the World Health Organization has put together a list of 200 essential drugs which might serve as a model for individual countries to identify their own drug priorities. This list has also been used as a guideline for the list of drugs for a refugee community of 10 000 for three months, published by the World Health Organization (WHO 1983; annotated in this review).

Environmental health

D. J. Bradley (1977). Health aspects of water supplies in tropical countries. *Water Wastes and Health in Hot Climates* (eds. Feachem, McGarry, and Mara). John Wiley, Chichester, 399 pp.

The relationship between water and health is often neglected in refugee communities. This is a basic reference to the epidemiology of diseases as related to the patterns of water utilization. It classifies infectious diseases in relation to water supplies, thus water-borne infections such as typhoid, cholera, or infective hepatitis will be limited by microbiological improvements of the water; water-washed infections such as the common diarrhoeas, both bacillary and viral, and skin and eye infections will be controlled by increasing the volume of water available; water-based diseases such as schistosomiasis and guinea worm need specific action to remove the intermediate host from the water and infections with water-related insect vectors such as sleeping sickness, yellow-fever, and malaria may be controlled by improvements in domestic water supplies. This classification is of great help when considering the improvements that need to be made regarding water quantity, quality, availability, sources, and distribution system according to disease patterns found in the camp or potential environment. The whole book makes worthwhile reading for those interested in studying the wider issues related to water, wastes, and health.

S. Cairncross and R. Feachem (1978). *Small water supplies*. Ross Bulletin No. 10, London School of Hygiene and Tropical Medicine, 78 pp.

It is often presumed by health workers that the subject of water supplies is the concern of environmental-health engineers, and there is very little or nothing a nurse or doctor can concern themselves with in this field. In refugee communities such an attitude can be disastrous. This booklet helps clarify in practical terms some of the issues involved in building or improving simple water supply systems, according to the source of water. Whether, for example, it is surface water, ground water, or water from a spring. It also gives guidelines on the principles of water treatment and storage on a domestic and community scale.

R. Feachem and S. Cairncross (1978). *Small excreta disposal systems*. Ross Bulletin No. 8, London School of Hygiene and Tropical Medicine, 54 pp.

Excreta disposal systems are not subjects that are covered in most medical training courses in the West, yet given an overcrowded refugee community in the rainy season, it is soon realized that they are priority subjects. This practical booklet reviews the various elements of excreta disposal systems and how they can be integrated in various combinations depending on local conditions and costs. The pit latrine will remain the main system in most refugee communities because it is easy to build and can be improved upon by adding ventilation pipes, or having composting pits, for example. Other systems that are described such as aqua privies, septic tanks, and sewerage treatment plants, may serve as a tool for improvements in permanent settlements, depending on cultural acceptability, availability of water, and nature of the environment.

D. Mara and R. Feachem (1980). Technical and public health aspects of low cost sanitation programme planning. *Journal of Tropical Medicine and Hygiene* **83**, 229–40.

Just as D. J. Bradley's paper (annotated above) reviews the relationship between water and health, so this paper, in the light of an environmental classification of excreta-related diseases, examines how sanitation improvements can be expected to reduce the incidence of certain diseases. Latency persistence and infective dose of the disease agents once they have been excreted with the faeces are major determinants of the efficiency of safe excreta disposal. Thus persistent and latent agents which are unable to multiply such as ascaris, hookworm, strongyloides, and taenia, will see their transmission limited by an effective sanitary system, while on the other extreme non-latent low infectious dose organisms such as amoebiasis and the enteric virus are better controlled by attention to domestic water supplies, personal hygiene, and better housing. Alternative excreta disposal technologies are discussed and the relevance of costs and socio-cultural factors are emphasized. Although some aspects of this paper do not apply to refugee communities, it provides a fundamental framework when thinking about sanitation issues.

J. P. W. Rivers and G. A. Brown (1979). Physiological aspects of shelter deprivation. *Disasters* **3**, 20–3.

Physiological factors need to be taken account of when planning the provision of shelter, although not in isolation from environmental and cultural factors. This interesting paper examines how exposure can affect both calorie and water requirements that can be lost through conduction, evaporation, convection, and radiation. Lack of adequate shelter and clothing during a famine, for example, where the night temperature falls to freezing point might require an extra 1000 kcal per person per day to prevent starvation and death. Living for 14 days at a temperature of between 34 and 38°C in an exceedingly dry atmosphere might cause one to lose 70 l of sweat and 750 g of salt. When discussing with administrators the relevance of appropriate shelter provision, especially where wide diurnal temperature fluctuations occur and when sudden showers are common, it should be stressed how heat losses may seriously worsen an already precarious nutritional condition.

Epidemiology

D. J. P. Barker (1982). *Practical Epidemiology*. Oxford University Press, London, 180 pp.

Epidemiology is one way of trying to understand what is happening to the pattern of diseases, and to the use being made of health services in refugee communities. This useful book makes epidemiology more understandable to those with little or no formal training in the subject. It covers topics such as making observations and counting diseases, samples, controls, selection of variables, design of record form, use of fieldwork techniques, and analysis of findings.

J. E. Brown and R. C. Brown (1975). The community census as a basis for health programmes. *Journal of Tropical Paediatrics and Environmental Child Health* **21**, 315–20.

A census is a pre-requisite to successful planning in a refugee community; the primary objective of which is to determine an accurate total number of persons. This information is required for planning quantities of food, shelter, water, and medical supplies, and can also be used as a frame for epidemiological surveillance. This paper outlines the formal steps such as ensuring community participation, a reasonably accurate estimate of the size of the population, determining the individuals and groups to be identified by the census, and the making of a map, that are needed to ensure reliable data recording and administrative organization for a census in any community. It provides fundamental guidelines for field workers.

N. M. Foege, R. C. Hogan, and L. H. Newton (1976). Surveillance projects for selected diseases. *International Journal of Epidemiology* **5**, 29–37.

Accurate and reliable data recording is often difficult to achieve, especially at the outset of a refugee crisis. To improve data collection and increase precision in monitoring intervention activities in any community, the authors suggest concentrating surveillance on a particular group of people selected by cluster sampling. This may be dangerous in a refugee community where people tend to congregate in ethnic, social, and cultural groups. Moreover, such a cluster is likely to receive more attention by repeated contacts with the health workers and therefore, soon cease to be representative of the rest of the community. This system can, nevertheless, be useful in ensuring reliable data in the initial stages of planning a health programme, and the paper provides useful information on how to organize such a prospective surveillance system.

Health aid

S. Aga Khan (1982). *Study on human rights and massive exoduses.* Commission on Human Rights, United Nations, Economic and Social Council, Geneva. E/CN.4/1503, 63 pp.

Increasing concern over the continued incidence of large-scale exoduses and displacements of populations and the resulting hardship both to the individuals and countries concerned prompted the United Nations to appoint the Aga Khan, a former High Commissioner for Refugees, 'to study the question of human rights and mass exoduses'.

The study makes fascinating reading on some of the wider issues which so closely interact with health. Nine recommendations are given and the sobering thought that a prerequisite to translate measures into reality is the political will of governments.

J. Briscoe (1980). Are voluntary agencies helping to improve health in Bangladesh?. *International Journal of Health Services* **10**, 47–69.

Little credit can be given to the 'community approach' if foreign agencies do not effectively allow the people they aim to help to organize and develop the programmes themselves. Many projects pay lip service to community health, having merely replaced one system of dependency with another. This stimulating paper serves as a reminder of the need to question the ultimate purpose of helping destitute people, and the method and outcome of aid as delivered by international agencies.

L. C. Chen (ed.) (1973). *Disaster in Bangladesh. Health crises in a developing nation.* Oxford University Press, 290 pp.

In 1970 a devastating cyclone hit Bangladesh and in 1971 civil war broke out, both contributing to a state of crisis in the country. This book reviews the main demographic and health characteristics of Bangladesh before those events and proceeds to analyse the specific problems that ensued and the lessons learnt. An interesting collection of papers that puts the crisis in perspective and outlines all its different aspects.

A. E. Ifekwunigwe (1976). Emergency assistance. The nature and organization of disaster relief. *Food and Nutrition* **2**, 6–13.

There are three components to planning in disaster situations; predisaster preparedness, emergency relief action, and rehabilitation. Although the first step is difficult where refugee problems are due to war, it is possible when people are displaced due to famine or drought. This paper briefly summarizes all the steps and topics that should be envisaged when planning and implementing relief work. Organization and operational guidelines for the emergency phase are given, with a strong emphasis on the importance of surveillance.

A. J. Taylor and F. C. Cuny (1979). The evaluation of humanitarian assistance. *Disasters* **3**, 37–42.

There is much to learn about the programmes implemented in refugee communities but very few individuals and even fewer agencies are systematic in their approach to assessing and learning from their experiences. This paper is a comprehensive review of the purpose, scope, and alternatives of evaluation, and also questions whether evaluation is better done within an organization or by outsiders. It succeeds in de-mystifying many aspects of evaluation and will, it is hoped, stimulate more people to attempt to evaluate their work in the field.

Health care

F. J. Bennett (ed.) (1979). *Community diagnosis and health action.* The Macmillan Press, London, 190 pp.

Good planning from the beginning is essential if health services are to be effective and appropriate, and respond to the changing environment. Part of the planning process involves undertaking an investigation of the community which will give an understanding of the social, cultural, economic, psychological, and environmental factors contributing to the health problems of that community. This book, although not specifically dealing with refugee camps, attempts to cover these aspects, giving a comprehensive view of community diagnosis, methods, and approaches to obtaining information, the analytical process following acquisition of data, the planning and evaluation of interventions, and finally the uses of community diagnosis for training programmes.

M. King (1973). *A medical laboratory for developing countries.* Oxford University Press, 519 pp.

To have access to basic laboratory investigations in a camp can be invaluable, both to the clinician and to those working on public health measures, in order to raise the standards of individual and community diagnosis. This useful book provides detailed yet simple methods of establishing a basic laboratory in the field with limited means and maximum reliance on locally made equipment. Particular emphasis is placed on basic laboratory techniques and information on the equipment required; indispensable when planning to implement a basic laboratory service in a camp.

M. King, F. King, and S. Martodipoero (1981). *Primary child care. A manual for health workers. Book One.* Oxford University Press, 315 pp.

In 'normal' times in developing countries as much as 40 per cent of the population is often less than 15 years of age and many children die before they are five years old. Due to political, socio-economic, and health and disease factors, these problems may be magnified in a refugee community. The care of healthy and sick children is, therefore, a priority issue. This book provides a comprehensive review of the common afflictions of children in tropical countries. In easily understood terms it describes the pathogenesis, clinical aspects, and treatment procedures in successive working steps, to allow logical teaching to health workers. Well illustrated, this is a useful book for helping develop tropical paediatric skills.

L. P. Medis and P. A. Fernando (1972). Health education in emergency situations: a cholera outbreak in Sri Lanka. *International Journal of Health Education* **20**, 200–4.

The term 'emergency situation' in this paper refers to a cholera outbreak in two villages, some 10 km from the capital of Sri Lanka, Colombo. Health education is always said to be important in emergency relief, but it is probably one of the most difficult aspects to implement. To be effective a health education programme needs to involve the community, be sensitive to social and cultural factors, and address different targets, such as the community, health workers, or medical personnel, with different topics and methods. This paper is an interesting example of how a health education programme was implemented following a definition of the general and specific objectives, matched to the target groups, content of programme, and method and material to be used.

G. Walt and P. Vaughan (eds.) (1981). *An introduction to the primary health care approach in developing countries: a review with selected annotated references.* Ross Institute Publication No. 13, London School of Hygiene and Tropical Medicine, 61 pp.

Primary health care, with its emphasis on extending and improving health care in populations with limited resources, on improving nutrition, on better environmental health, and the role of health in development, is highly relevant to the planning of health care in refugee camps. This useful bibliography gives references to the many facets of health and development which the primary health care approach encompasses, and serves as a guide to the readily available literature.

Immunization

D. N. McMurray, S. A. Loomis, L. J. Casazza, and H. Rey (1979). Influence of moderate malnutrition on morbidity and antibody response following vaccination with live, attenuated measles virus vaccine. *Bulletin of the Pan American Health Organization* **13**, 52–7.

Measles epidemics have devastating consequences among malnourished populations, a feature of many camps. There are, however, often doubts expressed in the field on the effectiveness of immunizing malnourished children. This paper reviews the effects of measles vaccination on antibody response and vaccine-related complications between normal and mal-nourished children. No difference was observed and a conclusion reached that attenuated live measles vaccine is an efficient and harmless tool to prevent severe effects from measles infection among malnourished children.

WHO (1980). *BCG vaccination policies.* Technical Report Series No. 652, World Health Organization, Geneva, 17 pp.

Recent BCG trials have shed some doubts on the effectiveness of BCG vaccination to protect against active tuberculosis. This short report reviews all the available evidence to date and concludes that BCG should still be administered in areas of high TB prevalence, especially as it probably does protect young infants and children.

WHO (1981). *An annotated cold chain bibliography.* EPI/CCIS/81.9, World Health Organization, Geneva, 8 pp.

As with other health interventions among refugee communities, the priority given to immunization depends not only on its intrinsic importance but on its feasibility. Factors such as cultural acceptance, community participation, and physical and climatic constraints have to be considered before an immunization programme can be implemented. This document, now in its third revision, lists 36 references covering different aspects of the cold chain. These range from product information sheets detailing equipment for the vaccine cold chain to a paper describing the 'state of the art' of solar refridgerators, an article on monitoring vaccine storage temperatures, a booklet describing the cold chain game, which is used as training material. and a set of colour slides with an accompanying text on vaccine handling.

International health workers

Council of Europe (1982). *European workshop on educational aspects of health in disasters.* Division for Higher Education and Research, Council of Europe, Strasbourg, 48 pp.

The Council of Europe and the World Health Organization with the help of the Ross Institute of Tropical Hygiene, London School of Hygiene and Tropical Medicine, and the School of Public Health, Catholic University of Louvain, Brussels, convened to review the needs in Europe for postgraduate training of health professionals and others in the management of health problems in acute catastrophe and longer-term refugee disasters. The workshop defined the training needs and drafted recommendations. Appendix III of the booklet outlines proposed course modules.

Ross Institute (1980). *Preservation of personal health in warm climates.* The Ross Institute of Tropical Hygiene, London School of Hygiene and Tropical Medicine, 108 pp.

When international health workers fall ill in a refugee community, not only is the sending agency deprived of the workers' sevices but it may be put to great trouble in procuring treatment. By the very nature of the environmental situation that may exist, camps are often potential personal health risks, but there are many ways in which the risk can be minimized. This booklet, now in its eighth edition, has proved invaluable to many travellers over the years, containing as it does, useful information on such aspects as the health hazards of the tropics, prophylactic inoculations, and the world distribution of tropical diseases.

S. W. A. Gunn, F. Parakatil, and C. Murcia (1983). *English–French vocabulary of emergency relief and disaster management.* Conseil International de la langue Francaise, Paris, France, 200 pp.

This vocabulary is the first compilation of all the technical and administrative abbreviations currently used and encountered in international relief work. Each term is explained in French in dictionary form and its equivalent given in English.

University of Louvain (1979). *Medico-nutritional information on disaster prone countries and glossary of common illnesses.* The Centre for Research on the Epidemiology of Disasters, School of Public Health, University of Louvain, Brussels, 167 pp.

One of the main problems when preparing to go to work in a foreign country is trying to get background information on the medical and nutritional situation of both the country the refugees have fled from and the host country. This book is a good base-line assessment of the predominant diet pattern, nutritional deficiencies, medical supply system, health services structure, and common illnesses, in countries prone to disasters. It is published as part of the *Country Fact Sheets* issued by the Licross/Volags Steering Committee for Disasters, in 1978.

E. Wauty, C. de Ville de Goyet, and S. Chaze (1977). Social integration among disaster relief volunteers: a survey. *Mass Emergencies* **2**, 105–9.

During the Sahel famine of 1968–1974, many foreign volunteers were recruited to work on various aspects of the relief development programme. One such group of volunteers worked in Niger in 1974, and as a result of the many social, psychological, and professional problems encountered within the group, a study was commissioned by the League of Red Cross Societies to look at such aspects as motivation, personality, professionalism and communication. The authors, who were staff of the Research Centre in Disaster Epidemiology at the University of Louvain, Brussels, analysed end of mission reports, anonymous questionnaires, and an evaluation report on each delegate. Their main conclusion was that when selecting volunteers more attention should be paid to practical qualifications, even at the expense of specialized abilities, in the belief that it would enhance the efficiency of relief agencies.

Nutrition

H. J. L. Burgess and A. Burgess (1975). A field worker's guide to nutritional status survey. *The American Journal of Clinical Nutrition* **28**, 1299–321.

One of the main objectives of a nutrition survey is to get a good estimate of the amount of malnutrition present. The information gained can then be used in various ways, including influencing policy changes. To be of value, therefore, the survey has to be carried out using a reliable reproducible technique. Although the approach described in this paper is probably too

complex for rapid nutritional assessment in refugee communities, it nevertheless provides a good reference and framework for the design of surveys.

L. C. Chen, A. K. M. Chowdhury, and S. L. Huffman (1980). Anthropometric assessment of energy–protein malnutrition and subsequent risk of
mortality among pre-school aged children. *American Journal of Clinical
Nutrition* **33**, 1836–45.

The assessment of malnourished children by anthropometric criteria in a
refugee community is useful in that it allows, amongst other things, for the
identification of those children exposed to an increased risk of death.
Preventive measures can subsequently be taken. This paper relates to a
survey done on more than 2000 children in Bangladesh, who were followed
for 2 years. Various anthropometric criteria were used including weight for
height, weight for age, height for age, and arm circumference for height. It
showed that the risk was not graduated with the intensity of malnutrition,
but that there was a definite threshold level over which the risk of death
would increase many times. Also that weight for age, and height for age
appeared to be far more discriminating criteria than weight for height, which
is the measurement used most often in refugee communities. An issue that
could become controversial.

C. de Ville de Goyet, J. Seaman, and V. Geijer (1978). *The management of
nutritional emergencies in large populations.* World Health Organization,
Geneva, 98 pp.

Nutrition relief does not rely solely on the provision of food. Aspects such
as assessment and surveillance of nutritional status, efficient and effective
feeding programmes, and camp administration are vital if the number of new
cases of malnutrition is not to increase. All these subjects and more are
discussed in this booklet, which is the most relevant, useful source of
information available despite its lack of emphasis on working 'with' the
community. To date the book is regarded by most relief workers as their
nutrition bible.

T. P. Eddy (1977). An error of medicine? Kwashiorkor and the protein gap.
Tropical Doctor **7**, 28–32.

Marasmus and kwashiorkor are no longer seen as two different diseases
due to radically different diets, but more as interchangeable conditions for
which a whole range of factors such as heredity, environment, illness,
maternal care, and food intake, intermingle. The consequences of this
concept lie mainly in the re-thinking of the treatment and prevention of
malnutrition in children; getting away from the supposition that an
extremely complicated syndrome attributed to protein deficiency 'can be

treated and controlled by a simple replacement therapy with a dose of protein, much as one would give an appropriate dosage of a vitamin in a vitamin-deficiency disease'. Instead more emphasis should be on education, child welfare, the promotion and maintenance of breast-feeding, improvement of the environment, and production of sufficient food of all kinds for the population.

M. Gebre-Medhin (1977). Sequence of events. Model of a consolidated food and nutrition information system ('Early warning system'). *Journal of Tropical Paediatrics and Environmental Child Health* **23**, 23–8.

Events that cause people to become displaced need to stimulate a preventive approach to future similar problems. Following an outline of the sometimes complicated, interlinked mechanisms operative in the evolution of famine the author goes on to describe a model of an early warning system for Ethiopia. This was devised as a result of the disastrous 1972–1974 drought and famine in the Wollo region and was based on the analysis of a shelter population (S. Belete *et al.*, annotated elsewhere in this review). A very interesting example of a practical early warning system that has identified measurable variables such as malnutrition, health and disease rates, and meteorological, agricultural, livestock and market information so as to attempt to assess the impact of drought and food production, distribution, and consumption on individuals and communities. Good coverage at both regional and national level is considered essential and the inter-disciplinary collection and analysis of data should be done as an integral part of the governments' planning system.

M. Gebre-Medhin, R. Hay, Y. Licke, and M. Maffi (1977). Initial experience of a consolidated food and nutrition information system. Analysis of data from the Ogaden area. *Journal of Tropical Paediatrics and Environmental Child Health* **23**, 29–37.

To devise an early warning system is one thing, to implement and evaluate it quite another task. In this paper the authors report a positive outcome of the previously described system, as applied to a different region in the country. The various recordings indicated a marked deterioration of the situation including delayed rainfall, a drastic fall in average livestock holdings, unusually high grain prices, a significant deterioration in the nutritinal condition of the population, and a higher than usual motality rate. This surveillance permitted a prediction of forthcoming events and led to a faster relief response than might have otherwise occurred.

P. Harman (1981). Measuring malnutrition in nutritional emergencies. *Nursing Times* **77**, 65–8.

The identification and assessment of malnutrition is one vital aspect of health work in refugee communities. Visual impressions are often accurate and should not be neglected, but it can also be extremely valuable for epidemiological purposes to be able to quantify the degree of malnutrition. This paper reviews in very clear terms the various types of malnutrition that may be encountered, the use of anthropometric assessments in the community and simplified techniques for the identification of wasted (thin) children.

D. B. Jelliffe (1969). Emergency feeding of young children. *Tropical Pediatrics* **75**, 153–4.

This is an advocation to stockpile appropriate supplementary foods to ensure immediate availability in times of disasters, for past experience has shown that most foods comprise an 'ad hoc collection of hastily gathered . . . food surpluses' which are not geared to the needs of young children. Rejecting dried skimmed milk because of its association with infections and nutritive problems, the author reviews and supports the development of preparations based on cereals, with added oil and vitamin supplements. A short paper of value and relevance more than 12 years after publication.

D. B. Jelliffe and E. F. Jelliffe (1977). Breast feeding: a key measure in large scale disaster relief. *Disasters* **1**, 199–203.

The promotion of breast-feeding should be an integral part of disaster relief planning. Based on a physiological analysis of the lactation phenomenon, this paper looks at simple, practical measures to induce and maintain breast-feeding by stimulating prolactin secretion and restoring the let-down reflex combined with simple priority management of common infections and the giving of additional rations.

J. Mayer (1975). The management of famine relief. *Science* **188**, 571–7.

There are probably four primary causes of famine, according to the author—drought, crop diseases or pests, the impact of war or civil disturbance, or a combination of disturbances hitting both crops and farmers, such as floods or earthquakes and in all of them the situation is made worse by lack of communication and social inequality. This often leads to increased death rates from starvation, severe social disruption, and loss of livestock and seeds. This is a fundamental reference paper on famine management and relief, covering factors such as food policy, treatment of starvation, and rehabilitation and development.

D. Nabarro and S. McNabb (1980). A simple new technique for identifying thin children. *Journal of Tropical Medicine and Hygiene* **83**, 21–33.

Weight for height is the accepted criteria for anthropometric assessment of malnutrition in emergency situations as it identifies thin children, who are classified as recent sufferers. It is, however, a fairly time-consuming process to execute in mass screening programmes and requires skill in the measurement of height and weight and for reading tables. This paper describes a simplified approach to weight/height reading that is from a wall-chart and requires only the measurement of weight. The child is placed against the chart at the point of his weight and a range of columns allow him to be categorized quickly into severe, moderate, or normal nutritional status.

S. Peel (1977). Practical relief and preventive methods. *Disasters*, **1**, 179–97; also published as *Selective feeding procedures* (1977). OXFAM Working Paper No. 1, OXFAM, Oxford, UK, 33 pp.

The decision to implement supplementary and therapeutic feeding programmes during emergencies will depend on the health and nutritional status of the population, the existing environmental health hazards, the effectiveness of the general feeding programme, and the resources available. Should it be decided that supplementary with or without therapeutic feeding is required then this thorough, clearly written paper will be of value, especially if used in conjuction with the book *Management of nutritional emergencies in large populations* (C. de Ville de Goyet *et al.* 1978, annotated in this section). The paper summarizes all the accepted principles in the organization and running of such programmes and also looks at the compounding problems encountered in the management of malnourished children. There are also annexes giving details on such things as tables of anthropometric standards, energy–protein values of useful relief and indigenous foods, food preparation, and the equipment required for such feeding programmes.

WHO (1981). *The treatment and management of severe protein–energy malnutrition*. World Health Organization, 47 pp.

This manual goes into slightly more depth on the treatment and management of severe protein–energy malnutrition than either of the previously annotated booklets, *Selective feeding procedures* and *Management of nutritional emergencies in large populations*. Of particular use are the tables on how to prepare high-energy feeds and the recipe for the stock solution of potassium supplement.

Training

F. R. Abbat (1980). *Teaching for better learning: a guide for teachers of primary health care staff*. World Health Organization, 137 pp.

Teaching health workers requires careful design of the curriculum. Attention must be given to ensure that the student is not only given information but equally the technical knowledge on how to apply the information. This document is a exposé on how to plan a teaching curriculum for health workers based on a task analysis of what their future duties are expected to be. Applicable to training interested refugees, and other levels of health workers for refugee communities.

J. P. Vaughan (1980). Barefoot or professional? Community health workers in the Third World: some important questions concerning their function, utilization, selection, training and evaluation. *Journal of Tropical Medicine and Hygiene* **83**, 3–10.

Much of the health work in refugee communities is often done by refugees with no previous training in the health sector, but who are trained 'on the spot' in certain aspects of the work. They then become key members of the health team and are not only invaluable but vital, if any degree of self-sufficiency is to be achieved. Before commencing such a training course it is imperative to consider certain issues. This paper reviews many of the issues that must be questioned concerning community and primary health care workers, including what will the workers' precise role be? How to select them? How should the training be done? And as part of their evaluation, what is their professional ability? All relevant to the training of interested refugees.

D. Werner (1980). *Where there is no doctor*. The Macmillan Press, 408 pp.

One of the main aims of a health programme in a refugee community is to help refugees to become as self-sufficient as possible, to manage programmes and to learn skills that will be useful on their return home. This interesting book is useful as a teaching tool for health workers, to help identify what the interested refugees should be taught as part of the process of developing preventive and curative skills.

D. Werner and B. Bower (1982). *Helping health workers learn*. The Hesperian Foundation, Palo Alto, California, USA, 593 pp.

This book of methods, aids, and ideas for instructors at the village level is an excellent companion to the book *Where there is no doctor* (annotated above). The refreshing approach to the training, role, and responsibilities of community health workers makes fascinating reading. Part One of the book looks at approaches to planning and carrying out a training programme; Part Two gives ideas for bringing learning to life; Part Three gives suggestions for helping people learn to use *Where there is no doctor*; Part Four covers activities with mothers and children, and Part Five looks at health in relation to food, land, and social problems.

A COUNTRY BIBLIOGRAPHY

Angola

S. P. Simmonds and H. Brown (1979). Angola: meeting health and health-related needs with refugees. *Disasters* **3**, 411–15.

Australia

A. J. Bourne, R. B. Dymock, W. D. H. Parry, and T. W. Turner (1980). Leprosy in Indo-Chinese refugees. *The Medical Journal of Australia* **1**, 275–6.

Bangladesh

C. Aall (1979). Disastrous international relief failure: a report on Burmese refugees in Bangladesh from May–December 1978. *Disasters* **3**, 429–34.

R. E. Brown (1972). Some nutritional considerations in times of major catastrophe. *Clinical Pediatrics* **11**, 334–42.

L. C. Chen and J. E. Rohde (1971). Famine and civil war in East Pakistan. *The Lancet* **2**, 557–60.

L. C. Chen (ed.) (1973). *Disaster in Bangladesh*. Oxford University Press, 290 pp.

M. P. Chisholm (1978). Lessons from a school building project, and refugee relief operations—Bangladesh 1975–77. *Disasters* **2**, 148–51.

C. P. Dodge and P. O. Wiebe (1980). Practical application of nutritional assessment: malnutrition in the flood area of Bangladesh. *Disasters* **4**, 311–14.

S. Franken and J. G. Anten (1976). The pattern of famine in Bangladesh. *Annales de la Societe Belge de Medecine Tropicale* **56**, 325–32.

J. Howard and B. Lloyd (1979). Sanitation and diseases in Bangladesh urban slums and refugee camps. *Progress in Water Technology* **11**, 191–200.

M. U. Khan and M. D. Shahidullah (1982). The role of water and sanitation in the incidence of cholera in refugee camps. *Transactions of the Royal Society of Tropical Medicine and Hygiene* **76**, 373–7.

T. Majors (1976). Conditions in a refugee camp in Bangladesh in 1972. *Tropical Doctor* **6**, 171–2.

S. Rahman (1981). Dispersing the disaster clouds. *Unicef News* **3**, 13–15.

E. M. Ressier (1979). Evaluation of CMU/INTERECT A-frames as emergency shelter in Bangladesh, March 1977. *Disasters* **3**, 457–9.

A. Sommer and W. H. Mosley (1972). East Bengal cyclone of November, 1970. Epidemiological approach to disaster assessment. *The Lancet* **1**, 1029–35.

M. D. Thompson (1980). Reliability of recorded death rates among Burmese refugees in Bangladesh (letter). *Disasters* **4**, 356–9.

E. Waldron (1977). Bangladesh—an unforgettable experience. *Nursing Times* **73**, 7–8.

Canada

L. M. Cathcart, P. Berger, and B. Knazan (1979). Medical examination of torture victims applying for refugee status. *Canadian Medical Association Journal* **121**, 179–84.

M. Korcok (1980). The Haitian and Cuban refugees: dealing with imported disease. *Canadian Medical Association Journal* **123**, 213–15, 218–20.

M. L. Schwartz (1980). Malaria in Vietnamese refugees. *Canadian Medical Association Journal* **123**, 968–71.

Cyprus

P. Loizos (1981). *The Heart Grown Bitter*. Cambridge University Press, 219 pp.

Denmark

F. Black, I. Bygbjerg, P. Effersoe, G. Gomme, S. Jepsen and A. Jensen (1981). Fansidar resistant falciparum malaria acquired in South East Asia. *Transactions of the Royal Society of Tropical Medicine and Hygiene* **75**, 715–16.

Ethiopia

M. Azbite (1981). A famine relief operation at Qorem, Ethiopia, in 1966. *Disasters* **5**, 6–18.

G. Barnabas (1982). Popcorn and fairies in the management of measles in Ethiopia (letter). *The Lancet* **1**, 450.

S. Belete, M. Gebre-Medhin, B. Hailemariam, M. Maffi, B. Vahlquist, and Z. Wolde-Gebriel (1977). Study of shelter population in the Wollo Region. *Journal of Tropical Paediatrics and Environmental Child Health* **23**, 15–36.

G. N. Brown (1977). Nutritional surveillance in the Ogaden. *The Lancet* **2**, 911–12.

N. Cohen (1977). Nutritional status and pressure on populations in the Awash Valley and Hararghe Mountains, Ethiopia. *Disasters* **1**, 59.

M. G. Davey (1976). Somali food shelters in the Ogaden famine. *The Lancet* **2**, 798.

J. Fitzpatrick (1978). Air transporting relief supplies: the Ethiopian experience. *Disasters* **2**, 193–5.

M. Gebre-Medhin and B. Vahlquist (1976). Famine in Ethiopia—a brief review. *American Journal of Clinical Nutrition* **29**, 1016–20.

M. Gebre-Medhin (1977). Sequence of events. Model of a consolidated food and nutrition information system (Early Warning System). *Journal of Tropical Paediatrics and Environmental Child Health* **23**, 23–8.

M. Gebre-Medhin, R. Hay, Y. Licke, and M. Maffi (1977). Initial experience of a consolidated food and nutrition information system. Analysis of data from the Ogaden area. *Journal of Tropical Paediatrics and Environmental Child Health* **23**, 29–37.

J. F. J. Holt, J. Rivers, and J. Seaman (1975). The Ethiopian famine of 1973–1974. 2. Harargh Province. *Proceedings of the Nutrition Society* **34**, 115A–16A.

R. J. McKerrow (1979). Drought in Ethiopia 1977/1979. *Disasters* **3**, 131–34.

J. B. Mason, R. W. Hay, J. Holt, J. Seaman, and M. R. Bowden (1974). Nutritional lessons from the Ethiopian drought. *Nature* **248**, 646–50.

J. B. Mason, R. W. Hay, J. Leresche, S. Peel, and S. Darley (1974). Treatment of severe malnutrition in relief. *The Lancet* **1**, 332–5.

A. Matheson (1981). The key word is 'basic'. *Unicef News* **3**, 20–1.

D. S. Miller and J. F. Holt (1975). The Ethiopian famine. *Proceedings of the Nutrition Society* **34**, 167–72.

M. J. Murray, A. B. Murray, M. B. Murray, and C. J. Murray (1976). Somali food shelters in the Ogaden famine and their impact on health. *The Lancet* **1**, 1283–5.

J. P. W. Rivers, J. F. Holt, J. A. Seaman, and M. R. Bowden (1974). Lessons for epidemiology from the Ethiopian famine. *Annales de la Societe Belge de Medecine Tropicale* **56**, 345–67.

J. Seaman and J. F. J. Holt (1975). The Ethiopian famine of 1973–1974. 1. Wollo Province. *Proceedings of the Nutrition Society* **34**, 114A–15A.

J. Seaman, J. Holt, and J. Rivers (1978). The effects of drought on human nutrition in an Ethiopian province. *International Journal of Epidemiology* **7**, 31–40.

J. Shepherd (1975). *The politics of starvation*. Carnegie Endowment for International Peace, New York, 101 pp.

R. Waiblinger (1976). German Red Cross effort in Ethiopia. *Deutsche Drankepflegez* **30**, 12–16.

W. H. Watson (1976). The Ogaden famine (letter). *The Lancet* **2**, 48.
R. Wooldridge (1976). Nursing in a famine. *Nursing Times* **72**, 166–7.

Gabon

T. C. Okeahialam (1972). Children with protein calorie malnutrition evacuated to Gabon during the Nigerian Civil War. *Journal of Tropical Paediatrics and Environmental Child Health* **18**, 169–84.
J. Thomas, G. Lebigot, P. Capdevieille, J. Girard, Y. Lassalle, and H. Sagnet (1971). Les manifestations neuro-psychiques et le comportement psychologique des enfants atteints de Kwashiorkor de famine. *Medecine Tropicale* **31**, 165–72.

Honduras

P. Isaza, Z. T. de Quinteros, E. Pineda, C. Parchment, E. Aguilar, and M. McQuestion (1980). A diarrheal disease control programme among Nicaraguan refugee children in Campo Luna, Honduras. *Bulletin of the Pan American Health Organization* **14**, 337–42.

Hong Kong

P. Anton, K. Arnold, G. K. Trnong, and W. T. Wong (1981). Bacterial enteric pathogens in Vietnamese refugees in Hong Kong. *Southeast Asian Journal of Tropical Medical Public Health* **12**, 151–6.
K. Arnold and T. G. Khanh (1980). Vietnamese refugee health status in Hong Kong (letter). *The Lancet* **2**, 475–6.
S. S. Lai (1980). Health of Vietnamese refugees in Hong Kong (letter). *The Lancet* **2**, 1308–9.
T. Philpot (1980). A harbour of hope. *Nursing Times* **151**, 24–7.

India

J. Barnes (1971). Nutrition in refugee camps (letter). *British Medical Journal* **3**, 528.
R. E. Brown (1972). Some nutritional considerations in times of major catastrophe. Observations following a recent visit to the Bangladesh refugee camps in North Eastern India. *Clinical Pediatrics* **11**, 334–42.
F. C. Cuny (1977). Refugee camps and camp planning. The state of the art. *Disasters* **1**, 125–43.
P. Gardner, J. E. Rohde, and M. B. Majumdar (1972). Health priorities among Bangladesh refugees. *The Lancet* **1**, 834–6.
R. Hickman (1971). Deteriorating health of refugee children in India. *The Lancet* **2**, 917–18.
D. Mahalanabis, A. B. Choudhuri, N. G. Bacchi, A. K. Bhattacharya, and T. W. Simpson (1973). Oral fluid therapy of cholera among Bangladesh refugees. *The Johns Hopkins Medical Journal* **132**, 197–205.
D. N. Mazumder and A. K. Chakrabarty (1973). Epidemic of smallpox among the evacuees from Bangladesh in Salt Lake area near Calcutta. *Journal of Indian Medical Association* **60**, 275–80.
S. K. Nayak and S. Patel (1977). Some physical observations among Tibetan refugees. *Journal of Indian Medical Association* **69**, 279–80.
B. Pastakia (1972). Relief for Bangladesh refugees in India (letter). *The Lancet* **2**, 1139.
J. Seaman (1972). Relief work in a refugee camp for Bangladesh refugees in India. *The Lancet* **2**, 866–70.

R. N. Srivastava (1973). Nutrition therapy centre: experience at a West Bengal refugee camp. *Indian Paediatrics* **10**, 503–6.

M. C. Swaminathan, K. Visweswara Rao, and D. Hanumantha Rao (1967). Food and nutrition in the drought affected areas of Andhra Pradesh. *Indian Journal of Medical Research* **55**, 768–78.

M. C. Swaminathan, K. Vijayaraghavan, and D. Hanumantha Rao (1973). Nutritional status of refugees from Bangla Desh. *Indian Journal of Medical Research* **61**, 278–84.

B. N. Tandon (1976). Monitoring emergency nutrition programmes in India. *Food and Nutrition* **2**, 19–22.

A. J. Taylor (1979). Emergency sanitation for refugees: experiences in the Bangladesh refugee relief camp, India 1971–1972. *Disasters* **3**, 435–42.

P. Thompson (1977). Saving the children in West Bengal. *Nursing Times* **68**, 715–16.

Iran

M. Lange (1975). Relief work in Kurdistan. *Nursing Mirror* **141**, 44–66.

Israel

L. Alexander (1968). Military psychiatry, occupation and refugee problems in Israel. *Military Medicine* **133**, 265–74.

C. Dworkin (1974). A volunteer nurse in Israel. *The Canadian Nurse* **70**, 30–2.

A. H. Guinena (1977). Protein–calorie malnutrition in young refugee children in the Gaza Strip. *Journal of Tropical Paediatrics and Environmental Child Health* **23**, 38–57.

Ivory Coast

R. E. Brown, D. Carroll, G. Mulvihill, M. Mulvihill, S. Silberstein, and S. Thacker (1974). Field nutrition survey of Nigerian children in Ivory Coast refugee camps. *Tropical Geographical Medicine* **26**, 152–6.

Jordan

A. G. Hill (1983). The Palestinian population of the Middle East. *Population and Development Review* **9**, 85–103.

Kampuchea

U. Bollag (1980). Practical evaluation of a pilot immunization campaign against typhoid fever in a Cambodian refugee camp. *International Journal of Epidemiology* **9**, 121–2.

W. D. Everett (1979). Malaria and beriberi: unresolved military medical problems contributing to the fall of Cambodia. *Military Medicine* **144**, 158–61.

J. Pilger (1979). The aid agencies play politics while a nation starves: the 'filthy affair' of denying relief. *New Statesman* **98**, 546.

M. van der Westhuizen (1980). Kampuchean refugees—an encounter with grief. *The Australia Nurses Journal* **10**, 53–6.

R. J. Weiss (1981). Michigan physician horrified by 'second holocaust' in Cambodia. *Michigan Medicine* **80**, 14.

Kenya

C. Capone, F. Jacob, and A. O'Laughlin (1978). Catholic relief services: nutrition intervention programme for the drought areas of Kenya. *Disasters* **2**, 225–58.

R. Hogg (1980). Pastoralism and impoverishment: the case of the Isiolo Boran of Northern Kenya. *Disasters* **4**, 299–310.
M. O'Leary (1980). Responses to drought in Kitui District, Kenya. *Disasters* **4**, 315–27.

Lebanon

A. G. Hill (1983). The Palestinian population of the Middle East. *Population and Development Review* **9**, 85–103.
J. H. Puyet, E. F. Downes, and R. Budeir (1963). Nutritional and growth characteristics of Arab refugee children in Lebanon. *American Journal of Clinical Nutrition* **3**, 147–57.
E. Roine (1980). Working with mothers and children in a Palestinian refugee camp. *Sykepleien* **67**, 18–19.
A. Sirhan (1975). Palestinian refugee camp life in Lebanon. *Journal of Palestine Studies* **4**, 91–107.
P. A. Wright (1971). Diarrhoea: a specific treatment programme in Palestinian refugee camps. *Nursing Times* **67**, 915–18.

Malaysia

J. Howard (1979). Survey on water supply and sanitation for Pulau Bidong. *Disasters* **3**, 461–7.

Mauritania

M. Engel (1981). A way of life is turned to dust. *Unicef News* **3**, 26–8.
M. H. Greene (1974). Impact of the Sahelian drought in Mauritania, West Africa. *The Lancet* **1**, 1093–7.
D. D. Hedley and J. E. Rohde (1978). The analysis of the results of supplementary feeding trials: an approach based on the evaluation of Swedish emergency foods during the famine in Mauritania. *Disasters* **2**, 259–64.

Niger

C. Aall and E. Helsing (1976). The Sahelian drought: experiences from a supporting programme in Niger for food provision, nutrition rehabilitation, prevention of malnutrition. *Journal of Tropical Paediatrics and Environmental Child Health* **22**, 69–83.
B. Camara (1976). Effects of drought: experience of Niger. *Annales de la Societe Belge de Medecine Tropicale* **56**, 293–304.
C. de Ville de Goyet (1977). Anthropometric measurements in a relief programme in Niger: a tool for decision making at the community level. *Disasters* **1**, 223–9.
K. A. Luker (1975). A food programme for drought stricken Niger. *Nursing Times* **71**, 368–70.
E. Wauty, C. de Ville de Goyet, and S. Chaze (1977). Social integration among disaster relief volunteers: a survey. *Mass Emergencies* **2**, 105-9.

Nigeria

C. Aall (1970). Relief, nutrition and health problems in the Nigerian/Biafran War. *Journal of Tropical Paediatrics and Environmental Child Health* **16**, 70–90.
R. E. Brown (1969). Mission to Biafra: a study and survey of a population under stress. *Clinical Paediatrics* **8**, 313–21.

R. E. Brown and J. Mayer (1969). Famine and disease in Biafra: an assessment. *Tropical and Geographical Medicine* **21**, 348–52.

L. E. Davis (1971). Epidemiology of famine in the Nigerian crisis: rapid evaluation of malnutrition by weight and arm circumference in large populations. *American Journal of Clinical Nutrition* **24**, 358–64.

B. Gans (1969). A Biafran relief mission. *The Lancet* **1**, 660–5.

R. E. Gribbin (1973). Two relief crisis: Biafra and Sudan. *Africa Today* **20**, 47–59.

J. M. Gurney (1969). The arm circumference as a public health index of protein-calorie malnutrition of early childhood. Rapid assessment in a refugee camp in Nigeria. *Journal of Tropical Paediatrics and Environmental Child Health* **15**, 241–2.

R. Hickman (1970). The relief operation in former Biafra. *The Lancet* **2**, 815–16.

M. S. Loewenstein and J. F. Phillips (1973). Evaluation of arm circumference measurement for determining nutritional status of children and its use in an acute epidemic of malnutrition: Owerri, Nigeria, following the Nigerian Civil War. *American Journal of Clinical Nutrition* **26**, 226–33.

J. P. Miller (1970). Medical relief in the Nigerian Civil War. *The Lancet* **1**, 1330–4.

M. J. Murray, A. B. Murray, N. J. Murray, and M. B. Murray (1978). Diet and cerebral malaria: the effect of famine and refeeding. *The American Journal of Clinical Nutrition* **31**, 57–61.

Pakistan

A. S. Ahmed (1980). Afghan refugees aid and anthropologists. *Overseas Development Institute Review* **2**, 1–13.

A. Hyman (1981). Afghan refugees: the awkward choice. *Unicef News* **3**, 24–5.

R. King (1981). Taking refuge. *Nursing Times* **77**, 1771–3.

S. York and K. Grant (1980). *Afghan refugees in Pakistan: a report on current conditions*. International Disasters Institute, London, 83 pp.

Sahel area

R. Baker (1977). The Sahel: an information crisis. *Disasters* **1**, 13.

B. J. Brown (1977). The UN and disaster relief in the Sahel 1973–5. *Disasters* **1**, 145.

C. de Ville de Goyet (1978). Disaster relief in Sahel. *Disasters* **3**, 79.

R. Hogan and S. P. Broske (1977). Sahel nutrition surveys 1974 and 1975. *Disasters* **1**, 117.

T. I. Kloth, W. A. Burr, J. P. Davis, G. Epler, C. A. Kolff, R. L. Rosenberg, N. W. Staehling, J. M. Lane, and M. Z. Nichaman (1976). Sahel nutrition survey, 1974. *American Journal of Epidemiology* **103**, 383–90.

W. E. Ormerod (1976). Drought in the Sahel: the debit side of development?. *Tropical Doctor* **6**, 163–7.

J. Roch (1975). Selective bibliography of the famines and drought in the Sahel. *African Environment* **1**, 94–116.

Somalia

A. S. Abbas (1978). *The health and nutrition aspect of the drought in Somalia*. Ministry of Health, Mogadishu, Somalia, 194 pp.

M. Bryant (1981). What happens when teams go home? *Unicef News* **3**, 16–17.

H. Christensen (1982). *Survival strategies for and by camp refugees*. United Nations Research Institute for Social Development, Geneva, 48 pp.

P. L. Henderson and R. J. Biellik (1981). Health and nutrition delivery to refugees in the Somali Democratic Republic, 1980. *Disasters* **5**, 104–12.

N. Lloyd (1981). Experiences in a Somali Refugee Camp. *Appropriate Technology* **8**, 4–6.

G. Melander (1980). *Refugees in Somalia.* Scandinavian Institute of African Studies, Uppsala, Sweden, Research Report No. 56, 48 pp.

Ministry of Health (1982). *Health guidelines for refugee camps.* Refugee Health Unit, Ministry of Health, Mogadishu, Somalia, 62 pp.

S. P. Simmonds (1980). Seminar on health and health-related needs of refugees. National Office of the Commissioner for Refugees, Somalia. *Disasters* **4**, 129–32.

F. Vertongen and M. Carael (1981). Refugee camps in Somalia: a micro survey (March 1980). *Disasters* **5**, 18–23.

W. H. Watson (1981). Personal view. *British Medical Journal* **282**, 1149.

Sudan

G. Barnabas (1982). Popcorn and fairies in the management of measles in Ethiopia (letter). *The Lancet* **1**, 450.

G. Barnabas and H. J. Lovel (1982). Bitter drugs replacing bitter plant juice to stop infants breast feeding (letter). *The Lancet* **1**, 1133.

M. Bizuneh (1980). An Ethiopian refugee camp in Sudan—the problem of tuberculosis. *Disasters* **4**, 167–70.

N. Cowan (1980). After the bullets . . . . *Nursing Mirror* **151**, 30–1.

K. Dahlin (1979). Maternal and child health among refugees in Sudan. *Lakartidningen* **76**, 2115–18.

R. E. Gribbin (1973). Two relief crises: Biafra and Sudan. *Africa Today* **20**, 47–59.

T. Johnson (1979). Eritrea refugees in Sudan. *Disasters* **3**, 417–21.

K. Wright (1980). News and views: Sudans refugees, 1967–1980. *Disasters* **4**, 157–66.

Thailand

J. Adler, E. Bodner, S. Borustein, J. Goldfarb, D. Engelhard, J. Naparstek, B. Norkiu, J. Sack, S. Shemer, and D. Weiler (1981). Medical mission to a refugee camp in Thailand. *Disasters* **5**, 23–31.

P. Bhiwandiwala (1980). Thai initiative in Kampuchean refugee camps (letter). *British Medical Journal* **281**, 812.

N. R. Buist (1980). Perspectives from Khao-I-Dang refugee camp. *British Medical Journal* **281**, 36–7.

N. R. Buist (1981). Genetic disease among Kampuchean Refugees (letter). *Journal Medical Association of Thailand* **64**, 51.

K. Dahlberg (1980). Medical care of Cambodian refugees. *Journal of the American Medical Association* **243**, 1062–5.

C. DeWitt (1981). Volunteers ease suffering in Thailand hospital. *Hospitals* **55**, 104–5.

S. Ebrahim (1980). Health needs of refugees (letter). *The Lancet* **1**, 1139.

C. Floriani (1980). Southeast Asian refugees: life in a camp. *American Journal of Nursing* **80**, 2028–30.

R. I. Glass, W. Cates, P. Nieburg, C. Davis, R. Russbach, H. Nothdurft, S. Peel, and R. Turnbull (1980). Rapid assessment of health status and preventive medicine needs of newly arrived Kampuchean refugees, Sa Kaeo, Thailand. *The Lancet* **1**, 868–72.

E. S. Hurwitz, D. Johnson, C. C. Campbell (1981). Resistance of *Plasmodium falciparum* malaria to sulfadoxine-pyrimethamine (Fansidar) in a refugee camp in Thailand. *The Lancet* **1**, 1068–70.

B. S. Levy (1981). Special report working in a camp for Cambodian refugees. *New England Journal of Medicine* **304**, 1440–4.

E. Rasche Gonzalez (1980). Practicing medicine on the edge of purgatory. *Journal of the American Medical Association* **244**, 1180–3.

R. A. Goodman and M. E. Speckhard (1980). Health needs of refugees. *The Lancet* **1**, 1139.

M. Grabe (1980). Report from Khao-I-Dang, Thailand: in this way the huge camp got efficient medical and health service. *Lakartidningen* **77**, 1765–8.

D. B. Jelliffe and E. F. P. Jelliffe (1980). Refugee health programme (letter). *British Medical Journal* **281**, 677.

G. Morch-Petersen (1980). Refugee camp Khao-I-Dang, Thailand: after hunger comes the fear for the future. *Sygeplejersken* **80**, 4–9.

J. G. Morris, G. R. West, S. E. Holck, P. A. Blake, P. D. Echeverria, and M. Karaulnik (1982). Cholera among refugees in Rangsit, Thailand. *The Journal of Infectious Diseases* **1**, 131–4.

H. Nelson (1981). Health care for refugees stirs resentment among Thais. *Los Angeles Times*, 29 January.

M. Reacher, C. C. Campbell, J. Freeman, E. B. Doberstyn, and A. D. Brandling-Bennett (1981). Drug therapy for *Plasmoidium falciparum* malaria resistant to pyrimethamine-sulfadoxine (Fansidar): a study of alternative regimens in Eastern Thailand, 1980. *The Lancet* **3**, 1066–9.

G. Smilkstein (1981). Refugees in Thailand and short-term medical aid. *Journal of American Medical Association* **245**, 1052–4.

G. O'Sullivan, S. Ebrahim, J. O'Sullivan, and C. Tafts (1980). Nutritional status of Laotian refugee children in Ubon camp, Thailand. *Journal of Epidemiology and Community Health* **34**, 83–6.

J. O'Sullivan, G. O'Sullivan, and S. Ebrahim (1980). Primary health care in Ubon refugee camp. *British Medical Journal* **280**, 779–81.

J. O'Sullivan (1981). *Thailand: medical care for Lao refugees in Ubon camp 1978–1979*. International Disaster Institute, London, 55 pp.

P. Patmann (1980). Refugee camps in Thailand: refugee camps lie in a zone which can remain combat zone continuously. *Sygeplejersken* **80**, 12–15.

P. Shillington (1981). Working at a camp in Thailand. *Nursing Times* **77**, 69–73.

G. Smilkstein (1981). Refugees in Thailand and short-term medical aid. *Journal of the American Medical Association* **245**, 1052–4.

E. A. Sumpter (1980). Teach a man to fish. *American Journal of Diseases of Children* **134**, 1025–7.

P. Temcharoen, J. Viboolyavatana, B. Tongkoom, P. Sumethanurugkul, B. Keittivuti, and L. Wanaratana (1979). A survey of intestinal parasitic infections in Laotian refugees at Ubon Province, Northeastern Thailand, with special reference to schistosomiasis. *South East Asian Journal of Tropical Medicine and Public Health* **10**, 552–4.

P. F. Walker (1980). Care of Cambodian refugees. *Journal of the American Medical Association* **244**, 1193–4.

Uganda

R. J. Bennett, D. B. Jelliffe, E. F. P. Jelliffe, and N. Moffat (1968). The nutrition and disease pattern of children in a refugee settlement. *East African Medical Journal* **45**, 229–46.

R. J. Biellik and P. L. Henderson (1981). Current famine in North-East Uganda (letter). *The Lancet* **2**, 697.

R. J. Biellik and P. Henderson (1981). Mortality, nutritional status and the diet during the famine in Karamoja, Uganda, 1980. *The Lancet* **21**, 1330–3.

L. Kristensen (1969). Vaccination tour to a Congolese–Sudanese refugee camp in Uganda. *Tiddskr Sygepl* **69**, 488–90.

S. Robinson, A. Streetly, M. Farrant, S. MacSweeney, and A. McCracken (1980). Famine relief in Karamoja, Uganda. *The Lancet* **2**, 849–51.

United Kingdom

P. Buisseret (1981). Tuberculosis among Vietnamese refugees (letter). *British Medical Journal* **282**, 1314–15.

Communicable Disease Surveillance Centre (1980). Epidemiology: Indo-Chinese refugees in Britain. *British Medical Journal* **280**, 1276.

A. Houston (1979). Sopley—medical services for refugees. *British Medical Journal* **2**, 1191–2.

E. Lam (1980). Health visiting Vietnamese refugees in Britain. *Health Visitor* **53**, 254–5.

P. Nuttall (1980). Light years away from the NHS: a recent course on refugee camps gave valuable insight to volunteer helpers. *Nursing Times* **76**, 1206.

R. J. Pearson (1980). Health visiting with a difference. *Journal of the Health Visitors Association* **53**, 257–8.

S. J. Phillips and R. J. Pearson (1981). Dealing with Vietnamese refugees: plans. *British Medical Journal* **282**, 525–7.

S. J. Phillips and R. J. Pearson (1981). Dealing with Vietnamese refugees: what we found. *British Medical Journal* **282**, 613–16.

S. Phillips (1981). Bizarre physical signs and traditional Vietnamese folk medicine. *Maternal and Child Health* **6**, 145–7.

T. Ross (1979). Enter the Boat People. *Nursing Mirror* **149**, 14–17.

P. Strong (1981). The recruitment and training of volunteers for emergency relief work. *Nursing Times* **77**, 62–4.

United States of America

F. Arfaa (1981). Intestinal parasites among Indochinese refugees and Mexican immigrants resettled in Contra Costa Country, California. *Journal Family Practitioners* **12**, 223–6.

P. M. Arnow, J. C. Hierholzer, J. Higbee, and D. H. Harris (1977). Acute hemorrhagic conjunctivitis: a mixed virus outbreak among Vietnamese refugees on Guam. *American Journal of Epidemiology* **105**, 68–73.

Center for Disease Control (1980). *Morbidity and mortality weekly report*, **29**, Center for Disease Control, Atlanta, USA, 12 pp.

W. G. Eckert (1981). Unexplained deaths in refugees newly arrived in America. *American Journal Forensic Medical Pathology* **2**, 185–6.

R. V. Erikson and G. N. Hoang (1980). Health problems among Indochinese refugees. *American Journal of Public Health* **70**, 1003–6.

A. M. Gallo, J. Edwards, and J. Vessey (1980). Little refugees with big needs. *Registered Nurse* **43**, 45–8.

J. C. Gaydos, L. E. Ashmore, T. J. McNeil, T. A. Mino, M. L. Bertsche, and B. Eisen, (1978). A preventive medicine team in a refugee relief operation—Fort Chaffee Indochina refugee camp (April–July 1975). *Military Medicine* **143**, 318–21.

R. A. Goodman, T. F. Nolan, and A. R. Hinman (1980). Immunization of Indochinese refugees. *Journal of the American Medical Association* **244**, 2046.

R. A. Goodman, T. J. Dondero, M. G. Schultz, J. F. Giordano, and D. R. Hopkins (1980). Indochinese refugees and infectious disease. *Annals of Internal Medicine* **93**, 375.

V. C. Gordon, I. M. Matousek, and T. A. Lang (1980). Southeast Asian refugees: life in America. *American Journal of Nursing* **80**, 2031–6.

R. K. Harding and J. G. Looney (1977). Problems of Southeast Asian children in a refugee camp. *American Journal of Psychiatry* **134**, 407–11.

M. J. Jones, J. H. Thompson, and N. S. Brewer (1980). Infectious diseases and Indochinese refugees. *Mayo Clinic Proceedings* **55**, 482–8.

J. D. Kinzie, K. A. Tran, Z. Breckenridge, and J. D. Bloom (1980). An Indochinese refugee psychiatric clinic: culturally accepted treatment approaches. *American Journal of Psychiatry* **137**, 1429–32.

D. Koval and A. M. W. Brennan (1980). Exotic diseases you're sure to see more of. *Registered Nurse* **43**, 73–81.

K. M. Lin, L. Tazuma, and M. Masuda (1979). Adaptational problems of Vietnamese refugees: health and mental health status. *Archives of General Psychiatry* **36**, 955–61.

K. P. Okura (1981). Refugees in America suffer from loss of community. *Michigan Medicine* **80**, 18.

K. Olness (1981). A health outreach to a refugee camp. Perspectives for would-be volunteers. *Pediatrics* **67**, 523–9.

S. M. Pickwell (1981). School health screening of Indo-chinese refugee children. *Journal School Health* **51**, 102–5.

K. E. Powell, R. A. Goodman, and L. S. Farer (1980). Tuberculosis in Indochinese refugees. *Annals of Internal Medicine* **93**, 375–6.

R. H. Rahe, J. C. Looney, H. W. Ward, T. M. Tung, and W. T. Liu (1978). Psychiatric consultation in a Vietnamese refugee camp. *American Journal of Psychiatry* **135**, 185–90.

L. V. Rocereto (1981). Selected health beliefs of Vietnamese refugees. *Journal of School Health* **81**, 63–4.

M. C. S. Santopietro (1981). How to get through to a refugee patient. *Registered Nurse* **44**, 43–8.

R. Shaw (1977). Preventive medicine in the Vietnamese refugee camps on Guam, *Military Medicine* **142**, 19–28.

R. Shaw (1979). Health services in a disaster: lessons from the 1975 Vietnamese evacuation. *Military Medicine* **144**, 307–11.

W. B. Shields (1981). Dentistry and the issue of Hepatitis B. *Journal American Dental Association* **102**, 180–2.

S. A. Stalcup, M. Oscherwitz, M. S. Cohen, F. Crast, D. Broughton, F. Stark, and R. Goldsmith (1975). Planning for a pediatric disaster—experience gained from caring for 1600 Vietnamese orphans. *The New England Journal of Medicine* **293**, 691–4.

H. Torjesen, K. Olness, and E. Torjesen (1981). *The gift of refugees.* The Garden, 6605 Rowland Road, Erlen Prairie, Minnesota 55344, USA, 30 pp.

E. B. Waldman, Sister B. Lege, B. Oseid, and J. P. Carter (1979). Health and nutritional status of Vietnamese refugees. *Southern Medical Journal* **72**, 1300–3.

A. M. Wiesenthal, M. K. Nickels, and K. G. Hasimoto (1980). Intestinal parasites in Southeast-Asian refugees: prevalence in a community of Laotians. *Journal of the American Medical Association* **244**, 2543–4.

R. M. Zweighaft, J. C. Hierholzer, and J. A. Bryan (1977). Epidemic kerato-conjunctivitis at a Vietnamese refugee camp in Florida. *American Journal of Epidemiology* **106**, 399–407.

Upper Volta

J. Seaman, J. Holt, J. Rivers, and J. Murlis (1973). An inquiry into the drought situation in Upper Volta. *The Lancet* **2**, 774–8.

Vietnam

M. Fast (1979). A nation of refugees. *Disasters* **3**, 342–7.

P. Hoheisel (1968). Michigan doctors describe Vietnam experiences as volunteers. *Michigan State Journal* **67**, 248–59.

M. Kaufman (1979). Vietnam 1978: crisis in food, nutrition and health. *Journal of the American Dietetic Association* **74**, 310–16.

B. Ryan (1975). General factors in the mortality among refugees in Vietnam. *Medical Journal of Australia* **1**, 625–9.

D. W. Stickney (1967). Vietnamese Province Hospital in the war zone. *Hospitals Journal of the American Health Authority* **41**, 67–71.

Zaire

W. D. Grenfell (1975). An account of refugees and refugee work on Kibentele Baptist Mission, Bas Zaire 1967. *Holborn II*, 1063–78.

J. Holt (1980). Famine prevention in Africa, a Conference/Workshop held in Kinshasa, Zaire, by the Centre National de Planification de Nutrition Humaine, 6–11 January 1980. *Disasters* **4**, 133–7.

Zambia

A. Hansen (1979). Once the running stops: assimilation of Angolan refugees into Zambian border villages. *Disasters* **3**, 369–74.

A. Hansen (1979b). Managing refugees: Zambia's response to Angolan refugees 1966–1977. *Disasters* **3**, 375–80.

A. Spring (1979). Women and men as refugees: differential assimilation of Angolan refugees in Zambia. *Disasters* **3**, 423–8.

Appendix 2: Summary of statistics and list of equipment and addresses

SUMMARY OF FIGURES

Estimating refugee populations

Random sampling numbers

	1	2	3	4	5	6	7	8	9	10	11	12	13	14	15	16
1	1	0	0	2	5	7	3	5	0	5	2	3	2	0	1	7
2	1	7	5	0	7	4	9	9	6	0	2	5	2	9	6	5
3	9	9	7	0	3	4	0	5	7	2	4	6	0	1	7	2
4	2	4	3	6	7	0	4	7	9	0	9	2	1	9	4	8
5	6	5	1	2	9	0	9	1	9	2	3	3	5	6	4	0
6	1	0	1	4	3	7	3	2	5	3	9	0	9	3	3	5
7	3	1	5	3	3	1	0	8	6	6	6	8	4	4	4	9
8	6	7	3	1	1	4	2	7	5	1	9	0	2	8	0	4
9	2	2	6	3	6	2	7	4	2	2	1	7	2	9	7	8
10	6	7	1	7	8	4	3	5	9	2	3	4	7	7	2	9
11	5	0	9	7	4	2	5	9	6	4	8	3	9	7	2	1
12	5	1	5	1	9	7	8	0	6	6	5	2	5	0	3	1
13	6	2	4	7	2	4	4	0	7	5	4	6	3	2	9	5
14	4	7	3	6	9	0	1	2	1	4	5	3	2	9	9	7
15	7	1	7	8	6	3	7	5	7	2	7	6	6	7	4	7
16	0	2	0	9	5	3	9	5	9	9	5	2	8	4	4	6
17	2	7	6	1	3	7	0	2	0	5	2	7	8	0	5	1
18	8	2	6	4	3	0	5	0	8	4	0	6	2	9	5	5
19	8	6	2	2	4	8	1	0	9	2	8	2	1	5	3	5
20	4	9	0	6	3	8	2	6	4	2	4	5	4	5	7	4
21	8	7	1	7	3	6	3	1	9	8	2	9	1	4	0	3
22	2	4	8	4	1	0	3	9	6	2	5	5	3	7	0	1
23	2	2	4	6	4	3	1	4	3	9	7	2	1	2	1	5
24	6	4	5	5	5	5	0	5	7	9	8	1	0	2	2	1
25	1	1	2	3	8	6	1	6	5	5	9	6	0	2	1	5
26	0	5	6	9	9	1	9	3	7	5	9	4	2	6	3	1
27	3	6	8	0	7	5	8	3	9	7	1	3	8	4	9	2
28	4	2	2	8	9	0	1	8	1	0	9	9	9	7	4	1
29	8	5	2	8	1	7	6	3	9	6	3	0	2	2	7	0
30	9	2	6	4	9	0	1	5	2	7	2	7	1	4	2	1

Random sampling numbers—contd.

	1	2	3	4	5	6	7	8	9	10	11	12	13	14	15	16
31	9	9	1	5	3	0	6	8	1	7	8	3	9	4	3	5
32	1	5	4	7	8	1	4	2	1	3	8	7	9	3	6	8
33	3	0	7	8	4	7	2	4	7	8	7	0	5	1	7	8
34	2	3	5	6	8	8	0	1	9	1	8	0	2	5	9	7
35	2	3	7	2	5	6	9	0	3	7	6	1	0	6	0	3
36	2	3	0	1	0	8	7	7	9	9	1	1	6	6	0	6
37	7	2	2	5	6	8	1	6	4	5	4	1	8	5	6	9
38	0	2	3	5	3	6	4	0	7	8	4	1	1	3	0	7
39	8	7	2	0	4	1	8	9	8	0	0	5	2	1	5	9
40	9	9	4	5	2	5	3	8	1	3	4	0	0	2	5	9

USE OF EDGE-PUNCHED CARDS

Figure A1 illustrates an edge-punched card. One card is completed for each
person in the survey. Detailed data collected in the survey are written on the
card. Around the edge of the card are holes which may be clipped out with
scissors (or with a special tool). Each hole is assigned a variable. An example
of such assignment is shown above the card in Fig. A1. For example, hole 24
is assigned 'sex—male?'. If the answer is 'yes' the hole is clipped out, if the
answer is 'no' it is not clipped. Thus when hole 24 has been 'clipped' or 'not
clipped' on each card for all persons in the survey we can sort out the males

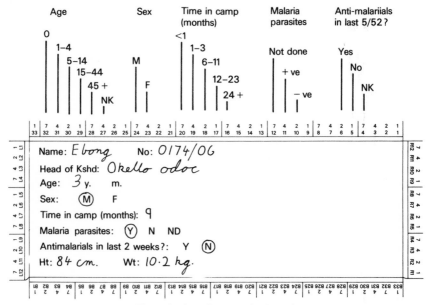

Fig. A1. An edge-punched card.

simply by putting all the cards together, inserting a knitting needle through hole 24 and shaking the cards until all those clipped in hole 24 drop off the needle. The cards that stay on the needle relate to females (which may be checked as all these cards should be clipped out in hole 23). We may then sort the males and females separately by age by inserting the needle in holes 27 to 32 successively, first for the cards relating to males and then for those relating to females. (In the example age has been divided into 6 groups and thus we will end up with 6 piles of cards for each sex. These may be counted (manually) to form a table showing the age and sex structure of the sample.)

Anthropometric reference figures

by

David Nabarro and Jane Rickleton
Prepared from the NCHS/CDC tables of normalized reference figures (sex averaged).

INTRODUCTION

Source of reference figures

The figures presented in the tables are derived from the normalized NCHS growth curves for children,[1] prepared as an anthropometric reference by the National Centre for Health Statistics and the Center for Disease Control, USA.[2] These reference values are now recommended by the World Health Organization for use in the analysis of data from developing countries.[3] For ease of use, the figures presented are a unisex version of the NCHS Reference.

Use of reference figures

These anthropometric reference figures are useful when comparisons are made between anthropometric measurements on children of different ages or heights. They can be used to help identify individual children in need of special attention or to assist those making comparisons between different groups of children. If common reference figures are used for these purposes, comparison between different locations or programmes becomes easy. There are, therefore, substantial advantages in using international reference figures. The choice of cut-off points used to identify children in need or to describe optimal growth will be influenced by the situation in which the references are used.[4] The NCHS reference figures are similar to the Harvard standards,[5] though the former are based on larger populations and have been subjected to more rigorous statistical analysis.

Nutritional indices available

Three sets of tables are presented. They can be used to calculate the following anthropometric indices:

1. Weight-for-length or weight-for-height.
   (The child's weight can be compared with the reference weight for a child of the same length or height.)
2. Length-for-age or height-for-age.
   (The child's length or height can be compared with the reference length or height for a child of the same age.)
3. Weight-for-age.
   (The child's weight can be compared with the reference weight for a child of the same age.)

In order to calculate these indices, the difference between the child's weight (height or length) has to be compared with the appropriate reference value. This can be done in two ways, which are described with respect to weight-for-age.

1. The difference between actual weight and reference weight for a child of the same age is divided by the standard deviation of the reference weight value. This yields a Z score.
2. The actual weight is expressed as a percentage of the reference weight for a child of the same age.

Z scores

These anthropometric reference values are, in fact, median values for child weight, length or height obtained from a large series of surveys in the USA. Because the anthropometric values have a normal frequency distribution, the median has the same value as the mean, and the spread of weight values at a particular age can be described with the help of the standard deviation. Among the children surveyed to provide this data, only one child in 20 would have a weight that is at least twice the standard deviation below the median. This is equivalent to a Z score of -2 or less. If a community is studied and a large number of children are found to have Z scores of less than -2, the weight-for-age values in that community will clearly be lower than the population used to describe the reference values.

The Z score technique has been recommended by the World Health Organization.[6] Its disadvantage is that users not only need to know the reference value for a particular age; they also need to know the standard deviation of weight values at that age. Explaining the Z score approach to people not familiar with statistical methods is quite difficult—indeed, the approach is considered by some to be unnecessarily complicated. Most health and nutrition workers want to know the size of the difference between a child's weight and the reference weight—they do not need to relate that difference to the distribution of weights in the original reference population in North America. Workers are more likely to be comparing weight differences of individual children and different groups of children in their own country. The Z score method is unnecessarily elaborate for such applications.

Percentage of reference

It is comparatively easy to express the child's weight as a percentage of the reference weight-for-age. However, a particular percentage of reference weight (say 80 per cent) will have different significance at different ages. The health risks faced by children who are 80 per cent weight-for-age will vary at different ages, during different seasons, and in different locations. The important lesson is that cut-off points used to decide action for individuals or groups need to be decided on in the context of the situation in which they are used.

Layout of tables

The tables are designed to enable users to classify children's weight-for-age, weight-for-height/weight-for-length and height-for-age and length-for-age into either a *range* of percentage of reference or a *range* of Z scores. For example, if a child is 86 cm high and weighs 95 kg, the weight is between 70 per cent and 80 per cent of the reference. It also has a Z score of between -2 and -3. The exact percentage of reference figures for a particular child can be obtained by dividing the child's weight, height or length by the appropriate reference value and multiplying by a hundred. The reference weight for a child 86 cm tall is 12.2 kg; 9.5 kg is 77.9 per cent of 12.2 kg. The exact Z score for a particular child can be obtained by subtracting the child's weight, height, or length from the appropriate value and dividing the difference by the standard deviation for the reference value. 9.5 kg is 2.7 kg less than 12.2 kg. The standard deviation for weight values of 86 cm children is 1.1 kg. A child 86 cm tall, weighing 9.5 kg, therefore has a Z score of -2.4.

References

1. Hamill, P. V. NCHS growth curves for children. US Department of Health, Education and Welfare (DHEW Publication number DHS–78–1650) (1977).
2. Normalized NCHS/CDC Anthropometric Reference, Centre for Disease Control, Atlanta, Georgia, USA (1980).
3. A guideline for the measurement of nutritional impact of supplementary feeding programmes aimed at vulnerable groups. Geneva: World Health Organization (Publication FAP/79.1) (1979).
4. Graitcer, P. L. and Gentry, E. M. Measuring children: one reference for all. *Lancet* **ii**, 297–9 (1981).
5. Jelliffe, D. B. The assessment of the nutritional status of the community. Geneva: World Health Organization (Monograph Series no. 53) (1966).
6. Waterlow, J. C. *et al.* The presentation and use of height and weight data comparing the nutritional status of groups of children under the age of 10 years. *Bull WHO* **55**, 489–98 (1977).

Table 1. *Percentage of reference weight-for-length (sexes averaged) in kg*

Length (cm)	Values for different percentages of reference weight-for-length						
	50%	60%	70%	80%	90%	100%	110%
49	1.6	1.9	2.2	2.6	2.9	3.2	3.5
50	1.7	2.0	2.4	2.7	3.1	3.4	3.7
51	1.8	2.1	2.5	2.8	3.2	3.5	3.9
52	1.9	2.2	2.6	3.0	3.3	3.7	4.1
53	2.0	2.3	2.7	3.1	3.5	3.9	4.3
54	2.1	2.5	2.9	3.3	3.7	4.1	4.5
55	2.2	2.6	3.0	3.4	3.9	4.3	4.7
56	2.3	2.8	3.2	3.7	4.1	4.6	5.1
57	2.4	2.9	3.4	3.8	4.3	4.8	5.3
58	2.6	3.1	3.6	4.1	4.6	5.1	5.6
59	2.7	3.2	3.7	4.2	4.8	5.3	5.8
60	2.8	3.4	3.9	4.5	5.0	5.6	6.2
61	3.0	3.5	4.1	4.7	5.3	5.9	6.5
62	3.1	3.7	4.3	5.0	5.6	6.2	6.8
63	3.3	3.9	4.6	5.2	5.9	6.5	7.2
64	3.4	4.0	4.7	5.4	6.0	6.7	7.4
65	3.5	4.2	4.9	5.6	6.3	7.0	7.7
66	3.7	4.4	5.1	5.8	6.6	7.3	8.0
67	3.8	4.6	5.3	6.1	6.8	7.6	8.4
68	4.0	4.7	5.5	6.3	7.1	7.9	8.7
69	4.1	4.9	5.7	6.6	7.4	8.2	9.0
70	4.3	5.1	6.0	6.8	7.7	8.5	9.4
71	4.4	5.2	6.1	7.0	7.8	8.7	9.6
72	4.5	5.4	6.3	7.2	8.1	9.0	9.9
73	4.6	5.5	6.4	7.4	8.3	9.2	10.1
74	4.8	5.7	6.7	7.6	8.6	9.5	10.5
75	4.9	5.8	6.8	7.8	8.7	9.7	10.7
76	5.0	5.9	6.9	7.9	8.9	9.9	10.9
77	5.1	6.1	7.1	8.1	9.1	10.1	11.1
78	5.2	6.2	7.3	8.3	9.4.	10.4	11.4
79	5.3	6.4	7.4	8.5	9.5	10.6	11.7
80	5.4	6.5	7.6	8.6	9.7	10.8	11.9
81	5.5	6.6	7.7	8.8	9.9	11.0	12.1
82	5.6	6.7	7.8	9.0	10.1	11.2	12.3
83	5.7	6.8	8.0	9.1	10.3	11.4	12.5
84	5.8	6.9	8.1	9.2	10.4	11.5	12.7
85	5.9	7.0	8.2	9.4	10.5	11.7	12.9
86	6.0	7.1	8.3	9.5	10.7	11.9	13.1
87	6.1	7.3	8.5	9.7	10.9	12.1	13.3
88	6.2	7.4	8.7	9.9	11.2	12.4	13.6
89	6.3	7.6	8.8	10.1	11.3	12.6	13.9
90	6.4	7.7	9.0	10.2	11.5	12.8	14.1
91	6.5	7.8	9.1	10.4	11.7	13.0	14.3
92	6.6	7.9	9.2	10.6	11.9	13.2	14.5
93	6.8	8.1	9.5	10.8	12.2	13.5	14.9
94	6.9	8.2	9.6	11.0	12.3	13.7	15.1
95	7.0	8.4	9.8	11.2	12.6	14.0	15.4
96	7.1	8.5	9.9	11.4	12.8	14.2	15.6
97	7.3	8.7	10.2	11.6	13.1	14.5	16.0
98	7.4	8.9	10.4	11.8	13.3	14.8	16.3
99	7.5	9.0	10.5	12.0	13.5	15.0	16.5
100	7.7	9.2	10.7	12.2	13.8	15.3	16.8

Table 2. *Percentage of reference weight-for-height (sexes averaged) in kg*

Height (cm)	Values for different percentages of reference weight-for-height						
	50%	60%	70%	80%	90%	100%	110%
55	2.3	2.8	3.2	3.7	4.1	4.6	5.1
56	2.4	2.9	3.4	3.8	4.3	4.8	5.3
57	2.6	3.1	3.6	4.1	4.6	5.1	5.6
58	2.7	3.2	3.8	4.3	4.9	5.4	5.9
59	2.8	3.4	3.9	4.5	5.0	5.6	6.2
60	3.0	3.1	4.1	4.7	5.3	5.9	6.5
61	3.1	3.7	4.3	5.0	5.6	6.2	6.8
62	3.3	3.9	4.6	5.2	5.9	6.5	7.2
63	3.4	4.1	4.8	5.4	6.1	6.8	7.5
64	3.6	4.3	5.0	5.7	6.4	7.1	7.8
65	3.7	4.4	5.2	5.9	6.7	7.4	8.1
66	3.8	4.6	5.4	6.2	6.9	7.7	8.5
67	4.0	4.8	5.6	6.4	7.2	8.0	8.8
68	4.1	4.9	5.7	6.6	7.4	8.2	9.0
69	4.3	5.1	6.0	6.8	7.7	8.5	9.4
70	4.4	5.2	6.1	7.0	7.8	8.7	9.6
71	4.5	5.3	6.2	7.1	8.0	8.9	9.8
72	4.6	5.5	6.4	7.4	8.3	9.2	10.1
73	4.7	5.6	6.6	7.5	8.5	9.4	10.3
74	4.8	5.8	6.7	7.7	8.6	9.6	10.6
75	4.9	5.9	6.9	7.8	8.8	9.8	10.8
76	5.0	6.0	7.0	8.0	9.0	10.0	11.0
77	5.2	6.2	7.2	8.2	9.3	10.3	11.3
78	5.3	6.3	7.4	8.4	9.5	10.5	11.6
79	5.4	6.4	7.5	8.6	9.6	10.7	11.8
80	5.5	6.5	7.6	8.7	9.8	10.9	12.0
81	5.6	6.7	7.8	8.9	10.0	11.1	12.2
82	5.7	6.8	7.9	9.0	10.2	11.3	12.4
83	5.8	6.9	8.1	9.2	10.4	11.5	12.7
84	5.9	7.1	8.3	9.4	10.6	11.8	13.0
85	6.0	7.2	8.4	9.6	10.8	12.0	13.2
86	6.1	7.3	8.5	9.8	11.0	12.2	13.4
87	6.2	7.4	8.7	9.9	11.2	12.4	13.6
88	6.3	7.6	8.8	10.1	11.3	12.6	13.9
89	6.4	7.7	9.0	10.3	11.6	12.9	14.2
90	6.5	7.9	9.2	10.5	11.8	13.1	14.4
91	6.6	8.0	9.3	10.6	12.0	13.3	14.6
92	6.8	8.2	9.5	10.9	12.2	13.6	15.0
93	6.9	8.3	9.7	11.0	12.4	13.8	15.2
94	7.0	8.4	9.8	11.2	12.6	14.0	15.4
95	7.2	8.6	10.0	11.4	12.9	14.3	15.7
96	7.3	8.7	10.2	11.6	13.1	14.5	16.0
97	7.4	8.9	10.4	11.8	13.3	14.8	16.3
98	7.5	9.0	10.5	12.0	13.5	15.0	16.5
99	7.7	9.2	10.7	12.2	13.8	15.3	16.8
100	7.8	9.4	10.9	12.5	14.0	15.6	17.2
101	7.9	9.5	11.1	12.6	14.2	15.8	17.4
102	8.1	9.7	11.3	12.9	14.5	16.1	17.1
103	8.2	9.8	11.5	13.1	14.8	16.4	18.0
104	8.4	10.0	11.7	13.4	15.0	16.7	18.4

Table 2.—contd.

Height (cm)	Values for different percentages of reference weight-for-height						
	50%	60%	70%	80%	90%	100%	110%
105	8.5	10.1	11.8	13.5	15.2	16.9	18.6
106	8.6	10.3	12.0	13.8	15.5	17.2	18.9
107	8.8	10.5	12.3	14.0	15.8	17.5	19.3
108	8.9	10.7	12.5	14.2	16.0	17.8	19.6
109	9.1	10.9	12.7	14.5	16.3	18.1	19.9
110	9.2	11.0	12.9	14.7	16.6	18.4	20.2
111	9.4	11.3	13.2	15.0	16.9	18.8	20.7
112	9.6	11.5	13.4	15.3	17.2	19.1	21.0
113	9.7	11.6	13.6	15.5	17.5	19.4	21.3
114	9.9	11.9	13.9	15.8	17.8	19.8	21.8
115	10.1	12.1	14.1	16.1	18.1	20.1	22.1
116	10.3	12.3	14.4	16.4	18.5	20.5	22.6
117	10.4	12.5	14.6	16.6	18.7	20.8	22.9
118	10.6	12.7	14.8	17.0	19.1	21.2	23.3
119	10.8	13.0	15.1	17.3	19.4	21.6	23.8
120	11.0	13.2	15.4	17.6	19.8	22.0	24.2
121	11.2	13.4	15.7	17.9	20.2	22.4	24.6
122	11.4	13.7	16.0	18.2	20.5	22.8	25.1
123	11.7	14.0	16.3	18.6	21.0	23.3	25.6
124	11.9	14.2	16.6	19.0	21.3	23.7	25.3
125	12.1	14.5	16.9	19.4	21.8	24.2	26.6
126	12.4	14.8	17.3	20.0	22.2	24.7	27.2
127	12.6	15.1	17.6	20.2	22.7	25.2	27.7
128	12.9	15.4	18.0	20.6	23.1	25.7	28.3
129	13.1	15.7	18.3	21.0	23.6	26.2	28.8
130	13.4	16.1	18.8	21.4	24.1	26.8	29.5
131	13.7	16.4	19.2	22.0	24.7	27.4	30.1
132	14.0	16.7	19.5	22.3	25.1	27.9	30.7
133	14.3	17.2	20.0	22.9	25.7	28.6	31.5
134	14.6	17.5	20.4	23.4	26.3	29.2	32.1
135	14.9	17.9	21.0	23.8	26.8	29.8	32.8
136	15.3	18.3	21.4	24.4	27.5	30.5	33.6
137	15.6	18.7	21.8	25.0	28.1	31.2	34.3

Table 3. *Percentage of reference length-for-age (sexes averaged) in cm*

Age (months)	Values for different percentages of reference length-for-age								
	70%	75%	80%	85%	90%	95%	100%	105%	110%
0	35.1	37.7	40.2	42.7	45.2	47.7	50.2	52.7	55.2
1	37.9	40.6	43.3	46.0	48.7	51.4	54.1	56.8	59.5
2	40.2	43.1	45.9	48.8	51.7	54.5	57.4	60.3	63.1
3	42.2	45.2	48.2	51.3	54.3	57.3	60.3	63.3	66.3
4	44.0	47.1	50.2	53.4	56.5	59.7	62.8	65.9	69.1
5	45.5	48.8	52.0	55.3	58.5	61.8	65.0	68.3	71.5
6	46.8	50.2	53.5	56.9	60.2	63.6	66.9	70.2	73.6

Table 3.—contd.

Age (months)	Values for different percentages of reference length-for-age								
	70%	75%	80%	85%	90%	95%	100%	105%	110%
7	48.0	51.4	54.8	58.2	61.7	65.1	68.5	71.9	75.4
8	49.0	52.5	56.0	59.5	63.0	66.5	70.0	73.5	77.0
9	50.0	53.6	57.1	60.7	64.3	67.8	71.4	75.0	78.5
10	50.9	54.5	58.2	61.8	65.4	69.1	72.7	76.3	80.0
11	51.8	55.5	59.2	62.9	66.6	70.3	74.0	77.7	81.4
12	52.6	56.4	60.2	63.9	67.7	71.4	75.2	79.0	82.7
13	53.5	57.3	61.1	64.9	68.8	75.3	76.4	80.2	84.0
14	54.3	58.1	62.0	65.9	70.0	73.6	77.5	81.4	85.3
15	55.0	59.0	62.9	66.8	70.7	74.7	78.6	82.5	86.5
16	55.8	60.0	63.8	67.2	71.7	75.7	79.7	83.7	87.7
17	56.5	60.5	64.6	68.6	72.6	76.7	80.7	84.7	88.8
18	57.2	61.3	65.4	69.4	73.5	77.6	81.7	85.8	89.9
19	57.8	62.0	66.1	70.2	74.3	78.5	82.6	86.7	90.9
20	58.5	62.7	66.9	71.1	75.2	79.4	83.6	87.8	92.0
21	59.2	63.4	67.6	71.8	76.1	80.3	84.5	88.7	93.0
22	60.0	64.1	68.3	72.6	76.9	81.1	85.4	90.0	93.9
23	60.3	64.7	69.0	73.3	77.6	81.9	86.2	90.5	94.8

Table 4. *Percentage of reference height-for-age (sexes averaged) in cm*

Age (months)	Values for different percentages of reference height-for-age								
	70%	75%	80%	85%	90%	95%	100%	105%	110%
24	60.0	63.8	68.0	72.3	76.5	80.8	85.0	89.3	93.5
25	60.1	64.4	68.7	73.0	77.3	81.6	85.9	90.2	94.5
26	60.7	65.0	69.4	73.7	78.0	82.4	86.7	91.0	95.4
27	61.3	65.7	70.1	74.5	78.8	83.2	87.6	92.0	96.4
28	61.9	66.3	70.7	75.1	80.0	84.0	88.4	92.8	97.2
29	62.4	66.9	71.4	75.8	80.3	84.7	89.2	93.7	98.1
30	62.9	67.4	71.9	76.4	80.9	85.4	89.9	94.4	98.9
31	63.5	68.0	72.6	77.1	81.6	86.2	90.7	95.2	99.8
32	64.1	68.6	73.2	77.8	82.4	86.9	91.5	96.1	100.7
33	64.5	69.2	73.8	78.4	83.0	87.6	92.2	96.8	101.4
34	65.1	69.8	74.4	79.1	83.7	88.4	93.0	97.7	102.3
35	65.6	70.3	75.0	79.6	84.3	89.0	93.7	98.4	103.1
36	66.1	70.8	75.5	80.2	85.0	89.7	94.4	99.1	103.8
37	66.6	71.3	76.1	80.8	85.6	90.3	95.1	99.9	104.6
38	67.1	71.9	76.6	81.4	86.2	91.0	95.8	100.6	105.4
39	67.6	72.4	77.2	82.0	86.9	91.7	96.5	101.3	106.2
40	68.0	72.9	77.8	82.6	87.5	92.3	97.2	102.1	106.9
41	68.5	73.4	78.2	83.1	88.0	92.9	97.8	102.7	107.6
42	69.0	73.9	79.8	83.7	88.7	93.6	98.5	103.4	108.4
43	69.4	74.4	79.4	84.3	89.3	94.2	99.2	104.2	109.1
44	70.0	74.9	79.8	84.8	89.8	94.8	99.8	104.8	109.8
45	70.3	75.3	80.3	85.3	90.4	95.4	100.4	105.4	110.4
46	70.8	75.8	80.9	85.9	91.0	96.0	101.1	106.2	111.2

Table 4.—contd.

Age (months)	70%	75%	80%	85%	90%	95%	100%	105%	110%
				Values for different percentages of reference height-for-age					
47	71.2	76.3	81.4	86.4	91.5	96.6	101.7	106.8	111.9
48	71.6	76.7	81.8	87.0	92.1	97.2	102.3	107.4	112.5
49	72.0	77.2	82.3	87.5	92.6	97.8	102.9	108.0	113.2
50	72.5	77.6	82.8	88.0	93.2	98.3	103.5	108.7	113.9
51	72.9	78.1	83.3	88.5	93.7	98.9	104.1	109.3	114.5
52	73.2	78.5	83.8	89.0	94.2	99.5	104.7	110.0	115.2
53	73.6	78.9	84.2	89.4	94.7	99.9	105.2	110.5	115.7
54	74.1	79.4	84.6	89.9	95.2	100.5	105.8	111.1	116.4
55	74.5	79.8	85.1	90.4	95.8	101.1	106.4	111.7	117.0
56	74.8	80.2	85.5	90.9	96.2	101.6	106.9	112.2	117.6
57	75.3	80.6	86.0	91.4	96.8	102.1	107.5	112.9	118.3
58	75.7	81.1	86.5	91.9	97.3	102.7	108.1	113.5	118.9
59	76.0	81.5	86.9	92.3	97.7	103.2	108.6	114.0	119.5
60	76.4	81.9	87.4	92.8	98.3	103.7	109.2	114.7	120.1
61	76.8	82.3	87.8	93.2	98.7	104.2	109.7	115.2	120.7
62	77.1	82.7	88.2	93.7	99.2	104.7	110.2	115.7	121.2
63	77.6	83.1	88.6	94.2	99.7	105.3	110.8	116.3	121.9
64	77.9	83.5	89.0	94.6	100.2	105.7	111.3	116.9	122.4
65	78.3	83.9	89.4	95.0	100.6	106.2	111.8	117.4	123.0
66	78.6	84.2	89.8	95.4	101.1	106.7	112.3	117.9	123.5
67	79.0	84.6	90.2	95.9	101.5	107.2	112.8	118.4	124.1
68	79.4	85.1	90.7	96.4	102.1	107.7	113.4	119.1	124.7
69	79.7	85.4	91.1	96.8	102.5	108.2	113.9	119.6	125.3
70	80.1	85.8	91.5	97.2	103.0	108.7	114.4	120.1	125.8
71	80.4	86.2	91.9	97.7	103.4	109.2	114.9	120.6	126.4
72	80.8	86.6	92.3	98.1	104.0	109.6	115.4	121.2	126.9
73	81.1	86.9	92.7	98.5	104.3	110.1	115.9	121.7	127.5
74	81.5	87.3	93.1	98.9	104.8	110.6	116.4	122.2	128.0
75	81.8	87.6	93.4	99.3	105.1	111.0	116.8	122.6	128.5
76	82.1	88.0	93.8	99.7	105.6	111.4	117.3	123.2	129.0
77	82.5	88.4	94.2	100.1	106.0	111.9	117.8	123.7	129.6
78	82.8	88.7	94.6	100.6	106.5	112.4	118.3	124.2	130.1
79	83.2	89.1	95.0	101.0	106.9	113.0	118.8	124.7	130.7
80	83.4	89.4	95.4	101.3	107.3	113.2	119.2	125.2	131.1
81	83.8	89.8	95.8	101.7	107.7	113.7	119.7	125.7	131.7
82	84.1	90.2	96.2	102.2	108.2	114.2	120.2	126.2	132.2
83	84.5	90.5	96.6	102.6	108.6	114.7	120.7	126.7	132.8
84	84.8	90.8	96.9	102.9	109.0	115.0	121.1	127.2	133.2
85	85.1	91.2	97.3	103.4	109.4	115.5	121.6	127.7	133.8
86	85.5	91.6	97.7	103.8	110.0	116.0	122.1	128.2	134.3
87	85.8	91.9	98.0	104.1	110.3	116.4	122.5	128.6	134.8
88	86.1	92.3	98.4	104.6	110.7	116.9	123.0	129.2	135.3
89	86.5	92.6	98.8	105.0	111.2	117.3	123.5	129.7	135.9
90	86.7	93.0	99.1	105.3	111.5	117.7	123.9	130.1	136.3
91	87.1	93.3	99.5	105.7	112.0	118.2	124.4	130.6	136.8
92	87.4	93.6	99.8	106.1	112.3	118.6	124.8	131.0	137.3
93	87.7	94.0	100.2	106.5	112.8	119.0	125.3	131.6	137.8
94	88.1	94.4	100.6	106.9	113.2	119.5	125.8	132.1	138.4
95	88.3	94.7	101.0	107.3	113.6	119.9	126.2	132.5	138.8
96	88.7	95.0	101.4	107.7	114.0	120.4	126.7	133.0	139.4

Table 4.—contd.

Age (months)	Values for different percentages of reference height-for-age								
	70%	75%	80%	85%	90%	95%	100%	105%	110%
97	89.0	95.3	101.7	108.0	114.4	120.7	127.1	133.4	139.8
98	89.3	95.7	102.1	108.5	114.8	121.2	127.6	134.0	140.4
99	89.7	96.1	102.5	108.9	115.3	121.7	128.1	134.5	140.9
100	90.0	96.4	102.8	109.2	115.7	122.1	128.5	134.9	141.4
101	90.3	96.8	103.2	109.7	116.1	122.6	129.0	135.5	141.9
102	90.6	97.1	103.5	110.0	116.5	122.9	129.4	135.9	142.3
103	91.0	97.4	103.9	110.4	116.9	123.4	129.9	136.4	142.9
104	91.2	97.7	104.2	110.8	117.3	123.8	130.3	136.8	143.3
105	91.6	97.7	104.6	111.2	117.7	124.3	130.8	137.3	143.9
106	91.9	98.5	105.0	111.6	118.2	124.7	131.3	137.9	144.4
107	92.2	98.8	105.4	111.9	118.5	125.1	131.7	138.3	144.9
108	92.5	99.2	105.8	112.4	119.0	125.6	132.2	138.8	145.4
109	93.0	99.5	106.2	112.8	119.4	126.1	132.7	139.3	146.0
110	93.2	99.8	106.5	113.1	119.8	126.4	133.1	139.8	146.4
111	93.5	100.2	106.9	113.6	120.2	127.0	133.6	140.3	147.0
112	93.9	100.6	107.3	114.0	120.7	127.4	134.1	140.8	147.5
113	94.2	100.9	107.6	114.3	121.1	127.8	134.5	141.2	148.0
114	94.5	101.3	108.0	114.8	121.5	128.3	135.0	141.8	148.5
115	94.9	101.6	108.4	115.2	122.0	128.7	135.5	142.3	149.0
116	95.2	102.0	108.8	115.6	122.4	129.2	136.0	142.8	149.6
117	95.6	102.4	109.2	116.0	122.9	129.7	136.5	143.3	150.2
118	95.8	102.7	109.5	116.4	123.2	130.1	136.9	143.7	150.6
119	96.2	103.1	109.9	116.8	123.7	130.5	137.4	144.3	151.1

Table 5. *Percentage of reference weight-for-age in kg*

Age (months)	Values for different percentages of reference weight-for-age			
	60%	75%	90%	100%
0	1.9	2.4	2.9	3.2
1	2.5	3.1	3.7	4.1
2	2.9	3.7	4.4	4.9
3	3.4	4.3	5.1	5.7
4	3.8	4.8	5.8	6.4
5	4.2	5.3	6.3	7.0
6	4.5	5.6	6.8	7.5
7	4.8	6.0	7.2	8.0
8	5.1	6.4	7.7	8.5
9	5.3	6.7	8.0	8.9
10	5.5	6.9	8.3	9.2
11	5.8	7.2	8.6	9.6
12	5.9	7.4	8.8	9.8

Table 5.—contd.

| Age (months) | Values for different percentages of reference weight-for-age | | | |
	60%	75%	90%	100%
13	6.1	7.6	9.1	10.1
14	6.2	7.7	9.3	10.3
15	6.4	8.0	9.5	10.6
16	6.5	8.1	9.7	10.8
17	6.6	8.3	9.9	11.0
18	6.7	8.3	10.0	11.1
19	6.8	8.5	10.2	11.3
20	6.9	8.6	10.4	11.5
21	7.0	8.8	10.5	11.7
22	7.1	8.9	10.7	11.9
23	7.3	9.1	10.9	12.1
24	7.3	9.1	10.9	12.1
25	7.4	9.2	11.1	12.3
26	7.5	9.4	11.3	12.5
27	7.6	9.5	11.4	12.7
28	7.7	9.7	11.6	12.9
29	7.9	9.8	11.8	13.1
30	8.0	10.0	12.0	13.3
31	8.1	10.1	12.2	13.5
32	8.2	10.2	12.2	13.6
33	8.3	10.4	12.4	13.8
34	8.4	10.5	12.6	14.0
35	8.5	10.7	12.8	14.2
36	8.6	10.8	13.0	14.4
37	8.7	10.9	13.1	14.5
38	8.8	11.0	13.2	14.7
39	8.9	11.2	13.4	14.9
40	9.0	11.3	13.5	15.0
41	9.1	11.4	13.7	15.2
42	9.2	11.6	13.9	15.4
43	9.3	11.6	14.0	15.5
44	9.4	11.8	14.1	15.7
45	9.5	11.9	14.3	15.9
46	9.6	12.0	14.4	16.0
47	9.7	12.2	14.6	16.2
48	9.8	12.2	14.7	16.3
49	9.9	12.4	14.9	16.5
50	10.0	12.5	14.9	16.6
51	10.1	12.6	15.1	16.8
52	10.1	12.7	15.2	16.9
53	10.3	12.8	15.4	17.1
54	10.3	12.9	15.5	17.2
55	10.4	13.1	15.7	17.4
56	10.6	13.2	15.8	17.6
57	10.6	13.3	15.9	17.7
58	10.7	13.4	16.1	17.9
59	10.8	13.5	16.2	18.0
60	10.9	13.7	16.4	18.2
61	11.0	13.7	16.5	18.3

Table 5.—contd.

Age (months)	Values for different percentages of reference weight-for-age			
	60%	75%	90%	100%
62	11.1	13.9	16.7	18.5
63	11.2	14.0	16.7	18.6
64	11.3	14.1	16.9	18.8
65	11.4	14.3	17.1	19.0
66	11.5	14.3	17.2	19.1
67	11.6	14.5	17.4	19.3
68	11.6	14.6	17.5	19.4
69	11.8	14.7	17.6	19.6
70	11.9	14.9	17.8	19.8
71	11.9	14.9	17.9	19.9
72	12.1	15.1	18.1	20.1
73	12.2	15.2	18.3	20.3
74	12.3	15.4	18.5	20.5
75	12.4	15.5	18.5	20.6
76	12.5	15.6	18.7	20.8
77	12.6	15.8	18.9	21.0
78	12.7	15.8	19.1	21.2
79	12.8	16.1	19.3	21.4
80	13.0	16.2	19.4	21.6
81	13.0	16.3	19.5	21.7
82	13.1	16.4	19.7	21.9
83	13.3	16.6	19.9	22.1
84	13.4	16.7	20.1	22.3
85	13.6	17.0	20.3	22.6
86	13.7	17.1	20.5	22.8
87	13.8	17.3	20.7	23.0
88	13.9	17.4	20.9	23.2
89	14.0	17.6	21.1	23.4
90	14.2	17.7	21.2	23.6
91	14.3	17.9	21.5	23.9
92	14.5	18.1	21.7	24.1
93	14.6	18.2	21.9	24.3
94	14.8	18.5	22.1	24.6
95	14.9	18.6	22.3	24.8
96	15.1	18.8	22.6	25.1
97	15.2	19.0	22.8	25.3
98	15.4	19.2	23.0	25.6
99	15.5	19.4	23.2	25.8
100	15.7	19.6	23.5	26.1
101	15.8	19.8	23.8	26.4
102	16.0	20.0	23.9	26.6
103	16.1	20.2	24.2	26.9
104	16.3	20.4	24.5	27.2
105	16.4	20.6	24.7	27.4
106	16.6	20.8	24.9	27.7
107	16.8	21.0	25.2	28.0
108	17.0	21.2	25.5	28.3
109	17.2	21.5	25.7	28.6
110	17.3	21.7	26.0	28.9

Table 5.—contd.

Age (months)	Values for different percentages of reference weight-for-age			
	60%	75%	90%	100%
111	17.5	21.9	26.3	29.2
112	17.7	22.1	26.6	29.5
113	17.9	22.4	26.8	29.8
114	18.1	22.6	27.1	30.1
115	18.2	22.8	27.4	30.4
116	18.4	23.0	27.6	30.7
117	18.6	23.3	27.9	31.0
118	18.8	23.5	28.2	31.3
119	19.0	23.8	28.5	31.7

Table 6. *Weight-for-height chart dimensions—sexes averaged* (*using percentage of reference values as cut-offs*)

Weight (kg)	Heights (cm) at given weight-for-height percentage points					
	110%	100%	90%	80%	70%	60%
5.0	54.25	56.5	58.75	61.0	64.0	68.5
5.5	56.5	58.5	60.5	63.5	66.5	71.75
6.0	58.5	60.5	62.75	65.5	69.0	75.25
6.5	60.0	62.0	64.5	67.5	72.0	79.5
7.0	61.75	64.0	66.5	70.0	75.0	83.75
7.5	63.0	65.5	68.5	72.25	78.5	87.75
8.0	65.0	67.25	70.75	75.25	82.0	91.75
8.5	66.5	69.0	72.75	78.25	85.5	95.0
9.0	68.0	71.0	75.25	81.5	88.75	98.0
9.5	69.5	73.0	78.0	84.75	92.0	101.5
10.0	71.25	75.25	80.75	87.75	95.0	104.0
10.5	73.25	77.5	83.5	90.25	97.5	107.0
11.0	75.25	80.25	86.25	93.0	100.0	109.75
11.5	77.5	82.75	89.0	95.5	103.0	112.25
12.0	79.75	85.25	91.25	98.0	105.25	114.5
12.5	82.25	87.75	93.5	100.0	107.75	117.0
13.0	84.25	89.75	95.5	102.5	110.0	119.0
13.5	86.75	92.0	98.0	105.0	112.25	121.25
14.0	88.75	94.0	100.0	107.0	114.25	123.0
14.5	90.75	96.0	102.0	108.75	116.25	125.0
15.0	92.5	98.0	104.0	110.75	118.0	126.5
15.5	94.5	100.0	106.0	112.75	120.0	128.5
16.0	96.25	101.5	107.75	114.5	121.5	130.0
16.5	98.0	103.5	109.5	116.25	123.0	131.5
17.0	99.5	105.25	111.25	118.0	124.75	132.75

Table 6.—contd.

Weight	Heights (vm) at given weight-for-height percentage points					
(kg)	110%	100%	90%	80%	70%	60%
17.5	101.5	107.0	112.75	119.5	126.25	134.0
18.0	103.0	108.5	114.5	121.0	127.75	135.5
18.5	104.5	110.0	116.0	122.5	129.0	136.5
19.0	106.25	111.5	117.5	124.0	130.5	138.0
19.5	107.75	113.0	119.0	125.5	131.5	139.0
20.0	109.25	114.5	120.5	126.5	132.75	140.25
20.5	110.5	116.0	121.75	127.75	133.75	141.25
21.0	112.0	117.5	123.0	129.0	135.0	142.45
21.5	113.5	118.5	124.25	130.25	136.0	143.25
22.0	114.5	120.0	125.5	131.5	137.0	144.25
22.5	116.0	121.5	126.5	132.25	138.0	—
23.0	117.25	122.5	127.5	133.25	139.0	—
23.5	118.25	123.5	128.75	134.25	140.0	—
24.0	119.5	124.5	129.75	135.5	141.5	—
24.5	120.75	125.5	130.75	136.0	142.25	—
25.0	121.75	126.0	132.0	137.0	143.25	—

Table 7. *Weight-for-length distribution (sexes averaged) by standard deviations (Z scores) weight in kg; length in cm*

Length (cm)	Lower S.D.	−3.0 S.D.	−2.0 S.D.	−1.0 S.D.	Mean	+1.0 S.D.
49.0	0.4	2.2	2.5	2.9	3.2	3.6
50.0	0.4	2.2	2.6	3.0	3.4	3.8
51.0	0.4	2.3	2.7	3.1	3.5	4.0
52.0	0.4	2.4	2.8	3.2	3.7	4.2
53.0	0.5	2.5	2.9	3.4	3.9	4.4
54.0	0.5	2.6	3.1	3.6	4.1	4.7
55.0	0.5	2.8	3.3	3.8	4.3	4.9
56.0	0.5	2.9	3.5	4.0	4.6	5.2
57.0	0.6	3.1	3.7	4.2	4.8	5.4
58.0	0.6	3.3	3.9	4.5	5.1	5.7
59.0	0.6	3.5	4.1	4.7	5.3	6.0
60.0	0.6	3.7	4.3	5.0	5.6	6.3
61.0	0.6	3.9	4.6	5.2	5.9	6.6
62.0	0.7	4.2	4.8	5.5	6.2	6.9
63.0	0.7	4.4	5.1	5.8	6.5	7.2
64.0	0.7	4.7	5.4	6.1	6.7	7.5
65.0	0.7	4.9	5.6	6.3	7.0	7.8
66.0	0.7	5.2	5.9	6.6	7.3	8.1
67.0	0.7	5.4	6.1	6.9	7.6	8.4
68.0	0.8	5.7	6.4	7.2	7.9	8.7
69.0	0.8	5.9	6.7	7.4	8.2	9.0
70.0	0.8	6.1	6.9	7.7	8.5	9.3

Table 7.—contd.

Length (cm)	Lower S.D.	−3.0 S.D.	−2.0 S.D.	−1.0 S.D.	Mean	+1.0 S.D.
71.0	0.8	6.4	7.2	7.9	8.7	9.5
72.0	0.8	6.6	7.4	8.2	9.0	9.8
73.0	0.8	6.8	7.6	8.4	9.2	10.1
74.0	0.8	7.0	7.8	8.7	9.5	10.3
75.0	0.8	7.2	8.1	8.9	9.7	10.6
76.0	0.8	7.4	8.3	9.1	9.9	10.8
77.0	0.8	7.6	8.5	9.3	10.1	11.0
78.0	0.9	7.8	8.6	9.5	10.4	11.2
79.0	0.9	8.0	8.8	9.7	10.6	11.5
80.0	0.9	8.1	9.0	9.9	10.8	11.7
81.0	0.9	8.3	9.2	10.1	11.0	11.9
82.0	0.9	8.5	9.4	10.3	11.2	12.1
83.0	0.9	8.7	9.6	10.5	11.4	12.3
84.0	0.9	8.8	9.7	10.6	11.5	12.5
85.0	0.9	9.0	9.9	10.8	11.7	12.7
86.0	0.9	9.2	10.1	11.0	11.9	12.9
87.0	0.9	9.3	10.3	11.2	12.1	13.1
88.0	0.9	9.5	10.5	11.4	12.4	13.4
89.0	1.0	9.7	10.7	11.6	12.6	13.6
90.0	1.0	9.9	10.8	11.8	12.8	13.8
91.0	1.0	10.1	11.1	12.0	13.0	14.0
92.0	1.0	10.3	11.3	12.2	13.2	14.3
93.0	1.0	10.5	11.5	12.5	13.5	14.5
94.0	1.0	10.7	11.7	12.7	13.7	14.8
95.0	1.0	10.9	11.9	12.9	14.0	15.0
96.0	1.0	11.1	12.2	13.2	14.2	15.3
97.0	1.0	11.3	12.4	13.4	14.5	15.6
98.0	1.1	11.6	12.6	13.7	14.8	15.8
99.0	1.1	11.8	12.9	14.0	15.0	16.1
100.0	1.1	12.1	13.2	14.2	15.3	16.4

Table 8. *Weight-for-height distribution (sexes averaged) by standard deviations (Z scores) weight in kg; height in cm*

Height (cm)	Lower S.D.	−3.0 S.D.	−2.0 S.D.	−1.0 S.D.	Mean	+1.0 S.D.
65.0	1.0	4.6	5.5	6.5	7.4	8.7
66.0	1.0	4.8	5.8	6.7	7.7	8.9
67.0	1.0	5.0	6.0	7.0	8.0	9.2
68.0	1.0	5.3	6.2	7.2	8.2	9.5
69.0	1.0	5.5	6.5	7.5	8.5	9.7
70.0	1.0	5.7	6.7	7.7	8.7	10.0
71.0	1.0	5.9	6.9	7.9	8.9	10.2
72.0	1.0	6.1	7.1	8.2	9.2	10.4
73.0	1.0	6.4	7.4	8.4	9.4	10.7
74.0	1.0	6.6	7.6	8.6	9.6	10.9

Table 8.—contd.

Height (cm)	Lower S.D.	−3.0 S.D.	−2.0 S.D.	−1.0 S.D.	Mean	+1.0 S.D.
75.0	1.0	6.8	7.8	8.8	9.8	11.1
76.0	1.0	7.0	8.0	9.0	10.0	11.4
77.0	1.0	7.2	8.2	9.2	10.3	11.6
78.0	1.0	7.4	8.4	9.4	10.5	11.8
79.0	1.0	7.6	8.6	9.7	10.7	12.0
80.0	1.0	7.8	8.8	9.9	10.9	12.3
81.0	1.0	8.0	9.0	10.1	11.1	12.5
82.0	1.0	8.2	9.2	10.3	11.3	12.7
83.0	1.1	8.4	9.4	10.5	11.5	12.9
84.0	1.1	8.6	9.6	10.7	11.8	13.2
85.0	1.1	8.7	9.8	10.9	12.0	13.4
86.0	1.1	8.9	10.0	11.1	12.2	13.6
87.0	1.1	9.1	10.2	11.3	12.4	13.8
88.0	1.1	9.3	10.4	11.5	12.6	14.1
89.0	1.1	9.5	10.6	11.7	12.9	14.3
90.0	1.2	9.6	10.8	11.9	13.1	14.5
91.0	1.2	9.8	11.0	12.2	13.3	14.8
92.0	1.2	10.0	11.2	12.4	13.6	15.0
93.0	1.2	10.2	11.4	12.6	13.8	15.3
94.0	1.2	10.4	11.6	12.8	14.0	15.5
95.0	1.3	10.5	11.8	13.0	14.3	15.8
96.0	1.3	10.7	12.0	13.3	14.5	16.0
97.0	1.3	10.9	12.2	13.5	14.8	16.3
98.0	1.3	11.1	12.4	13.7	15.0	16.6
99.0	1.3	11.3	12.6	14.0	15.3	16.9
100.0	1.4	11.5	12.8	14.2	15.6	17.1
101.0	1.4	11.7	13.0	14.4	15.8	17.4
102.0	1.4	11.9	13.3	14.7	16.1	17.7
103.0	1.4	12.1	13.5	14.9	16.4	18.0
104.0	1.5	12.3	13.7	15.2	16.7	18.3
105.0	1.5	12.5	14.0	15.5	16.9	18.6
106.0	1.5	12.7	14.2	15.7	17.2	19.0
107.0	1.5	12.9	14.5	17.0	17.5	19.3
108.0	1.6	13.2	14.7	16.3	17.8	19.6
109.0	1.6	13.4	15.0	16.6	18.1	20.0
110.0	1.6	13.6	15.2	16.8	18.4	20.3
111.0	1.6	13.9	15.5	17.1	18.8	20.7
112.0	1.6	14.2	15.8	17.4	19.1	21.1
113.0	1.7	14.4	16.1	17.8	19.4	21.4
114.0	1.7	14.7	16.4	18.1	19.8	21.8
115.0	1.7	15.0	16.7	18.4	20.1	22.2
116.0	1.7	15.3	17.0	18.7	20.5	22.7
117.0	1.8	15.6	17.3	19.1	20.8	23.1
118.0	1.8	15.8	17.6	19.4	21.2	23.6
119.0	1.8	16.2	18.0	19.8	21.6	24.0
120.0	1.8	16.5	18.3	20.2	22.0	24.5
121.0	1.9	16.8	18.7	20.5	22.4	25.0
122.0	1.9	17.1	19.0	20.9	22.8	25.6
123.0	2.0	17.4	19.4	21.3	23.3	26.1
124.0	2.0	17.7	19.7	21.7	23.7	26.7
125.0	2.0	18.1	20.1	22.2	24.2	27.3

Table 8.—contd.

Height (cm)	Lower S.D.	−3.0 S.D.	−2.0 S.D.	−1.0 S.D.	Mean	+1.0 S.D.
126.0	2.1	18.4	20.5	22.6	24.7	27.9
127.0	2.1	18.7	20.9	23.0	25.2	28.5
128.0	2.2	19.1	21.3	23.5	25.7	29.2
129.0	2.3	19.4	21.7	24.0	26.2	29.9
130.0	2.3	19.7	22.1	24.4	26.8	30.6
131.0	2.4	20.1	22.5	24.9	27.4	31.4
132.0	2.5	20.4	22.9	25.4	27.9	32.2
133.0	2.6	20.7	23.3	25.9	28.6	33.0
134.0	2.7	21.1	23.8	26.5	29.2	33.8
135.0	2.8	21.4	24.2	27.0	29.8	34.7
136.0	2.9	21.7	24.7	27.6	30.5	35.6
137.0	3.0	22.1	25.1	28.2	31.2	36.6

Table 9. *Length-for-age distribution (sexes averaged) by standard deviations (Z scores) length in cm*

Age (months)	Lower S.D.	−3.0 S.D.	−2.0 S.D.	−1.0 S.D.	Mean	+1.0 S.D.
0.0	2.2	43.5	45.7	47.9	50.2	52.4
1.0	2.4	46.9	49.3	51.7	54.1	56.4
2.0	2.5	50.0	52.4	54.9	57.4	59.9
3.0	2.6	52.6	55.2	57.8	60.3	62.9
4.0	2.6	55.0	57.6	60.2	62.8	65.4
5.0	2.6	57.1	59.7	62.3	65.0	67.6
6.0	2.7	58.9	61.5	64.2	66.9	69.5
7.0	2.7	60.5	63.2	65.9	68.5	71.2
8.0	2.7	62.0	64.7	67.3	70.0	72.7
9.0	2.7	63.3	66.0	68.7	71.4	74.1
10.0	2.7	64.6	67.3	70.0	72.7	75.4
11.0	2.7	65.8	68.5	71.2	74.0	76.7
12.0	2.8	66.9	69.7	72.4	75.2	78.0
13.0	2.8	68.0	70.8	73.6	76.4	79.2
14.0	2.8	69.0	71.8	74.7	77.5	80.4
15.0	2.9	69.9	72.8	75.7	78.6	81.5
16.0	2.9	70.8	73.8	76.7	79.7	82.6
17.0	3.0	71.7	74.7	77.7	80.7	83.7
18.0	3.1	72.5	75.6	78.6	81.7	84.7
19.0	3.1	73.3	76.4	79.5	82.6	85.7
20.0	3.2	74.1	77.2	80.4	83.6	86.7
21.0	3.2	74.9	78.1	81.3	84.5	87.7
22.0	3.2	75.6	78.9	82.1	85.4	88.6
23.0	3.3	76.4	79.6	82.9	86.2	89.5

Table 10. *Height-for-age distribution (sexes averaged) by standard deviations (Z scores) height in cm*

Age (months)	Lower S.D.	−3.0 S.D.	−2.0 S.D.	−1.0 S.D.	Mean	+1.0 S.D.
24.0	3.2	75.4	78.6	81.8	85.0	88.2
25.0	3.3	76.1	79.4	82.6	85.9	89.1
26.0	3.3	76.8	80.1	83.4	86.7	90.0
27.0	3.4	77.5	80.8	84.2	87.6	90.9
28.0	3.4	78.1	81.5	84.9	88.4	91.8
29.0	3.5	78.8	82.2	85.7	89.2	92.6
30.0	3.5	79.4	82.9	86.4	89.9	93.5
31.0	3.6	80.1	83.6	87.2	90.7	94.3
32.0	3.6	80.7	84.3	87.9	91.5	95.1
33.0	3.6	81.3	84.9	88.6	92.2	95.9
34.0	3.7	81.9	85.6	89.3	93.0	96.7
35.0	3.7	82.5	86.3	90.0	93.7	97.4
36.0	3.8	83.1	86.9	90.7	94.4	98.2
37.0	3.8	83.7	87.5	91.3	95.1	98.9
38.0	3.8	84.3	88.2	92.0	95.8	99.7
39.0	3.9	84.9	88.8	92.6	96.5	100.4
40.0	3.9	85.5	89.4	93.3	97.2	101.1
41.0	3.9	86.0	90.0	93.9	97.8	101.8
42.0	4.0	86.6	90.6	94.5	98.5	102.5
43.0	4.0	87.2	91.2	95.2	99.2	103.2
44.0	4.0	87.7	91.7	95.8	99.8	103.8
45.0	4.1	88.2	92.3	96.4	100.4	104.5
46.0	4.1	88.8	92.9	97.0	101.1	105.2
47.0	4.1	89.3	93.4	97.6	101.7	105.8
48.0	4.2	89.8	94.0	98.1	102.3	106.4
49.0	4.2	90.4	94.5	98.7	102.9	107.1
50.0	4.2	90.9	95.1	99.3	103.5	107.7
51.0	4.2	91.4	95.6	99.8	104.1	108.3
52.0	4.3	91.9	96.1	100.4	104.7	108.9
53.0	4.3	92.4	96.7	100.9	105.2	109.5
54.0	4.3	92.8	97.2	101.5	105.8	110.1
55.0	4.4	93.3	97.7	102.0	106.4	110.7
56.0	4.4	93.8	98.2	102.6	106.9	111.3
57.0	4.4	94.3	98.7	103.1	107.5	111.9
58.0	4.4	94.7	99.2	103.6	108.1	112.5
59.0	4.5	95.2	99.7	104.1	108.6	113.1
60.0	4.5	95.6	100.1	104.6	109.2	113.7
61.0	4.5	96.1	100.6	105.2	109.7	114.2
62.0	4.6	96.5	101.1	105.7	110.2	114.8
63.0	4.6	97.0	101.6	106.2	110.8	115.4
64.0	4.6	97.4	102.0	106.7	111.3	115.9
65.0	4.7	97.8	102.5	107.1	111.8	116.5
66.0	4.7	98.2	102.9	107.6	112.3	117.0
67.0	4.7	98.7	103.4	108.1	112.8	117.6
68.0	4.8	99.1	103.8	108.6	113.4	118.1
69.0	4.8	99.5	104.3	109.1	113.9	118.7
70.0	4.8	99.9	104.7	109.5	114.4	119.2
71.0	4.9	100.3	105.2	110.0	114.9	119.7
72.0	4.9	100.7	105.6	110.5	115.4	120.3

Table 10.—contd.

Age (months)	Lower S.D.	−3.0 S.D.	−2.0 S.D.	−1.0 S.D.	Mean	+1.0 S.D.
73.0	4.9	101.1	106.0	110.9	115.9	120.8
74.0	5.0	101.5	106.4	111.4	116.4	121.3
75.0	5.0	101.9	106.9	111.9	116.8	121.8
76.0	5.0	102.3	107.3	112.3	117.3	122.3
77.0	5.1	102.7	107.7	112.8	117.8	122.9
78.0	5.1	103.0	108.1	113.2	118.3	123.4
79.0	5.1	103.4	108.5	113.7	118.8	123.9
80.0	5.2	103.8	108.9	114.1	119.2	124.4
81.0	5.2	104.2	109.4	114.5	119.7	124.9
82.0	5.2	104.5	109.8	115.0	120.2	125.4
83.0	5.3	104.9	110.2	115.4	120.7	125.9
84.0	5.3	105.3	110.6	115.8	121.1	126.4
85.0	5.3	105.6	111.0	116.3	121.6	126.9
86.0	5.4	106.0	111.4	116.7	122.1	127.4
87.0	5.4	106.4	111.8	117.1	122.5	127.9
88.0	5.4	106.7	112.2	117.6	123.0	128.4
89.0	5.5	107.1	112.6	118.0	123.5	128.9
90.0	5.5	107.5	112.9	118.4	123.9	129.4
91.0	5.5	107.8	113.3	118.9	124.4	129.9
92.0	5.6	108.2	113.7	119.3	124.8	130.4
93.0	5.6	108.5	114.1	119.7	125.3	130.9
94.0	5.6	108.9	114.5	120.1	125.8	131.4
95.0	5.7	109.2	114.9	120.6	126.2	131.9
96.0	5.7	109.6	115.3	121.0	126.7	132.4
97.0	5.7	110.0	115.7	121.4	127.1	132.9
98.0	5.8	110.3	116.1	121.8	127.6	133.3
99.0	5.8	110.7	116.5	122.3	128.1	133.8
100.0	5.8	111.0	116.9	122.7	128.5	134.3
101.0	5.9	111.4	117.3	123.1	129.0	134.8
102.0	5.9	111.8	117.6	123.5	129.4	135.3
103.0	5.9	112.1	118.0	124.0	129.9	135.8
104.0	6.0	112.5	118.4	124.4	130.3	136.3
105.0	6.0	112.8	118.8	124.8	130.8	136.8
106.0	6.0	113.2	119.2	125.2	131.3	137.3
107.0	6.1	113.6	119.6	125.7	131.7	137.8
108.0	6.1	113.9	120.0	126.1	132.2	138.3
109.0	6.1	114.3	120.4	126.5	132.7	138.8
110.0	6.2	114.7	120.8	127.0	133.1	139.3
111.0	6.2	115.0	121.2	127.4	133.6	139.8
112.0	6.2	115.4	121.6	127.9	134.1	140.3
113.0	6.3	115.8	122.0	128.3	134.5	140.8
114.0	6.3	116.2	122.5	128.7	135.0	141.3
115.0	6.3	116.6	122.9	129.2	135.5	141.8
116.0	6.3	116.9	123.3	129.6	136.0	142.3
117.0	6.4	117.3	123.7	130.1	136.5	142.8
118.0	6.4	117.7	124.1	130.5	136.9	143.3
119.0	6.4	118.1	124.5	131.0	137.4	143.9

Table 11. *Weight-for-age distribution (sexes averaged) by standard deviations (Z scores) weight in kg*

Age (months)	Lower S.D.	−3.0 S.D.	−2.0 S.D.	−1.0 S.D.	Mean	+1.0 S.D.
0.0	0.5	1.9	2.3	2.8	3.2	3.7
1.0	0.6	2.2	2.9	3.5	4.1	4.7
2.0	0.8	2.6	3.4	4.2	4.9	5.7
3.0	0.8	3.1	4.0	4.8	5.7	6.5
4.0	0.9	3.7	4.6	5.5	6.4	7.2
5.0	0.9	4.2	5.2	6.1	7.0	7.9
6.0	0.9	4.8	5.7	6.6	7.5	8.5
7.0	0.9	5.2	6.2	7.1	8.0	9.0
8.0	1.0	5.6	6.6	7.5	8.5	9.5
9.0	1.0	6.0	6.9	7.9	8.9	9.9
10.0	1.0	6.3	7.3	8.2	9.2	10.3
11.0	1.0	6.5	7.5	8.5	9.6	10.6
12.0	1.0	6.7	7.8	8.8	9.8	10.9
13.0	1.1	6.9	8.0	9.0	10.1	11.2
14.0	1.1	7.1	8.2	9.3	10.3	11.5
15.0	1.1	7.2	8.4	9.5	10.6	11.7
16.0	1.1	7.4	8.5	9.6	10.8	11.9
17.0	1.2	7.5	8.7	9.8	11.0	12.1
18.0	1.2	7.6	8.8	10.0	11.1	12.3
19.0	1.2	7.7	8.9	10.1	11.3	12.5
20.0	1.2	7.9	9.1	10.3	11.5	12.7
21.0	1.2	8.0	9.2	10.5	11.7	12.9
22.0	1.3	8.1	9.4	10.6	11.9	13.1
23.0	1.3	8.3	9.5	10.8	12.1	13.3
24.0	1.1	8.6	9.8	10.9	12.1	13.6
25.0	1.2	8.7	9.9	11.1	12.3	13.8
26.0	1.2	8.8	10.0	11.3	12.5	14.1
27.0	1.3	8.9	10.2	11.4	12.7	14.3
28.0	1.3	9.0	10.3	11.6	12.9	14.5
29.0	1.3	9.1	10.4	11.7	13.1	14.8
30.0	1.4	9.2	10.5	11.9	13.3	15.0
31.0	1.4	9.3	10.7	12.1	13.5	15.2
32.0	1.4	9.4	10.8	12.2	13.6	15.4
33.0	1.5	9.5	10.9	12.4	13.8	15.6
34.0	1.5	9.6	11.0	12.5	14.0	15.8
35.0	1.5	9.7	11.2	12.7	14.2	16.0
36.0	1.5	9.8	11.3	12.8	14.4	16.2
37.0	1.6	9.9	11.4	13.0	14.5	16.4
38.0	1.6	10.0	11.5	13.1	14.7	16.6
39.0	1.6	10.0	11.7	13.3	14.9	16.8
40.0	1.6	10.1	11.8	13.4	15.0	17.0
41.0	1.7	10.2	11.9	13.6	15.2	17.2
42.0	1.7	10.3	12.0	13.7	15.4	17.4
43.0	1.7	10.4	12.1	13.8	15.5	17.6
44.0	1.7	10.5	12.3	14.0	15.7	17.8
45.0	1.7	10.6	12.4	14.1	15.9	18.0
46.0	1.8	10.7	12.5	14.3	16.0	18.2
47.0	1.8	10.8	12.6	14.4	16.2	18.3
48.0	1.8	10.9	12.7	14.5	16.3	18.5

Table 11.—contd.

Age (months)	Lower S.D.	−3.0 S.D.	−2.0 S.D.	−1.0 S.D.	Mean	+1.0 S.D.
49.0	1.8	11.0	12.8	14.7	16.5	18.7
50.0	1.8	11.1	13.0	14.8	16.6	18.9
51.0	1.9	11.2	13.1	14.9	16.8	19.1
52.0	1.9	11.3	13.2	15.1	16.9	19.3
53.0	1.9	11.4	13.3	15.2	17.1	19.5
54.0	1.9	11.5	13.4	15.3	17.2	19.6
55.0	1.9	11.6	13.5	15.5	17.4	19.8
56.0	1.9	11.7	13.7	15.6	17.6	20.0
57.0	2.0	11.8	13.8	15.7	17.7	20.2
58.0	2.0	11.9	13.9	15.9	17.9	20.4
59.0	2.0	12.0	14.0	16.0	18.0	20.6
60.0	2.0	12.1	14.1	16.1	18.2	20.8
61.0	2.0	12.2	14.2	16.3	18.3	21.0
62.0	2.1	12.3	14.4	16.4	18.5	21.2
63.0	2.1	12.4	14.5	16.6	18.6	21.3
64.0	2.1	12.5	14.6	16.7	18.8	21.5
65.0	2.1	12.6	14.7	16.8	19.0	21.8
66.0	2.1	12.7	14.8	17.0	19.1	22.0
67.0	2.2	12.8	14.9	17.1	19.3	22.2
68.0	2.2	12.9	15.0	17.2	19.4	22.4
69.0	2.2	12.9	15.2	17.4	19.6	22.6
70.0	2.2	13.0	15.3	17.5	19.8	22.8
71.0	2.3	13.1	15.4	17.7	19.9	23.0
72.0	2.3	13.2	15.5	17.8	20.1	23.2
73.0	2.3	13.3	15.6	18.0	20.3	23.5
74.0	2.3	13.4	15.8	18.1	20.5	23.7
75.0	2.4	13.5	15.9	18.3	20.6	23.9
76.0	2.4	13.6	16.0	18.4	20.8	24.2
77.0	2.4	13.7	16.1	18.6	21.0	24.4
78.0	2.5	13.8	16.2	18.7	21.2	24.7
79.0	2.5	13.8	16.4	18.9	21.4	24.9
80.0	2.5	13.9	16.5	19.0	21.6	25.2
81.0	2.6	14.0	16.6	19.2	21.7	25.4
82.0	2.6	14.1	16.7	19.3	21.9	25.7
83.0	2.7	14.2	16.8	19.5	22.1	26.0
84.0	2.7	14.3	17.0	19.7	22.3	26.3
85.0	2.7	14.4	17.1	19.8	22.6	26.6
86.0	2.8	14.4	17.2	20.0	22.8	26.8
87.0	2.8	14.5	17.3	20.2	23.0	27.1
88.0	2.9	14.6	17.5	20.3	23.2	27.5
89.0	2.9	14.7	17.6	20.5	23.4	27.8
90.0	3.0	14.8	17.7	20.7	23.6	28.1
91.0	3.0	14.8	17.8	20.9	23.9	28.4
92.0	3.1	14.9	18.0	21.0	24.1	28.7
93.0	3.1	15.0	18.1	21.2	24.3	29.1
94.0	3.2	15.1	18.2	21.4	24.6	29.4
95.0	3.2	15.1	18.4	21.6	24.8	29.7
96.0	3.3	15.2	18.5	21.8	25.1	30.1
97.0	3.3	15.3	18.6	22.0	25.3	30.4
98.0	3.4	15.4	18.8	22.2	25.6	30.8
99.0	3.5	15.4	18.9	22.4	25.8	31.2

Table 11.—contd.

Age (months)	Lower S.D.	− 3.0 S.D.	− 2.0 S.D.	− 1.0 S.D.	Mean	+ 1.0 S.D.
100.0	3.5	15.5	19.0	22.6	26.1	31.5
101.0	3.6	15.6	19.2	22.8	26.4	31.9
102.0	3.7	15.6	19.3	23.0	26.6	32.3
103.0	3.7	15.7	19.4	23.2	26.9	32.7
104.0	3.8	15.8	19.6	23.4	27.2	33.1
105.0	3.9	15.8	19.7	23.6	27.4	33.4
106.0	3.9	15.9	19.9	23.8	27.7	33.8
107.0	4.0	16.0	20.0	24.0	28.0	34.2
108.0	4.1	16.1	20.1	24.2	28.3	34.7
109.0	4.2	16.1	20.3	24.4	28.6	35.1
110.0	4.2	16.2	20.4	24.7	28.9	35.5
111.0	4.3	16.3	20.6	24.9	29.2	35.9
112.0	4.4	16.4	20.7	25.1	29.5	36.3
113.0	4.4	16.4	20.9	25.3	29.8	36.7
114.0	4.5	16.5	21.0	25.6	30.1	37.2
115.0	4.6	16.6	21.2	25.8	30.4	37.6
116.0	4.7	16.7	21.4	26.0	30.7	38.0
117.0	4.8	16.8	21.5	26.3	31.0	38.5
118.0	4.8	16.9	21.7	26.5	31.3	38.9
119.0	4.9	17.0	21.9	26.8	31.7	39.4

Table 12. *Weight-for-height chart dimensions—sexes averaged (using standard deviations, or Z scores, as cut-offs)*

Weight (kg)	Heights (cm) at given Z score points				
	−3.0 S.D.	−2.0 S.D.	−1.0 S.D.	Mean	+1.0 S.D.
4	63.0	59.25	55.75		
4.5	65.0	61.5	58.0		
5	67.0	63.25	60.0		
5.5	69.0	65.25	61.75		
6	71.0	67.25	63.5	60.25	56.0
6.5	73.25	69.0	65.25	62.25	58.0
7	75.5	71.0	67.25	63.75	59.5
7.5	78.25	73.0	69.0	65.5	61.0
8	80.75	75.5	71.0	67.25	62.75
8.5	83.75	77.75	73.0	69.0	64.5
9	86.75	80.75	75.5	71.0	66.25
9.5	89.75	83.25	77.75	73.0	68.0
10	92.5	86.25	80.25	75.25	70.0
10.5	95.0	88.75	83.25	77.5	72.0
11	97.5	91.5	85.75	80.25	74.0
11.5	100.25	93.75	88.25	82.75	76.25
12	102.75	96.25	90.75	85.25	78.75
12.5	105.25	98.5	92.75	87.75	81.0
13	107.25	100.75	95.0	90.0	83.5
13.5	109.5	103.25	97.25	92.25	86.0
14	111.25	105.25	99.25	94.25	88.0
14.5	113.25	107.0	101.25	96.0	90.25
15	115.0	109.0	103.25	98.0	92.25
15.5	116.75	110.75	105.25	99.75	94.0
16	118.5	112.5	107.0	101.75	95.5
16.5	120.0	114.25	108.75	103.75	97.5
17	121.5	116.0	110.5	105.25	99.25
17.5	123.25	117.5	112.0	107.0	101.0
18	124.75	119.0	113.75	108.5	102.75
18.5	126.25	120.5	115.25	110.0	104.5
19	127.75	122.0	116.5	111.75	106.0
19.5	129.25	123.5	118.0	113.0	107.5
20	131.0	124.5	119.5	114.5	109.0
20.5	132.5	126.0	121.0	116.0	110.5
21	134.0	127.5	122.0	117.5	112.0
21.5	135.5	128.5	123.5	118.5	113.25
22	137.0	129.75	124.5	120.0	114.5
22.5		131.0	125.75	121.25	115.5
23		132.25	127.0	122.5	117.0
23.5		133.5	128.0	123.5	118.0
24		134.5	129.0	124.5	119.0
24.5		135.5	130.25	125.75	120.0
25		137.0	131.25	127.75	121.0

Nutrition surveys

Table 1. *Weight-for-height percentages at different weights and heights (sexes combined, NAS (NCHS) standards)*

Weight (kg)	Heights (cm) at given weight-for-height percentage points					
	110%	100%	90%	80%	70%	60%
5.0	54.25	56.5	58.75	61.0	64.0	68.5
5.5	56.5	58.5	60.5	63.5	66.5	71.75
6.0	58.5	60.5	62.75	65.5	69.0	75.25
6.5	60.0	62.0	64.5	67.5	72.0	79.5
7.0	61.75	64.0	66.5	70.0	75.0	83.75
7.5	63.0	65.5	68.5	72.25	78.5	87.75
8.0	65.0	67.25	70.75	75.25	82.0	91.75
8.5	66.5	69.0	72.75	78.25	85.5	95.0
9.0	68.0	71.0	75.25	81.5	88.75	98.0
9.5	69.5	73.0	78.0	84.75	92.0	101.5
10.0	71.25	75.25	80.75	87.75	95.0	104.0
10.5	73.25	77.5	83.5	90.25	97.5	107.0
11.0	75.25	80.25	86.25	93.0	100.0	109.75
11.5	77.5	82.75	89.0	95.5	103.0	112.25
12.0	79.75	85.25	91.25	98.0	105.25	114.5
12.5	82.25	87.75	93.5	100.0	107.75	117.0
13.0	84.25	89.75	95.5	102.5	110.0	119.0
13.5	86.75	92.0	98.0	105.0	112.25	121.25
14.0	88.75	94.0	100.0	107.0	114.25	123.0
14.5	90.75	96.0	102.0	108.75	116.25	125.0
15.0	92.5	98.0	104.0	110.75	118.0	126.5
15.5	94.5	100.0	106.0	112.75	120.0	128.5
16.0	96.25	101.5	107.75	114.5	121.5	130.0
16.5	98.0	103.5	109.25	116.25	123.0	131.5
17.0	99.5	105.25	111.25	118.0	124.75	132.75
17.5	101.5	107.0	112.75	119.5	126.25	134.0
18.0	103.0	108.5	114.5	121.0	127.75	135.5
18.5	104.5	110.0	116.0	122.5	129.0	136.5
19.0	106.25	111.5	117.5	124.0	130.5	138.0
19.5	107.75	113.0	119.0	125.5	131.5	139.0
20.0	109.25	114.5	120.5	126.5	132.75	140.25
20.5	110.5	116.0	121.75	127.75	133.75	141.25
21.0	112.0	117.5	123.0	129.0	135.0	142.45
21.5	113.5	118.5	124.25	130.25	136.0	143.25
22.0	114.5	120.0	125.5	131.5	137.0	144.25
22.5	116.0	121.5	126.5	132.25	138.0	—
23.0	117.25	122.5	127.5	133.25	139.0	—
23.5	118.25	123.5	128.75	134.25	140.0	—
24.0	119.5	124.5	129.75	135.5	141.5	—
24.5	120.75	125.5	130.75	136.0	142.25	—
25.0	121.75	126.0	132.0	137.0	143.25	—

Diarrhoea and rehydration

Examples of calculations of the fluid required by children with diarrhoea.

1. A 10 kg child aged 1 year old (infant) is moderately dehydrated.

   (a) Detailed calculation.

Replacement volume 75 ml × 10 kg in 4–6 hours	= 750 ml ORS
Continuing loss, e.g. 4 stools, approx. 100 ml each	= 400 ml ORS
Maintenance volume 120 ml per kg i.e. × 10	= 1200 ml water and other liquids
Total intake in 24 hours	2350 ml

   (b) Approximate volume.

200 ml per kg in 24 hours 200 × 10 plus breast milk	= 2000 ml dilute ORS or sugar–salt solution

2. A 24 kg child aged 10 years is severely dehydrated.

   (a) Detailed calculation.

Replacement volume 100 ml × 25 kg in 4–6 hours	= 2500 ml ORS
Continuing loss, e.g. 4 stools, approx. 200 ml each	= 800 ml ORS
Maintenance volume 80 ml per kg i.e. × 25	= 2000 ml water and other liquids
Total intake in 24 hours	4300 ml

   (b) Approximate volume.

150 ml per kg in 24 hours 150 × 25	= 3750 ml dilute ORS or sugar–salt solution

Note: for a severely dehydrated child oral rehydration should be started and the patient transferred to a unit which can give intravenous fluid if this becomes necessary.

GUIDELINES FOR REHYDRATION IN SEVERE DEHYDRATION (PLAN C, p. 162)

If Ringer's lactate is not available use whatever other I.V. solutions are available. Give in the same volumes as shown except for half strength Darrow's solution, for which the volumes should be increased by 50 per cent.

	Type of fluid and route	Volume of fluid (per kg body weight)	Time of administration
Infants	Ringer's lactate I.V. (Note 1)	30 ml/kg	Within 1 hour
	Followed by: Ringer's lactate I.V. (Note 1)	40 ml/kg	Within next 2 hours
	Followed by: ORS solution by mouth	40 ml/kg	Within next 3 hours
Older children and adults	Ringer's lactate	110 ml/kg	Within 4 hours initially as fast as possible until radial pulse is palpable
	Followed by: ORS solution by mouth	15–30 ml/kg	Within next 3–4 hours depending on amount of diarrhoea

LISTS OF EQUIPMENT

Emergency Health Kit: drugs and clinic equipment for 10 000 persons for 3 months

EXPLANATION

1. There are *two drug lists* (*lists A and B*) and *one equipment list* (*list C*). Together, the items make up one complete emergency kit. The drugs are selected from WHO Technical Report Series 641 (1979): *The selection of essential drugs*. Consecutive numbers are allocated to facilitate reordering. The WHO reference numbers are shown on lists A and B. The equipment in list C is generally available, standard clinic equipment.

2. The purpose of the lists and emergency kit is twofold: to encourage an appropriate standardization of drugs and equipment for refugees and to enable swift outside supply in a refugee emergency if local supply is not possible.

3. Vaccines and drugs for the control of certain communicable diseases have not been included in the lists because:

(1) many countries have national disease control programmes, e.g. for tuberculosis, leprosy, schistosomiasis; it is necessary, therefore, first to

investigate the incidence of these diseases among the refugees and then discuss the problem with the national authorities so that any disease control programme implemented conforms to national policies;

(2) many countries have an expanded programme of immunization (EPI) and use can be made of this, including the cold chain system; it is necessary, therefore, first to discuss the programme with the authorities before deciding on the type of vaccine and equipment required; also under adverse conditions a cold chain may not be immediately available.

List A: Basic drug requirements for 10 000 refugees for 3 months

4. This list is based on:

(1) a population structure of 0–14 years of age = 5000
15+ years of age = 5000;

(2) four contacts (informal or formal) per person per year for all age groups:
= 10 000 in 12 weeks
= 5000 in 6 weeks
= 800–900 per week;

(3) the possible incidence of symptoms and suggested treatment as detailed in Table 14;

(4) the possible standardized treatment schedule as detailed in Table 2;

(5) a rounding up of the total drug quantities to simplify packaging;

(6) the likelihood that the clinic will be staffed routinely by basically trained health workers who on the whole will be treating symptoms rather than clearly defined diseases, and referring patients who need more sophisticated treatment;

(7) the realization that the supply of drugs on the list will only suffice as a help during the early life of a camp until a thorough assessment has been made.

List B: Drugs for use by doctors and senior health workers

5. These drugs are intended as an emergency supply of second line professional management/more sophisticated drugs until more work has been done/information is available.

6. If a nearby national hospital is acting as the referral point, and the drugs on list B are not immediately required within the refugee community, consideration should be given to providing them to that hospital.

General considerations

7. When prescribing any of the drugs on the two lists, as for all drugs, careful attention must be paid to patient-specific considerations such as contra-indications, the possibility of adverse reactions, drug interactions, irritant factors, and prescribing constraints in pregnancy, children, especially neonatals, the undernourished, elderly and those with renal or hepatic diseases. *The patient must be given clear instructions in his or her language on how to take/use the drug.*

8. Cost effectiveness in prescribing is important, but it must take into account factors such as frequency of dose and duration of treatment. The use of more expensive drugs may be justified, especially if it results in better and quicker treatment of the patient.

9. With regard to the supply of drugs for refugees generally, it is important that:

(1) no drugs are sent from a donor country without prior clearance;
(2) no drug should arrive with an expiry date of less than six months;
(3) the labelling on each drug should also be in the main language of the country of asylum;
(4) details on the label include the full pharmacopoeial (non-proprietary) name plus the strength and quantity of the drug;
(5) bottles are packaged in leakproof containers and all the drugs packaged in waterproof, durable containers;
(6) the need for the regular supply of an adequate quantity of soap for personal hygiene, is not forgotten.

Re-ordering

10. An example of a re-order form is shown on p. 338. Much time and trouble may be saved by adapting this to the needs of the situation and then standardizing re-order procedures for all locations/health teams, regardless of whether supplies are available locally or must come from abroad.

List A: *Basic drug requirements for 10 000 persons for 3 months*

Ref. No. A/	Drug (WHO reference)	Pharmaceutical form and strength	Total required for 3 months (rounded up)
1.	*Analgesics* (2)		
	1 acetylsalicylic acid	tab 300 mg	17 000 tabs
	2 paracetamol	tab 500 mg	5000 tabs
2.	*Anthelmintic* (6.1)		
	1 piperazine	syrup 500 mg/5 ml (30 ml bottle)	5.1 litres
	2 mebendazole	tab 100 mg	2100 tabs
3.	*Antibacterial* (6.3)		
	1 ampicillin	suspension 125 mg/5 ml	420 bottles 60 ml
	2 benzylpenicillin	inj 0.6 g (1 million IU)	500 vials
	3 phenoxymethylpenicillin	tab 250 mg	9500 tabs
	4 procaine benzylpenicillin	inj 3.0 g (3 million IU)	375 vials
	5 sulfamethoxazole plus trimethroprim	tab 480 mg	4000 tabs
	6 tetracycline	tab 250 mg	9000 tabs
4.	*Antimalarial** (6.7)		
	1 chloroquine	tab 150 mg/base	8000 tabs
	2 chloroquine	syrup 50 mg/5 ml base	3 litres
5.	*Antianaemia* (10.1)		
	ferrous salt and folic acid	tab 60 mg iron with 0.25 mg folic acid	30 000 tabs
6.	*Dermatological* (13)		
	1 benzoic acid and salicylic acid	oint 25 g tube	100 tubes
	2 benzyl benzoate	lotion 25%	35 litres
	3 gentian violet	crystals	200 g (8 bottles)
	4 neomycin and bacitracin	oint 25 g tube	50 tubes
	5 calamine lotion	lotion	50 litres
7.	*Antacid* (17.1)		
	aluminium hydroxide	tab 500 mg	5000 tabs
8.	*Cathartic* (17.5)		
	senna	tab 7.5 mg	400 tabs
9.	*Diarrhoea* (17.6.2)		
	oral rehydration salts	sachet 27.5 g/litre	6000 sachets
10.	*Ophthalmological* (21.1)		
	tetracycline	eye oint 1%, 5 g tube	750 tubes
11.	*Solutions* (26)		
	1 water for injection	2 ml	500 amps
	2 water for injection	10 ml	500 amps
12.	*Surgical disinfectants* (15)		
	chlorhexidine	solution 20%	5 litres
13.	*Vitamin* (27)		
	1 retinol (vitamin A)	caps 60 mgh 200 000 IU	500 caps
	2 retinol (vitamin A)	caps 7.5 mg 10 000 IU	400 caps

* For chloroquine resistant treatment see List B item 6.2.

Table 14. *Likely symptoms and proposed treatment* (*List A*)

Symptoms 0–14 years of age (5000)	Possible percentage/ numbers receiving treatment	Treatment

Respiratory	30% = 1500	750 upper respiratory tract:
		  400 paracetamol
		  350 acetylsalicylic tab
		750 lower respiratory tract:
		  650 phenoxymethylpenicillin tab
		  100 benzylpenicillin injections

Diarrhoea	30% = 1500	1500 rehydration sachets
Malaria	15% = 750	200 chloroquine syrup 550 chloroquine tabs
Helminths	20% = 1000	250 piperazine syrup (under 2 years of age) 750 mebendazole (over 2 years of age
Skin, trauma	10% = 500	200 benzyl benzoate lotion 150 chlorhexidine solution 100 benzoic acid and salicylic acid cream 50 calamine lotion
Anaemia	10% = 500	500 ferrous salt and folic acid tab
Eyes	10% = 500	500 tetracycline ointment 100 vitamin A caps (100 000 IU) 400 vitamin A caps (200 000 IU)
Ears	5% = 250	250 ampicillin suspension
15 years of age+ (5000)		
Respiratory	20% = 1000	700 upper respiratory tract acetylsalicylic acid tabs 300 lower respiratory tract tetracycline tabs
Musculo-skeletal	15% = 750	500 acetysalicylic acid tabs 250 paracetamol tabs
Digestive	15% = 750	300 mebendazole tabs 250 aluminium hydroxide tabs 200 senna tabs
Diarrhoea	10% = 500	500 oral rehydration sachets
Genito-urinary	15% = 750	375 sulfamethoxazole plus trimethroprim tabs 375 procaine benzylpenicillin injections
Malaria	10% = 500	500 chloroquine tabs
Skin, trauma	5% = 250	125 benzyl benzoate lotion 25 gentian violet 25 chlorhexidine 50 neomycin and bacitracin ointment
Anaemia	5% = 250	250 ferrous salt and folic acid tabs
Eyes	5% = 250	250 tetracycline ointment 100 vitamin A caps (200 000 IU)

Table 15. *Standardized treatment schedules (List A)*

Drug	Form	Course			Quantity/course	Total requirement*
acetylsalicylic acid	tab 300 mg	adult	2 tds 2/7		= 12 tabs	= 14 400 tabs
acetylasalicylic acid	tab 300 mg	paed	1/2–1 tds 2/7		= 6 tabs	= 2100 tabs
aluminium hydroxide	tab 500 mg	adult	1 qds 5/7		= 20 tabs	= 5000 tabs
ampicillin	suspension 125 mg/5 ml	paed	125 mg qds 5/7		= 100 ml	= 420 bottles (60 ml)
benzoic acid and salicylic acid	oint 25 g	(external use)				100 tubes
benzyl benzoate	lotion 25%	both	100 ml		= 100 ml	= 35 litres
benzylpenicillin	inj 0.6 g (1 million IU)	paed	1 od 5/7		= 5 vials	= 500 vials
calamine lotion	lotion bath	(external use)				= 50 litres
chlorhexidine	solution 20%	(external use)				= 5 litres
chloroquine	tab 150 mg/base	adult	varies		= 10 tabs (full dose)	= 5000 tabs
chloroquine	tab 150 mg/base	paed	varies		= 5 tabs (full dose)	= 2750 tabs
chloroquine	syrup 50 mg/5 ml/base	paed	10 mg/kg		= avg 15 ml	= 3 litres
ferrous salt and folic acid	tab 60 mg/base	adult	1 bd 30/7		= 60 tabs	= 15 000 tabs
ferrous salt and folic acid	tab 60 mg/base	paed	1 od 30/7		= 30 tabs	= 15 000 tabs
gentian violet	25 g bottles	(external use)				= 8 bottles
mebendazole	tab 100 mg	both	2 stat		= 2 tabs	= 2100 tabs
neomycin and bacitracin	oint 25 g	adult	bd 7/7		= 1 tube	= 50 tubes
oral rehydration	sachets 27.5 g/litre	both	3 sachets		= 3 sachets	= 6000 sachets
paracetamol	tab 500 mg	adult	2 tds 2/7		= 12 tabs	= 3000 tabs
paracetamol	tab 500 mg	paed	1/4–1/2 tds 2/7		= 4 tabs	= 1600 tabs
piperazine	syrup 500 mg/5 ml	paed	20 ml stat		= 20 ml	= 4 litres
phenoxymethyl-penicillin	tab 250 mg	paed	125 mg qds 7/7		= 14 tabs	= 9100 tabs
procaine benzyl-penicillin	inj 3 g (3 million IU)	adult	1 stat		= 1 vial	= 375 vials
retinol	caps 200 000 IU	children and adults	1 stat		= 1 cap	= 500 caps
retinol	caps 25 000 IU	infants	4 stat		= 4 caps	= 400 caps
senna	tab 7.5 mg	adult	2 stat		= 2 tabs	= 400 tabs
sulfamethoxazole plus trimethroprim	tab 480 mg (400 + 80)	adult	2 bd 5/7		= 10 tabs	= 3750 tabs
tetracycline	tab 250 mg	adult	1 qds 7/7		= 28	= 8400 tabs
tetracycline	eye oint 1% 5 g tube	both	g 7/7		= 1 tube	= 750 tubes

* Using numbers of patients from Table 1. Quantities are rounded up in List A.

Key: od = take daily; bd = twice a day; tds = 3 times a day; qds = 4 times a day; stat = at once; X/7 = number of days per week.

List B: *Drugs for use by doctors and senior health workers*

Ref. No. B/	Drug (WHO reference)	Pharmaceutical form and strength	Total amount
1.	*Anaesthetic* (1.2) lidocaine (local) 1 %	inj vial/50 ml	10 vials
2.	*Analgesic* (2.2) pethidine*	inj vial 50 mg	10 vials
3.	*Antiallergic* (3) chlorphenamine	tab 4 mg	100 tabs
4.	*Antiepileptic* (5) diazepam	inj 5 mg/ml 2 ml amp	10 amps
5.	*Antiinfective* (6) 1 benzylpenicillin	inj 3.0 g (5 million IU)	100 vials
	2 chloramphenicol	caps 250 mg	2000 caps (2 qds 5/7 for 50 patients)
	3 cloxacillin	caps 500 mg	1500 caps (1 qds 7/7 for 50 patients)
	4 mebendazole	caps 100 mg	100 caps (2 stat)
	5 metronidazole	tab 250 mg	1500 tab (2 tds 5/7 for 50 patients)
6.	*Antimalarial* (6.7) 1 quinine	inj 300 mg/ml	20 amps (2 ml) (avg of 4 ml per patient)
	2 sulfadoxine and pyrimethamine	tab 525 mg	150 tabs (2–3 stat for 50 patients)
7.	*Blood substitute* (11) dextran 70	inj sol 6%/500 ml, with 10 giving sets	5 litres
8.	*Cardiovascular* (12) 1 digoxin	inj 0.25 mg/ml, 2 ml amp	10 amps
	2 digoxin	tab 0.25 mg	100 tabs
	3 glyceryl trinitrate	tab 0.5 mg	100 tabs
	4 epinephrine	inj 1 mg/ml, 1 ml amp	10 amps
	5 propranolol	tab 40 mg	100 tabs
9.	*Dermatological* (13) 1 hydrocortisone	1 % cream, 30 g tube	10 tubes
	2 nystatin	cream 100 000 IU, 30 g tube	10 tubes
10.	*Diuretics* (16) 1 furosemide	tab 40 mg	100 tabs
	2 furosemide	inj 10 mg/ml, 2 ml amp	10 amps
11.	*Gastrointestinal* (17) 1 promethazine	tab 25 mg	100 tabs
	2 promethazine	syrup 5 mg/5 ml, bottle of 250 ml	10 bottles
	3 codeine*	tab 30 mg	100 tabs
12.	*Hormones* (18) hydrocortisone	inj 100 mg	10 vials
13.	*Ophthalmological* (21.1) sulfacetamide	eye oint 10%	250 5 g tubes

List B–contd.

Ref. No. B/	Drug (WHO reference)	Pharmaceutical form and strength	Total amount
14.	*Oxytocics* (22)		
	1 ergometrine	tab 0.2 mg	100 tabs
	2 ergometrine	inj 0.2 mg/ml	10 amps
15.	*Psychotherapeutic* (24)		
	diazepam	tab 5 mg	100 tabs
16.	*Respiratory* (25)		
	1 aminophylline	inj 25 mg/ml, 10 ml amp	10 amps
	2 beclomethasone	oral inhalation 0.05 mg	5 aerosols
	3 salbutamol	oral inhalation 0.1 mg	5 aerosols
17.	*Solutions* (26.2)		
	1 water for injection	inj 10 ml amp	100 amps
	2 sodium chloride	0.9% inj sol/isotonic, with 10 giving sets	5 litres
	3 glucose for injection	inj 50% hypertonic 10 ml amp	10 amps
	4 compound solution of sodium lactate	solution/500 ml	10 litres

*Subject to international control under the Single Convention on Narcotic Drugs (1961) and the Convention on Psychotropic Substances (1971). *Not included in the kit*: to be obtained locally in accordance with national procedures.

List C: *Basic medical equipment for a clinic*

(equipment marked with an asterisk may need replacing every 3 months)

Ref No. C/	Description	Quantity
1	Sterile disposable syringes, Luer 2 ml	4000*
2	Sterile disposable syringes, Luer 10 ml	1000*
3	Sterile disposable needles 0.8 × 40 mm/G21 × 1½″	2500*
4	Sterile disposable needles 0.5 × 16 mm/G25 × ⅝″	2500*
5	Interchangeable glass syringes, Luer 2 ml	5
6	Interchangeable glass syringes, Luer 10 ml	5
7	Interchangeable needles, 144 assorted, Luer	2 pkts
8	Sterile swabs	5000
9	Emergency suture sets with needles, pkt 12	15 pkts*
10	Needle-holder	1
11	Scalpel handle No. 3 size	2
12	Artery forceps	2
13	Dissecting forceps	2
14	Blades, disposable size 10	100*
15	Scissors, straight	6

List C—contd.

Ref No. C/	Description	Quantity
16	Scissors, suture	1
17	Thermometers	10*
18	Stethoscope, standard and fetal	2 of each
19	Sphygomanometer, anaeroid	1
20	Diagnostic set (auroscope, ophthalmoscope)	1
21	Battery alkaline dry cell 'D' type 1–5 v for item 20	4*
22	Vaginal speculum, Graves	2
23	Metal syringes for ear washing, 90 ml	1
24	Tongue depressor, metal	1
25	Nasogastric tubes size Ch. 5 (premature), polyethylene	5*
26	Nasogastric tubes size Ch. 8 (infant), polyethylene	10*
27	Nasogastric tubes size 12, polyethylene	5*
28	Scalp vein needles	50
29	Gloves, reusable small	100
30	Gloves, reusable medium	100
31	Gloves, reusable large	100
32	Dressing tray with lid, stainless steel	4
33	Basin, kidney 350 ml, stainless steel	2
34	Bowls, round with lid 240 ml, stainless steel	4
35	Bowls, round 600 ml, stainless steel	4
36	Gauze swabs 5 × 5 cm in packets of 100	10 pkts
37	Gauze swabs 10 × 10 cm in packets of 100	10 pkts*
38	Sterile gauze swabs 10 × 10 cm in packets of 5	50 pkts*
39	Eye pads (sterile)	6 pkts*
40	Paraffin gauze dressings 10 × 10 cm in tins of 36 pieces	3 tins*
41	Sanitary towels	200*
42	White cotton wool, rolls of 500 gms	2 rolls*
43	Zinc oxide plaster 25 mm × 0.9 m roll	120 rolls*
44	Gauze bandage, 25 mm × 9 m	50*
45	Gauze bandage, 50 mm × 9 m	50*
46	Gauze bandage, 75 mm × 9 m	50*
47	Plaster of Paris bandages 3″ × 3 yds, packs of 1 dozen	1 pkt*
48	Pneumatic splint sets, multipurpose	1 of each*
49	Safety pins, 40 mm	500*
50	Hand towels	2*
51	Soap, cleansing	60 bars*
52	Nail brush, surgeons	5*
53	Health cards with plastic envelopes	10 000*
54	Plastic envelopes for drugs	10,000*
55	Plastic sheeting 910 mm wide	2 m
56	Apron, plastic	2
57	Tape measure 2 m/6′	2
58	Weighing scale, adult 140 kg × 100 g	1
59	Weighing scale, infant 25 kg × 20 g	1
60	Height measuring board	1
61	Sterilizer dressing pressure type, 350 mm diameter × 380 mm	1
62	Stove for 61, kerosene single burner pressure	1
63	Basic laboratory kit and spares	1
64	Filter, water candle aluminium, 9 litres	1
65	Clinitest tabs	5 bottles*
66	Multistix	5 bottles*
67	Airway (children's set)	1

Example of a standard re-order form

Serial No. of order ....
Date of order...
Country .... Refugee location ....
Total number of refugees at location ....
Requirement expected to last from .... (date needed by) for .... (months)
Last order: serial No. .... date of order .... date received ....

List A

Reference No. (always prefix by A/ in any separate reference)	Quantity required (in form and strength as in list unless otherwise indicated)	Quantity supplied	Remarks
1.1			
1.2			
2.1			
2.2			
3.1			
3.2			
3.3			
3.4			
3.5			
3.6			
4.1			
4.2			
5			
6.1			
6.2			
6.3			
6.4			
6.5			
7			
8			
9			
10			
11.1			
11.2			
12			
13.1			
13.2			

List B

Reference No. (always prefix by B/ in any separate reference)	Quantity required (in form and strength as in list unless otherwise indicated)	Quantity supplied	Remarks
1			
2			
3			
4			
5.1			
5.2			
5.3			
5.4			
5.5			

List B—contd.

Reference No. (always prefix by B/ in any separate reference)	*Quantity required* (in form and strength as in list unless otherwise indicated)	*Quantity supplied*	*Remarks*
6.1			
7			
8.1			
8.2			
8.3			
8.4			
8.5			
9.1			
9.2			
10.1			
10.2			
11.1			
11.2			
11.3			
12			
13			
14.1			
14.2			
15			
16.1			
16.2			
16.3			
17.1			
17.2			
17.3			
17.4			

Other drugs

Ref. no (always prefix by WHO/)	*Drug*	*Pharmaceutical form and strength*	*Quantity required*	*Supplied*	*Remark*

Notes
1. Equipment on list C may be ordered in the same way.
2. In an emergency, *orders can be placed in the same way by telex, but it is imperative that each separate item reference number be prefixed by A/, B/, C/, or WHO/ as appropriate.*

Ordered by:..
(Name and title)

Signature: ....

NUTRITION KITS

The following kits are available from OXFAM, 274 Banbury Road, Oxford, UK. The list of equipment is also intended as a guide as to what equipment is needed to undertake a nutrition survey and implement supplementary and therapeutic feeding programmes. Much of this equipment can often be purchased locally.

Kit No. 1

Nutritional assessment and surveillance kit.

This is designed to enable relief workers to measure the nutritional status of refugee children and those in village communities, immediately on arrival in a given situation. If there is a need for nutritional intervention, then the kit can be used to identify potential feeding programme recipients and also for ongoing monitoring of the situation.

Equipment

For nutritional surveys and ongoing monitoring.

1 height stick (150 cm) and 1 'read off' marker ⎫
1 length board (100 cm)   ⎬ wooden
                                                 ⎭
1 salter spring scales: 25 kg
1 salter spring scales: 50 kg
10 fibreglass tape measures
2 instruction leaflets for shakir strips
2 registers
10 exercise books
2 pairs scissors
10 pens, 10 pencils, 2 rubbers, 2 pencil sharpeners
2 rulers, 2 clip boards, 1 box drawing pins
1 packet of graph paper
1500 identity bracelets
2 dymo machines
2 boxes dymo tape (red) ⎫ for insertion into identity braclets
2 boxes dymo tape (blue) ⎭
50 height for weight graph sheets
1 holdall (heavy duty nylon)

Books

Selective feeding by Sue Peel × 2. *Management of nutritional emergencies in large populations* by De Ville de Goyet *et al.* × 2. *Nutrition for developing countries* by Maurice King *et al.* × 2. *Control of communicable diseases* by Benenson (also available in French) × 2. Packed in one Triwall container 106 cm × 37 cm × 27 cm.

Kit No. 2
Supplementary feeding kit

This is designed to cater for 250 recipients. This hopefully will give greater flexibility and if large numbers are involved, then two or more kits can be used in conjunction with each other. The kit contains nutritional surveillance equipment (Box A) and feeding and cooking equipment (Box B).

Stoves and other sources of heat are not included as conditions vary from one situation to another.

Supplementary feeding kit (Box A)

Oxfam Nutritional Surveillance Equipment as described on previous page plus:

Supplementary feeding kit (Box B)

1 cooking pot 100 litres (with lid)
1 cooking pot 50 litres (with lid)
2 wooden paddles for stirring food
300 cups (plastic)
300 bowls (plastic)
500 plastic teaspoons
30 metal spoons
2 scoops
2 measuring jugs
2 ladles
2 metal whisks
2 tin openers (1 heavy duty and 1 ordinary)
1 scrubbing brush
3 buckets with lids
2 large jerry cans
500 water sterilizing tablets

Books

Selective feeding procedure by Sue Peel × 2. *Guidelines for training community health workers in nutrition* WHO × 2. *Medical care in developing countries* by Maurice King × 1. Packed in one Triwall container 105 cm × 73 cm × 63 cm.

Kit No. 3
Therapeutic feeding kit

This is designed to enable the rapid establishment of a Therapeutic Feeding Programme to cover up to 100 severely malnourished people. For use, this kit needs supervision by medical/nursing personnel or nutritionists with medical knowledge. It is not envisaged that this kit will be used as frequently as the other kits (Nos. 1 and 2).

Equipment

PART A
As nutritional surveillance equipment

PART B
2 cooking pots (50 litres) + lids
2 paddles for stirring food
120 cups
120 bowls
50 metal teaspoons
250 plastic teaspoons
2 measuring jugs (2 litres)
2 scoops
2 ladles
2 whisks
1 tin opener and 1 heavy duty tin opener
1 food scales
1 alarm clock
1 scrubbing brush
2 large plastic jerry cans
2 buckets with lids
4 hurricane lamps $\begin{cases} 2 \text{ tilley lamps} \\ +2 \text{ hurricane} \end{cases}$
12 candles (nightlights) + matches
2 torch and batteries
500 water purifying tablets

Packed in one Triwall container 105 cm × 73 cm × 63 cm.

IMMUNIZATION EQUIPMENT
Equipment to immunize 5000 children between the ages of 0 and 5 years and 1000 pregnant women.

Electric powered cold chain kit for use in refugee areas—advice should be sought from the national EPI programme or from EPI, WHO in Geneva on the most appropriate makes and suppliers.

The list is in two parts: equipment kept and used in a central store/central sterilizing area; equipment used by the two vaccinators.

Central store equipment

1. 1 iced lined refrigerator
2. Thermometer with 4 °C to 8 °C range
3. 1 ice lined freezer
4. Thermometer with − 20 °C to 0 °C range
5. 2 cold boxes
6. 2 sets of ice packs for each box above
7. 2 sets of ice packs for the vaccine carriers
8. 1 pressure cooker
9. 2 containers with a lid for sterile needles (to prepare sterile packs for collection by the vaccinators)
10. 2 containers with a lid for sterile syringes
11. 1 large container with a lid for used syringes and needles
12. 1 dressing forceps
13. 1 container for dressing forceps
14. $\frac{1}{2}$ kg gauze for wrapping syringes and needles
15. 4 syringes 10 cc
16. 6 syringes BCG
17. 100 syringes 2 cc
18. 4 needles (18 gauge) for mixing
19. 9 dozen needles size 22 short gauge
20. 1 packet of 10 needles for BCG
21. 5000 vaccination cards and/or records and/or Road-to-Health cards
22. 50 vaccine stock cards

Field equipment

Note: All the quantities below are for two vaccinators. Each vaccinator would, therefore, have half these quantities in his (her) kit.

1. 2 vaccine carriers
2. 2 sets of ice packs for the carriers above
3. 2 thermometers with 4 °C to 8 °C range
4. 2 containers with lid for 50 sterile needles
5. 2 containers with lid for sterile syringes
6. 2 containers for used equipment
7. 2 containers for dressing forceps
8. 2 spirit lamps for flaming
9. 2 wind shields
10. 2 containers with spirit
11. 4 syringes 10 cc
12. 6 syringes BCG
13. 100 syringes 2 cc
14. 4 needles (18 gauge) for mixing

15. 10 dozen needles size 22 short gauge 30 mm 7/10
16. 1 packet of 10 needles 10 mm 25 or 26 gauge for BCG
17. 2 carrying cases
18. 4 wooden vaccine vial holders
19. 2 plastic cups
20. 2 cotton wool containers (or plastic bag)
21. 2 plastic soap containers with soap
22. 2 methylated spirit
23. 2 boxes of matches
24. 12 files for cutting the ampoules
25. 100 vaccination cards and/or records and/or Road-to-Health cards (replenished each working day) from central stores

ENVIRONMENTAL HEALTH EQUIPMENT

Soap-making kit

Scales, sprung balance, 25 kg
Measuring jug, enamel
Mixing bowls or buckets made of enamel, iron or stone
Mixing spoons or sticks made of wood or enamel
Strainer or sieve—50 mesh gauge
Thermometer—18 °C to 65 °C
Cooling frames of wood or strong cardboard 5 cm to 7.5 cm deep or use gourds or coconut shells
Cotton cloth or waxed paper to line cooling frames
Knife or piece of wire to cut soap into bars
Safety equipment for caustic soda, e.g. gloves and goggles

Supplies for 10 000 people

Water

Test equipment
2   pump + petrol engine, skid mounted (see Fig. 5)
            capacity 20 m 3/hr, pumping head 20–30 m
75 mm and 50 mm polythene pipe + fittings as required
1   floating suction strainer
1   suction strainer
5   10 m 3 liquidrum tank
GI pipe and taps for manifolds (40 taps total) plus 50 mm valves for fire hydrants
5 × 100 m lengths flexible 50 mm hose for fire-fighting
Timber, nails, tools (carpentry and plumbing)
picks and shovels

500   plastic buckets
Augers for well-drilling
2   drip feeders plus mixing tank 20 L/Hr capacity
1   SWS filter box plus hose
1   diatomite filter 20 m 3/hr capacity
20   'family-size' silver impregnated ceramic filter assemblies
100 kg Calcium hypochlorite (monthly)
100 kg Alum   (monthly)
500 kg Diatomaceous earth (monthly)
1   Comparator or colour card + DPD tablets for measuring chlorine levels

Sanitation

15 sets moulds for concrete/ferrocement squatting plates, plus boards onto which to turn out slabs
25 tonnes cement
1 tonne 8 mm reinforcement bar *or* 500 kg calcium chloride
Sand, aggregate, lubricating oil assumed locally obtainable
Timber, tools (carpentry)
50 picks and shovels
Galvanized iron sheeting (20 tonnes)
50 barrels cresol-based disinfectant

Transport

1   Landrover (long wheelbase)
1   5T truck

General

Oil drum, timber, GI sheets
Water and sanitation equipment

Oxfam sanitation unit

The unit has been developed to provide a self-contained package sanitation-sewerage system and provides all the materials required to install the system, including pipes, fittings, and tools and has a capacity for 500–1000 persons a day. The kit is best suited for places where there is a very high water table and large quantities of water for flushing available.

Oxfam water kit

This kit is being developed in the form of a series of modules to suit different water sources.

LABORATORY SERVICES EQUIPMENT

Equipment

Much of the following equipment can be obtained nationally or through supplies such as (1) ECHO, 4 West Street, Ewell, Surrey, UK. (2) UNIPAC, Copenhagan, Denmark.

Equipment and reagents required for the following tests:
TB, malaria, and intestinal parasites

Equipment required in all tests:
Microscope

   Examples:
   (1) Vickers M16 student microscope
   (2) Nikon Labophot
   (3) Leitz Labolux 11

Slide name marker (pencil or diamond pen)
Immersion oil

REQUIRED FOR 1500 TB SLIDES

3″ × 1″ glass slides	1500
22 × 40 mm glass coverslips No. 1	1500
Bacteriological wire loop	1
Absorbent cotton wool rolls	3
Staining rack to fit over sink	1
Blotting paper or filter paper—large sheets	100
Ziehl–Nielsen (strong) carbon fuchsin stain	15 × 500 ml
Concentrated sulphuric acid	4 × 2.5 litres
95% alcohol	3 × 2.5 litres
Loffler's methylene blue stain or dilute Malachite green stain	15 × 500 ml
Mountant (DPX)	3 × 100 ml

REQUIRED FOR 5000 MALARIA FILMS

3″ × 1″ glass slides	5000
Staining rack	1
10 ml measuring cylinder	2
Methanol	8 × 2½ litres
Buffer tablet—50 per bottle	1
Giemsa stain	3 × 500 ml

REQUIRED FOR 5000 STOOL EXAMINATIONS (FORMOL-ETHER CONCENTRATION METHOD)

Stool sample containers	5000

Wooden tongue depressors	5000
3″ × 1″ glass slides	5000 ⎫ fewer required if
22 × 40 mm glass coverslips No. 1	5000 ⎭ washed and re-used
10 ml glass graduated centrifuge tubes	10
Tube rack	1
Pasteur pipettes	5000
Mesh sieve	1
4″ filter funnel	2
10 % formol saline solution	42 litres
Ether	18 × 500 ml
Lugol's iodine stain	100 ml
1 % eosin stain	100 ml.
Centrifuge (hand, battery or main)	

EDUCATION AIDS AND PUBLICATIONS

UNESCO coupons are available in the Third World for purchases which require payment by sterling, dollar or some other foreign currency.

Ross Institute Publications, Ross Institute of Tropical Hygiene, London School of Hygiene and Tropical Medicine, Keppel Street, London WC1, UK.

● Preservation of personal health in warm climates

Bulletins:

No. 1. *Insecticides*
No. 2. *Anti-malarial drugs*
No. 5. *The housefly and its control*
No. 7. *Malaria and its control*
No. 8. *Small excreta disposal systems*
No. 9. *The inflammatory diseases of the bowel*
No. 10. *Small water supplies*
No. 11. *Anaemia in the tropics*
No. 12. *Protein calorie malnutrition in children*

Publications:

No. 13. *An introduction to the primary health care approach in developing countries. A review with selected annotated references.*
No. 14. *Refugee camp health care: selected annotated references.*

Numbers 8, 10, 13, and 14 are of particular relevance.
● Two charts on diarrhoea

TALC, Teaching Aids at Low Cost, PO Box 49, St. Albans, Herts, UK.
A mail order scheme that sells teaching aids for health workers especially those in the developing countries at or below cost price. Books, sets of

slides, and other equipment as detailed on the order forms available from the above address.

World Health Organization, 1211 Geneva 27, Switzerland, Telex 27821.

WHO publications may be obtained from the above address, or the back page of most WHO publications lists booksellers who maintain stocks in many countries.

Author index

Subject index